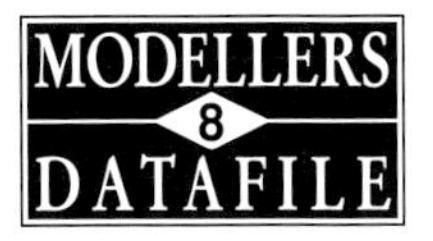

THE GLOSTER & AW METEOR

A COMPREHENSIVE GUIDE FOR THE MODELLER

by Richard J. Caruana & Richard A. Franks

SAM Publications

The cover artwork depicts a Meteor F Mk 8 of the Israeli Air Force and was created exclusively for this publication by Michele Marsan

Modellers Datafile No.8
The Gloster & Armstrong-Whitworth Meteor
by Richard J. Caruana & Richard A. Franks

First published in 2004 by SAM Publications
Media House, 21 Kingsway, Bedford, MK42 9BJ, United Kingdom

ISBN 0 9533465 8 7

Typeset by SAM Publications, Media House, 21 Kingsway, Bedford, MK42 9BJ, United Kingdom
Series Editor Richard A. Franks
Designed by Simon Sugarhood
Printed and bound in the United Kingdom by Printhaüs, Scirocco Close, Moulton Park, Northampton, NN3 6HE, United Kingdom

The Modellers Datafile Series:

- No.1 – De Havilland Mosquito - Out of Print
- No.2 – Hawker Hurricane - Out of Print
- No.3 – Supermarine Spitfire (Part 1 Merlin-Powered)*
- No.4 – Avro Lancaster (Inc Manchester & Lincoln) *
- No.5 – Supermarine Spitfire (Part 2 Griffon-Powered) *
- No.6 – Bristol Beaufighter *
- No.7 – English Electric Lightning *
- No.8 – Gloster (& Armstrong-Whitworth) Meteor
- No.9 – Hawker Tempest & Sea Fury – Due late 2004

* Available

Acknowledgments

A word of thanks must go to the following people and organisations, without whose help and encouragement this title would never have happened:
The Department of Records & Information Services, Royal Air Force Museum, Hendon; The Aircraft & Exhibits Department, Royal Air Force Museum, Hendon; The Conservation Centre, Royal Air Force Museum, Cosford; RAF Museum, Cosford; Midland Air Museum, Coventry; Rudy Binnemans (Belgium); Bill Coffman (Canada); Jim Grant (Australia); Glenn Sands (UK)

Also a large vote of thanks to the following organisations and firms that readily supplied products for inclusion in this title:
Aeroclub, 5, Silverwood Avenue, Ravenshead, Nottingham, NG15 9BJ • Tel: 44 (0)115 967 0044 • Fax: 44 (0)115 967 1633
Airfix, Humbrol Ltd, Marfleet, Hull, North Humberside, HU9 5NE • Tel: 44 (0)1482 701191 • Fax: 44 (0)1482 712908
CzechMaster Resin (CMR), Czech Republic
Classic Airframes, PO Box 577580, Chicago, IL 60657-7580, USA • Tel/Fax: 773-588-5161
Eduard M.A., 435 21 Obrnice 170, Czech Republic • Tel: 420 35 6118259 • Fax: 420 35 6118186
Hannants (Xtradecal), Harbour Road, Oulton Broad, Lowestoft, Suffolk, NR32 3LZ • Tel: 01502 517444 • Fax: 01502 500521

Contents

Contents

Preface

NF Mk 14, WS744 in the colours of No.85 Squadron. This machine was later converted to a NF(T) Mk 14 and operated by Nos. 1 and 2 Air Navigation Schools before going to RAF Leeming as Inst. Airframe 7962M
(© R.J. Caruana)

Military aircraft that do not carve their niche in wartime, rarely make it into the annals of aviation history; the Gloster Meteor is an exception. With a service life spanning some thirty odd years, all those who, in one way or another, were associated with the Meteor remember it with affection and nostalgia. Born during the bitter years of the Second World War, George Carter's elegant design formed the basis of Fighter Command (Royal Air Force) for the best part of the decades that followed. It also served to bridge old technology and the far more sophisticated requirements of future jet aircraft development. It was only when jet engine technology outstripped the Meteor's development capabilities that new fighters began to appear. Still, during its lifetime the Meteor saw a metamorphosis difficult to find in any other contemporary aircraft. The emergence of new air forces just after the war and the rebuilding of those that had disappeared during the conflict owe much to the Meteor – Egypt, Syria, Israel, Denmark, The Netherlands and Belgium just to mention a few. And the number of surviving Meteors preserved in museums all over the world are the best memorial to those who designed and flew it.

Richard J. Caruana
Malta, 2004

This F Mk 8 (WH456) of No.616 Squadron carries the individual letter L on the nose door. This photo was take during their annual Summer Camp detachment, which was to Ta'Qali, Malta in this instance
(© R.J. Caruana)

It is unusal to have two prefaces in a title, but with this Modellers' Datafile I feel I must make mention of someone by way of recognition and thanks. Way back in October 1988 in the second edition of the 'new' Airfix magazine, Jim P. Wood did a series of articles on building the Meteor. In them was a series of sketches that showed the modeller how to make eleven versions. At this time I had only been back in modelling for about a couple of years and I have to say that I felt this article was stunning. It showed you how to build the versions in such a clever and concise manner. The memory of that article stayed with me and some ten years later my thoughts turned to what became the Modellers' Datafile series you see before you now. That article by Jim Wood had stuck with me over the intervening ten years and helped me to formulate this new book series. I wanted to show modellers how to make every version of a specific aircraft type and show them in a way that was easy to understand and of use. I never had the good fortune to meet Jim Wood, who is sadly no longer with us, but through that one article I was encouraged to create this series of books. To me that is what modelling is all about and I can only hope that our work today will encourage another batch of modellers in the future, as Jim Wood's article did for me back in 1988.

Richard A. Franks
Bedford, 2004

Glossary

AA . . . . .Anti-Aircraft
A&AEE . . . .Aeroplane & Armament Experimental Establishment
AACU . . . . .Anti-aircraft Cooperation Unit
Air Cdre . . .Air Commodore (RAF)
ACM . . . . . .Air Chief Marshal (RAF)
AFC . . . . . . .Air Force Cross (RAF)
AFDU . . . . .Air Fighting Development Unit
AI . . . . .Airborne Interception (radar)
Air Mshl . . .Air Marshal (RAF)
ASC . . . . . . .Air Support Control
AVM . . . . . .Air Vice-Marshal (RAF)
BAFO . . . . .British Air Forces of Occupation
BEF . . . . . . .British Expeditionary Force
BS . . . . .British Standard
Capt . . . . . .Captain
CMF . . . . . .Central Mediterranean Force
CO . . . . .Commanding Officer
Do . . . . .Dornier
DFC . . . . . . .Distinguished Flying Cross
DFM . . . . . .Distinguished Flying Medal
DSO . . . . . . .Distinguished Service Order
DTD . . . . . .Directorate of Technical Development
FAA . . . . . . .Fleet Air Arm
FEAF . . . . . .Far East Air Force
Fg Off . . . . .Flying Officer (RAF)
Flt Sgt . . . . .Flight Sergeant (RAF)
Flt Lt . . . . . .Flight Lieutenant (RAF)
FRU . . . . . . .Fleet Requirements Unit
FS . . . . .Federal Standard
FTS . . . . . . .Flying Training School
GLO . . . . . . .Ground Liaison Officer
Gp Capt . . .Group Captain (RAF)
HAL . . . . . .Hawker Aircraft Ltd.
HF . . . . .High-Altitude Fighter
HMS . . . . . .His/Her Majesty's Ship
HQ . . . . . . .Headquarters
IFF . . . . . . .Identification Friend or Foe
kg . . . . .Kilogram
KG . . . . .Kampfgeschwader (Luftwaffe)
JG . . . . .Jagdgeschwader (Luftwaffe)
lb . . . . .Pound
LF . . . . .Low-Altitude Fighter
L.G. . . . . . . .Landing Ground
lt . . . . .Litre
Lt Cdr . . . . .Lieutenant Commander (Royal Navy)
Lt Col . . . . .Lieutenant Colonel
MAC . . . . . .Mediterranean Air Command
Maj . . . . . . .Major
MAP . . . . . .Ministry of Air Production
Me. . . . . . . .Messerschmitt (also Bf)
Mk . . . . . . .Mark
ML . . . . . . .ML Aviation Ltd
MU . . . . . . .Maintenance Unit (RAF)
NF . . . . .Night Fighter
No. . . . . . . .Number
NCO . . . . . .Non-commissioned Officer
NEAF . . . . .Near East Air Force
OTU . . . . . .Operational Training Unit
PFF . . . . . . .Pathfinder Force
Plt Off . . . . .Pilot Officer (RAF)
PR . . . . .Photographic reconnaissance
PRU . . . . . . .Photo-reconnaissance Unit
RAAF . . . . .Royal Australian Air Force
RAE . . . . . .Royal Aircraft Establishment
RAF . . . . . . .Royal Air Force
RATO . . . . .Rocket Assisted Take-Off
RCAF . . . . .Royal Canadian Air Force
RNAS . . . . .Royal Naval Air Station
Sgt . . . . . . .Sergeant
Sqn . . . . . . .Squadron
Sqn Ldr . . .Squadron Leader (RAF)
T . . . . .Trainer
TI . . . . .Target Indicator
UK . . . . . . .United Kingdom
USAAC . . . .United States Army Air Corps
USAAF . . . .United States Army Air Force
USS . . . . . . .United States Ship
VC . . . . .Victoria Cross
VE-Day . . . .Victory in Europe Day
VJ-Day . . . .Victory in Japan Day
Wg Cdr . . . .Wing Commander (RAF)
W/O . . . . . .Warrant Officer
/G . . . . .Suffix letter added to aircraft serial number denoting that it carried special equipment and was to be guarded at all times.

Categories of accident - military

Cat.3 . . . . . .The aircraft damage is considered to be beyond unit resources but may be repairable on site by a service working party or a contractor's working party.
Cat.4 . . . . . .The aircraft damage needs special facilities or equipment for repair which is not available on site.
Cat.5 . . . . . .The aircraft is considered to be beyond economical repair.

This RNethAF F Mk 4 coded I-69 was originally VZ409 in RAF service
(© R.J. Caruana)

Birth of a New Era

Chapter 1

A well-known image of the Gloster E.28/39, probably taking off from Farnborough
(© R.J. Caruana)

Gas Turbine Development

The development of turbine engines in England began during the mid-twenties, when Rolls-Royce was considering an axial flow turbine to drive a propeller in 1926. W.C. Clothier carried out tests on a single-stage compressor and a single-stage turbine the following year. No more serious investigations and studies were conducted in this area for several years, until Frank Whittle provided the necessary drive to bring the jet engine into practical reality. Whittle had begun thinking about gas turbines in 1929, taking out his first patent on 16th January 1930. It was only six years later that his dream began to materialise, having gained the financial support of O.T. Falk & Company, when Power Jets Ltd was incorporated in March 1936 with an authorised capital of £10,000.

Under Whittle's direction, British Thomas Houston Co Ltd (BTH) designed and built the first experimental jet engine that was test run on 12th April 1937. Results obtained by the 'U'- type engine immediately proved that both project and development were on the right track. By July 1939, the revolutionary engine was ordered into production as the Welland W.1, by which time L.J. Cheshire and D.N. Walker from BTH had been loaned to Power Jets Ltd. The Air Ministry began to take notice of developments and even provided some funding for further research.

During a visit to the Gloster factory, Sqn Ldr Whittle was shown a twin-boom fighter project mock-up (the F.18/37) on which Chief Designer W.G. Carter was working. Carter had already come to know of Whittle's propulsion project, and during this visit was able to obtain first-hand information on jet engines. In fact, Whittle even commented that such a twin-boom layout would be ideal for the installation of his engine in place of the projected Napier Sabre.

Carter returned the compliment of Frank Whittle's visit by going over to visit the Power Jets' establishment at Lutterworth in August 1939, accompanied by T.O.M. Sopwith, director of the Hawker-Siddeley Group of which Gloster Aircraft had become a part in 1934. Before going there, however, Carter had been summoned to the Air Ministry where he was asked to design an aircraft to test Whittle's engine. By that time, the Air Ministry had placed an initial contract for an engine designated W.1, similar to the U-1, as the U-type engine was now known. Since Power Jets had no production facilities, it was decided that the company would be entirely devoted to design and development, while production of the engines would be contracted to other companies.

Whittle himself suggested in January 1940 that the Rover Motor Company Ltd should undertake construction work of the new engine, while Sir Henry Tizard mentioned Vauxhall Motors Ltd as another possibility. Vauxhall declined the offer due to pressure of work. Unfortunately, throughout 1940 relations between Power Jets, Rover and BTH deteriorated to such an extent that only Whittle's determination managed to get the jet engine to fly! Credit must also go to his dedicated team, which included Cheshire, W.R. Hawthorne, G.B.R. Feilden and G.W. Bone. Part of the problem was financial, as the Government, through the Ministry of Aircraft Production (MAP), did not take full responsibility for development costs before March 1940. In August, MAP placed the first order with Rover, who had been contracted for quantity production. They worked from designs supplied by Power Jets, modifying wherever necessary to ease production.

Proving the Theory

Contract SB.3229 (to Specification E.28/39) for the design and construction of an aircraft to test the new engine in flight was placed with Gloster on 3rd February 1940. It was intended to be a basis for a fixed-gun interceptor "as far as the limitations of size and weight imposed by the power unit permit". The four 0.303in (7.7mm) Browning guns were not required for the testing stage, though space and weight provisions had to be allowed. The specification called for a maximum speed of 380mph (611km/h) with an engine thrust of 1,200lb.

Carter and Whittle worked very closely to design a small low-wing monoplane with the engine buried behind the pilot's cockpit. It was to have a tricycle undercarriage, and air for the engine would enter through an intake in the nose, passing through ducts on either side of the cockpit. Any serious consideration of using the F.18/37 twin-boom design that Whittle had seen at Gloster in 1939 had been discarded, as with the power

DG202/G, the first prototype powered by Rover W.2B engines. When this image was taken in July 1943 this aircraft lacked the fin/tailplane acorn fillet

available the aircraft offered little potential for the future fighter the Air Ministry was seeking. It was becoming increasingly obvious that E.29/39 could only serve as a test bed.

Work on two E.28/39 prototypes, bearing Gloster's designation G.40, commenced at Brockworth. W4041 was soon moved to Regent Motors in Cheltenham for fear of enemy raids against aircraft factories. The 'Pioneer', as the prototype E.28/39 was referred to by Gloster, was of all-metal construction with a monocoque fuselage of nearly circular section practically built around the Whittle engine. The pilot sat in a cockpit covered with a rear-sliding hood and an 81Imp. Gal. (306lt) fuel tank was placed between the rear end of the cockpit and the engine. Two wings were designed, one having a NACA 23012-series section and another of EC1240 section, both of which were built as two-spar cantilever structures tapering in chord and thickness towards the tips. All moving control surfaces (except the flaps) were fabric-covered.

Progress of the W.1 engine progressed in parallel, with a second engine largely made up of reject parts from the W.1 being designated W.1X. Tests were run with the latter engine and it was even fitted to the prototype for taxying trials. This enabled the W.1 to be conserved for the actual flight test programme.

W4041 was completed in March 1941, fitted with the NACA 23012 wing. It was taken from Crabtree's Garage in Cheltenham to Brockworth where Gloster's Chief Test Pilot Flt Lt P.E.G. Sayer commenced taxying trials on the evening of 7th April. Controllability was found to be good, but acceleration was poor. The following day the engine ran at 16,000rpm as compared to the 13,000rpm it had achieved before, and the aircraft managed three hops of about 6ft (1.82m) height during fast runs. Whittle himself performed some short taxying runs that same afternoon.

After taxying trials at Brockworth had been concluded, W4041/G (G standing for 'Guarded', indicating that the aircraft had to be guarded at all times while unattended on the ground) returned to Cheltenham where the W.1 engine was installed. From there it was taken to Cranwell by road where by 14th May it was ready for taxying trials. After a few ground runs on 15th May 1941, Sayer decided that the aircraft was ready for its first flight. This could not begin until late that evening due to poor weather conditions, but at 7.45pm the aircraft ran down the Cranwell runway and took off for a flawless 17-minute flight.

Over the following thirteen days, fourteen more flights were flown with W4041/G, proving even to the most sceptical that jet propulsion was not only feasible and practical, but that it was also going to open a completely new chapter in aviation history. Altitudes of up to 25,000ft (7,605m) were reached, recording a maximum speed of 300mph (482.4km/h) and an endurance of 56 minutes with a full tank.

Well before this flight Carter was convinced that the first jet fighter had to be a twin-engined design, as a single engine could not possibly provide the necessary power to make any marked improvement over conventionally powered aircraft.

The F.9/40

In August 1940, George Carter had prepared a detailed study concerning the possibility of designing a real jet fighter aircraft and his recommendations were grouped into a brochure presented to the Air Ministry. He therefore recommended the use of a twin-engined layout, the power plants being encased in wing pods that made their replacement a fairly simple matter. There appears to have been some indecision as to whether the engine pods should be under-slung or mid-mounted. The choice fell on the latter solution, especially after wind-tunnel tests at RAE Farnborough.

This arrangement, in turn, resulted in a shift of the aircraft's centre of gravity further aft in comparison with that of nose-mounted piston-engined fighters. The tricycle undercarriage layout as fitted to the 'Pioneer' was a partially successful solution, as the new fighter would fly for quite a few years with useless ballast in the nose. Carter had also argued that as the engines were buried in wing pods, the main airframe design would not need to undergo radical changes whenever engine updates were necessary.

A high tail configuration appeared as most logical, keeping

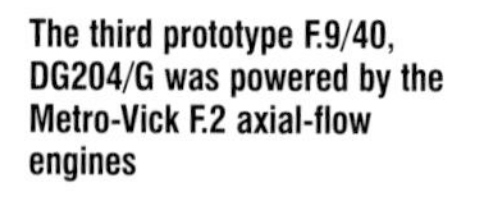

The third prototype F.9/40, DG204/G was powered by the Metro-Vick F.2 axial-flow engines

Fourth prototype DG205/G with (from left to right) John Crosby-Warren, Michael Daunt, Frank McKenna, Frank Whittle and George Carter

the tail well away from the stream of engine exhausts. This, in turn, entailed a complicated and heavy structure. Although the Air Ministry had specified a six-cannon installation with 150 rounds per gun (rpg), Carter opted for a four-gun arrangement in the nose (a pair on either side), with the other pair installed underneath. He actually cautioned against the latter pair, as though 18,000lb thrust was being expected from the Whittle engines, he was not so optimistic that such thrust would be available.

By October 1940, most of these points had been thoroughly debated and decided in consultation with the MAP, with Specification F.9/40 being written around the outcome of these talks in November. The original six-cannon arrangement eventually gave way to four 20mm cannon with 150rpg in a move to save weight and avoid putting the aircraft's performance at risk.

A full-scale wooden mock-up of the fuselage, including the cockpit layout and one complete wing, was ready for inspection in January 1941, and after some slight modifications it was fully approved on 11th February. Detail design studies continued throughout that year, Gloster having received an order from MAP (Contract SB21179/C.23 (a) of 7th February 1941) for the construction of twelve 'Gloster Whittle Aeroplanes' (allocated serials DG202 to DG213) as development aircraft. The order specified the installation of two 1,400lb (630kg) thrust Rover W.2B turbojets.

The order included the manufacture of jigs and tooling for the production of the new fighter, at the rate of 80 aircraft per month. This was not an easy task as Gloster's facilities were deeply involved in design, development and production of the Hurricane Mk II and the Typhoon Mk I. MAP turned to the smaller firms, such as Parnall Aircraft, Boulton-Paul Aircraft Ltd and a number of motor-manufacturers for sub-contract work. Fate thankfully spared the F.9.40 from suggestions such as Terrifier, Scourge, Tyrant and Wrathful when a name was being chosen! MAP apparently settled for 'Meteor' in February 1942.

The first twelve pre-production aircraft were practically hand-built. By September 1941, some of the sub-contractors fell behind schedule; so did Rover Motors who had planned to have thirty W.2B engine components ready by the end of that year. A real shot in the arm for the Meteor programme arrived on 21st June 1941 when MAP placed an order for 300 F.9/40 fighters with Gloster, to be produced at a rate of forty airframes per month. In parallel to this, MAP placed another order with Rover for thirty engines followed by full production of the W.2B, at the rate of twenty engines per week.

Production plans turned out to be over-optimistic; though the first prototype DG202/G was complete by early May 1942, the first Rover W.2B/26 engine arrived on 20th May, the second on 9th June. Moreover, they fell below the specified thrust, providing only 1,000lb (450kg) each and were installed only to permit the prototype to perform its taxying trials. Meanwhile, Gloster had to cope with the failure of the wing's rear centre section spar. Rather than risk further delays due to a complete redesign of the unit, the problem was solved by strengthening its 'O' section by using high tensile steel. By 26th June, the revised wing structure passed through all its tests and three days later the engines were run.

DG202/G was then finished in all other details, dismantled and transferred from Bentham to Newmarket Heath on 3rd July 1942 for taxiing trials. Gerry Sayer began these tests on 10th July, during which he also managed a couple of short hops. In his report Sayer commented favourably on the aircraft's stability although it was clear that power was still inadequate.

Improving Thrust

Sayer's report had made it evident that F.9/40 could not fly with the Rover engines; the supply of Rover W.2/500s (which were to offer 1,500lb (675kg) thrust) was severely delayed. MAP had envisaged such problems and had already contracted de Havilland Aircraft and Metropolitan-Vickers to develop their own jet engines. Most promising at that stage were the de Havilland Halford H.1, initially rated at around 1,600lb (720kg) but with a potential of 2,300lb (1,045kg). Metro-Vick was also registering good progress with its F.2.

At the end of August 1942, an H.1 mock-up was delivered to Gloster in preparation of the fifth airframe (DG206/G), the project receiving maximum priority under the designation F.9/40H. The wings required modification due to the wider cross-section of the Halford (15in [38cm]), calling also for larger nacelles and, therefore, a longer span.

Further failure in the development of the Welland W.2B and W.2/500 placed the whole Meteor project in jeopardy, with Gloster trying to find equitable solutions for its future production programme. Another major setback was the loss of Gerry Sayer on 21st October while test-flying a Typhoon. The first good news arrived on 23rd November when Halford announced that their H.1 had run successfully, and that two units would be delivered to Glosters by the first week of December. On 8th December, however, MAP cancelled all orders for the Meteor F Mk I it had placed with Gloster, due to Rover's failure in delivering its W.2B engines. Furthermore, the order for 12 prototypes was reduced to six, later raised to eight. Everything else had to depend on the F.9/40's first flight and subsequent test results.

Although the first Halford engine arrived at Gloster on 28th November 1942, the other was delayed until 12th January 1943. By 26th January ground runs of DG206/G's engines had begun. On 12th February it was taken to Cranwell, where more ground tests

The seventh prototype, DG208/G, was fitted with an enlarged fin and rudder, plus air brakes to try and cure directional instability

followed its reassembly. Glosters' Chief Test Pilot Michael Daunt performed a series of taxying trials on 3rd March, after having gained some previous experience in taxying the W.2B-powered DG202/G; the H.-engined DG206/G immediately impressed him with its far superior 'kick'. All went well during the first flight performed on 5th March, Daunt complaining only of some directional instability.

For security reasons, the aircraft was moved to Newmarket Heath from where Michael Daunt flew a seven-minute test flight on 17th April, followed by five more flights during May with the longest lasting some eighteen minutes. Due to the confined limitations at Newmarket, a move to Moreton Valence was contemplated, but expansion works there meant that an alternative had to be found. On 28th May 1943, DG206/G's fuel tanks were completely filled up for the first time and it took off for its first cross-country flight to its new home at Barford St John, in Oxfordshire. Here it joined DG202/G and DG205/G, which had arrived on 22nd and 23rd May respectively.

• DG207/G Originally fitted with the W.2B/37s and a pressure cabin. Was used for flat-sided rudder and airbrake tests.

Into Production

F Mk I production began and was going smoothly and at a good pace. By late 1942, Rolls-Royce took over production and further development of the W.2B/23 from Rover, with their first engine being test-flown in a Wellington.

It was planned that EE210 to EE229 would be powered by the 1,700lb (765kg) Rolls-Royce W.2B/23 named Welland I, as fitted to prototype DG205. The first F Mk I, EE210, flew on 12th January 1944, and the following month it was dispatched to America in exchange for a Bell YP-59A Airacomet. This Airacomet, the first of which had flown on 2nd October 1942, was tested alongside the Meteor at Moreton Valence for some months.

Of the remaining nineteen Meteors in the pre-production batch, the RAF received EE213 to EE222 and EE224 to EE229. They were practically armed versions of the F.9/40 prototypes

DG207/G was powered by the Halford H.1 (later DH Goblin) engines and was the prototype for the proposed Meteor F Mk II series

The Meteor Prototypes

Of the originally planned 12 prototypes only eight were eventually built. These were:

• DG202/G Already mentioned in some detail above. It was later fitted with Rover W.2B/23 engines and made its first flight on 24th July 1943. It became an instructional airframe as 578H and is now preserved at the RAF Museum, Cosford.

• DG203/G Originally fitted and tested with 1,640lb (738kg) thrust Power Jets W.2/500s, it was later re-engined with 2,000lb (900kg) thrust W.2/700s. Became instructional airframe 5928M.

• DG204/G Chosen to flight test the Metropolitan-Vickers axial flow turbo-jet engines. It was first fitted with 1,900lb (860kg) thrust F.2s and made its first flight on 13th September 1943. It was later re-engined with 2,000lb (900kg) F.3/1s. These engines were of a relatively narrow cross-section and instead of being mid-mounted as was usual practice they were slung under the wings.

• DG205/G Originally fitted with Rover W.2Bs. Later it was fitted with Rolls-Royce W.2B/23s of 1,600lb (720kg) thrust and kept by this company for further engine trials.

• DG206/G The first to fly, and already described in detail above.

and those not received by the RAF were retained for further trials. EE211/G went to RAE Farnborough where its W.2B/23Cs were exchanged for Power Jets W.2/700 engines in March 1945. It was also the first to be fitted with long-chord engine nacelles. EE212/G, which had flown on 15th April 1944, was used for directional stability trials featuring revised tail surfaces and had the tail bumper removed. EE214/G performed a number of trial flights with a fixed ventral fuel tank while EE215/G was used for exhaust reheat experiments that started towards the end of 1944. Of the others, EE221/G flew with Power Jets W.2/700 engines which were evaluated operationally; EE224 was converted to twin-seat configuration and EE227 was fitted with Trent turbo-props.

The Meteor Airframe

Construction of the Meteor was fairly straightforward by contemporary standards. It had been designed in such a way that it could be built in small sections in as many dispersed factories as possible, rendering the airframe easy to dismantle, transport, repair or salvage for spares. Since the construction of the Meteor remained fairly unaltered throughout its career the following description serves most versions, unless otherwise specified. Differences in the different mark numbers are described in detail in their appropriate sections.

The fuselage was built in three major sections with the foremost part comprising the cockpit section, armament and nose wheel gear. This section was formed out of two vertical webs and three bulkheads. The front bulkhead carried the nose wheel mounting blocks and hydraulics, and served as the front wall to the cockpit pressure cabin (on the versions where this was installed). The rear bulkhead formed the rear wall and seat attachment and extended to a point just ahead of the main spar. Originally the cockpit canopy was formed from three parts: a fixed forward windshield, another fixed rear fairing, and an opening middle section which on the F Mk I was hinged to starboard. On the F Mk 3 the centre section was made to slide aft while on later versions a single aft-sliding teardrop canopy became standard fit to all single-seaters.

Armament consisted of two 20mm Hispano cannon on either side of the cockpit with the ammunition tanks to the rear. Extensive panelling in this area facilitated accessibility to guns and ammo bays. The centre section housed the 300Imp. Gal. (1,364lt) tank and carried the wing centre section, the front and rear spar bulkheads that formed the fore and aft undercarriage bay walls. Quickly detachable doors situated above the fuselage permitted easy access to the main fuel tanks. The rear fuselage was a semi-monocoque construction with hoop pressed light alloy frames and rolled stringers. The last two frames formed the basis of the lower fin to which the tailplane and top fin construction could be attached.

Forming part of the centre fuselage section was the main (centre section) wing, built on two spars spaced by six major ribs, inter-spaced with lighter ribs and stress-skinned. Two hoop frames attached to the spars formed the engine mounts. The rear spar was deepened at this section to take the engine tailpipe and the engine nacelle was built in such a way that the section between the spars and the intake lips could be completely detached allowing full access to the engine. Perforated air brakes were fitted on both upper and lower surfaces, hinged to the rear spar. The outer wing sections were of similar construction to the centre section and were joined at the two main spars; wing tips were detachable. The top tail unit had a split rudder, the upper and lower halves being joined internally by a tubular spar. The elevators were similarly joined and all tail control surfaces had trim tabs.

Controls were conventional and followed contemporary practice except for the rudder pedals which were mounted independently due to lack of forward space that was taken up by the nose wheel well. All trim tabs could be operated from the cockpit through handwheels on the left of the seat. Hydraulics operated the flaps, undercarriage and air brakes, with a secondary manual pump also being provided.

The undercarriage was very unusual for its time. The Dowty lever suspension units had proved themselves excellent on the E.28/39, being strong yet compact, especially when in the retracted position. A shortening device was incorporated through which the legs were reduced in length during retraction. The steerable nose wheel had as a visual lock-down indicator a red rod that protruded from the nose in front of the windscreen, apart from the normal electrical cockpit indicators. No such visual means were provided for the main gear, as this was clearly visible from the cockpit once it was fully extended. All three wheels were fitted with mudguards.

All fuel was housed inside the two-cell self-sealing tank in the fuselage just aft of the cockpit rear bulkhead. No provision for internal wing tanks was ever made, but on later marks (F Mk 4 onwards) under-wing and under-fuselage tanks were introduced. Fuel from the external tanks was first pumped into the main fuselage tank and then pumped back to the engines, the front tank cell feeding the port engine and the rear cell feeding the starboard. However, a balance cock could supply all the fuel to one engine, this due to the fact that it was standard practice to cruise the Meteor on one engine to maximise flying time. An inverted flight trap was also provided in the main tank.

Armament consisted of four Hispano 20mm cannon (Mark number varied slightly between Meteor versions), these being cocked by compressed air, originally from two ground-charged bottles (that also operated the main wheel brakes). From the F Mk 4 onwards, this air system was replaced by a Heywood compressor, which kept the air bottles continuously charged while the engines were running. Shell cases and links were ejected through holes in the under-fuselage skin. After a while, this was found to be the cause of surface damage, and ejector chutes were installed (F Mk 8) to clear the links and cases as far away from the fuselage as possible, especially as damage to the belly tank could prove disastrous. Cannon could be fired all together, top pair or bottom pair only. A gun camera (cine) was a standard fit in the front of the nose.

Cabin pressure was supplied directly from the engine's compressor casings, joined with a non-return valve and then through a single pipe to the cockpit. A control valve on the last part of the pipe bled the airflow up to 7,000ft (2,134m) and then progressively closed the air bleed up to the full cabin 3lb per square inch differential at 24,000ft (7,315m).

A technical fault that dogged early Meteors was the amount of dead weight carried in the nose and engine nacelle fronts as ballast. On the Meteor F Mk 4 more than 1,000lb (450kg) of ballast were needed to keep the nose on the ground (modellers take note)! The problem persisted until a 30in (76cm) extension was fitted to the front fuselage to house a second seat in the T Mk 7. So successful was this operation that it led to the extended front fuselage of the F Mk 8, curing the problem once and for all.

The first pre-production F Mk I, EE210/G was sent to America in February 1944 for evaluation in exchange for a Bell P-59 Airacomet

Meteor F Mk 1 to Mk 7

Chapter 2

This shot is of an Argentinian F Mk 4 coded C-084. The use of the 'C' prefix denotes that this photo was taken after 1950
(© R.J. Caruana)

Meteor F Mk I (G.41A)

Of the small batch of 20 Gloster G.41A Meteors F Mk I produced only fifteen saw active service. Within No.616 'South Yorkshire' Squadron, rumours were rife with stories of an impending re-equipment on a radically new fighter, something far superior to the unit's Spitfires F Mk VII. Squadron Leader Andrew McDowall and five other pilots from the squadron were summoned to Farnborough where they found two brand new Meteors awaiting them (EE213/G and EE214/G).

With the arrival of EE216/G, EE217/G and EE218/G a jet pilot training unit under the leadership of Wing Commander H.J. Wilson was formed, whereby high-speed handling tuition was undertaken as from 22nd June 1944. On 1st July, EE219 joined the flight and within a relatively short period the new 'jets' clocked 150 flying hours. The small force was soon augmented with the arrival of EE215/G on 23rd July and the absorption of Wilson's four-aircraft unit when No.616 moved to Manston towards the end of the month. EE213/G and EE214/G were returned to Gloster for conversion to full operational standard in August, by which time the squadron's strength had risen to thirteen Meteors. Apart from some slight difficulty in getting accustomed to the Meteor's tricycle undercarriage, conversion work was uneventful, thirty-two pilots going through the changeover within the first week of August.

The Meteor was still in its infancy development-wise and there were many instances where aircraft were taken from the squadron for conversions or modifications. EE215/G was sent to the RAE for reheat experiments where maximum speed rose from 420 to 460mph (672-736km/h). EE227/G (at one time coded YQ•Y) also left for the RAE Farnborough, for stability trials and was later fitted with the Rolls-Royce Trent turbo-prop engines in February 1945, receiving the unofficial appellation of 'Trent Meteor'. Eric Greenwood performed the first flight of the Meteor in this configuration on the 20th September 1945 at Church Broughton.

Though the Meteor was the fastest fighter aircraft at low level in operational service, a decision had already been taken that the new jet fighter would not be committed to combat duty, for fear of loss or capture. The Meteor was therefore given the task of countering the V-1 flying bomb menace. On 27th July 1944, Fg Off 'Dixie' Dean scrambled to intercept one of these 'doodlebugs', only to be recalled as it had entered an area mushrooming with balloon barrages, where it was feared that the Meteor might be endangered. Operational patrols commenced on 2nd August by which time No.616 Squadron had eight Meteors F Mk I on strength.

Two days later, Fg Off Dean managed to close up on one of these bombs south of Tornbridge at around 10,000ft (3,050m). The pilot found his guns had jammed, so he carefully edged one of the wings of Meteor EE216/G under the V1 and, by pulling sharply, flipped the missile out of control. It exploded about four miles from Tenterden making it the first enemy 'aircraft' brought

Meteor T Mk 7 '14' named 'Sa'ar' (Tempest) which was one of the first two Meteors delivered
(© R. Weiss)

F Mk 4 EE549 is one of the modified aircraft used by the High Speed Flight. Today it belongs to the RAF Museum and is currently on show at Tangmere
(© R J. Caruana)

down by an Allied fighter jet. This technique became a favourite way of confronting V-1s.

Twenty-four minutes later, Fg Off Rodger, also flying a Meteor, brought down a second V-1 with two bursts of cannon fire close to where the first had fallen. By 10th August, Dean's score had risen to three and towards the end of that month German forces had been driven away from the main launch sites along the Pas de Calais and the V-1 menace abated. No.616 had meanwhile totalled thirteen 'kills'. Five aircraft and their crews were transferred to Debden, in Essex, where they flew mock attacks against Mustangs and Thunderbolts escorting USAAF bombers, enabling American pilots to work out tactical procedures on how to tackle Messerschmitt Me 262 attacks.

Meteor F Mk II (G.41B)

The F Mk II was an attempt to standardise the Meteor power plant by installing the de Havilland-Halford Goblin engines of 2,700lb (1,230kg) thrust, already tested on DG206. The only F Mk II (DG207) had already gone through considerable experimental modifications. Completely fitted to the established F Mk II standard, it flew for the first time on 24 July 1945. Meteor F Mk II production was abandoned as the Goblin engine had, by that time, been completely reserved for the de Havilland Vampire.

Performance and specifications of the F Mk II were very similar to the F Mk I.

Meteor F Mk III (G.41C/D/E)

Efforts continued relentlessly to improve the turbojet's performance. By July 1945 Rolls-Royce had taken over development of the Rover N.2B engine and produced the W.2B/37 Derwent I with a straight through flow arrangement, increasing thrust to 2,000lb (900kg). With the availability of this engine the F Mk III was fitted with the new Derwent in place of the planned Welland 1. Apart from an increase in internal fuel capacity, the F Mk III featured a revised windscreen highly influenced by studies conducted on a captured Focke-Wulf Fw 190. Another canopy modification consisted of the replacement of the side-hinged central section with a rear-sliding, one-piece unit of cleaner design. The rear (fixed) canopy transparency was reduced in size, eliminating the complex framing of the F Mk I.

A general strengthening of the airframe and the introduction of slotted upper and lower wing air brakes were amongst the other modifications for the F Mk III. DG209, the last prototype to fly, was powered by Derwent I (W.2B/37) engines and performed its maiden flight on 18th April 1944. At that time it wasn't even considered as a prototype in the real sense of the word, being rather more of a modified F.9/40.

By August 1944, the first production F Mk III, EE203, was ready to begin flight trials. However, the Derwent had only just entered production and, as MAP were eager to get the jet fighter into wider RAF service, it was decided to power the initial batch of fifteen production F Mk IIIs (EE230 to EE244) with Welland I W.2B/23C engines of 1,700lb (772kg) thrust. EE230, in fact, took to the air for the first time powered by Wellands in September 1944. Power was switched to the Derwent on the 16th example off the line (EE245). To distinguish between the two engines, Gloster type numbers were G.41C for those powered by the Welland and G.41D for those fitted with the Derwent which produced 2,000lb (900kg) thrust. A number of Meteors from the initial batch were retrofitted with the Derwent as well. A final batch of fifteen production Meteors F Mk III (EE497 to EE493) were fitted with long-chord cowlings developed for the F Mk 4, bearing Gloster type number G.41E. Performance improved considerably with the result that they were fitted to a number of earlier F Mk IIIs as well.

First deliveries of Welland-powered F Mk IIIs in December 1944 went to No.616 Squadron, which in January 1945 moved to Colerne. A flight was soon sent on 4th February on detachment to Melsbroek (Brussels), in Belgium, operating within the 2nd Tactical Air Force (84th Group). Though the move was intended to counter the Messerschmitt Me 262 menace, Meteor pilots were severely restricted in their flying, prohibiting them from crossing over into enemy lines. During the early months of 1945, some of the Squadron's F Mk IIIs had been painted overall in a white distemper paint during the heavy snowy winter months. The flight moved first to Gilze-Rijen in Holland on 27th March and then to Nijmegen on 13th April.

Operational flying, however, reaped a number of positive results, such as the first ever attack by an Allied jet against German transports by Fg Off Cooper. On 20th April the Meteors were venturing deeper into German territory, flying from Quackenbrück, a Ju 88 being destroyed on the ground during a raid against Nordholz. Tragedy struck just after the squadron moved to Fassburg when Sqn Ldr Watts and Flt Sgt Cartmel collided in thick cloud. On 1st May the squadron flew 26 sorties, destroying 13 German transports with a further 25

A Meteor T Mk 7 being prepared for flight
(© R. Weiss)

One of the first four Meteors T Mk 7 to arrive in Israel. This aircraft was numbered A 15 (The A letter is for the first Hebrew letter - Alef, which indicated at that time that it was a training aircraft). This aircraft was named Ra'am (Thunder)
(© R. Weiss)

claimed as damaged. No.616 disbanded on 29th August 1945 at Lübeck, in Germany.

No.504 became the second Meteor Squadron to receive the F Mk III. In January 1945 six of its pilots then flying Spitfires Mk IX were posted to Gloster for jet conversion. By the end of March the Spitfires were relinquished and the Squadron joined No.616 at Colerne to take a consignment of F Mk IIIs on 10th April. Jet conversion and training continued well into May and, though fully operational by the end of the war, the squadron had no opportunity to go into action. In July it transferred its Meteors to Lübeck where it flew some impressive formation displays before being disbanded on 10th August, its aircraft and most of its personnel going to No.245 Squadron.

In May 1945 No.74 Squadron joined Nos. 616 and 504 at Colerne to form the first jet fighter Wing of the RAF. After a working-up period the unit left for the East Coast of England and in October 1946 became permanently based at Horsham St. Faith. Its last Meteor F Mk III was relinquished in March 1948. No.74, together with Nos.56 and 245 Squadrons formed RAF Fighter Command's first jet fighter Wing in the UK, flying the Meteor.

During 1945, most of the pre-war 'Auxiliaries' that had become regular units with the RAF during the war were disbanded until the Royal Auxiliary Air Force (RAuxAF) was reformed. No.500 (County of Kent) Squadron was the first RAuxAF unit to equip with the Meteor F Mk III in peacetime on 14th August 1948.

Among the interesting trials conducted on numerous Meteors of this version were the pioneering tests of Martin-Baker ejector seats on about thirty examples reserved for this purpose. Some aircraft were assigned for cold weather trials in Canada and deck landing assessments on *HMS Implacable*. Others included EE240/G (to USA); EE246, EE338, EE416 (used for ejector seat trials); EE249/G (pressurised cabin trials); EE311 (winter trials in Canada); EE337 & EE338 (deck landing trials); EE360/G (F Mk 4 prototype); EE397 (flight-refuelling trials); EE445 (Griffith's wing installation); EE395 (to RNZAF as NZ6001); EE427 (to RAAF as A77-1, tropical trials by No.1 Air Performance Unit at Darwin, crashed 14/02/47, used as spares); EE429 (to South Africa). Total production of the F Mk III ended with the 280th example.

Meteor T Mk 7 'Shfifon'. The pilot is former IAF commander General (Res) Herzel Bodinger
(© R. Weiss)

The Meteor F Mk 4 (G.41F/G)

The increased thrust of Derwent 1s pushed the airframe of the F Mk III into compressibility problems. Further investigation and wind tunnel testing suggested that the nacelle design required extensive revision resulting in a much larger unit.

Trials were conducted on the second prototype (EE211) whose engine cowlings were at first extended forward. It flew in this form in November 1944 and results were so encouraging that the cowlings were also extended aft of the wings. The Derwents were exchanged for a pair of Power Jets W.2/700 units providing 2,000lb (900kg) of thrust, with which it resumed flight-testing in March of the following year. The last fifteen in the F Mk III production run were, therefore, converted to take the longer nacelles on the assembly line, and the long-chord nacelles became a permanent feature on all subsequent marks.

In their search for higher-powered engines Gloster showed interest in the Rolls-Royce Nene designed for a maximum thrust of 4,000lb (1,814kg). Its power was intended for single-engined aircraft then being developed, such as the Gloster E.1/44 and the Supermarine E.10/44 (later Attacker). Rolls-Royce managed to scale down the Nene to produce the Derwent 5, with a thrust of 3,500lb (1,575kg), in a relatively short time. By mid-1945 the new engine had already passed its 100-hour bench test mark and in September the thrust had been increased to 4,000lb (1,814kg).

Rolls-Royce immediately placed the Derwent 5 into production, and Eric Greenwood flew the first Meteor F Mk 4 (EE360) early in August 1945. The powerful Derwent 5 provided the Meteor with a spectacular leap in performance, top speed rising to 585mph (940km/h) at sea level; climb to 40,000 ft (12,200m) took eight minutes. Other improvements included a fully operational pressurised cockpit and external (under-wing and ventral) fuel tanks.

An intensive investigation followed an accident when an F Mk 4 flown by Gloster's test pilot Moss broke up in the air. It was decided to reduce the aircraft's wingspan by 5ft 10in (178cm) to lessen stress on the centre-section spars. A hundred F Mk 4s had already been delivered with the standard wings when the ninth production aircraft, EE525, was modified and tested with the new short-span wings. New-build Meteors with the clipped wings were

EE211 with the long-chord engine nacelles and Power Jets W.2/700 engines installed

designated G.41G. No other significant changes were introduced on this mark of Meteor which all pilots, eventually, agreed was a sheer delight to fly.

Gloster built a total of 539 examples of the F Mk 4, together with a further 44 being built by Armstrong-Whitworth who, although involved in the Meteor programme since 1946, were only now building the complete aircraft.

No.222 at Tangmere became the first operational squadron on the Meteor F Mk 4 in December 1947 after having returned to the UK from Lübeck (Germany) in July; it returned there for a detachment in June-July of the following year. The last production F Mk 4 (VZ437) was delivered from Armstrong-Whitworth's Baginton works on 29th April 1950.

Records

Two F Mk IIIs (EE454 and EE455) were modified (to F Mk 4 standard) for an attempt at the World Speed Record, then still standing at 469mph (753km/h) from pre-war days. EE454 piloted by Gp Capt H.J. Wilson established a 606mph (975km/h) speed record on 7th November 1945 at Herne Bay, Kent. EE455, with Eric Greenwood at the controls, managed 603mph (969km/h). The first example, named 'Britannia' (EE454), retained its camouflage, while the second (EE455), finished in an all-yellow scheme, became known as 'Yellow Peril'.

The RAF High Speed Flight, 'officially' reformed at Tangmere on 14th June 1946, realised that the recently established Meteor records would not stand for long, as a Lockheed F-80 was being prepared in America for such an attempt. So two operational Meteors (EE549, EE550) F Mk 4s were prepared in August for another record run. The aircraft were highly modified: all gun armament and equipment was removed, panel joints filled and smoothed down, canopies replaced by metal units with small windows. A special set of Derwent 5 engines providing 4,200lb (1,890kg) thrust were also prepared. Gp Capt. E.M. Donaldson raised the record to 616mph (990km/h) on the evening of 7th November 1946 on EE549. Sqn Ldr Waterton took off a little later in EE550, but his attempt fell 2mph (3.2km/h) short of Donaldson's record.

Other records set by Meteors F Mk 4 included the Paris-London flight in November 1946 by EE549 on its return from the Paris Air Show (520mph-835km/h), bettered by the same aircraft on the 19th January 1947 to 618.4mph (993.3km/h); both flights were flown by Sqn Ldr Waterton. Meteor F Mk 4 VT103 established a new world record for the 100km closed circuit averaging 542.9mph (872km/h) on 6th February 1948, at Moreton Valence. Coates Preedy broke the Brussels-Copenhagen record with an average run of 630mph (1,011km/h) in Gloster's private Meteor G-AIDC, which was basically of F Mk 4 standard.

Test Aircraft

RA490 was highly modified to take the Metropolitan-Vickers F.2/4 Beryls, with higher undercarriage legs enabling the deeper nacelles to clear the ground. Rolls-Royce RA2 and RA3 Avons were tested on RA491, cutting down the climb to 40,000ft (12,200m) from 8 to a spectacular 2.7 minutes and 3.65 minutes to 50,000ft (15,250m)! RA490 fitted with a Mk 8-style tail unit eventually went to Westlands to test Nenes with jet deflectors for short take-off and landing trials, an arrangement considered to be too cumbersome and complicated for service use. RA435 and CT196 were fitted with reheat units (afterburners) on their Derwent 5 and 8 engines. RA438 and VZ389 were used for flight refuelling trials with the first successful transfer being effected on 2nd April 1950.

VT510 was chosen to test the Martin-Baker ejection seat installation. F Mk III EE416 had already proved the ejector seat as a sound practical proposition but the retrofit to the F Mk 4 was abandoned in favour of its installation on the forthcoming F Mk 8. RA382, which had a 30in. (76cm) plug inserted just aft of the cockpit in an attempt to cure the nose ballast problems, was not entirely successful, due to the shift in centre of gravity as ammunition was expended. Other interesting test aircraft included EE521 and EE524 converted to U Mk 15 unmanned targets, EE530 and RA382 used for T Mk 7 nose development, RA418 and RA430 fitted with camera noses and EE531 tested with a set of folding wings.

Exports

The export potential of such a revolutionary aircraft as the Meteor was not neglected by Gloster who could boast of the most highly-developed contemporary jet fighter in the form of the F Mk 4.

A late 60s photo showing Meteor T Mk 7 number 15 in service with the 'Knights of the North' Squadron for training pilots for the Vautours that were also in the same squadron. The squadron operated alongside the Vautours, two Meteor T Mk 7s numbered '17' and '15' and a Meteor T Mk 7.5 numbered '21'. These aircraft got names the same as the Vautours in the squadron, these being the names of snakes. This machine was therefore 'Shfifon' which was painted in red with black shadows
(© R. Weiss)

The eighteenth F Mk I, EE227/G was used for a number of stability trials and in one the entire upper fin and rudder were removed as seen here. The airframe later became the 'Trent Meteor'

Argentina was the first foreign buyer with an order for 100 examples in May 1947, serialled I-001 to I-100. The first 68 examples were taken from airframes already allocated for the RAF, the rest being specially built. On arrival in Argentina, Gloster technicians reassembled the aircraft until the last machine was delivered in September 1948. These Meteors were blooded in the 1955 revolution and some were even lost in action. They were eventually reserialled C-001 to C-100 and were operated by I, II and III Gruppos de Caza, VII Brigada Aérea. The last machine was struck off service in August 1971.

On 27th June 1947, the Royal Netherlands Air Force ordered five F Mk 4s, first of a total of 60, serialled I-21 to I-81. Nos.322, 323, 326, 327 and 328 Squadrons operated these aircraft at Leeuwarden and Soesterberg. Belgium followed in 1949 with an order for forty-eight machines (EF-1 to EF-48) that went to Nos.349 and 310 Squadrons, until withdrawn in 1957.

A contract was signed on 23rd May 1949 between Denmark and Gloster for twenty Meteors F Mk 4, (D.461 to D.480). The Third Air Flotilla (Naval Service) was formed on 20th October with the first three aircraft delivered (D.461 to D. 463), moving to Karup where the second consignment arrived on 13th November. By 14th April 1950, all twenty had been delivered. On 31st January 1951, the Third Air Flotilla was renumbered No.723 Squadron.

Egypt had to wait for an arms embargo to be lifted before it took delivery of its twelve Meteors, starting in October 1949 (1401 to 1412). France received two interesting Meteors, the first being EE523, ex-RAF High Speed Flight, re-registered F-WEPQ (later F-BEPQ) in 1948. RA491, the Avon and Atar test aircraft, was also sent to France in 1952, converted to Atar engines and fitted with an F Mk 8-style nose section.

Meteor PR Mk 5 (G.41H)

Meteor F Mk 4 VT347 was fitted with two F37 oblique cameras positioned in the rear fuselage and an F24 camera inside the nose. The latter was housed behind three flat windows, one in front, and one on either side. Choice of position had to be determined before flight. Normal armament was retained, the cameras' weight and equipment, which practically offset the nose ballast, hardly affecting the aircraft's performance.

The prototype flew for the first time on 13th July 1949, designated PR Mk 5. It was not to be a straightforward test flight, like most others, as it broke up during a high-speed pass over Moreton Valence killing the pilot, Rodney Dryland.

With the F Mk 8 already in production and entering service the following month, it became obvious that a reconnaissance version of the Meteor should be based on the latest mark available. Thus no PR Mk 5s were ever produced although it brought reconnaissance into the jet age and the installation design did help to produce the later FR Mk 9 and PR Mk 10.

Meteor F Mk 6 (G.41J)

No F Mk 6 aircraft was ever produced. It was projected that this type of Meteor would be externally very similar to the F Mk 8 that superseded it into production. At one time it was contemplated giving the F Mk 6 sweptback wings, although a general arrangement drawing dated February 1946 shows a much more conventional layout, powered by Derwent 7 engines.

The Meteor T Mk 7 (G.43)

For the specific task of promoting the Meteor overseas, Gloster had built a special F Mk 4 which, with armament removed and increased internal fuel tankage, enjoyed a much wider range. G-AIDC, painted a bright vermilion, left England in April 1947 for a tour of the continent earning orders from Belgium, Denmark and Holland as detailed above. However, the aircraft suffered severe damage after a flight by a Belgian pilot, when one of the main undercarriage members collapsed on landing at Melsbroek. It was obvious that pilots inexperienced in jet-flying should not have been allowed to fly the aircraft, and as a second sales tour was being planned, serious thought was given to the development of a two-seat, dual-control version then already on the drawing boards.

In fact, discussions between the Air Ministry and Gloster led to the definitive draft specification of T.1/47 on 2nd May 1947. Cost of conversion of two Meteor T Mk 7 prototypes (including a mock-up) was quoted at £27,000 per aircraft, to which a further £5,000 for cockpit canopy jettison research had to be added. Final mock-up inspection took place on 30th May.

Work began to convert a pair of F Mk 4 airframes to serve as T Mk 7 prototpyes (EE530, EE573). The new front fuselage section had a 30in. (76cm) extension inserted between the rear cabin bulkhead and the main wing spar-to-fuselage joint. Instruments and controls were duplicated for both crew members sitting in a cockpit enclosed by a new heavily framed canopy. Dead weight fitted in the nose of previous versions had been eliminated and an extra fuel tank installed. Provision was also made for the installation of the standard 180Imp. Gal. (680lt) ventral tank plus two 100Imp. Gal. (378lt) drop tanks under each wing. While the T Mk 7 prototype was powered by a pair of Derwent 5 engines, the Derwent 8 was fitted to subsequent production aircraft.

The camera port in the nose was retained; R.3121 and TR1430 radio equipment was fitted. Engine intake lips were slightly enlarged and the aileron trim tab that extended beyond the trailing edge in single-seat versions was replaced by two trim tabs along the whole length of the aileron trailing edge without extending further aft.

The first example, bearing new serial VW410, was inspected by the Air Ministry at Bentham on 7th May 1948, and flew for the first time on 26th October of the same year. Work was also taken in hand to refurbish G-AIDC's wings, rear fuselage and tail unit, mated to a new front fuselage housing the two-seat layout. In this form, it re-emerged from Gloster's works carrying civil registration G-AKPK.

The type entered service with No.203 Advanced Flying School at Driffield. Courses of some three and a half months duration began the following year during which student pilots were also required to fly four hours dual before going solo.

Most pilots who joined the RAF in the early 'fifties flew the Meteor T Mk 7 as part of their training course, especially with Nos.226 and 228 Operational Conversion Units (OCU). However, one or two Meteor T-birds were also to be found with most front-line RAF units. This was not limited to Meteor-equipped squadrons, either. In fact the type could also be found in service with a number of Vampire-equipped squadrons. Most of the RAuxAF units also had the T Mk 7 on their inventory.

The Meteor trainers supplied to RAF and RAuxAF units were intended for continuation training of pilots after joining a particular squadron. Other duties performed by the T Mk 7s included instrument rating checks, target-towing and even liaison.

XF279 became the last to be delivered to the RAF in July 1957. The Royal Navy, too, used the Meteor T Mk 7, the last example in service, WS103, being retired at Yeovilton in January 1967.

T Mk 7 Exports

Brazil received ten examples of the two-seat version later known in service as Meteor TF-7s. The first batch of four left the UK in March 1953 arriving in Brazil the following month. First flight in that country of the two-seat Meteor took place on 22nd May 1953. In February 1962 restrictions were put on their use, most aircraft having logged more than 2,280 flying hours. Inspections undertaken during 1965 revealed cracked wing spars on a number of them, limiting the number that could remain in service even further. Nonetheless, the last flight of a TF-7 (FAB-4309) in Brazil was recorded on 7th October 1971.

France acquired two new-build T Mk 7s for the *Centre d'Essais en Vol*, serialled No.91 and No.92, in February 1951. Another T Mk 7 was F-BEAR, ex-WA607/G-7-133, in 1955. A further twelve examples were bought between 1952 and 1956 (all ex-RAF machines), serialled F1 to F11. Syria ordered a pair of T Mk 7s (91, 92) on 28 January 1950 but these were diverted to France (see above) on 7th February 1951 due to an arms embargo. In September 1952, two ex-RAF T Mk 7s were eventually delivered to Syria, marked as 91 and 92.

Denmark received nine T Mk 7s delivered in three batches, the first on 20th January 1950, the second on 4th August of the same year and the third on 25th November 1952. The Belgian Air Force took delivery of a total of thirty-nine Meteor trainers, nineteen of which came from ex-RAF stocks and the rest converted from surplus F Mk 4s. By far the biggest user of the T Mk 7 outside the RAF was the Royal Netherlands Air Force. A total of forty-five examples were acquired, including Private Venture G-AKPK that received the first serial in the batch (I-1), delivered on 27th February 1949. Nineteen of the other T Mk 7s were new-build machines that came directly from Gloster, the balance being made up from ex-RAF stocks.

EE227 the 'Trent Meteor' seen with the cropped Rotol propellers fitted

Egypt received its first T Mk 7 (1400) on 19th July 1949 after the lifting of an arms embargo, followed by another pair (1413, 1414) in February and May 1950. Further supplies of the Meteor trainer consisted of three examples (1439, 1440, 1441). Israel purchased four T Mk 7s, the first pair arriving at Ramat David air base on 17th June 1953 ferried by British pilots. Official sources show a further two examples (111 and 112) acquired from Avions Fairey in Belgium, fitted with the E.1/44 (F Mk 8-type) tail unit. Israeli sources, however, claim that the number received from Avions Fairey was, in fact, four. Their designation is also referred to as T.7 1/2. The first pair arrived on 4th December 1957 and the second on 25th January 1958. Two Israeli Meteor trainers were converted for photo-reconnaissance missions toward the end of that same year. Recce T Mk 7s participated in Operation Kadesh (Israel's participation in the Suez Campaign) when a pair flew a diversion deep into Egyptian territory on 29th October 1956. It has been reported that the T Mk 7 continued to fly with the Israeli Air Force well into the late 1950s.

Australia received an initial batch of T Mk 7s (A77-701 to A77-707) towards the end of 1951 to train pilots of No.77 Squadron Royal Australian Air Force (RAAF) then being equipped with the Meteor F Mk 8. In February 1952, another T Mk 7 (ex VW410 reserialled A77-2) was acquired for use with the Aircraft Research and Development Unit (ARDU). Another T Mk 7 delivered to Australia in December 1953 was A77-4 (ex-WN321). Some of the RAAF T Mk 7s were posted to Royal Navy Air Station Hal Far, in Malta, between 1952 and 1955. A77-702 was still in service with No.38 Squadron (Communications Flight) at Richmond in 1963.

Meteor T Mk 7s operated by Svenska Flygtjänst, a private company contracted by the Swedish Air Force for target-tug duties, were converted to the T.T. role by Flight Refuelling Ltd. The first example (SE-CAS) was delivered on 29th July 1955 (ex-VF883), while the second, registered as SE-CAT (ex-WH128), was delivered on 1st March 1956. The latter was lost on 21st January 1959 at Visby and replaced by SE-DCC on 11th August. SE-DCC was in fact Gloster's G.44 'Reaper' (ex-G-7-1, ex-G-ANSO).

A number of T Mk 7s earmarked for export went through extensive refurbishment and conversion work by Flight Refuelling Ltd at its Tarrant Rushton plants, including a number delivered to France, Israel and Egypt, apart from those that went to Sweden.

F Mk 4 VZ389 seen here taking fuel from a Lincoln tanker during in-flight refuelling trials

Meteor F Mk 8, FR Mk 9 & PR Mk 10

Chapter 3

VZ517 was fitted with an Armstrong-Siddeley Screamer rocket motor. The portion aft of the cockpit is stainless steel as this area was the fuel tank for the wide-cut gasoline used by the Screamer engine

The Meteor F Mk 8 (Gloster G.41K) became the most representative of the long line of Meteors and its ultimate single-seat fighter version. Between 1950 and 1955 it was to constitute the backbone of the RAF, not to mention the important status it earned with a great number of foreign air arms.

Ballast in the Meteor's nose remained an unresolved problem until Meteor F Mk 4 RA382 was modified with a 30 inch (762mm) extension between the existing front-to-centre fuselage break bulkhead. This balanced the Meteor when fully loaded, but with the expenditure of some 800lb (360kg) of ammunition pitch problems reappeared. The next problem was to cure this pitch-up attitude and studies centred on the redesign of the tail unit. E.1/44, a single-engined project aircraft, provided the answer in its fin and tailplane design, which proved to be perfectly suitable. The only change consisted in the substitution of the top wooden section of the E.1/44's tail with a metal section.

Experience gained on RA382 was passed on to the true prototype, VT150 (also an ex-F Mk 4), which flew for the first time on 12th October 1948. Handling improved considerably over that of earlier marks and, as a bonus, performance increased dramatically. However, the airframe required strengthening to meet the stress induced by the improved performance. Power for the F Mk 8 was provided by a pair of Rolls-Royce Derwent 8s of 3,500lb (1,575kg) thrust. The canopy of VT150 was modified further with the introduction of a fully blown transparent unit. Although the rear metal fairing had been eliminated on the prototype, it continued to appear on a number of early production examples. Most important of all, the long-awaited introduction of an ejector seat was finally achieved.

Meteor F Mk 8 production was immediately taken in hand. Some 1,183 examples for the RAF were to be produced, with initial deliveries going to No.43 Squadron on 2nd August 1949. The first aircraft on the production line (VZ438) however, went to No.1 Squadron on 10th December of that same year. No.245 Squadron at Horsham St. Faith was to become the first fully operational unit on this version of the Meteor on 29th June 1950, thus beginning a long association with the type that was to last up to April 1957. WH398 was to become the last operational F Mk 8 with the RAF, leaving Singapore in 1962 after it had been flying at Seletar since 1954 (at one time it became a TT Mk 8).

Experimental F Mk 8s

The list of experimental Meteor F Mk 8s is extensive, although the following deserve special mention:

- VT150 Prototype F Mk 8. Later tests included spin parachute installation designed for the Javelin.
- VZ438 First production aircraft used for FR Mk 9 development tests at Farnborough. Used for conversion trials to TT Mk 8 configuration (a number of F.8s were converted to target-tugs as TT Mk 8s after they had completed regular service.
- VZ439 High-altitude tests with strengthened canopy.
- VZ460 Underwing bomb and rocket pylon acceptance trials; spring tab ailerons; went to the Central Fighter Establishment.
- VZ468 London-Copenhagen record flight.
- VZ500 Auto-stabiliser trials.
- VZ517 Used by Rolls-Royce (Hucknell) for surge tests on the

Derwent 8 and later tested with an Armstrong-Whitworth Screamer rocket engine.
- VZ657 Used for trials to investigate the damage caused to the belly tank by spent cannon cartridges.
- VZ442 Canopy fastenings trials.
- WA775 Nose radar for Firestreak missile guidance (for the Hunter).
- WA820 Most powerful Meteor ever built, fitted with two Armstrong-Whitworth Sapphire engines of 7,600lb (3,420kg) thrust each. Airframe and engine nacelles highly modified.
- WA823 Probe and drogue flight-refuelling trials.
- WA828–WA830 Probe and drogue flight-refuelling trials.
- WA832 Probe and drogue flight-refuelling trials.
- WA834 Probe and drogue flight-refuelling trials.
- WA837 Probe and drogue flight-refuelling trials.
- WA936 Probe and drogue flight-refuelling trials.
- WA941 Probe and drogue flight-refuelling trials.
- WA946 Probe and drogue flight-refuelling trials.
- WA952 Probe and drogue flight-refuelling trials.
- WA982 Fitted with Rolls-Royce Soar lightweight engine at port wing tip; the starboard unit originally fitted was a dummy, later also fitted making it a four-engined Meteor!
- WE855 Over-run airfield barrier tests.
- WH301 Converted to advance trainer configuration. Several F Mk 8s similarly converted becoming T Mk 8s.
- WH483 Spring-loaded tab aileron trials for improved manoeuvrability.
- WK935 Also known as the 'Prone Meteor' due to the addition of a prone position in the lengthened nose, for the Bristol 185 rocket interceptor project.
- G-AMCJ Private venture ground attack version with RATOG, underwing stores and tip tanks.

The Meteor Goes to War

The United States Air Force (USAF) found itself heavily committed in Korea with regard to personnel and material. Although the F-86 Sabre had already made its mark in the air battles over North Korea, production at that stage could not permit its supply to other air arms engaged in the fighting. The Royal Australian Air Force's (RAAF) need for more modern equipment was becoming urgent as since the beginning of the war in Korea it was still flying the P-51 Mustang.

One hundred Meteors were shipped to Australia in February 1951, ninety-seven F Mk 8s together with three T Mk 7s, to re-equip No.77 Squadron (RAAF), and following a short work-up period at Iwakuni, in Japan, the unit flew its first operational sorties on 29th July 1951. Under the command of Sqn Ldr Pete Crosswell, the squadron included within its flying personnel six experienced RAF pilots. Of the British pilots, Fg Off Berg was shot down by a MiG-15 and captured while Flt Sgt Lamb was killed in August in a mid-air crash. The first MiG kill by No.77 Squadron was recorded on 1st December 1951.

Misgivings about the Meteor's suitability were confirmed on 29th August when during a sweep over Chongju, the F Mk 8 proved no match for the far superior MiG-15. A77-21 was lost that day, and after another rough brush with MiGs the following week, 'MiG Alley' was declared a prohibited zone for the squadron. Meteor pilots henceforth concentrated on fighter sweeps and bomber escort duties keeping well to the south of the Chongchan River.

Once again the Meteor's role was switched, this time to ground attack. On 8th January 1952, No.77 Squadron flew its first such sortie against Chongdan, followed by no fewer than 1,773 sorties by the end of February, during which four pilots were lost. Ground attack missions were successful mainly due to the near total lack of enemy opposition. Originally use was made of 60lb HE rockets during these attacks but napalm bombs were also fitted later.

No.77 returned to fighter sweeps in May 1952 with the last MiG combat being recorded in March of the following year, when Sgt J. Hale was awarded another kill. When the war ended on 27th July 1953, 18,872 sorties had been flown during which fifty-four Meteors and thirty-two pilots had been lost. Three confirmed MiG kills appears to be a rather poor record in comparison. However, the damage inflicted on enemy ground positions by RAAF Meteors more than makes up for the apparent imbalance.

This underside view of VZ620, a PR Mk 10, clearly shows the ventral camera positions

This F Mk 8 (WA851, 'B') was operated by No.500 Squadron from its West Malling base, although this photograph shows this machine during one of the squadron's Summer Camps to Ta'Qali, Malta
(© R.J. Caruana)

Ground crew replacing the ammunition boxes in an F Mk 8 Meteor ('04'). To do this they need to lift the canopy in order to get access to the ammunition bay
(© R. Weiss)

Exports

On return to Australia, No.77 Squadron exchanged its Meteors for CAC-built F-86 Sabres. Other RAAF units to operate the Meteor were Nos.22 and 23 Squadrons, and No.75's three-ship aerobatic team known as the 'Meteorites'. Some F Mk 8s were eventually converted to pilotless drones as U Mk 16, 21 and 21A, or target-tugs.

Belgium received an initial order of twenty-three ex-RAF F Mk 8s (EG-201-EG-223) in 1949. Avions Fairey built 150 examples (EG-1-EG-150) under licence, assembled from components supplied by Fokker and the Fabrique Nationale Belge who also produced the Derwents. Sixty-seven examples were built later on - beginning with EG-224 - in two batches of thirty and thirty-seven respectively. These Meteors were operated by the 1st, 7th and 9th Wings and were eventually replaced by Hawker Hunters F Mk 4 and Republic F-84F Thunderstreaks.

Brazil received sixty examples (4400-4459) to replace the P-47 Thunderbolts in service with the two squadrons of 1° GavCa, as from 23rd October 1953. An additional Meteor F Mk 8 (4460) was built from spares available by Parque de Aeronáutica of Sao Paolo and delivered to 1° GAvCa for target-tug duties; eventually it was taken to the Museu Aerospacial for preservation on 22nd April 1974. Meteors F Mk 8 were grounded due to metal fatigue on 24th April 1965 and their number was drastically reduced until all were retired from service between 1966 and 1968.

Denmark ordered twenty examples (481-500) in April 1950, the first arriving in January of the following year. Esk 724 was formed, at first flying Meteors F Mk 4 on loan from Esk 723, until the arrival of the first four F Mk 8s on 15th January 1951. By 4th June deliveries had been completed and on 16th June 1952 the unit moved to Aalborg. In June 1954 all remaining F Mk 4s, T Mk 7s and F Mk 8s were integrated into Esk 724. On 12th March 1956, 724 Esk was reformed into two flights, one flying the Hawker Hunter, the other the Meteor F Mk 8. On 27th June the seventeen Meteors F Mk 8 still in service were retired, six being taken into storage while the others were distributed to various station flights for target-towing and liaison duties.

In October 1949, Egypt ordered nineteen Meteors F Mk 8 from Gloster, with a second batch of five being placed in December of the same year. Delivery of these aircraft was stalled by an arms embargo until seven aircraft were delivered in December 1952. The remaining twelve of the original contract did not reach Egypt until 1955.

Israel had ordered eleven F Mk 8s in February 1953. These were fitted with cannon armament supplied by Israel and HVAR rocket projectiles. Apart from their normal fighter role these aircraft could be easily converted to act as target-tugs as required. Israeli Meteors were serialled 2166 to 2169 and 2172 to 2178.

Syria ordered twelve F Mk 8s in 1950 (101 to 112). WK814 to WK817, 824 to 827, and 862 to 865 were originally marked for delivery but were diverted to the RAF due to the 1951 arms embargo. The ordered Meteors were delivered during the following year from ex-RAF stocks supplemented, in 1956, by a further seven examples.

The Royal Netherlands Air Force (RNAF) began to exchange its F Mk 4s for F Mk 8s in January 1951. Fokker initiated licence

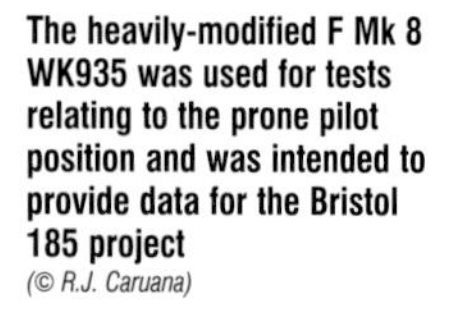

The heavily-modified F Mk 8 WK935 was used for tests relating to the prone pilot position and was intended to provide data for the Bristol 185 project
(© R.J. Caruana)

VT150 was the prototype F Mk 8 and was converted from a Gloster-built F Mk 4

production of 155 Meteors F Mk 8, sub-contracting considerable work to Aviolanda and De Schelde. An order for fifty examples placed on 21st April 1949 was to be assembled by Fokker from components supplied by Gloster, delivering the first example on 12th January 1951. The last, and 155th, Meteor F Mk 8 for the RNAF (I-255) was completed on 15th February 1956. Fokker also delivered 145 F Mk 8s to Belgium and thirty sub-assemblies for construction in Belgium by Avions Fairey. The RNAF Meteors F Mk 8 served with the following units (unit codes in parenthesis): No.322 (3W), No.323 (9Y), No.324 (3P), No.325 (4R), No.326 (9I), No.327 (7E) and No.328 (8S) Squadrons, and were retired from service in 1956.

The Meteor FR Mk 9 (G.41L)

A reconnaissance version of the highly successful F Mk 8 was a logical progression in the development of a fully armed photographic version. Conversion work required only slight remodelling of the nose section to hold one of the F.24 cameras that could be remotely operated from the cockpit to take pictures from all three windows. Hot air bled from the starboard engine was piped into this compartment to keep the nose-cone windows clear from condensation and the camera swivelling gear from freezing.

Prototype VW360 flew for the first time on 22nd March 1950, proving to possess an excellent performance. Designated FR Mk 9, the recce Meteor served mostly with the RAF outside the UK, particularly with Nos.2, 7 and 54 Squadrons in Germany, and No.208 Squadron in the Middle East. No.208 received the first FR Mk 9 to be delivered, VW363, on 28th July 1950. During the Suez Crisis, a detachment was transferred to Ta'Qali, in Malta, from where they flew daily reconnaissance flights.

VZ608, was originally used for tests on the Derwent 8, delivered to Rolls-Royce Flight Test Unit at Hucknall in March 1951 direct from Gloster. By September1952 it had flown 98 hours with an afterburner, and a reverse thrust unit was fitted on one of the engines in 1956. At Miles Aircraft it was fitted with an RB.108 lift engine in the centre fuselage designed for the Short SC.1, a vertical take-off project aircraft; the Meteor flew this engine in the air on 18th May 1956. A total of 162 FR Mk 9s was built, production ending with WX981 on 24th August 1952.

Twelve examples from ex-RAF stocks (701-712) were reconditioned and exported to Ecuador, the first going to Escuadrón de Combate 2111 on 9th July 1954. Deliveries were completed on 19th November of the same year. At least one example is preserved at the Museo Aéreo de la FAE, bearing the serial FF-123.

Syria received a pair of FR Mk 9s together with a batch of F Mk 8s between December 1952 and March 1953. Israel ordered nine Meteors of this mark in 1954 with the first pair arriving from Flight Refuelling Ltd in January 1955. Again here records are not quite clear, for only seven ex-RAF serialled machines are attributed to the Israeli order while Israeli sources claim that all nine had been delivered by May 1955. These FR Mk 9s enabled Israel to collect extensive data not only over Egyptian territory but also of Iraq's airfield facilities. As a number of T Mk 7s had been converted into photo-reconnaissance machines, most of the Israeli FR MK 9s were stripped of their cameras and used as fighters.

The Meteor PR Mk 10 (G41M)

Distinguishable by its early F Mk 4 style tail, the Meteor PR Mk 10 was virtually identical to the FR Mk 9 in front fuselage design. However, this version was fitted with the 43ft (13.11m) span wings as it was intended to replace the Spitfire PR Mk XIs and PR Mk 19s in the high-altitude reconnaissance role. Additional cameras were fitted in the fuselage and as no armament was fitted, the PR Mk 10 was a pure reconnaissance machine.

The first PR Mk 10, VS968, flew for the first time on 29th March 1950. Production of this type totalled fifty-eight examples, the first going to No.54 Squadron based at Gütersloh, in Germany, in February of 1951. Other squadrons that operated the PR Mk 10 included No.13, Middle East Air Force and No.81, Far East Air Force. The last PR Mk 10 was retired by No.81 Squadron in July 1961. There were no exports of the PR 10.

VW360 was the prototype FR Mk 9

Long-Nosed Meteors & Target Tugs

Chapter 4

This NF Mk 13 Meteor served with the 'Bat' Squadron
(© R. Weiss)

The night-fighter version of the Meteor was born more out of necessity than by design, as a replacement for the ageing Mosquito night fighter versions became a pressing need. Moreover, the RAF was conscious of the need for a jet-powered nocturnal interceptor for its squadrons. Work on a fully-fledged all-weather radar-equipped fighter was already in hand, and eventually led to the Gloster Javelin. However, the parent company realised that this new fighter would require a long gestation period in both design and flight development and proposed a radar-equipped Meteor as a stop-gap measure.

An AI radar had already been tested in a single-seat F Mk 3 in response to Air Ministry Specification F.44/46, which called for a two-seat all-weather fighter. In October 1946 the company submitted a detailed proposal for a night fighter based on the T Mk 7 fuselage with a radar operator occupying the rear seat. Gloster found itself fully committed both in the production and development of other Meteor versions as well as design of the far more advanced Javelin. By that time it had also become part of Hawker-Siddeley Aircraft, so the task of developing the night fighter Meteor was passed on to a company within the group, Armstrong-Whitworth Aircraft of Coventry. This company had been connected with the Meteor programme practically since its inception, producing several assemblies as one of the subcontractors, and in 1949 had also begun to build complete examples of the F Mk 8.

NF Mk 11 (G.47) Development

Detail design work, initiated in 1946, had been completed by the end of that year, together with a full-scale mock-up, around which Specification F.24/48 was written. The fourth production T Mk 7, VW413, was allocated for development purposes and fitted with the long-span F Mk 3 wings. By 23rd December 1948, flight-tests had begun but the aircraft was not, as yet, a true prototype as it could only be used to obtain aerodynamic data. Retaining the use of as many of the existing jigs, tooling and airframe components already available was essential in order to achieve low costs and early delivery dates.

The prototype closely resembled its trainer ancestor, fitted with long-span wings. By early 1949 it had acquired a lengthened bulbous nose to house the AI Mk 10 radar which, however, was not fitted at that stage. With this four-foot extension (1.20m), VW413 performed its first flight as the true NF Mk 11 prototype on 23rd January 1949, piloted by Armstrong-Whitworth's test pilot William H. Else.

Further external changes included the substitution of the T Mk 7 type tail with that of E.1/44, as introduced on the F Mk 8. Fitted with this tail unit, the prototype was flight-tested on 8th April by Armstrong-Whitworth's Chief Test Pilot Eric G. Franklin. Radar was fitted later on, as the final choice fell on the AI Mk 9c that required an additional 15 inches (38cm) to the nose length and a chin blister to accommodate the lower radar-mounting bracket of the dish and the scanner motor drive. Radar scanner diameter was 28 inches (71cm). Trials with this nose started early in December.

As the nose section was completely taken up by radar equipment, the four Hispano Mk 5 20mm cannon with 160 rounds per gun (rpg) were mounted in the outer wing section

Another view of Meteor NF Mk 13 '57' at the IAI during the testing of the 'Gabri'el' Air-Sea missile. Note the addition of the missile's head to the radome
(© R. Weiss)

TT Mk 20 WS767 was operated by A&AEE and RAE Llanbedr before being shipped to Woomera in 1970. This machine was subsequently preserved in the Mildura Museum
(© R.J. Caruana)

(two per wing). A cine gun camera was fitted to the starboard inboard wing section.

By July 1950 VW413 had been delivered to the A&AEE at Boscombe Down where it was evaluated by the establishment's pilots on the 18th and 19th of that month. It later returned to Bitteswell for a further nose extension of 9.5 inches (24cm). Finally VW413 went to RAE Farnborough in July of 1952.

The True Prototypes

Following tests with VW413, Armstrong-Whitworth received an order for three production-standard prototypes and 200 aircraft. The first true prototype (WA546) performed its first flight from Baginton on 31st May 1950 with Sqn Ldr Eric Franklin as test pilot, embodying all the refinements that were progressively developed through VW413. Although the basic T Mk 7 cockpit remained largely unchanged, the cabin was sealed and pressurised to equal the pressure at 24,000ft (7,301m) when the aircraft was at 40,000ft (12,168m). Air was tapped and piped into the cockpit from the Derwent's compressors.

Installation of ejection seats would have required extensive modifications, so none were fitted. The original AI Mk 10 radar chosen was now fitted but still lacked full instrumentation. In this form, J.O. Lancaster displayed the aircraft in the air at Farnborough on 7th and 8th July 1950. Flight-testing proceeded smoothly at Bitteswell after a full instrumentation fit that included IFF 10, GEE 3 navigational radar, AYF radio altimeter and VHF radio.

The second prototype (WA547) was ready and joined the test programme after its first flight on 11th August. Armament trials were carried out in September, but real firing trials were held at Boscombe Down in October. The third NF Mk 11 (WB543) appeared with strengthened wings, a feature embodied on all subsequent Meteors of this mark, and performed its maiden flight on 23rd September 1950. One of the trials involved testing a pair of 100Imp. Gal. (378lt) drop tanks under the wings. Although these had been cleared for use on the Meteor FR Mk 9 and PR Mk 10, they were found to collapse when at high speed on the NF Mk 11 and had to be fitted with a strengthened nose cap.

Production and Service

Although production began in September 1950 the NF Mk 11's entry into service had to be postponed for another year. WD585, the first production NF Mk 11, flew for the first time on 19th October 1950. Together with most of the early production night fighters it was assigned to further development studies. Others to join the development programme directly on leaving the production line included WD588, WD594 and WD595 which went to the Central Flying Establishment, followed by WD586, WD587, WD589, WD591, WD593 and WD596.

Further refinements before the type's entry into service included the replacement of the gear-tab ailerons with spring-loaded tabs and a clear-vision panel was fitted to the port side of the windscreen. Some modifications took much longer to be

A Meteor U Mk 21A. Note the areas of red paint applied to this aircraft
(© Courtesy of the Aviation Heritage Museum of WA)

The first U Mk 21 for Australia was WL136

officially sanctioned and were retrofitted to aircraft when already well advanced in construction on the production line.

Though the NF Mk 11 was some 3,000lb (1,326kg) heavier than the F Mk 8, it was only marginally slower; however, it proved to be more cumbersome during its initial climb. Pilot handling remained excellent, especially at low level.

The RAF took consignment of its first Meteor NF Mk 11 on 20th August 1951 when WD599 was delivered to No.24 Squadron at Tangmere to replace the venerable, though ageing, Mosquitoes NF Mk 36. The second RAF unit to receive the night fighter Meteor was No.141 Squadron at Coltishall. Re-equipping continued throughout 1951, with No.85 at West Malling and No.264 at Linton-on-Ouse. Nos.68 and 85 Squadrons were formed on 1st January 1952 at Wahn, in Germany, the first to be equipped with the type within the 2nd Tactical Air Force. Two more NF Mk 11 squadrons were added to North Atlantic Treaty Organisation (NATO) forces in Germany with No.96 on 1st October and No.256 on 17th November 1952, both based at Ahlhorn. By the end of that year, the night-fighter conversion course on the Meteor with No.228 OCU at Leeming had been well established.

NF Mk 11 WM239 goes vertical. This machine was operated by Nos.96 and 256 Squadron before being scrapped in May 1958 (©via J.L Bilcliffe)

A follow-on order for a further 192 was awarded to Armstrong-Whitworth, although not all destined for the RAF. This enabled No.151 Squadron at Leuchars in 1953 to exchange its Vampires NF Mk 10 with the Meteors NF Mk 11. Several examples were also supplied to the Central Flying Establishment (CFE) at West Raynham for the development of night fighter tactics. Others were delivered to the Central Signals Establishment (Watton), the Telecommunications School (Farnborough), the RAF Handling Squadron (Manby), as well as those on trials at Farnborough and Boscombe Down.

Exports

Meteors NF Mk 11 WM381 to WM403 from the second contract were released for the Royal Danish Air Force bearing serials H-501 to H-520. The first example (H-501) performed its maiden flight on 22nd October 1952. All the Danish Meteor night fighters had been delivered by 28th March of the following year and were assigned to Esk 723 at Aalborg. They remained in service until the US Government offered two squadrons of F-86Ds as replacements in May 1959.

France ordered twenty-five examples (NF11-1 to NF11-25), the first two leaving for Le Bourget on 7th January 1953. NF11-1 to NF11-9 went to the *Centre d'Essais en Vol* (CEV), the French Flight Evaluation Centre. A second order for sixteen aircraft was supplied from refurbished ex-RAF NF Mk 11s bearing codes NF11-26 to NF11-41, delivered between September 1954 and 21st April of the following year. These joined NF11-10 to NF11-25 which, in the meantime, had been assigned to the *Escadron Chasse de Nuit* (night fighter squadron) ECN-30. Some of these were eventually transferred to ECN 1/7, operating from Algeria, North Africa. When retired from frontline service they were mainly deployed with the CEV and it is interesting to mention that NF11-6 served as chase-plane during early Concorde flights.

Belgium's order in 1952 for twenty-four Meteors NF Mk 11 was entirely supplied by refurbished ex-RAF machines (EN-1 to EN-24) to equip Nos.10 and 11 Squadrons (No.1 Wing) in 1956. They were retired from service on 31st October 1958, except for nine examples converted to target-tugs and sold to civilian operators.

Little known is the fact that three production NF Mk 11s (WM372, WM373 and WM374) were acquired by Australia and used by the Air Research and Development Unit. These were never allocated RAAF (A77-) serials.

The Meteor NF 12

Meteors NF Mk 11 WD670 and WD687 were allocated for modification trials that were to lead to the NF Mk 12. The main difference consisted in the installation of the American APS AI.21 radar supplied under the Mutual Aid Defense Program (MDAP) that possessed an improved range, though heavier in weight than the AI Mk 10 radar of the NF Mk 11. The nose was further lengthened by 17 inches (43cm) while the chin fairing was eliminated.

To counter the extra weight, Armstrong-Whitworth installed

WM361 was the prototype NF Mk 14 converted from a NF Mk 11

Rolls-Royce Derwent 9 engines that provided 3,800lb (1,724kg) of thrust. Further strengthening to the wings was also considered necessary due to the higher limiting Mach number of these engines.

The Derwent 8-powered WD680 was test-flown in June 1952, immediately exhibiting dangerous tendencies attributed to fin stalling. WD687 was fitted with fillets ahead of the fin leading edges, below and above the bullet fairing, which cured the dangerous vices of the earlier test aircraft and became a characteristic recognition feature of the final line of Meteors.

One-hundred examples of the NF Mk 12 were ordered into production, the first (WS590) flying on 21st April 1953 at Baginton with Armstrong-Whitworth's Chief Test Pilot Sqn Ldr Eric Franklin at the controls. The first production Meteor NF Mk 12 eventually went to No.238 OCU. Early the following year No.85 Squadron began to replace the Meteor NF Mk 11 with the new mark of night fighter, followed by No.25 Squadron. No Meteors of this mark were ever exported.

The Meteor NF Mk 13

A tropicalised version was planned very early in the NF Mk 11's career, as its need in the Middle East was being felt. A cold air unit was fed through air intakes underneath the fuselage centre section, thus keeping cockpit temperatures at bearable levels. The refrigeration unit was, in fact, found to be too effective, especially at higher altitudes! A weight penalty of some 450lb (205kg) had a slightly adverse effect on performance. Externally the Meteor NF Mk 11 and NF Mk 13 were practically identical.

Production run of the NF Mk 13 consisted of forty conversions from the NF Mk 11 production line during assembly. The first NF Mk 13, WM308, flew for the first time on 23rd December 1952, piloted by J. Lancaster.

Delivery commenced soon afterwards, in January 1953, with the first examples being delivered to No.8 MU at Little Rissington. No.39 Squadron was the first unit to equip with the NF Mk 13 at Fayid the following March, followed by No.219 Squadron at Kabrit in April. With the Suez Crisis gathering momentum, No.219 was disbanded while No.39 Squadron moved to Luqa, Malta, in January 1955. These Meteors NF Mk 13 were detached to Nicosia in Cyprus during *'Operation Musketeer'* of November 1956 and returned to Malta on 30th June 1958, where the squadron disbanded to reform as a PR unit.

Production came to an end in March 1953 with WM367, which was assigned to the A&AEE at Boscombe Down, remaining in use up to 1972 (coded 'S'). The type found great favour with Middle East Air Forces and Armstrong-Whitworth eventually bought back half the NF Mk 13 production from the RAF for refurbishing and resale. Six such examples were supplied to Syria in June and July 1954 (serials 471-476) with a further six going to Egypt between June and August of the following year (serials 1427-1432). Three of these were lost during the fighting over Suez in 1956.

Having supplied Egypt and Syria, Israel requested six NF Mk 13s for its own use in 1956. The story of their delivery is rather amusing as they were delivered in the guise of civil-registered machines in two batches of three aircraft! The first trio was delivered on 5th September 1956, marked as 4X-FNA, 4X-FNB and 4X-FND, while the second batch (4X-FNC, 4X-FNE,

WA372 was modified in relation to trials with the Fairey Fireflash missile. Note the wing tip launch rails and the modified radome

4X-FNF) was withheld until March 1958. They were assigned to the 119th 'Atalef' Squadron that had been formed in August 1956. By the time the last three examples arrived it had been moved to Tel-Nof airbase.

France bought two, NF-F364 (ex-WM364) and NF-F365 (ex-WM365) in June 1956. They both went to the *Centre d'Essais en Vol* (CEV), presumably joining the unit's NF Mk 11s purchased earlier.

The Meteor NF Mk 14

The first two-seat Meteor to receive the elegant one-piece transparent canopy was WM261, a Meteor NF Mk 11 that served

WA546 was the first of two true prototypes for the NF Mk 11 series

U Mk 16 WH453 is seen in the colours of No.5 CAACU during a piloted flight
(©Glenn Sands)

as NF Mk 14 prototype, performing flight-tests at Baginton and later at Boscombe Down. The new canopy was electrically operated, sliding back to afford much easier access to the cockpit. In-flight jettison trials were also undertaken in October 1953.

Armstrong-Whitworth received orders for 100 examples, the first of which (WS722) was flown for the first time by Bill Else on 23rd October 1953. Following minor refinements introduced by AV Roe Ltd at Langar, the first examples were delivered to No.25 Squadron at West Malling in January 1954. The last NF Mk 14 was withdrawn from service with No.60 Squadron in 1961 at Tengah, Singapore, where they were used in the all-weather role. A small number of NF Mk 14s were converted to the trainer role with all armament removed for Air Navigation Schools and redesignated NF(T) Mk 14. At least two NF Mk 14 examples ended up on the civil register: G-AXNE that was used as a camera ship by Enterprise Films Ltd in 1969 and G-ASLW was owned by Rolls-Royce. The latter was mysteriously lost off the coast of Portugal.

Only one NF Mk 14 is believed to have been exported, this being WS747 that was acquired by France for its *Centre d'Essais en Vol* (CEV) and believed to have been still flying in the mid-1970s.

The Meteor TT Mk 20

This target tug version of the Meteor, based on the NF Mk 11, was produced mainly to fulfil the Royal Navy's requirement for a high-speed target tower to replace the ageing Firefly and Sturgeon. With the introduction of the NF Mk 12, 13 and 14 into service, NF Mk 11s came up for disposal and WD767 was used for the conversion work. A Type G wind-driven winch which could trail 6,100ft (1,800m) of cable and towing as many as four sleeve targets was fitted in a fairing onto the starboard inboard wing section. The occupant of the rear seat handled all operations connected with the target and winch. Though the nose radar was removed its fairing was retained. WD767, now designated TT Mk 20, flew for the first time on 5th December 1956.

Following several successful trials at Boscombe Down, eighteen conversions were approved, beginning with WM147 that was completed just over a year later. The A&AAE retained this example, together with four other TT Mk 20s, for further development and trials while the rest were delivered to RNAS Lossiemouth beginning in 1958. Conversion work on the Meteors TT Mk 20 fell on Armstrong-Whitworth Aircraft, but most of the later NF Mk 11s were converted by the Royal Navy at Belfast, Northern Ireland.

No.728 Squadron Fleet Air Arm (FAA) was the first unit to receive the TT Mk 20 at Hal Far, Malta, in 1958. Its task was to provide target facilities for shore and ship batteries all over the central Mediterranean, until withdrawn on 7th April 1967. In the UK, TT Mk 20 operations were passed on to civilian contractors Airwork Services Ltd, based at the Fleet Requirements Unit at Hurn, between 1958 and 1970. Some time after 1968 the TT Mk 20s operated by them were modified to tow the Rushton high-speed target developed by Flight Refuelling Ltd. Other units operating TT Mk 20s for the FAA were No.700 Trials Squadron at Ford and Yeovilton, and the Brawdy, Yeovilton and Lossiemouth Station Flights. The RAF also used a civilian contractor for UK operations, No.3 Civilian Anti-Aircraft Co-operation Unit (CAACU) at Exeter, and No.1574 Target Facility Flight at Seletar, in Singapore.

France acquired six Meteors TT Mk 20 in 1974 after the type's retirement from UK service, three of which had been refurbished by No.5 MU at RAF Kemble. Assigned to the *Centre d'Essais en Vol*, the TT Mk 20s were immediately stripped for spares to keep the other NF Mk 11s flying and were never flown as target tugs. Their empty shells were finally scrapped in October 1975.

Six of the Royal Danish Air Force (RDAF) NF 11s that had been acquired between November 1952 and March 1953 were converted to TT Mk 20 standard by Armstrong-Whitworth and delivered in February, 1959. Four of these were passed on to Svenska Flygtjänst AB in 1962, being given civilian registrations as follows: H-512 (ex-WM395) SE-DCF; H-517 (ex-WM400) SE-DCG; H-508 (ex-WM391) SE-DCH; H-519 (ex-WM402) SE-DCI. They were delivered with these registrations between 27th August and 3rd September 1962. Of these, SE-DCH and SE-DCF were sold to K. Mortenson for use as target tugs in Germany in March 1969.

Unmanned Meteors - U Mk 15, U Mk 16, U Mk 21

A number of F Mk 4s and F Mk 8s were converted to the 'unmanned' drone role after their retirement from service. The conversion project began in 1959 and by the following year a number of such aircraft were handed over to Flight Refuelling Ltd (FRL) to be fitted out. The new designations were U Mk 15 for aircraft converted from ex-F Mk 4s and U Mk 16 for those originating from F Mk 8s. Some of the U Mk 15 conversions replaced Fairey Fireflies used for the same purpose at Hal Far, Malta.

FRL supplied fifty-nine examples of the U Mk 15 to the RAAF, where the original RAF serials were retained (e.g. RA438). Most of these were to end their days at Woomera.

The U Mk 21 was a further conversion from the U Mk 16 by FRL, the first example flying on 3rd May 1961. Ten such aircraft were actually delivered as U Mk 16s with the necessary modifications supplied in kit form for final assembly by Fairey Aviation in Australia. With their conversion to U Mk 21 standard these aircraft received 'A' serials, including A77-157 and A77-884, in February 1963.

Today all that remains of NF Mk 13 WM367 is the nose section at the South Yorkshire Aviation Museum. This aircraft was originally delivered directly to France for the CEV
(©Glenn Sands)

The Meteor in Belgium

by Rudy Binnemans

Chapter 5

Meteor F Mk 4s of No.349 Squadron refuelling at Beauvechain in 1950
(©via Rudy Binnemans)

Demonstration Tour of the Meteor F Mk 4

To promote international sales of the Meteor F Mk 4, Gloster arranged a tour through several European capitals. On the 18th April 1947 the demonstration aircraft was at Evere/Brussels and while there it was test-flown by several Belgian pilots including Lt Col. Mike Donnet and Majors Lallemant, Mullenders and Van Lierde. The entire European tour concluded in Brussels where the demonstration Meteor (G-AIDN) was flown against a de Havilland Vampire. The Meteor was flown by Major Mullenders but unfortunately during a high speed, low-level flight part of the undercarriage was lost and the aircraft sustained serious damage during the ensuing emergency landing. The aircraft was returned to the UK by road and sea and parts from this machine were used in the production of the Meteor T Mk 7 demonstrator.

Initially Belgium did not place orders for the Meteor F Mk 4, however with the increase in the political tension between East and West and the creation of the Western Union Pact on the 17th March 1948, the Belgian Government was soon looking to purchase the type. On the 12th March 1948 Belgium ordered forty-eight Meteor F Mk 4s with a unit price of £29,400 and delivery before the 30th November 1949. The first of these forty-eight aircraft arrived in April 1949, while the last was delivered in September of that year. They carried serials EF-1 to EF-48 and although they had all initially been produced to meet an RAF order, they were all delivered straight to Belgium. The first two squadrons to use the type were Nos.349 and 350, both of which re-equipped from Spitfire Mk XIVs in May and July 1949 respectively. Both of these units were stationed at Beauvechain and both received sixteen aircraft while the rest of the airframes were stored at Melsbroek. On the 12th June 1949 the 35th anniversary of the Belgian Military Aviation was marked at Evere/Brussels with an International Air Meeting. For this event the Meteor F Mk 4 was demonstrated by Majors Arends and Geerts, after which there was a simulated ground attack mission performed by nine Meteors from both squadrons. At the end of

NF Mk 11, EN-1, ND•L in 1952. This later became KT•L
(©via Rudy Binnemans)

F Mk 4, EF-12, GE•R of No.349 Squadron is seen on the hardstanding at Beauvechain in 1951
(©via Rudy Binnemans)

1949, another day fighter squadron was activated at Beauvechain. This was No.4 Squadron and it utilised the remaining aircraft that had been stored at Melsbroek. The squadron received its first aircraft on the 20th December 1949.

During the summer of 1950 there was an international exhibition held at the Centenaire Halls, Heysel in Brussels and F Mk 4s EF-38 and 47 were present for this event. 1950 also saw the participation by Belgian Air Force Meteors in Western Union Pact air exercises such as 'Cupola' in April and 'X-Ray' in June. On the 25th June 1950 there was an international air show at Deurne/Antwerp where all three Meteor squadrons participated. During 1951 the F Mk 4s took part in Western Union Pact air exercises 'Umbrella' in May and 'Cirrus' in September. During this year No.350 Squadron exchanged its Meteor F Mk 4s for F Mk 8s. During 1952 the remaining F Mk 4 squadrons (Nos 4 & 349) participated in Exercise 'Coronet' during March, while in June No.349 Squadron took part in Excercise 'June Primer' because at this time No.4 Squadron was at Koksijde for its annual APC (Armament Practice Camp). By the end of 1952 there were still forty-one Meteor F Mk 4s in the Belgian Air Force.

1953 saw the re-equipping of No.349 Squadron with the Meteor F Mk 8 followed by No.4 Squadron doing the same in February. All remaining airworthy aircraft went to the Fighter School OCU at Koksijde and these included EF-3, 5, 6, 8, 14, 20, 24, 29, 31, 33, 34, 36, 37, 38, 44, 45, 47 and 48. During this period Fairey Aviation in Belgium suggested that they rebuild the F Mk 4 into T Mk 7s. A contract for 20 aircraft followed in 1953 and those aircraft rebuilt as T Mk 7s included EF-4, 7, 9, 10, 11, 12, 13, 15, 16, 18, 19, 21, 23, 25, 28, 30, 32, 39, 41 and 42. The remaining F Mk 4s stayed at the Fighter School until the 15th January 1957, by which time only EF-6, 8, 20, 34, 38, 44 and 48 were still flying. Later all of these airframes were sold for scrap, while those F Mk 4 airframes that had been converted to T Mk 7s remained in active service well into the 1960s.

The F Mk 8

At the end of 1949 the Belgian Government placed its first order in the UK for twenty-three F Mk 8s. All of these machines came from RAF stocks and were mostly brand new. Most of these aircraft were stored at No.38 MU Llandow and they were flown to Belgium from there by Belgian ferry pilots at the end of 1950 and the beginning of 1951. Once in Belgium they were stored at Melsbroek for some months until delivery to No.350 Squadron started in July 1951.

RAF SERIAL	BAF SERIAL	DELIVERED	STATUS/FROM
VZ450	EG-201	15/11/50	New
VZ457	EG-205	22/11/50	Gloster Aircraft Co.
VZ459	EG-206	24/11/50	New
VZ499	EG-203	22/11/50	New
VZ553	EG-211	11/12/50	Ex-74 Sqn
VZ562	EG-204	22/11/50	New
VZ600	EG-217	17/01/51	New
WA755	EG-220	24/11/50	New
WA870	EG-208	30/11/50	Ex-19 Sqn
WA876	EG-210	30/11/50	New
WA878	EG-209	30/11/50	Gloster Aircraft Co.
WA881	EG-202	14/11/50	New
WA883	EG-207	24/11/50	New
WA884	EG-213	11/12/50	New
WA887	EG-214	12/01/51	New
WA888	EG-215	11/12/50	OCU
WA889	EG-216	12/01/51	Ex-600 Sqn
WA892	EG-212	12/01/51	New
WA895	EG-218	19/01/51	New
WA898	EG-219	19/01/51	New
WA900	EG-221	23/01/51	New
WA901	EG-222	9/02/51	Ex-RAAF
WA902	EG-223	26/0/151	Ex-600 Sqn

The First Operational Meteor F Mk 8 Squadron

No.350 Squadron was the first equipped with the new Meteor F Mk 8. Squadron Code: MN

B EG-207	C EG-203	D EG-210
E EG-201	F EG-205	H EG-202
K EG-204	L EG-206	P EG-208
R EG-211	V EG-214	X EG-215
Y EG-216	Z EG-217	

There were also three aircraft that carried personal codes:

EG-212 MLD for Col. Mike Donnet
EG-219 ALW for Sqn Ldr Windskill in 1952
EG-220 GCA for Grp Cpt Atherton in 1953

Both of the above British pilots were allocated to the 1st Wing and did the job as Senior Flying Officer in above-mentioned year. In 1953 EG-212 became MN•A and EG-219 MN•M.

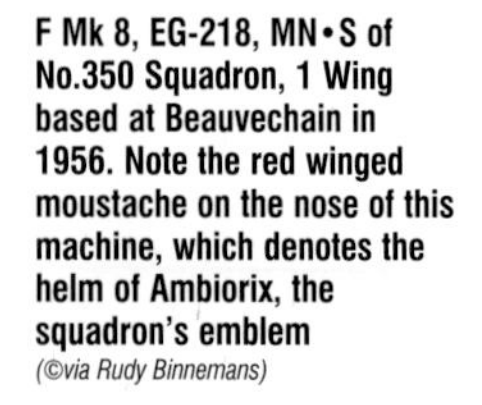

F Mk 8, EG-218, MN•S of No.350 Squadron, 1 Wing based at Beauvechain in 1956. Note the red winged moustache on the nose of this machine, which denotes the helm of Ambiorix, the squadron's emblem
(©via Rudy Binnemans)

Line-up of F Mk 8s of No.33 Sqn, 13 Wing, with EG-47, MS•G in the foreground
(©via Rudy Binnemans)

The Follow-up Order for the Meteor F Mk 8

After the first order for the F Mk 8 during 1949 a further order was placed to construct or assemble F Mk 8s in Belgium and Holland (Fairey Belgium and Fokker/Aviolanda). In total 150 aircraft were ordered in the Netherlands and sixty-seven in Belgium. The order was as follows:

EG-1 to EG145 — Built by Fokker and Aviolanda, delivered between October 1951 and February 1954.
EG-146 to EG-150 — Ex-RAF aircraft delivered by Fokker in October 1951.
EG-151 to EG-180 — Built by Fokker and assembled by Fairey Belgium.
EG-201 to EG-223 — From the UK.
EG-224 to EG-260 — Built by Gloster but assembled in Belgium by Fairey personnel at Beauvechain in the years 1952/53.
EG-261 to EG-270 — Cancelled, never delivered. The intention for their construction was the same as with EG-224/260.

1st Day Fighter Wing at Beauvechain – 1953/1957

In February 1953 No.349 Squadron changed its F Mk 4s for the F Mk 8, and they were followed by No.4 Squadron. Because No.4 Squadron was the last to receive the F Mk 8 it received the modified ones with the enlarged air intakes, one-piece canopy and twin trim tabs on the wings. No.349 Squadron was also to receive these later versions, but No.350 Squadron soldiered on with the earlier ones. Eventually, after Nos.4 and 349 Squadron had fully re-equipped with the modified F Mk 8s No.350 at last also received them. In April 1957 Nos.349 and 350 Squadrons exchanged their Meteors for the Hunter F Mk 4, while No.4 Squadron disbanded in May 1957.

The F Mk 8 in the 7th Day Fighter Wing

The 7th Day Fighter Wing consisted of the following squadrons:

- **No.7 Squadron** – **Sqn Code**: 7J
  Emblem: Red Cocotte
  No.7 Squadron was formed at Chièvres on the 1st December 1950. On the 22nd December 1950 it took charge of its first aircraft, not a Meteor but an Avro Anson Mk 1 (AN-8). The first Meteor F Mk 8 was collected at Melsbroek in May 1951.
- **No.8 Squadron** – **Sqn Code**: OV
  Emblem: Blue Cocotte
  This squadron was formed on the 16th July 1951.
- **No.9 Squadron** – **Sqn Code**: S2
  Emblem: Green Cocotte
  This squadron was formed on the 17th March 1952.

In 1951 the 1st and the 7th Wing merged into a new group, No.69 Group. This group was made up with squadrons from the Belgian, Dutch and British Air Forces and the headquarters of the Group was at Deurne/Antwerp. All the Senior Flying Officers in the 1st and 7th Wing were from the RAF.

1956 was the last year the Meteor served at Chièvres and on the 12th June 1956 the first Hunter F Mk 4s replaced the ageing Meteors. The last Meteor left Chièvres by the end of the year.

The 9th Day Fighter Wing, Bierset/Liège

When the 9th Wing was set up it was a Fighter-Bomber Wing equipped with the F-84E/G Thunderjet. In 1956 it was decided to change its role to that of a Day Fighter Wing equipped with the new Hawker Hunter. But because of delays and problems with the Hunter the Air Staff decided to use the Meteor F Mk 8 as an interim fighter. The Wing flew the Meteor from mid-1956 to the end of 1957.

The 9th Day Fighter Wing consisted of the following squadrons:

- **No.22 Squadron** – **Sqn Code**: IS
  Emblem: Silver eagle in a blue circle
  Sqn Colour: Light blue
  This squadron flew Meteors from the 1st July 1956 to the end of 1957.
- **No.26 Squadron** – **Sqn Code**: JE
  Emblem: Silver bison in a red circle
  Sqn Colour: Red
  This squadron flew Meteors from the 1st July 1956 to the end of 1957.
- **No.30 Squadron** – **Sqn Code**: EB
  Emblem: Panther in a yellow circle
  Sqn Colour: Yellow
  This squadron flew Meteors from the 1st July 1956 to its disbandment in October 1956.

Meteor F Mk 4, EG-27, MN•O of No.350 Squadron
(©via Rudy Binnemans)

Line-up of F Mk 8s of No.8 Squadron, 7 Wing at Chièvres in 1951. As may be apparent, these are all brand new machines
(©via Rudy Binnemans)

The 13th Day Fighter Wing, Koksujde/Brustem

In August 1953 the 13th Day Fighter Wing was established at Koksijde and on the 22nd December 1953 it moved to Brustem. At that time the Advanced Flying School which operated the Harvard left Brustem for Kamina (Belgian-Congo) and the 13th Wing took its place on the airfield. On the 8th January 1957 the wing moved again to Koksijde where it remained until its disbandment on the 1st July 1958.

The 13th Day Fighter Wing consisted of the following squadrons:

- **No.25 Squadron – Sqn Code**: K5
  Emblem: Blue swallow in a red circle
  Sqn Colour: Red
  This squadron flew Meteors from the 22nd December 1953 until the disbandment of the squadron on the 1st July 1958.
- **No.29 Squadron – Sqn Code**: VT
  Emblem: Chequerboard on a light blue shield, surrounded by a yellow circle. The chequerboard was enveloped by two green wings
  Sqn Colour: Green
  This squadron flew Meteors from the 22nd December 1953 to its disbandment on the 1st July 1958
- **No.33 Squadron – Sqn Code**: MS
  Emblem: A silver-winged red arrow
  Sqn Colour: Black
  This squadron flew Meteors from the 22nd December 1953 to its disbandment in May 1957

The 5th Day Fighter Wing

It was the intention to station the 5th Day Fighter Wing at Ursel with three squadrons: Nos.24, 28 and 32. In the end No.24 Squadron only had a short life, not as a fighter squadron but as a target-towing squadron.

- **No.24 Squadron – Sqn Code**: X0
  Emblem: None
  Sqn Colours: Orange/black
  The squadron was established at Chièvres in 1954 but was disbanded on the 25th August 1954. The decision was made to change the squadron's role and move it to Sylt, Germany. RAF Germany had an Armament Practice Camp for air-to-air gunnery training at Sylt. In that period it was also used by the Belgian Air Force for the same role. No.24 Squadron was used there as a target-towing squadron until its disbandment on the 6th May 1955. Most of its aircraft were old Meteors from the first order. The squadron had fifteen Meteor F Mk 8s on its strength, from which twelve had to be operational at any time.

The Fighter Pilot School – O.T.U.

From the 1st September 1954 an OTU with the Meteor F Mk 8 was established at Koksijde. The aircraft carried no squadron codes, just serials on the fuselage sides. They also carried the OTU badge on the engine nacelle and this took the form of a yellow vulture with black outline on a red/black arrow in a blue circle. They also sometimes carried a red arrow on the nose. After a move to Brustem the Meteor F Mk 8 OTU was disbanded and the Lockheed T-33 took over the job.

The Target-Towing Flight at Koksijde

After the disbandment of No.33 Squadron on the 2nd May 1957, a 13th Wing Target-Towing Flight was formed at Koksijde with its aircraft. After disbandment on the 1st July 1958 of the 13th Wing with its two squadrons, Nos.25 and 29, a Target-Towing Flight was formed at Koksijde. This Flight was of squadron strength and it continued flying the Meteors from the 13th Wing. The squadron code carried by these aircraft was now B2. This Flight (Squadron)

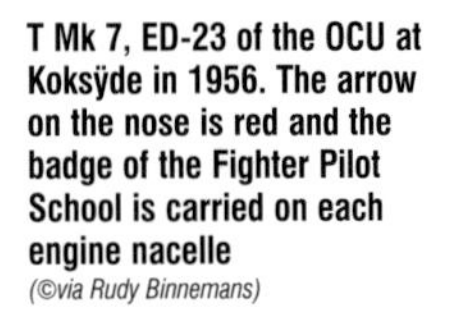

T Mk 7, ED-23 of the OCU at Koksÿde in 1956. The arrow on the nose is red and the badge of the Fighter Pilot School is carried on each engine nacelle
(©via Rudy Binnemans)

Meteor T Mk 7, ED-37 seen here off the coast in 1955-6
(©via Rudy Binnemans)

flew the Meteor TT Mk 8 until 1963 when they were flown not only in the target-towing role but also as target aircraft for interception sorties. For the first two years of its life it was permanently part of the flight at RAF Sylt in Germany and from 1960 onwards it was initially based at Cazaux (France) followed by Slenzara (Corsica). By the end of 1960 the Target-Towing Flight still had twenty-three Meteors. The last public demonstration of their machines was at Chièvres on the 23rd June 1963 when the demonstration aircraft for this occasion was EG-225/B2•H. The Target-Towing Flight itself was disbanded on the 9th November 1963.

The End of the Meteor F Mk 8

Most Meteors were sold for scrap. A civilian company, COGEA, who also bought Meteor NF Mk 11s, also bought three Meteor F Mk 8s and these were allocated civilian registrations. They were:

EG-162	00-ARU
EG-164	00-ART
EG-178	00-ARV

These aircraft were initially stored at Ostend airfield, but they never flew and were eventually scrapped. By the end of 1963 there were still forty-seven Meteor F Mk 8s stored at Koksijde awaiting scrapping. Some survivors include:

Brussels Air Museum	EG-224 K5•K
To the 1st Wing	EG-22 & EG-226
To the 10th Wing	EG-237
To Brustem	EG-259

A company named 'Star' bought thirty-one F Mk 8s.

At the time of writing the following airframes still exist in Belgium:

EG-224	K5•K	Brussels Air Museum
EG-247	B2•R	1972, Brussels Air Museum 1978, Brustem, to be painted as EG-244 MN-A of the Red Devils Aerobatic Team 1984, Stored in Belgium in a hangar for the Brussels Air Museum 1985, Bierset, to be painted as EG-244, OV-A of No.8 Squadron
EG-237		Repainted as EG-79, S2-R at Brustem (No.9 Sqn). After closure of the base at Brustem in 1996 the aircraft was presented to be displayed at the 1st Wing Historical Center/Beauvechain
EG-18		Repainted as OV-T (No.8 Sqn)
EG-162		This machine was at the citadel of the city of Dinant on the playing ground, but it was in a bad condition

Gloster Meteor T Mk 7

The first three T Mk 7 trainers were ordered from Gloster Aircraft in May 1948. Delivery to the Belgian Air Force was on the 1st March 1949, thus arriving in the country before the first F Mk 4s. These machines went to the 1st Day Fighter Wing at Beauvechain for transitional training of the Spitfire Mk XIV pilots. As there was still a need for even more trainers, the Belgian Air Force ordered more Meteor T Mk 7s from the UK, where they came from unused RAF stocks and were serialled ED-4 to ED-12. They were used in all the Day Fighter Wings and the OCU for conversion training, based at Beauvechain, Chièvres, Bierset and Koksijde. At the same time a contract was signed with Fairey Aviation Belgium to convert redundant F Mk 4s to T Mk 7 standard. These machines received the serials ED-13 to ED-32 and all were delivered in the 1954/55 period. A further eleven Meteor T Mk 7s were taken over from RAF stocks and they received serials ED-33 to ED-43. Fairey Aviation also converted an unknown number of F Mk 4/T Mk 7 conversions into the Meteor T Mk 7A, which was better known as the 'Mulet'. These machines had the high tail of the Meteor F Mk 8. One of these, ED-28, crashed before delivery to the Air Force. Of the remainder it is known that ED-7 and ED-29 to 32 were converted from T Mk 7 to T Mk 7A 'Mulets'. Two of these were delivered in 1958 to the Israeli Air Force and it is most probable that ED-14 and ED-15 were also transferred to the IAF.

The Operational Life of the Gloster Meteor T Mk 7

The first trainers were distributed between the Day Fighter Wings for use as pilot transitional training for two-engined aircraft. 1954 was the last year of the Operational Training Unit with the Spitfire Mk XIV. From this point onwards young pilots were to be graded on jet aircraft and therefore the Meteor T Mk 7 was used in Koksijde in the company of the F Mk 4. In 1955 two training units were established at Koksijde, an OCU with the Meteor T Mk 7 and F Mk 4 and an OTU with the Meteor T Mk 7. There were also some T Mk 7s in the OTU used for instrument training.

In the early fifties half of the Belgian pilots were trained in the USA. Returning to Belgium half of their number went to the Fighter-Bomber Wings, the other half to the Day Fighter Wings. As they had no experience on twin-engined aircraft, they had to do transitional training on the T Mk 7. In 1955 the 9th Fighter-Bomber Wing at Bierset became the 9th Day Fighter Wing. All the pilots had to be converted from the F-84G Thunderjet to the Gloster Meteor F Mk 8 and for this job the Meteor T Mk 7 was a very welcome addition. Some T Mk 7s remained at Koksijde in the new target-towing Flight until 1962,

Meteors being dismantled in 1957. Visible are T Mk 7 ED-12, EN-24 (ND•M) and EG-84 of the OTU
(©via Rudy Binnemans)

but the Meteors of the OCU and OTU were replaced by the Lockheed T-33 from 1957. The remaining aircraft went to Brustem (base of the 13th Day Fighter Wing) to form a special instrument training flight. Every pilot had just one attempt a year to prove his knowledge on instrument flying to get his green card. The Meteor T Mk 7 was used in this role until 1959, when it was replaced by the Lockheed T-33.

The End of the Gloster Meteor T Mk 7

After their operational life as a trainer in Belgium the remaining T Mk 7s, except two that went to Israel and those converted by Fairey Aviation, were one-by-one sold for scrap. The following aircraft crashed during service:

ED-21, 27, 30, 35 and 36

Those scrapped:
- 1956 ED-13
- 1957 ED-14, 15, 19 & 25 (the first two were actually sold to Israel)
- 1958 ED-2, 4, 6, 12, 16, 17, 18, 20, 23, 24, 26, 31, 32, 38, 39
- 1962 ED-1, 3, 5, 7, 8, 10, 11, 22, 28, 29, 33, 34, 37, 40, 41, 42 and 43

A formation of four NF Mk 11s in 1952 including EN-10 (KT•U), EN-6 (KT•W), EN-11 (KT•T) and EN-2 (KT•E)
(©via Rudy Binnemans)

Night-Fighters – The Meteor NF Mk 11

Due to the Soviet threat the 'Pact of Brussels' was signed on the 17th March 1948 between the UK, France, Belgium, Holland and Luxembourg. The development of Belgian Military Aviation was planned as follows: twelve squadrons of day fighters with sixteen aircraft each; three squadrons of night fighters with sixteen aircraft each; two squadrons of transport aircraft with twenty aircraft each. When the 'Accords of Luxembourg' were signed in July 1949, Belgian commitment was to create three squadrons of night fighters with eight aircraft each. The first squadron, No.10 Squadron, was equipped with the Mosquito NF Mk 30. On the 1st July 1951 a second night-fighter squadron was set up, also with the Mosquito. To replace the ageing Mosquitoes Belgium ordered the Meteor NF Mk 11. The first order for these aircraft was for twelve, which arrived in the summer of 1952 at Beauvechain. The first aircraft carried the squadron code ND for No.10 Squadron, but a little later these machines went to No.11 Squadron (code: KT). The Belgian Air Staff had decided to keep the Mosquito NF Mk 30s in No.10 Squadron while No.11 Squadron would fly the Meteor NF Mk 11. When in 1953 the Mosquitoes were grounded due to fatigue, the pilots of No.10 Squadron flew the Meteor NF Mk 11s of No.11 Squadron. In 1956 a second batch of twelve Meteor NF Mk 11s was ordered. But this time these machines were not new, having been in RAF service for a number of years before they were supplied to the Belgian Air Force. They all carried the code of No.10 Squadron (code: ND) and were serialled EN-13 to 24. Those aircraft were not completely identical to the previous ones and as a result there were a lot of technical problems to overcome. During this year there were also a number of accidents, one of which was unfortunately fatal and was caused by water in the fuel. During one night two aircraft crashed due to fuel starvation, and unfortunately one crash was fatal for one of the crew. The Meteor NF Mk 11 was replaced in 1958 with the Avro Canuck CF-100 Mk 5 All-Weather Fighter. In 1958 No.10 Squadron was disbanded, followed soon after by No.11 Squadron which took the Canuck onto its inventory, together with Nos 349 and 350 Squadrons. Ten Meteor NF Mk 11s were stored at Koksijde and sold publicly to the COGEA company for modification to target-tugs. However, the modification did not take place and the aircraft remained rotting in the open air in a corner of the airfield at Ostend. Some years later they were sold and scrapped.

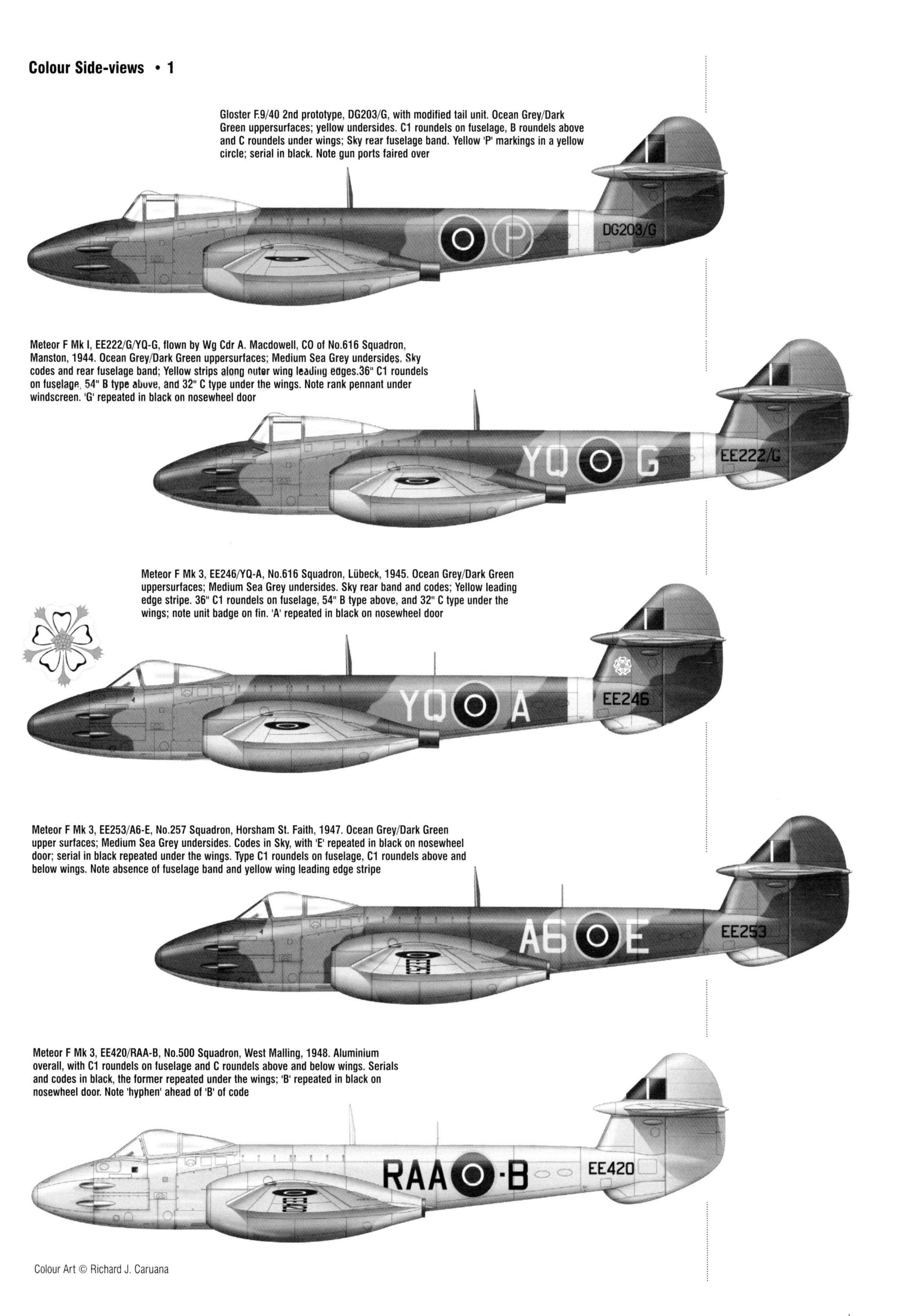

Gloster F.9/40 2nd prototype, DG203/G, with modified tail unit. Ocean Grey/Dark Green uppersurfaces; yellow undersides. C1 roundels on fuselage, B roundels above and C roundels under wings; Sky rear fuselage band. Yellow 'P' markings in a yellow circle; serial in black. Note gun ports faired over

Meteor F Mk I, EE222/G/YQ-G, flown by Wg Cdr A. Macdowell, CO of No.616 Squadron, Manston, 1944. Ocean Grey/Dark Green uppersurfaces; Medium Sea Grey undersides. Sky codes and rear fuselage band; Yellow strips along outer wing leading edges.36" C1 roundels on fuselage, 54" B type above, and 32" C type under the wings. Note rank pennant under windscreen. 'G' repeated in black on nosewheel door

Meteor F Mk 3, EE246/YQ-A, No.616 Squadron, Lübeck, 1945. Ocean Grey/Dark Green uppersurfaces; Medium Sea Grey undersides. Sky rear band and codes; Yellow leading edge stripe. 36" C1 roundels on fuselage, 54" B type above, and 32" C type under the wings; note unit badge on fin. 'A' repeated in black on nosewheel door

Meteor F Mk 3, EE253/A6-E, No.257 Squadron, Horsham St. Faith, 1947. Ocean Grey/Dark Green upper surfaces; Medium Sea Grey undersides. Codes in Sky, with 'E' repeated in black on nosewheel door; serial in black repeated under the wings. Type C1 roundels on fuselage, C1 roundels above and below wings. Note absence of fuselage band and yellow wing leading edge stripe

Meteor F Mk 3, EE420/RAA-B, No.500 Squadron, West Malling, 1948. Aluminium overall, with C1 roundels on fuselage and C roundels above and below wings. Serials and codes in black, the former repeated under the wings; 'B' repeated in black on nosewheel door. Note 'hyphen' ahead of 'B' of code

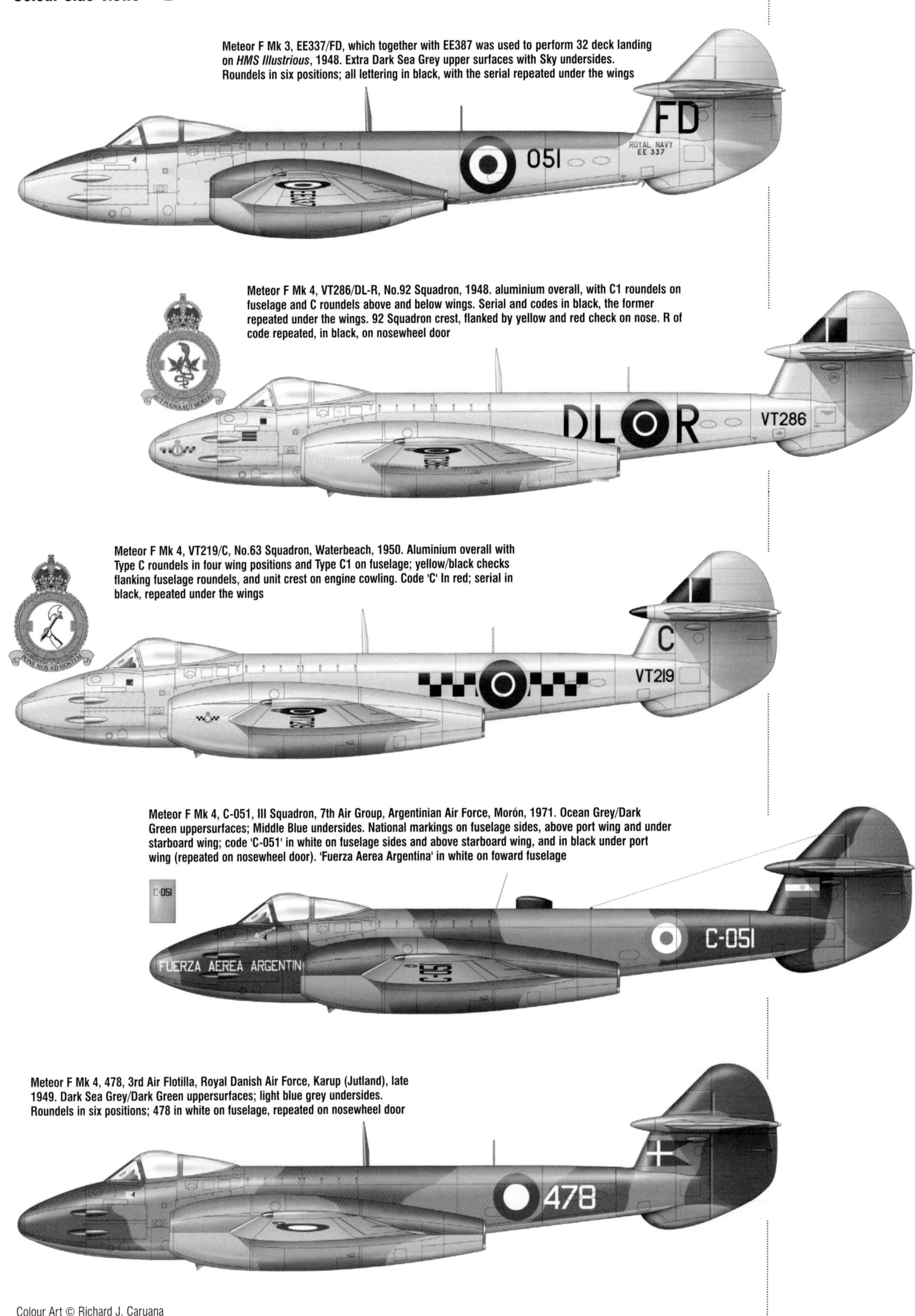

Meteor F Mk 3, EE337/FD, which together with EE387 was used to perform 32 deck landing on *HMS Illustrious*, 1948. Extra Dark Sea Grey upper surfaces with Sky undersides. Roundels in six positions; all lettering in black, with the serial repeated under the wings

Meteor F Mk 4, VT286/DL-R, No.92 Squadron, 1948. aluminium overall, with C1 roundels on fuselage and C roundels above and below wings. Serial and codes in black, the former repeated under the wings. 92 Squadron crest, flanked by yellow and red check on nose. R of code repeated, in black, on nosewheel door

Meteor F Mk 4, VT219/C, No.63 Squadron, Waterbeach, 1950. Aluminium overall with Type C roundels in four wing positions and Type C1 on fuselage; yellow/black checks flanking fuselage roundels, and unit crest on engine cowling. Code 'C' In red; serial in black, repeated under the wings

Meteor F Mk 4, C-051, III Squadron, 7th Air Group, Argentinian Air Force, Morón, 1971. Ocean Grey/Dark Green uppersurfaces; Middle Blue undersides. National markings on fuselage sides, above port wing and under starboard wing; code 'C-051' in white on fuselage sides and above starboard wing, and in black under port wing (repeated on nosewheel door). 'Fuerza Aerea Argentina' in white on foward fuselage

Meteor F Mk 4, 478, 3rd Air Flotilla, Royal Danish Air Force, Karup (Jutland), late 1949. Dark Sea Grey/Dark Green uppersurfaces; light blue grey undersides. Roundels in six positions; 478 in white on fuselage, repeated on nosewheel door

Colour Art © Richard J. Caruana

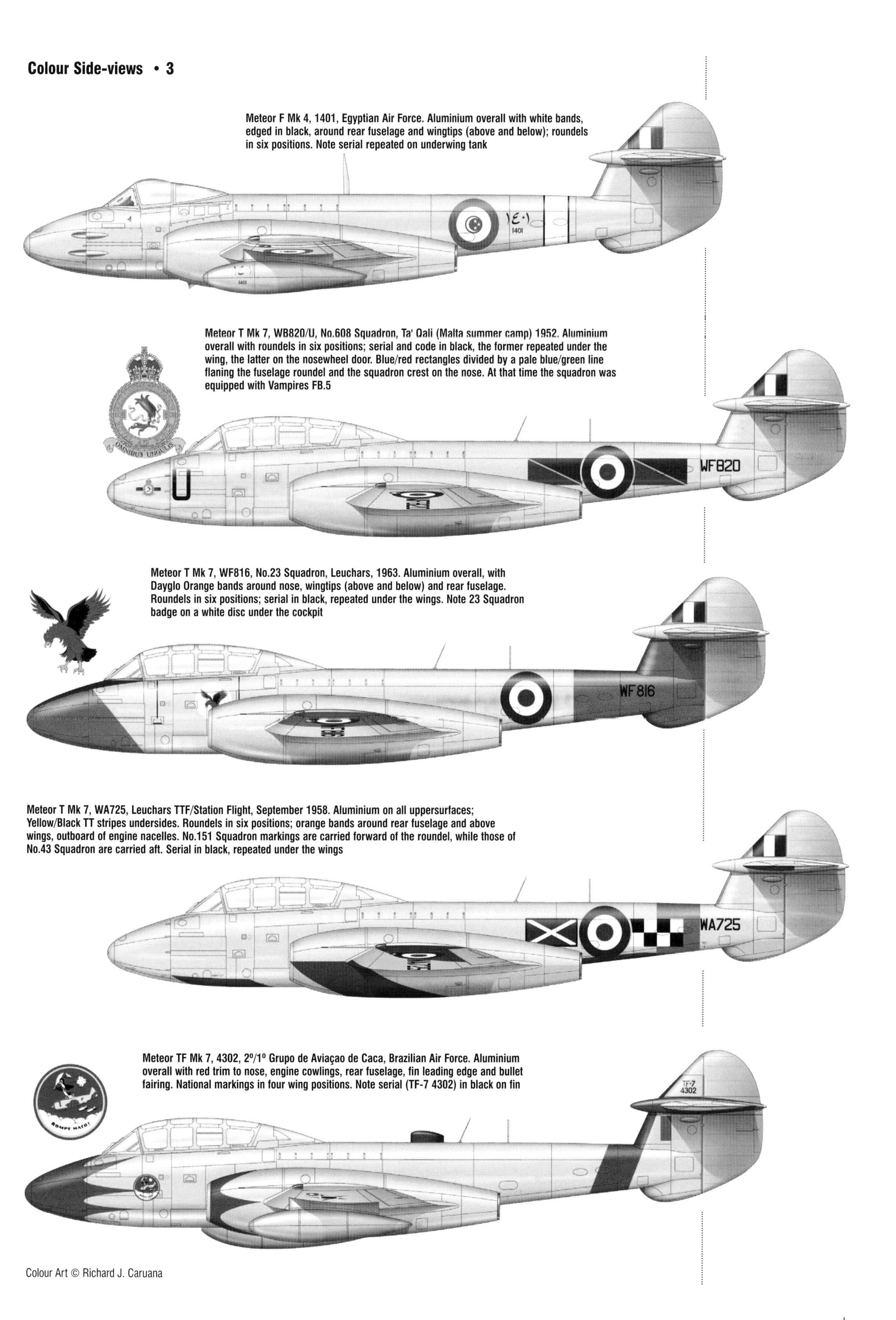

Meteor F Mk 4, 1401, Egyptian Air Force. Aluminium overall with white bands, edged in black, around rear fuselage and wingtips (above and below); roundels in six positions. Note serial repeated on underwing tank

Meteor T Mk 7, WB820/U, No.608 Squadron, Ta' Qali (Malta summer camp) 1952. Aluminium overall with roundels in six positions; serial and code in black, the former repeated under the wing, the latter on the nosewheel door. Blue/red rectangles divided by a pale blue/green line flaning the fuselage roundel and the squadron crest on the nose. At that time the squadron was equipped with Vampires FB.5

Meteor T Mk 7, WF816, No.23 Squadron, Leuchars, 1963. Aluminium overall, with Dayglo Orange bands around nose, wingtips (above and below) and rear fuselage. Roundels in six positions; serial in black, repeated under the wings. Note 23 Squadron badge on a white disc under the cockpit

Meteor T Mk 7, WA725, Leuchars TTF/Station Flight, September 1958. Aluminium on all uppersurfaces; Yellow/Black TT stripes undersides. Roundels in six positions; orange bands around rear fuselage and above wings, outboard of engine nacelles. No.151 Squadron markings are carried forward of the roundel, while those of No.43 Squadron are carried aft. Serial in black, repeated under the wings

Meteor TF Mk 7, 4302, 2º/1º Grupo de Aviaçao de Caca, Brazilian Air Force. Aluminium overall with red trim to nose, engine cowlings, rear fuselage, fin leading edge and bullet fairing. National markings in four wing positions. Note serial (TF-7 4302) in black on fin

Colour Art © Richard J. Caruana

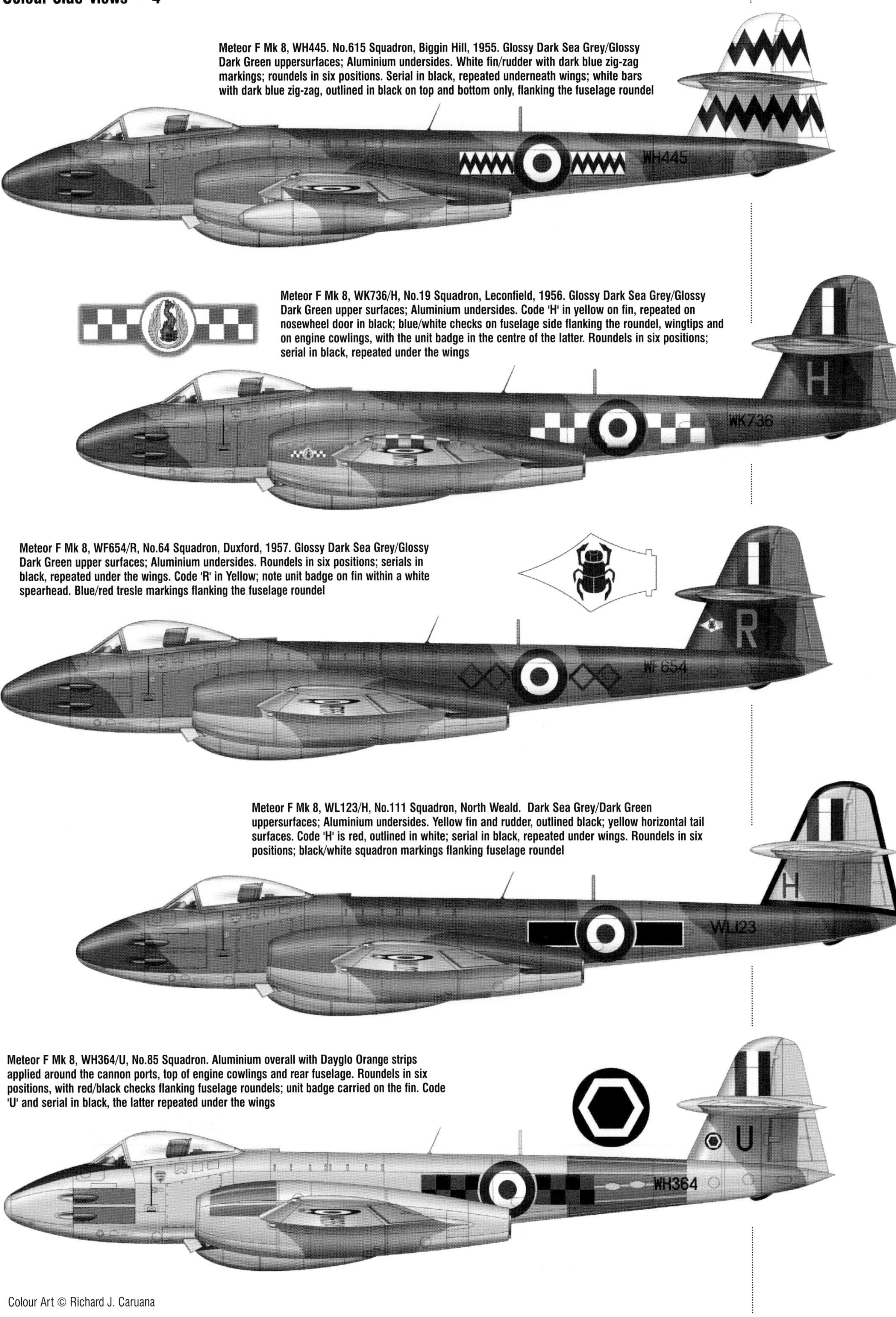

Meteor F Mk 8, WH445. No.615 Squadron, Biggin Hill, 1955. Glossy Dark Sea Grey/Glossy Dark Green uppersurfaces; Aluminium undersides. White fin/rudder with dark blue zig-zag markings; roundels in six positions. Serial in black, repeated underneath wings; white bars with dark blue zig-zag, outlined in black on top and bottom only, flanking the fuselage roundel

Meteor F Mk 8, WK736/H, No.19 Squadron, Leconfield, 1956. Glossy Dark Sea Grey/Glossy Dark Green upper surfaces; Aluminium undersides. Code 'H' in yellow on fin, repeated on nosewheel door in black; blue/white checks on fuselage side flanking the roundel, wingtips and on engine cowlings, with the unit badge in the centre of the latter. Roundels in six positions; serial in black, repeated under the wings

Meteor F Mk 8, WF654/R, No.64 Squadron, Duxford, 1957. Glossy Dark Sea Grey/Glossy Dark Green upper surfaces; Aluminium undersides. Roundels in six positions; serials in black, repeated under the wings. Code 'R' in Yellow; note unit badge on fin within a white spearhead. Blue/red tresle markings flanking the fuselage roundel

Meteor F Mk 8, WL123/H, No.111 Squadron, North Weald. Dark Sea Grey/Dark Green uppersurfaces; Aluminium undersides. Yellow fin and rudder, outlined black; yellow horizontal tail surfaces. Code 'H' is red, outlined in white; serial in black, repeated under wings. Roundels in six positions; black/white squadron markings flanking fuselage roundel

Meteor F Mk 8, WH364/U, No.85 Squadron. Aluminium overall with Dayglo Orange strips applied around the cannon ports, top of engine cowlings and rear fuselage. Roundels in six positions, with red/black checks flanking fuselage roundels; unit badge carried on the fin. Code 'U' and serial in black, the latter repeated under the wings

Colour Art © Richard J. Caruana

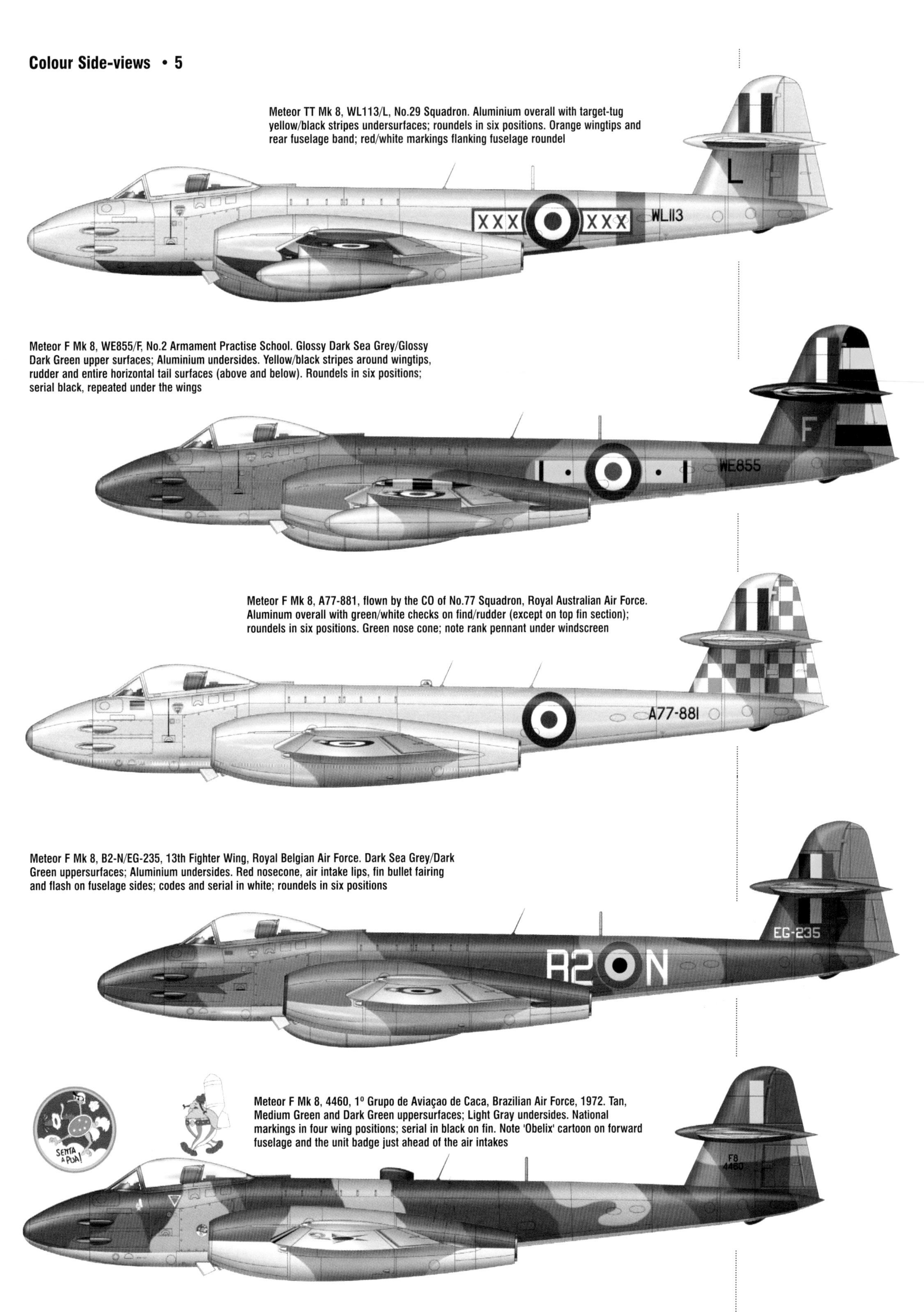

Meteor TT Mk 8, WL113/L, No.29 Squadron. Aluminium overall with target-tug yellow/black stripes undersurfaces; roundels in six positions. Orange wingtips and rear fuselage band; red/white markings flanking fuselage roundel

Meteor F Mk 8, WE855/F, No.2 Armament Practise School. Glossy Dark Sea Grey/Glossy Dark Green upper surfaces; Aluminium undersides. Yellow/black stripes around wingtips, rudder and entire horizontal tail surfaces (above and below). Roundels in six positions; serial black, repeated under the wings

Meteor F Mk 8, A77-881, flown by the CO of No.77 Squadron, Royal Australian Air Force. Aluminum overall with green/white checks on find/rudder (except on top fin section); roundels in six positions. Green nose cone; note rank pennant under windscreen

Meteor F Mk 8, B2-N/EG-235, 13th Fighter Wing, Royal Belgian Air Force. Dark Sea Grey/Dark Green uppersurfaces; Aluminium undersides. Red nosecone, air intake lips, fin bullet fairing and flash on fuselage sides; codes and serial in white; roundels in six positions

Meteor F Mk 8, 4460, 1º Grupo de Aviaçao de Caca, Brazilian Air Force, 1972. Tan, Medium Green and Dark Green uppersurfaces; Light Gray undersides. National markings in four wing positions; serial in black on fin. Note 'Obelix' cartoon on forward fuselage and the unit badge just ahead of the air intakes

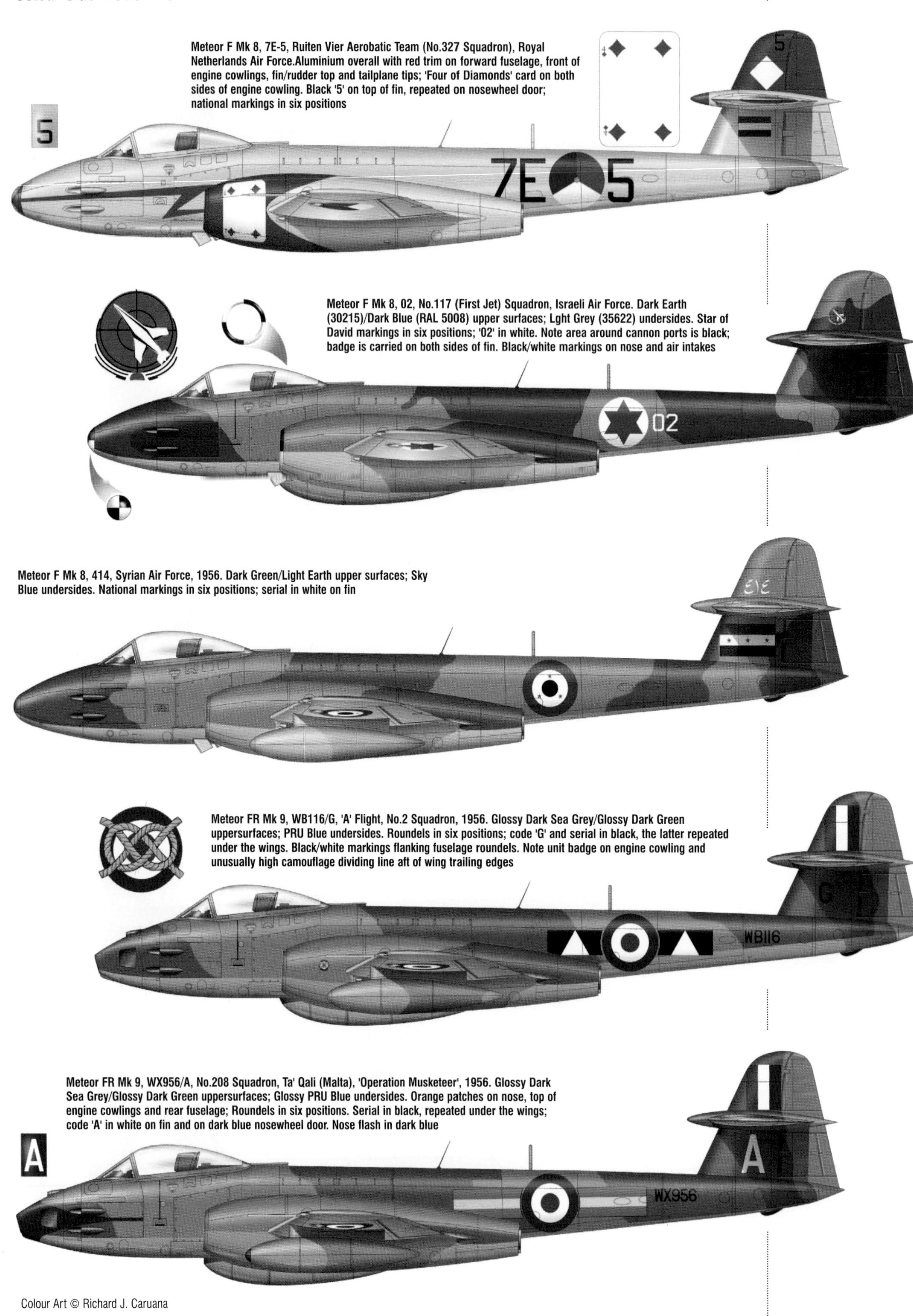

Meteor F Mk 8, 7E-5, Ruiten Vier Aerobatic Team (No.327 Squadron), Royal Netherlands Air Force.Aluminium overall with red trim on forward fuselage, front of engine cowlings, fin/rudder top and tailplane tips; 'Four of Diamonds' card on both sides of engine cowling. Black '5' on top of fin, repeated on nosewheel door; national markings in six positions

Meteor F Mk 8, 02, No.117 (First Jet) Squadron, Israeli Air Force. Dark Earth (30215)/Dark Blue (RAL 5008) upper surfaces; Lght Grey (35622) undersides. Star of David markings in six positions; '02' in white. Note area around cannon ports is black; badge is carried on both sides of fin. Black/white markings on nose and air intakes

Meteor F Mk 8, 414, Syrian Air Force, 1956. Dark Green/Light Earth upper surfaces; Sky Blue undersides. National markings in six positions; serial in white on fin

Meteor FR Mk 9, WB116/G, 'A' Flight, No.2 Squadron, 1956. Glossy Dark Sea Grey/Glossy Dark Green uppersurfaces; PRU Blue undersides. Roundels in six positions; code 'G' and serial in black, the latter repeated under the wings. Black/white markings flanking fuselage roundels. Note unit badge on engine cowling and unusually high camouflage dividing line aft of wing trailing edges

Meteor FR Mk 9, WX956/A, No.208 Squadron, Ta' Qali (Malta), 'Operation Musketeer', 1956. Glossy Dark Sea Grey/Glossy Dark Green uppersurfaces; Glossy PRU Blue undersides. Orange patches on nose, top of engine cowlings and rear fuselage; Roundels in six positions. Serial in black, repeated under the wings; code 'A' in white on fin and on dark blue nosewheel door. Nose flash in dark blue

Colour Art © Richard J. Caruana

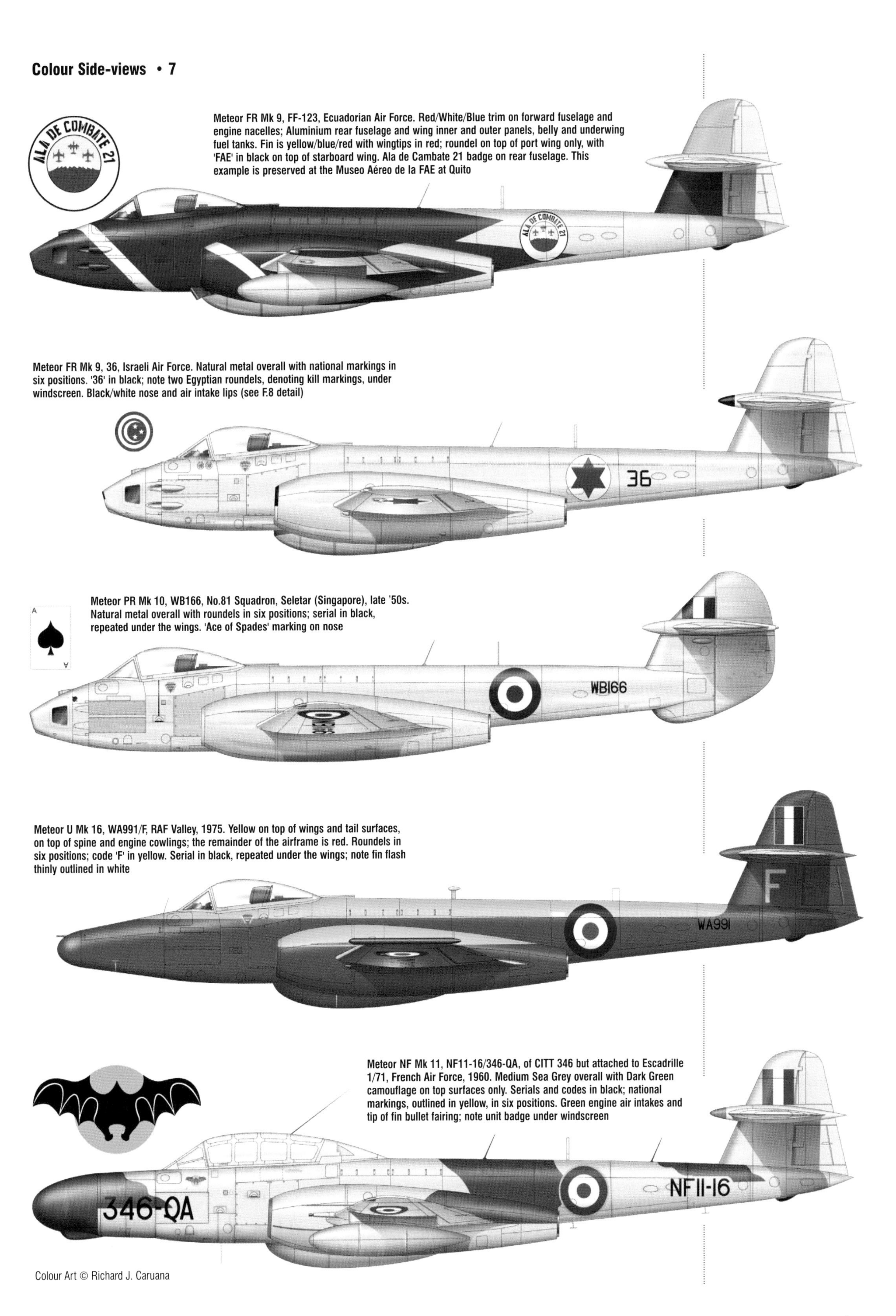

Meteor FR Mk 9, FF-123, Ecuadorian Air Force. Red/White/Blue trim on forward fuselage and engine nacelles; Aluminium rear fuselage and wing inner and outer panels, belly and underwing fuel tanks. Fin is yellow/blue/red with wingtips in red; roundel on top of port wing only, with 'FAE' in black on top of starboard wing. Ala de Cambate 21 badge on rear fuselage. This example is preserved at the Museo Aéreo de la FAE at Quito

Meteor FR Mk 9, 36, Israeli Air Force. Natural metal overall with national markings in six positions. '36' in black; note two Egyptian roundels, denoting kill markings, under windscreen. Black/white nose and air intake lips (see F.8 detail)

Meteor PR Mk 10, WB166, No.81 Squadron, Seletar (Singapore), late '50s. Natural metal overall with roundels in six positions; serial in black, repeated under the wings. 'Ace of Spades' marking on nose

Meteor U Mk 16, WA991/F, RAF Valley, 1975. Yellow on top of wings and tail surfaces, on top of spine and engine cowlings; the remainder of the airframe is red. Roundels in six positions; code 'F' in yellow. Serial in black, repeated under the wings; note fin flash thinly outlined in white

Meteor NF Mk 11, NF11-16/346-QA, of CITT 346 but attached to Escadrille 1/71, French Air Force, 1960. Medium Sea Grey overall with Dark Green camouflage on top surfaces only. Serials and codes in black; national markings, outlined in yellow, in six positions. Green engine air intakes and tip of fin bullet fairing; note unit badge under windscreen

Colour Side-views • 8

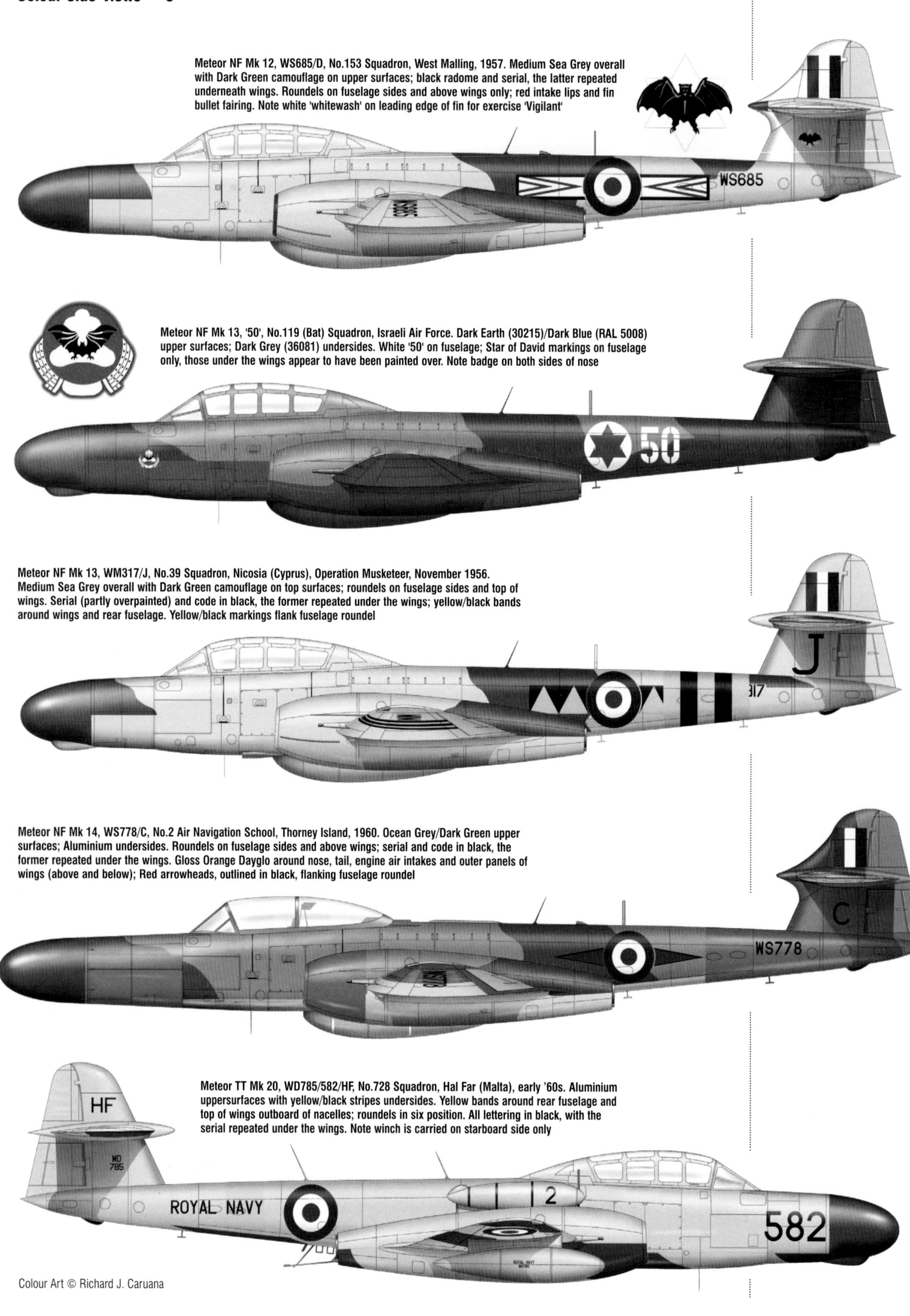

Meteor NF Mk 12, WS685/D, No.153 Squadron, West Malling, 1957. Medium Sea Grey overall with Dark Green camouflage on upper surfaces; black radome and serial, the latter repeated underneath wings. Roundels on fuselage sides and above wings only; red intake lips and fin bullet fairing. Note white 'whitewash' on leading edge of fin for exercise 'Vigilant'

Meteor NF Mk 13, '50', No.119 (Bat) Squadron, Israeli Air Force. Dark Earth (30215)/Dark Blue (RAL 5008) upper surfaces; Dark Grey (36081) undersides. White '50' on fuselage; Star of David markings on fuselage only, those under the wings appear to have been painted over. Note badge on both sides of nose

Meteor NF Mk 13, WM317/J, No.39 Squadron, Nicosia (Cyprus), Operation Musketeer, November 1956. Medium Sea Grey overall with Dark Green camouflage on top surfaces; roundels on fuselage sides and top of wings. Serial (partly overpainted) and code in black, the former repeated under the wings; yellow/black bands around wings and rear fuselage. Yellow/black markings flank fuselage roundel

Meteor NF Mk 14, WS778/C, No.2 Air Navigation School, Thorney Island, 1960. Ocean Grey/Dark Green upper surfaces; Aluminium undersides. Roundels on fuselage sides and above wings; serial and code in black, the former repeated under the wings. Gloss Orange Dayglo around nose, tail, engine air intakes and outer panels of wings (above and below); Red arrowheads, outlined in black, flanking fuselage roundel

Meteor TT Mk 20, WD785/582/HF, No.728 Squadron, Hal Far (Malta), early '60s. Aluminium uppersurfaces with yellow/black stripes undersides. Yellow bands around rear fuselage and top of wings outboard of nacelles; roundels in six position. All lettering in black, with the serial repeated under the wings. Note winch is carried on starboard side only

Colour Art © Richard J. Caruana

The Basics

As you would expect with such a famous type, there have been a large number of kits produced of the Meteor. Most of these were in 1/72nd scale, but there are also a few in 1/48th. To date though we are all still awaiting the release of an injected kit of any version of the Meteor in 1/32nd scale.

The Meteor in 1/72nd Scale

AEROCLUB

Meteor F Mk 8

This kit was originally released in the 1990s and has remained available ever since.

Our example had the following colour options:

- 1. WK884, No.616 Squadron.
- 2. WH307, No.504 Squadron.
- 3. WA780, No.66 Squadron.
- 4. A77-728, No.77 Squadron, RAAF, Korea.

Verdict

Aeroclub's kit is limited-run injection moulded plastic with white-metal and a vac-formed canopy. The injected parts are lovely, easily as good as some of the mainstream manufacturers' and in many ways as easy to work with. The fuselage length and profile are spot-on as is the wingspan and engine nacelle shape. The wings have panel lines I cannot confirm (see comments at end of this section) and the round panel for access to the drop tank and bomb release unit is missing on each upper surface. I am also not sure of the twin panels seen on the inboard section (some plans show a single narrow panel, others a much larger panel) and the shape and location of the bulge over the wheel well. The wheel wells have moulded internal detail and the oleo legs themselves are cast in white-metal with the wheels separate. The cockpit interior has a floor and bulkhead supplied in plastic with all other details as white-metal components. These include a lovely little ejection seat and instrument panel. The nose wheel and oleo is a single piece and in metal once again, but the level of detail on this is a little poor in comparison with the main wheels. To complete the model you get two lovely clear vac-formed canopies.

As I have said this model is easily as well-moulded as many mainstream manufacturers', but the fact that it is limited-run and includes metal parts and a vac-formed canopy may well put some off. This is a shame as I have to say that it is the pick of the bunch as far as 1/72nd scale kits go at the time of writing.

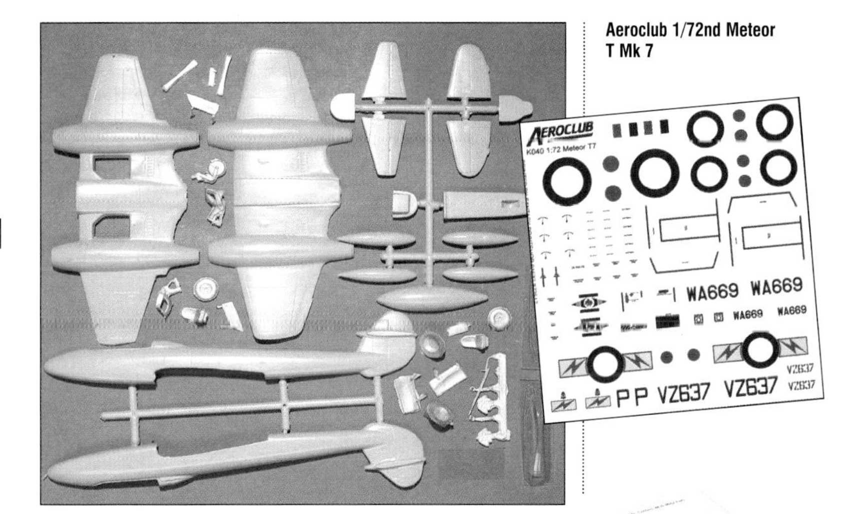

Aeroclub 1/72nd Meteor T Mk 7

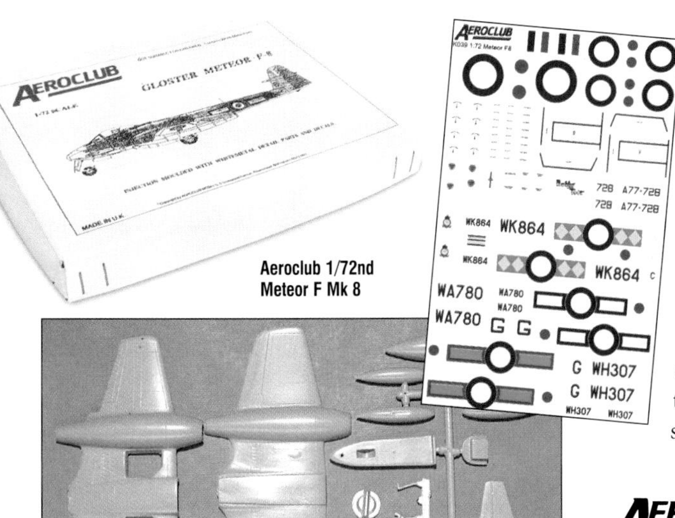

Aeroclub 1/72nd Meteor F Mk 8

AEROCLUB

Meteor T Mk 7

This kit was originally released in the 1990s and has remained available ever since.

Our example had the following colour options:

- 1. VZ837, No.502 Squadron.
- 2. WA669, CFS, Vintage Pair.

Verdict

This kit is in a similar vein to the F Mk 8 version reviewed previously. It is limited-run injection moulded plastic with

Airfix 1/72nd Meteor Mk III

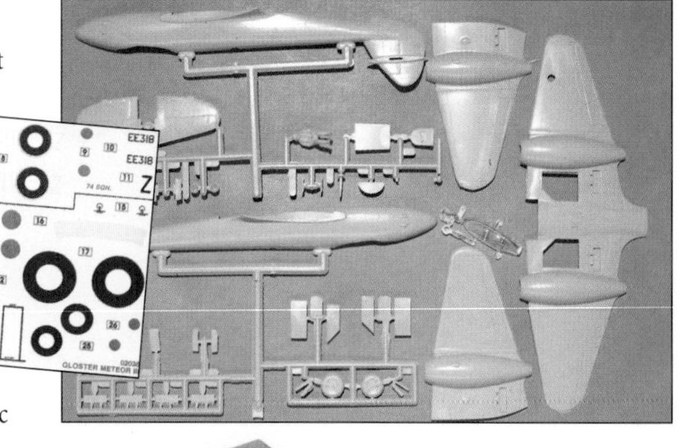

white-metal and a vac-formed canopy. The fuselage length and profile are spot-on at 43ft 6in. The wingspan is also correct at 37ft 2in and the engine nacelle shape and profile look good to me. Once again my previous comments about the wing panel lines and bulge over the wheel well apply here, as this kit has identical surface panel lines on the wing as the F Mk 8 kit. The wheel wells have moulded internal detail and the oleo legs themselves are cast in white-metal with the wheels separate.

The cockpit interior has a floor and bulkhead supplied in plastic with all other details as white-metal components. These include two seats, instrument panels and two control columns. The nose wheel and oleo is a single piece and in metal once again. All of the white-metal components in the example we had suffered from flash in different degrees, which although not a real problem, is surprising from the likes of Aeroclub. To complete the model you get a clear vac-formed canopy which has frame lines on it that are so faint that you are unlikely to see them.

As with the F Mk 8 this model is easily as well-moulded as many mainstream manufacturers'. It is certainly the best and only real option for a T Mk 7 in 1/72nd scale at present.

Mk III

This kit was originally released in 1970 and has remained available on an irregular basis ever since. At the time of writing (2004), it is still available.

We had two examples, both item number 02038, one of them was probably around the mid-1990s, while the other is the current (2003) release. The decal options in these were as follows:

1990s Edition

- 1. YQ•Q, EE239, No.616(F) Squadron, RAuxAF.

2003 Edition

- 1. YQ•Q, EE239, No.616(F) Squadron, RAuxAF based at RAF Manston in December 1944.
- 1a. Same as above but as seen at Lübeck, Germany in June 1945.
- 2. EE239, No.616(F) Squadron, RAuxAF based at Melsbroek, Belgium in January 1945. This is the overall white distemper scheme.
- 3. EE318, 4D•Z of No.74(F) Squadron based at RAF Colerne in 1945.

Airfix 1/72nd Meteor Mk III

Verdict

Being a product of the 1970s this kit is, of course, covered in rivets. All of the panel lines are also raised, so sanding will remove these and the rivets if you want to rescribe your model. Overall fuselage shape is good, but it is approximately 2mm too short and the chord of the rudder is where this discrepancy occurs, so it is therefore easy to rectify if you have to. Overall the entire tail area of this model is undersize. The span is also about 1mm too short, but the profile of the wing and position of the engines are such that you can correct this by adding a shim of plastic at the root and modifying the lower one-piece wing to correspond to it. The ailerons have an odd 'dog-leg' hinge line that does not correspond to any drawings or photos of the F Mk III that I have seen (this may be the often referred-to style seen on the F Mk I, although it should therefore not apply to the mid and late production F Mk IIIs). The aileron trim tabs are in the wrong place, being set to the inboard hinge line instead of being mid-aileron, and the surface effect on the ailerons is more akin to fabric covering than metal, which is again more representative of the F Mk I, so is best sanded off. The air brakes are separate items, but the bulge at the back of the wheel wells on the lower wing surface is far too subtle even for this scale, in fact it looks more like an unintentional moulding flaw than the extended bulge from the wheel doors. By the way, the undercarriage doors are flat and feature no hint of the bulge that should be on them. The canopy profile is fine for the windscreen and sliding section, but the fixed rear section is too shallow and slopes too steeply. Both undercarriage and cockpit detail are sparse. The former features oleo and wheel units that are all moulded as one, and each suffers with sink marks. The latter comprises a floor, bulkhead, seat, instrument panel and pilot, which was fine in 1970 but today it looks very bare.

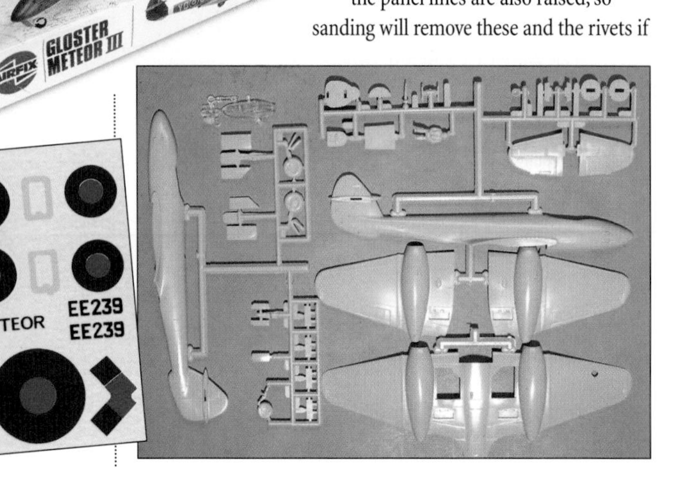

The decals in the later example (which we think first arrived in 1999) are far superior to any previous ones. They offer four potential options and even include the black walkway markings for the wings.

Overall this is a good kit, certainly worth a little added attention and full of potential for conversions, but it is now 30+ years old and really starting to show its age.

Meteor F Mk 8/FR Mk 9

This kit was originally released in the 1990s and has remained available on and off ever since.

Our example had the following colour options:

- 1. F Mk 8, WK738, 'M', No.66 Squadron, RAF.
- 2. F Mk 8, A77-15, No.77 Squadron, RAAF, flown by W/O Bob Turner from Kimpo Air Base, Korea. 1952.

• 3. F Mk 8, A77-85, No.77 Squadron, RAAF, flown by George Hale (a MiG killer having shot down two MiG-15s) from Kimpo Air Base, Korea, 27th March 1953.
• 4. FR Mk 9, '36', 117th Squadron, Israeli Air Force.
• 5. FR Mk 9, '36', flown by Rharon Yoeli, 1st September 1955.
• 6. F Mk 8, Israeli Air Force, Suez Crisis, 1956.

Verdict

This is a resin kit with a vac-formed canopy. The quality of the resin is stunning, with fine recessed panel lines and crisp casting. Checking with plans and scale dimensions the fuselage comes up almost spot on, the only comment I would make is that the vertical tail is slightly narrow in chord. Surface detail and panel lines on the fuselage are the best of the bunch in this scale, but the mid-fuselage panel on either side just behind the wing trailing edge is oversized and the two smaller ones aft of it are too oval in shape (they should be octagonal with rounded ends). The span is bang on at 37ft 2in, but oddly there are some anomalies with regard to panel lines once again. This kit features the panel line on the outer wing panel like the Aeroclub kit, but those on the inboard panel are very odd and on the example we had the scribing of the air brakes was of a different size on each wing. I know it was only slightly different, but it was really noticeable. The nacelles are OK for overall length and cross-section, but the forward intakes are too small in diameter. Separate noses for the F and FR versions and separate rockets are also included.

The cockpit interior is nicely detailed with moulded sidewalls, a seat, instrument panel, control column and rudder pedals. The seat is better than that in the PJ kit, but not as detailed as that in the Aeroclub kit. Overall shape and style of this seat is better, but not really too reminiscent of the early Martin-Baker units fitted to this version. This is a kit that offers the undercarriage legs and wheels all in resin. However, the assembly does not use as many parts and there is no etched brass unlike the PJ Productions versions. The wheel wells in the wings have very limited detail, but they are nice and deep so more could be added if you wanted to.

Overall this is a beautiful kit which is accurate in overall shape and dimensions. With a little extra attention to detail a lovely F Mk 8 or FR Mk 9 can be built.

F Mk IV

This kit was originally released in 1970 and remained available until Frog went out of production in 1977. It has been reboxed on a number of occasions since (see Appendix I), but at the time of writing was only available via the secondhand market.

We had two examples, both item number F200, one of them features the Frog logo in the second style, which was used from 1963 through to 1973, while the other is in the third (final) style, which was used from 1974 to 1977. The decal options are the same in each version and they are as follows:
• 1. Y9•8 of No.323 Squadron, RNethAF, 1950.
• 2. VT328, No.263 Squadron, RAF, 1950.

Verdict

Being a product of the 1970s this kit is, of course, covered in raised panel lines, but unlike the Airfix kit of the same era, no rivets. Overall fuselage shape is good, but the length is 2mm too long giving 41ft 6in instead of 41ft. Once again this error seems to be all centred around the chord of the rudder and the width of the vertical fin. The former needs to be reduced while the latter needs extra added to it at the leading edge. The profile of the leading edge of the fin is incorrect, as is the shape of the top of the rudder; it should be flatter with a distinct 'step' in the contour from the fin leading edge to the rounded top. Strangely the circumferential panel lines on the fuselage are missing. The access panels on the

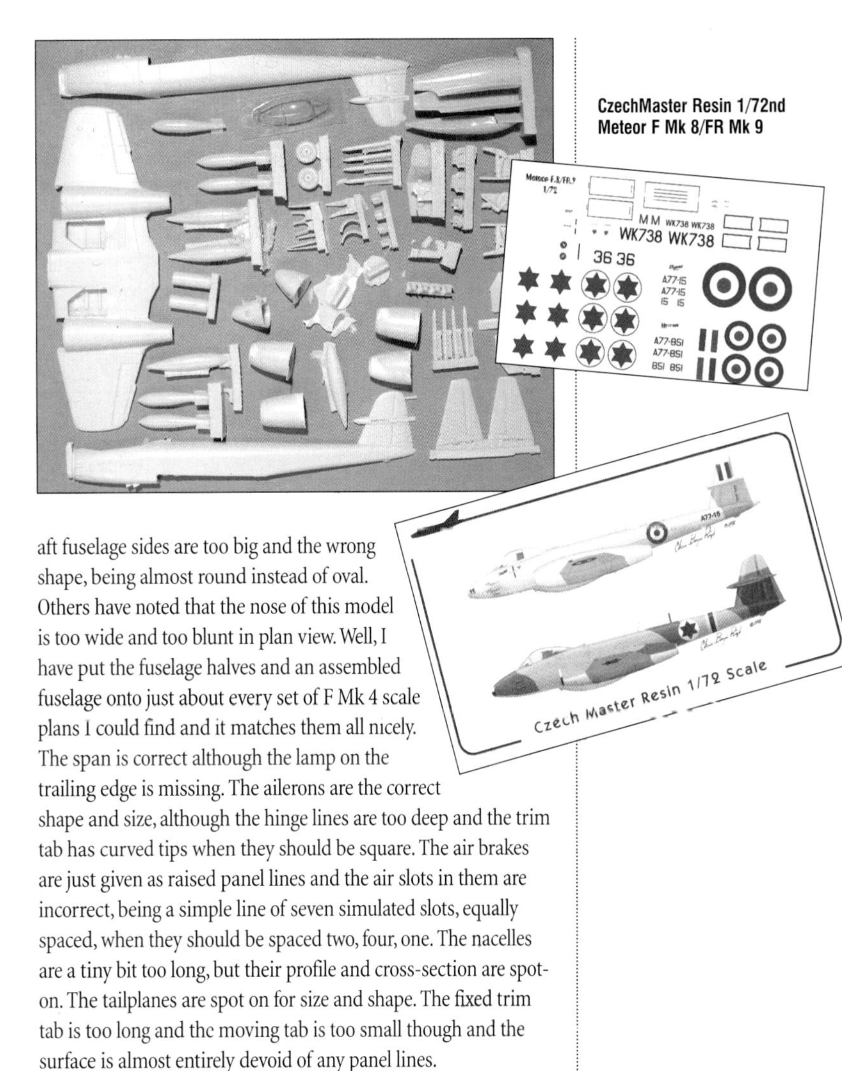

CzechMaster Resin 1/72nd Meteor F Mk 8/FR Mk 9

aft fuselage sides are too big and the wrong shape, being almost round instead of oval. Others have noted that the nose of this model is too wide and too blunt in plan view. Well, I have put the fuselage halves and an assembled fuselage onto just about every set of F Mk 4 scale plans I could find and it matches them all nicely. The span is correct although the lamp on the trailing edge is missing. The ailerons are the correct shape and size, although the hinge lines are too deep and the trim tab has curved tips when they should be square. The air brakes are just given as raised panel lines and the air slots in them are incorrect, being a simple line of seven simulated slots, equally spaced, when they should be spaced two, four, one. The nacelles are a tiny bit too long, but their profile and cross-section are spot-on. The tailplanes are spot on for size and shape. The fixed trim tab is too long and the moving tab is too small though and the surface is almost entirely devoid of any panel lines.

The undercarriage doors feature the distinctive bulge and the truncated extension of this behind the bays is included, if a little overdone this time. Wheel well and interior detail is very sparse. The former has no boxed-in wells and no interior details. The former is just a floor, 'couch' for a seat, control column and a pilot figure - there is huge scope for adding detail here! The main wheels are moulded separately from the oleos, a great improvement in comparison with the Airfix kit, but the wheels themselves lack any form of detail even though there is a four-spoke hub effect on one side. The nose wheel and oleo is one unit and suffers from lack of detail and poor moulding. The canopy is quite thick and the windscreen slope is too steep and too long. Drop tanks for the wing are included, but these are rather nondescript. There is no 180 Imp. Gal. drop tank for the centreline included though.

Overall this is a good kit and a sound basis

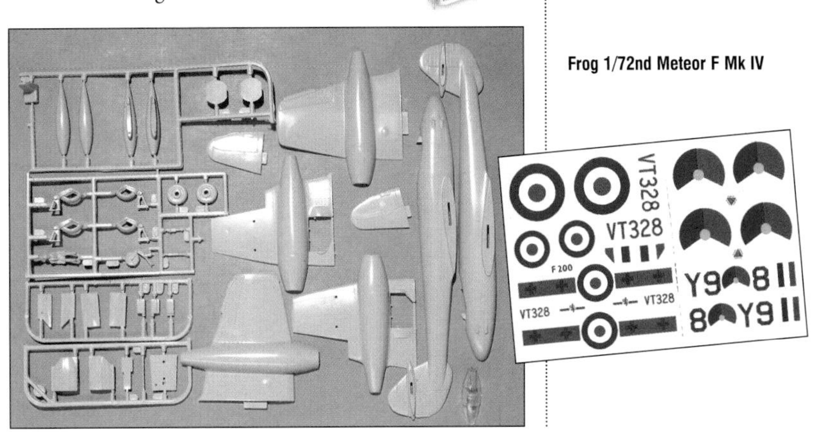

Frog 1/72nd Meteor F Mk IV

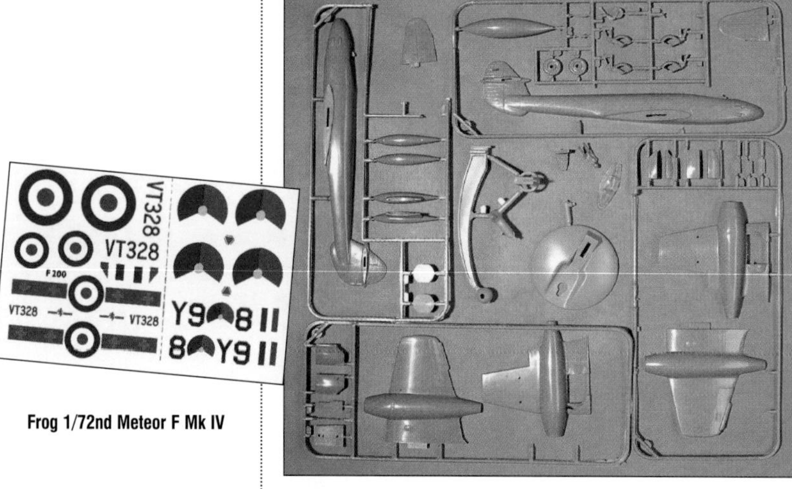

Frog 1/72nd Meteor F Mk IV

for many conversions. The age of the moulding is quite evident and strangely many of the panel lines on the real machine are not included in this kit at all. The level of detail, age of tooling and quality and finesse of detail mean that truly this kit should only be for the collector by now, but we are still waiting for a new Meteor in this scale in injection moulded plastic so this one will have to soldier on!

Meteor F Mk 8

This kit was originally released in 1955 and remained available until Frog replaced it with the F Mk IV in 1970. This is a very collectable item, which surely few would dare build today!
Our example, item number 326P, offers the following decal option:
• 1. WF753, 'F'.
No other identification is offered, but going by the fuselage bands this machine was operated by No.600 Squadron, RAuxAF. Apparently at some time this kit came with an option for a No.43 Squadron machine, although we cannot confirm this as we have not actually seen an example of that kit.

Verdict

Being a product of the 1950s this kit is covered in raised panel lines and rivets. Overall fuselage shape is good, but the length is 45ft 3in instead of the correct 44ft 7in, although this discrepancy is just 2mm in this scale. The rudder is correct in shape and size and all the panel lines, although overdone in this scale, all seem accurate. Strange thing is that the 'rivets' for things like the fuselage access panels on the aft fuselage are all outside of the panels, when they should be inside - maybe in the 1950s they could not fit them into such small areas, so went for the soft options instead! The wings are over 2mm too short in span each and the ailerons feature hinge lines like those of a shed door! There are no wheel wells, no cockpit interior and not even a hint of dive brakes. The former area also contains an elongated (squarish) bulge to replicate the bulge over the undercarriage area in the real thing. The main undercarriage legs are moulded in two parts, one of which is integral with the undercarriage door. These doors are more akin to pylons in their shape, and are nothing like the real thing. The wheels are simple 'buttons' with no detail. The nose wheel is multi-part, but very simplified and nothing like the real thing. As already mentioned the cockpit does not exist, this is a product of the 1950s, so the upper torso and head of the pilot is just moulded to each half of the fuselage.

Being from the 1950s this kit features that strangest of phenomena, raised lines to indicate the location of the decals! This is fine in a sense, but the manufacturer ensured there was nothing to impede their application, so made these areas devoid of any other panel lines or rivets, resulting in a very 'odd' look.

This is a kit that deserves to be collected but never built. It was very accurate and a good example of how things used to be, but the best way to appreciate this kit is to keep it in the box unbuilt.

Frog 1/72nd Meteor F Mk 8

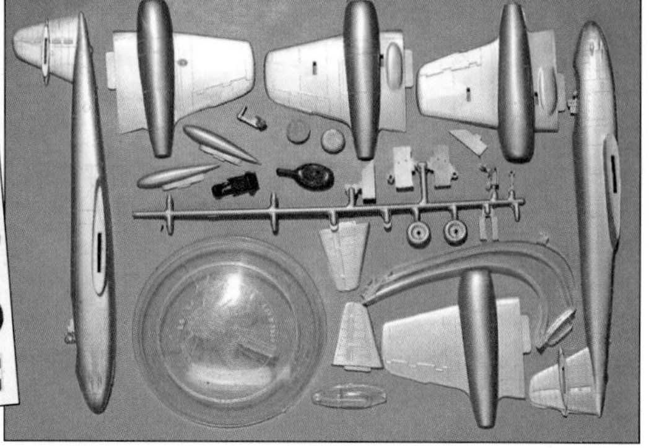

Meteor NF Mk 11/12/14

This kit was originally released in 1977 and remained available until the kit side of Matchbox was sold off to Revell-Monogram (Odyssey Partners) in 1991. The last known reissue of this kit with the Matchbox label was in 1998, and in 2000 Revell AG relinquished the license to use the Matchbox brand, so this kit will never be seen in a Matchbox box again (although it will certainly appear in a Revell box before too long!). Apparently this kit was originally intended as a 1/48th scale version, although I can't recall any mention of it at that scale.

We had two examples, one from Matchbox numbered PK-129, the other from Revell numbered 40124. They each feature different decal options as follows:

Matchbox #PK-129
• 1. NF Mk 12, WS743, No.84 Squadron.
• 2. NF Mk 14, WS593, No.85 Squadron.
• 3. NF Mk 11, EN6, KT•W, No.11 Squadron, No.1 Wing Belgian Air Force, Bevekom, 1953.

Revell #40124
• 1. NF Mk 11, EN6, KT•W, No.11 Squadron, No.1 Wing Belgian Air Force, Bevekom, 1953.
• 2. NF Mk 14, WS810, 'B', No.264 Squadron, RAF Linton-on-Ouse, 1957.
• 3. NF Mk 12, WS685, No.153 Squadron, RAF West Malling, 1955.

Verdict

Being a Matchbox kit you would expect it to be covered in their notorious 'trench' panel lines but this one is covered in fine raised lines. The multi-mark options means that the breakdown of parts is quite complex, with the upper decking and cockpit opening as a separate part to allow the NF Mk 11/13 and NF Mk 12/14 to be built. The short nose of the NF Mk 11/13 and the long nose of the NF Mk 12/14 are also included as separate parts as well as the very short nose fitted to the Belgian NF Mk 11. Overall fuselage shape is very good and the length of the NF Mk 12/14 is correct at 51ft 4in, while the NF Mk 11/13 is also spot-on at 49ft 11in. Both long and short engine front cones are included, both of which are pretty much spot-on. The span is also bang-on and the profile and shape of the engines nacelles looks OK in plan, but maybe a little less 'bulbous' in cross-section than it should be. The fin and rudder for both the NF Mk 11/13 and NF Mk 12/14 versions are correct, although the upper trim tab on the latter is missing and on the former is still there even when it should not be (the trailing edge has a 'kink' in it that should not be there). The hinge lines on the rudder, tailplanes and wings are all correct, although the trim tabs on the ailerons are somewhat oversimplified. The air brakes are simple indentations and panel lines, but sufficient for this scale. The ejector ports on the lower outer wing panels are moulded as raised lumps and should be removed and drilled out.

The main wheel wells feature nice interior details (on the inner upper wing panels) and the doors feature the correct 'bump' in them. This bump is carried through to be truncated by the air brakes, quite rightly. The main wheels are moulded with the oleos and the wheels themselves include some nice hub detail. The nose wheel and oleo is a single unit and suffers from lack of detail and poor moulding.

Cockpit interior detail is very sparse with just a floor, two 'arm chair' seats, control column, central instrument panel and two main instrument panels. The latter two items come in two different styles for each version, although the dials are simple raised circles. There are two styles of canopy included in this kit, both are quite thick, but have the windscreen separate from the main sliding section. The profile of both canopies and windscreens is excellent. Drop tanks for the wing are included along with a 180Imp. Gal. drop tank for the centreline.

Overall this is a great kit and a sound basis for many conversions. The age of the moulding is quite evident but at least it is not covered in the usual 'trenches' we all expect from a Matchbox kit. The level of detail, age of tooling and quality and finesse of detail are acceptable and for now, until someone does something new, this is your best bet for any late-series Meteor in this scale. Note that with the later Revell release of this kit the decals are a vast improvement on those included in the original issue. They even include a full set of walkway markings and various stencils and symbols. The Revell version also benefits from being moulded all in grey, while the original Matchbox kit came in three colours (dark grey, light grey and green!).

Meteor F Mk 8

This kit was originally released in the early to mid-1980s but at the time of writing is not readily available and can only be obtained via secondhand dealers.

Our example had the following colour options:

- 1. WA923, RAF.
- 2. A77-881, RAAF.

Neither of these are identified to a squadron but they should be No.56 for the RAF machine and No.77 for the RAAF example.

Verdict

Humm, what can I say really. This kit looks like it is moulded in old white sauce mix that was mixed in a blender! The plastic used is pretty abysmal and the model lacks detail. The fuselage is split into two parts and overall length is spot on at 44ft 7in. The wings are solid, not in two halves, but dimensionally they are once again spot on at 37ft 2in. The engine nacelles are supplied in upper and lower halves to wrap around the solid wing. They are the correct length and have the correct profile and diameter. The wheel wells are quite shallow, even in a solid wing, and the undercarriage doors are shapeless blobs.

The cockpit interior is non-existent, all you get is a rather oversized and bare looking white-metal seat! The canopy is sort of clear, but very 'limited' in how it has been made and would be better replaced with a vac-formed one (maybe it is so poor to hide the lack of interior!). The undercarriage legs and wheels are supplied in white-metal. Each oleo leg and wheel is a single unit and detail is compromised as a result. The mudguards on the main wheels do not look as if they are separate from the tyres, the moulding is that indistinct.

Many people have slammed this kit as it was made by a firm that did not have a good reputation for 'quality'. However, as you can see, dimensionally the kit is fine, it is just the bulky nature of the injected parts and total lack of detail that make it one that is truly only fit to be collected and never built. By the way, the decals in the example we had were all totally out of register, with the red dots nowhere near the centres of the roundels!

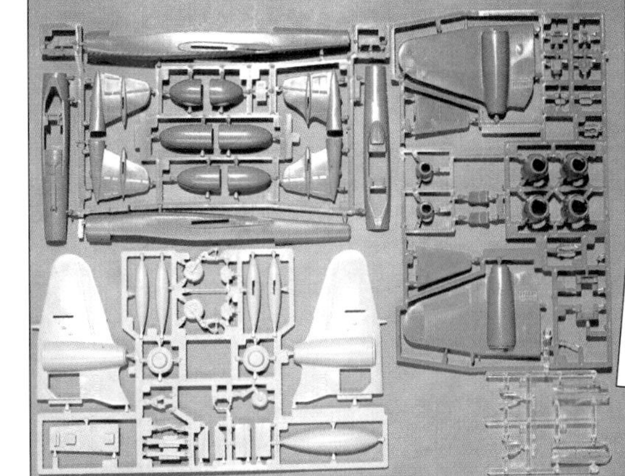

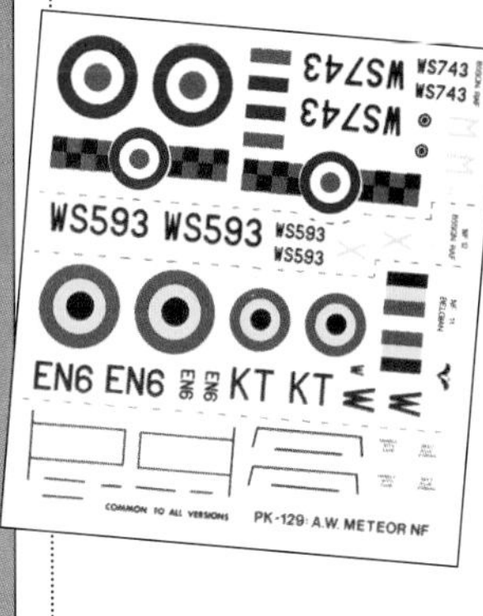

Matchbox 1/72nd Meteor NF Mk 11/12/14

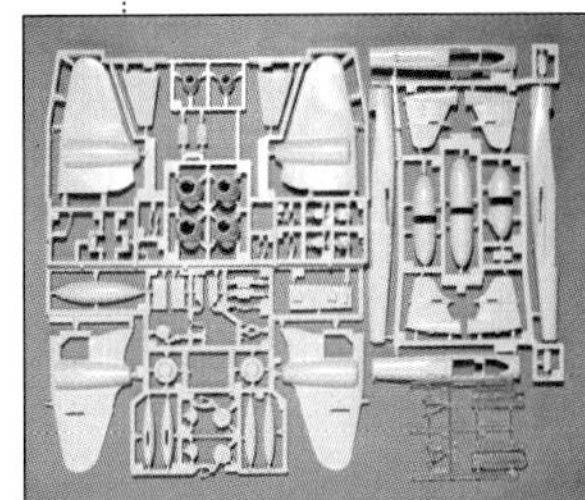

Matchbox 1/72nd Meteor NF Mk 11/12/14

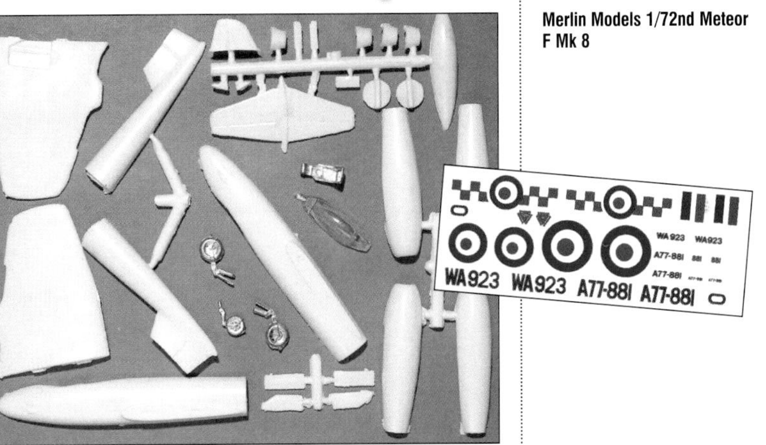

Merlin Models 1/72nd Meteor F Mk 8

PJ Productions 1/72nd Meteor F Mk 8

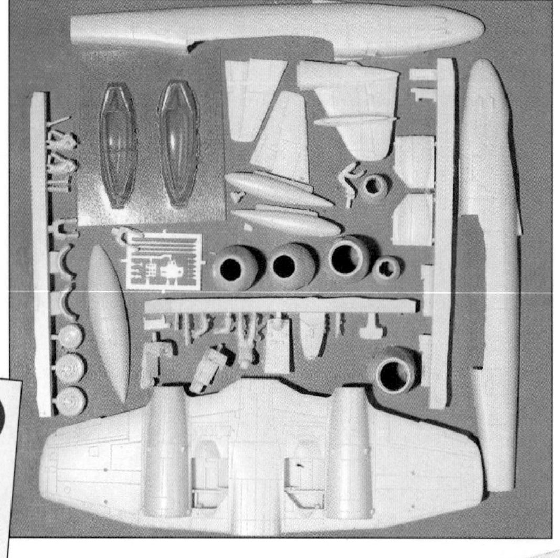

Meteor F Mk 8

This kit was originally released in the mid-1990s and has remained available ever since.

Our example had the following colour option:

• 1. WK784.

There are no indications on the instructions as to what squadron this machine was operated by, but going by the fuselage bands it was No.604 Squadron.

Verdict

This is a resin kit, with etched brass detail parts for the cockpit interior and a vac-formed canopy. The quality of the resin is stunning, easily as good as a CzechMaster kit and all looks well. However, on checking with plans and scale dimensions the fuselage comes up short, at just 43ft 3in instead of 44ft 7in. This makes it about 5mm short, but thankfully because the tail is separate all you have to do is add a 5mm plug at this point and all is well. The span is approximately 36ft 10in, while it should be 37ft 2in, but in this scale that is 1mm. The nacelles forward of the wing trailing edge are 2mm too long, but don't worry as you can use the spare fronts from a Matchbox kit here anyway, as they fit perfectly.

The cockpit interior is nicely detailed with moulded sidewalls, a floor, seat and bulkhead in resin. The seat is nice, but the headbox is too small. The etched parts are all used in the cockpit interior, with the instrument panel front and control levers all in brass. The undercarriage legs are all resin and multi-part. This does not make for easy assembly or a very strong unit, and when you think that the mudguards also have etched brass support bars you can see how fiddly this is all getting. Oh, and finally, the 180 Imp. Gal. drop tank is about 2mm too long and is not wide or bulbous enough.

Overall this is a beautifully moulded kit. The dimensional errors may well be down to the production, as resin shrinks, but I have tried to be fair here and used scale measurements against the dimensions of the real thing instead of just putting the parts over a set of scale plans. With a little attention to detail and correction of that short fuselage a nice F Mk 8 can be built, but once again there is some dispute with the panel lines on the upper wings.

Note that PJ also offer this kit with Belgian Air Force markings (#72 1006).

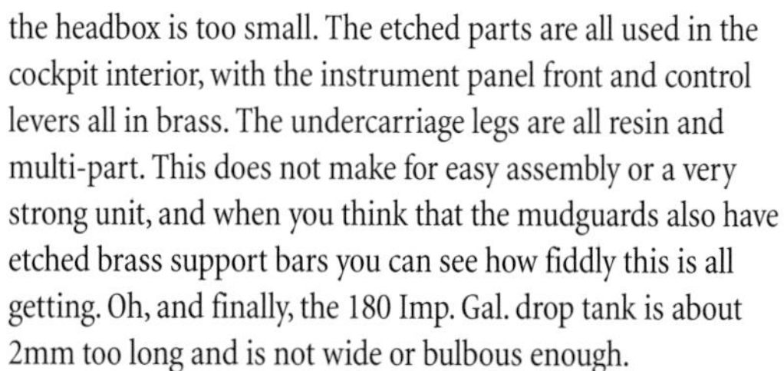

Meteor T Mk 7

This kit was originally released as a special edition for the IPMS/UK Nationals in 1998 and is as a result no longer available.

Our example had the following colour option:

• 1. Belgian Air Force, ED-40 based at Koksijde in 1958.

Verdict

This is a resin kit, with etched brass detail parts for the cockpit interior and a vac-formed canopy. On checking with plans and scale dimensions the fuselage comes up short, at just 42ft instead of 43ft 6in. This makes it about 7mm short, but thankfully because the tail is separate all you have to do is once again add a 7mm plug at this point. Strangely the span is over at 37ft 6in, while it should be 37ft 2in, although that is just 1.5mm in this scale. The nacelles are the correct length and profile.

The cockpit interior is nicely detailed with a separate cockpit 'tub', seats, instrument panels and control columns all in resin. There are no etched details in this kit, as all the instrument panels and cockpit sidewalls have the detail already moulded onto them. The undercarriage legs are all resin and multi-part, just like the F Mk 8. This does not make for easy assembly or a very strong unit, although this time the mudguard stays are not etched brass, the modeller has to add them from wire. And finally, once again the 180 Imp. Gal. drop tank is about 2mm too long and is not wide or bulbous enough.

This is another beautifully moulded kit but those dimensional errors may put a few off. Once again I have tried to be fair in my assessment of these and have used scale measurements against the dimensions of the real thing instead of just putting the parts over a set of scale plans. With a little attention to detail and correction of that short fuselage a nice T Mk 7 can be built, although once again there are some disputes with the panel lines on the upper wings.

PJ Productions 1/72nd Meteor T Mk 7

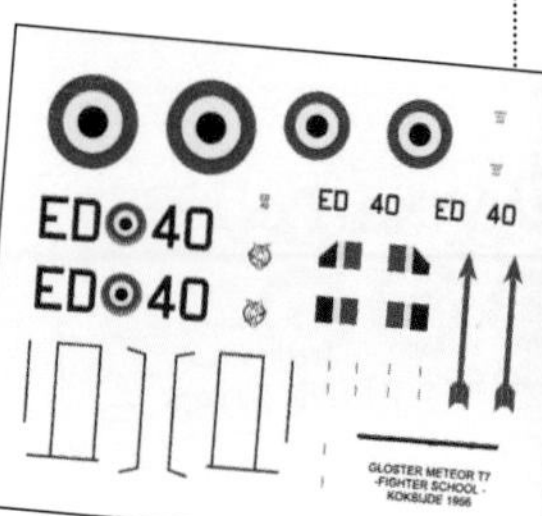

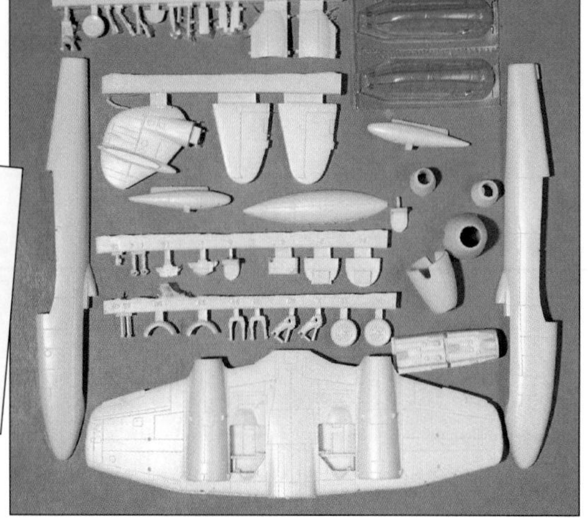

Meteor F Mk 8

This kit was originally released in the 1970s and remained in production until the Rareplanes brand was sold to Hannants in the 1980s. Although we believe this mould is still intact, the kit has never been reissued, to our knowledge, by Hannants and as a result is no longer available.

The kit came without decals although the instructions include profiles of WH291 of No.79 Squadron, RAF Chivenor in April 1972.

Verdict

This is a vac-formed plastic kit in its barest form without detail parts in the form of injected or resin components. This was what Rareplanes was all about as they offered those subjects not covered by the mainstream manufacturers and did so in their basic form so the modeller could add as much as he wanted. It is sad to say that even though some 25+ years have passed since this kit was produced, we still do not have a mainstream injected kit of the Meteor F Mk 8 from a major manufacturer in 1/72nd scale!

On checking with plans and scale dimensions the fuselage comes up spot-on at 43ft 6in. The span is also spot-on at 37ft 2in. The nacelles are the correct length and profile and depict the long-chord, small diameter units.

The cockpit interior consists of a simple floor, seat, bulkhead and instrument panel.

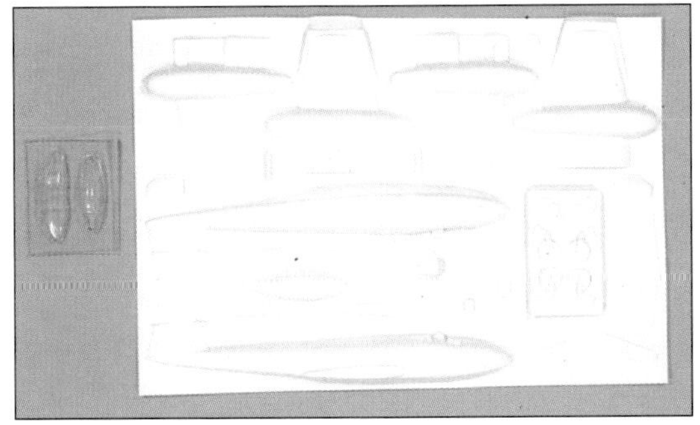

Rareplanes 1/72nd Meteor F Mk 8

These are all fine but you can always enhance this area further with items from the F Mk III etched detail set from Eduard. Strangely the seat is not an ejection seat, so here you will need to purchase a white-metal or resin example from the likes of Aeroclub or Pavla. The undercarriage legs are a bit of a 'no go' as they are moulded as complete units (legs and wheels) and as such are best replaced. Here you should really go for those from a Matchbox NF-series kit, as the heavier F Mk 8 used the strengthened legs not seen on the previous F Mk III and IV series. The up-side is that the undercarriage doors, being vac-forms, are actually better than you would see in even a mainstream injected kit as they are of a more 'scale' thickness. The kit includes a single one-piece canopy and an optional FR/PR-series nose, also in clear plastic. This latter item is very useful if you are backdating any other kit, or it can be used in place of injected or resin versions. The 180 Imp. Gal. drop tank is good in overall length and looks of the correct bulbous shape to me.

This is actually a nice little kit. So many modellers hate vac-forms that they dismiss them without a second glance, but this kit certainly deserves a second look. I picked this one up in 2004 for £3 and it is worth it as it can assist you to convert other injected kits to an F Mk 8 as well as allowing the FR Mk 9 and PR Mk 10 to be made. Well worth considering, as are so many Rareplanes kits.

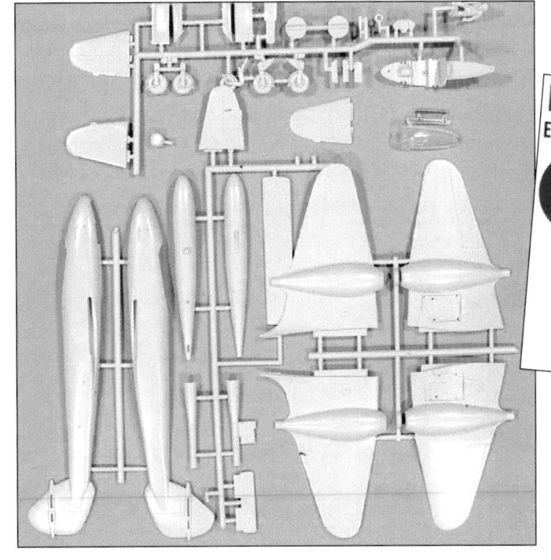

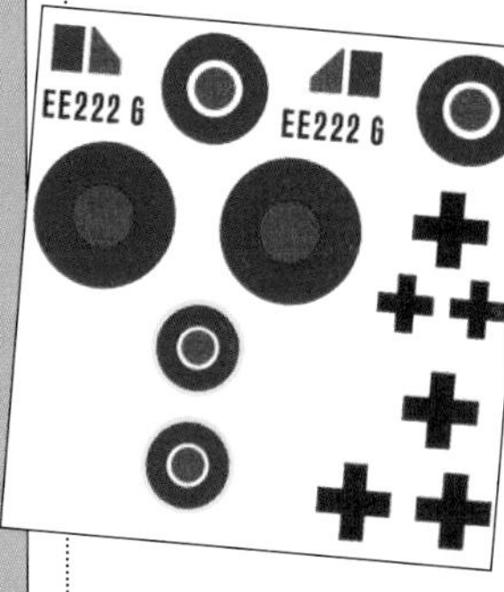

AMT 1/48th Meteor Mk I & Buzz Bomb

The Meteor in 1/48th Scale

Mk I

This kit was originally released in 1975 and remained in production on and off for about three years. It may have come back out again since then, but I cannot recall ever seeing more than one box, so I presume it has not. AMT was sold to Matchbox in the late 1970s and then on to Ertl in the mid-1980s. Ertl still hold the moulds for this kit although to date they have never reissued it. It is not therefore currently available at the time of writing.

Our example had the following colour option:

• 1 YQ•G, EE222/G of an unidentified squadron.

This machine was from No.616 Squadron.

Verdict

This injected kit also came with a Fi 103 V-1 'Buzz Bomb' and although it is not identified as such, it is an F Mk I. The fuselage should scale in at 41ft 3in, but is slightly short at around 41ft. This is nothing to worry about in this scale, as 3in in 1/48th scale is less than 2mm. The overall shape of the fuselage is slightly suspect, being almost 'squared off' and slightly 'boxy'. All panel lines are raised and each fuselage half is a mirror image of the other, which is unfortunately not correct. The cockpit interior features raised detail on each sidewall, a complete floor and bulkhead assembly, control column, instrument panel and pilot figure. All sounds good but there is no seat, the pilot figure just sits on a 'ledge' in the floor unit, the control column is more like something your kids blow bubbles through and the instrument panel is not much like the real thing, although AMT did try. Nice touch is that the canopy, although in one piece, is of the early style with the blister – very useful before the new Tamiya kits came along.

The wings are the major downside to this kit as they not only make no attempt at depicting the engines, but the wheel wells are completely wrong. First of all the engines have no internal detail, all you get is a blanking plate to cover the resulting hole and this is placed too near the front of the nacelle to be mistaken for the spar etc that is in the real machine. The wheel wells are a disaster, as they are about 1mm deep and full of the sort of ribs and pipework you would expect in a stereo system, not a 1940s jet! The main undercarriage parts just plug into these wells and they are also very basic. They depict the undercarriage OK, but the wheels are basic with no hub detail at all. The mudguards are included, but of course because it is all moulded as one with the oleo and wheel, it is very basic. The nose wheel does not fare much better, being a single piece once again with no hub detail and a moulded-on mudguard assembly. In their favour, AMT have moulded the correct bulges over the wheel doors and have NOT included the air brakes unlike Tamiya did first time around!

This is an old kit, it shows its age only in the finesse of the detail. The parts themselves are well moulded and pretty accurate, but are let down by a lack of attention to detail. That said, in the 1970s when this model was tooled, early Meteors were not that common in the USA. This is certainly one for the collector, as it has been surpassed by the (revised) F Mk I from Tamiya.

Classic Airframes

Now I can deal with all four of these kits in one go, as they are all based on the same main components.

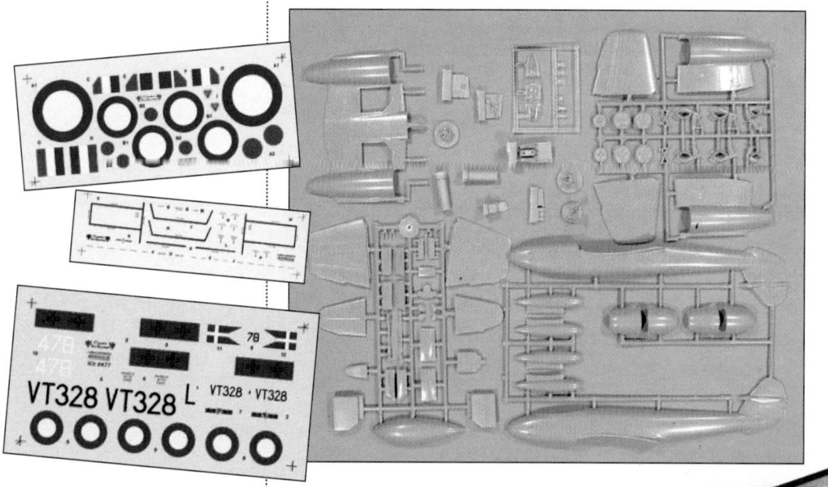

Classic Airframes 1/48th Meteor F Mk 4

F Mk 4

This kit was released in 2003, and at the time of writing was still readily available.
It offered the following colour options:
- 1. VT328 of No.263 Squadron, RAF Wattisham in 1950*.
- 2. 'White 47' of No.723 Eskadrille, Royal Danish Air Force, 1951.

* The fuselage bars on the decals for this kit seem to show the crosses on the red bars as being black. This is, I suspect, because they are in fact blue (which is correct according to M.J. Bowyer's book on the Meteor), but because the blue was printed over the red they have gone black.

Classic Airframes 1/48th Meteor F Mk 8 (Early Version)

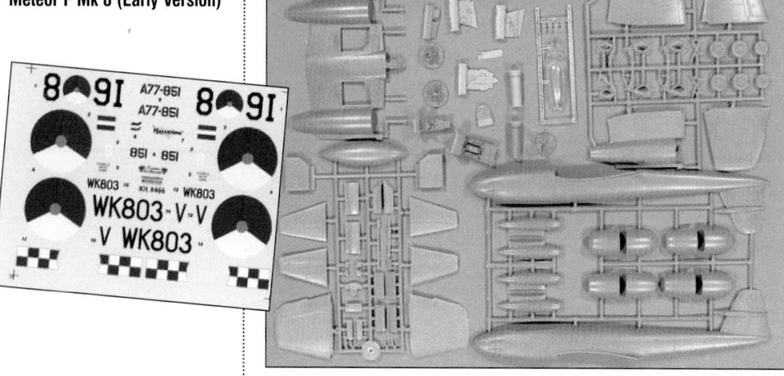

F Mk 8 (Early Version)

This kit was released in early 2004, and at the time of writing was still readily available.
It offered the following colour options:
- 1. WK803, 'V' of No.56 Squadron, RAF Waterbeach, 1953.
- 2. A77-851, 'Halestorm', flown by Sgt George Hale of No.77 Squadron, RAAF based in Korea in March 1953.
- 3. 8•91 of No.326 Squadron, Royal Netherlands Air Force based at Soesterberg in the early 1950s.

F Mk 8

This kit was released in 2003, and at the time of writing was still readily available.
It offered the following colour options:
- 1. VZ494 of No.501 Squadron, RAuxAF based at Filton in 1957.
- 2. VZ531, 'K' of No.609 Squadron, RAuxAF based at RAF Church Fenton in 1956.
- 3. 'White 106' of the Israeli Defence Force in the early 1960s.

FR Mk 9

This kit was released in late 2003, and at the time of writing was still readily available.
It offered the following colour options:
- 1. WL265, 'L' of No.79 Squadron, RAF Gütersloh, late 1950s.
- 2. WB116, 'G' of No.2 Squadron, 2nd TAF, Geilenkirchen, Germany, 1955.
- 3. 'Black 36' of the Israeli Defence Force in 1956.

Verdict

Each of these kits shares common sprues with unique parts added and some others taken away in each instance. The only real big differences are the F Mk 4 and F Mk 8/FR Mk 9 fuselages, the big and small diameter engine nacelles and the F Mk 4 and F Mk 8 early and later style canopies, all of which I will make note of in the assessment below.

The fuselage of the F Mk 4 is bang on at 41ft with the aircraft sitting on the ground. The kit only features the small diameter engine intakes and long nacelles of this mark, which is again correct. The air brakes feature the correct number of slots on each (seven on top and nine underneath) but these are equally spaced when they should not be. The single trim tabs on the ailerons are correctly depicted and the cockpit has no ejection seat, all of which is correct. Wheel well detail is nice and there is even detail on the inside of the main and nose wheel doors. Resin is used for the cockpit interior, front bulkhead and nose wheel support, engine fronts and exhaust pipes. All are well cast and nicely detailed although that front bulkhead and nose wheel support is fragile. The lower outer wing panels feature a panel line inboard of the tip that does not tie up with any examples I have seen, nor does it tie up with the diagrams in the types Air Publication.

The F Mk 8s (early and standard) are slightly underscale in length, working out at just under 44ft, when they should be 44ft 7in. The difference is about 5mm. If you take the quoted 44ft 7in as being the 'in flight' length then the kit measures 44ft 3in and is 3mm short - the choice is yours! Both kits feature big and small diameter intakes plus the long nacelles. The clear sprues come with both early (solid rear section) and later ('blown') canopies, which is a nice touch. The cockpit this time comes with a resin ejection seat but all my previous comments on the F Mk 4 also apply here. The wings feature only a single trim tab, so a later version of the F Mk 8 can't truly be built, as those machines had twin trim tabs.

The FR Mk 9 must have struck many as an odd choice, as there were not that many built. The kit is identical to the previous F Mk 8s and in fact uses the same fuselage halves which have to be cut off at a panel line for the replacement PR nose to be fitted. There is no change in the official length of the FR Mk 9 in comparison with the F Mk 8; however, if you put the new clear FR nose of the kit on top of the standard nose you will see the former is about 5mm longer, making this version accurate at 44ft 7in! Everything else about this kit is identical to the F Mk 8 so my comments on that kit apply here also.

Classic Airframes 1/48th Meteor F Mk 8

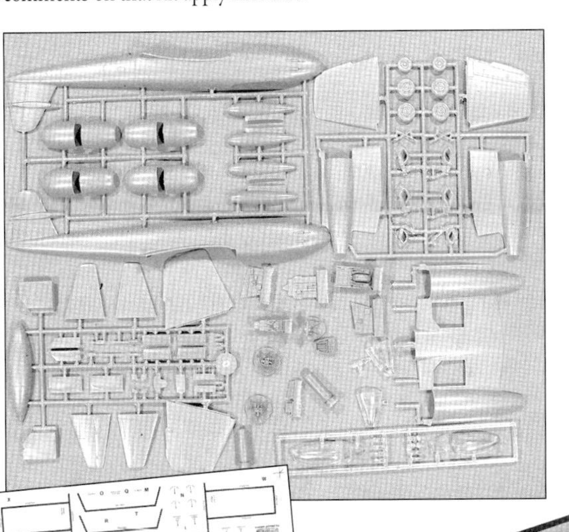

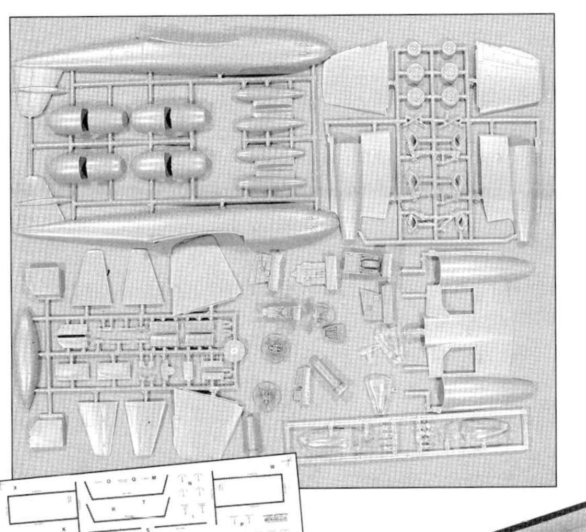

Classic Airframes 1/48th Meteor FR Mk 9

T Mk 7

This kit was released in 2003, and at the time of writing was still readily available.

It offers the following colour options:

- 1. WS103, '709' of the Station Flight at RNAS Yeovilton, late 1960s.
- 2. WL380 of No.74 Squadron, RAF Horsham St. Faith in February 1958.

Verdict

This kit shares a lot of common parts with the others, but many items relating to the fuselage all have to be new to reproduce the two-seater configuration. The fuselage is bang on for an 'on the ground' measurement of 43ft 6in. The wing sprues only contain the small diameter intakes, which is a shame, as that means you can only make an early T Mk 7. The gap left by them is obvious and it would have been nice if these had been left. The wings feature single trim tabs on the ailerons which again means this kit only allows for an early T Mk 7 to be built. There is lots of resin for the interior, but strangely in this kit the main wheels have also been replaced in resin and the corresponding parts clipped off the injected sprues. I have no problem with this, as they are far superior to the injected parts, but they would be welcome in the other kits as well.

Overall impressions of the entire Classic Airframes range of Meteors is that they are very nice, well detailed and moulded, but because of their limited-run nature and the inclusion of resin etc, they are for the experienced modeller only.

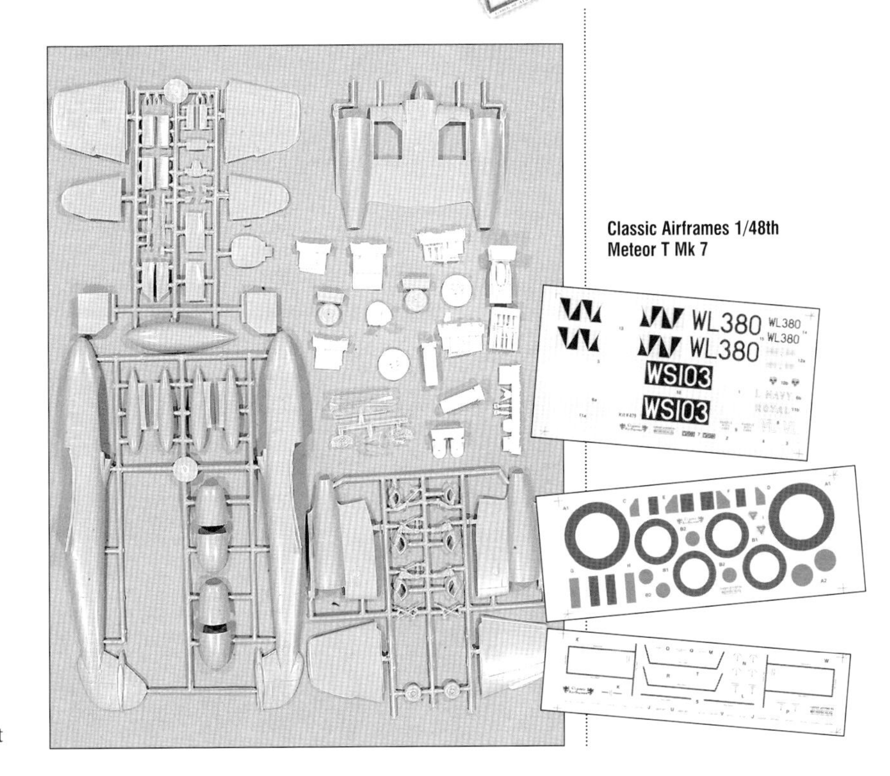

Classic Airframes 1/48th Meteor T Mk 7

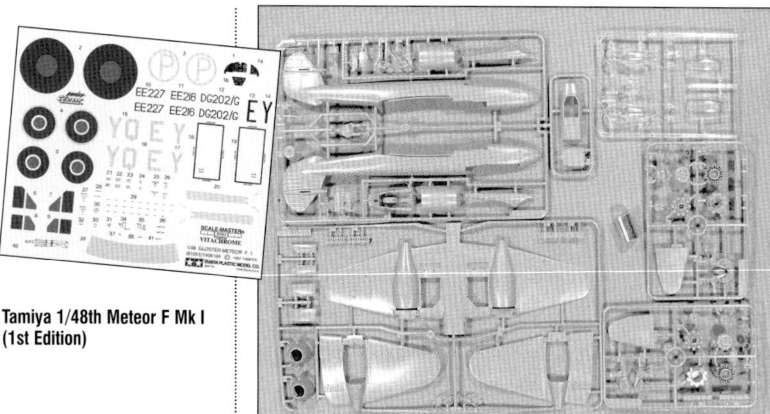

Tamiya 1/48th Meteor F Mk I (1st Edition)

an unusual mistake from Tamiya, but in their usual thoroughness they soon recalled the kit and revised the tooling to correctly depict the wing of the F Mk I, after all, they needed to do the air brake wing for their F Mk III anyway!

Overall this kit is extremely good. The fuselage length is bang-on for an 'on the ground' measurement of 41ft 3in. Span is actually a little under at only 42ft 6in, when it should be 43ft. This deficiency is 3mm in this scale, so nothing drastic. The wings feature the short nacelles and small diameter intakes that are correct for an F Mk I and there are even separate (clear) access panels and two complete engines in this kit. Wheel well detail is nice and deep and there is detail even inside the main and nose wheel doors. The kit does feature two styles of canopy, one with and one without the bulge associated with the fitment of a rear-view mirror, which is a nice touch. Probably the neatest touch in this kit is the inclusion of a shaped nose weight that sits within the completed cockpit insert. This ensures your model sits on all three wheels with ease.

F Mk I (1st Edition)

This kit was originally released in 1998 but was shortly withdrawn and revised (see revised version elsewhere). Be warned though, the only way you can tell that the model inside (they both have the same item number - #61051) is the early (incorrect) one from the (corrected) later one is to look at the illustrations on the side of the box. If the air brakes are shown in the illustration, it is the old kit, if they are not it is the revised edition!

The decal options in this first kit were as follows:

- 1. EE216, YQ•E of No. 616 Squadron, flown by Fg Off Dean.
- 2. EE227, YQ•Y of No.616 Squadron.
- 3. DG202/G, 2nd Prototype (see note in Verdict).

Verdict

Of course all of the details relating to the inclusion of air brakes on this machine mean that in fact you can only build one machine, that being the 2nd prototype as it is today at the RAF Museum, Cosford. None of the operational schemes are suitable because none of the F Mk Is had air brakes. This was

F Mk I (Revised Edition)

This kit (#61051) was originally released in 1999 and represented a revised version of the previous inaccurate first release. At the time of writing it is still currently available in the Tamiya range and was also released with a Fieseler Fi 103 (V-1) in 2000 (#61065).

The decal options in this revised kit were as follows:

- 1. EE216, YQ•E of No. 616 Squadron, flown by Fg Off Dean.
- 2. EE227, YQ•Y of No.616 Squadron.
- 3. DG202/G, 2nd Prototype (see note in Verdict).

The Meteor and V-1 (#61065) version offered the following colour options:

- 1. EE216, YQ•E of No. 616 Squadron, flown by Fg Off Dean.
- 2. EE219, YQ•D of No.616 Squadron.
- 3. EE222/G, YQ•G of No.616 Squadron.

Verdict

With this revised version at least all the operational schemes are suitable this time around, and the 2nd prototype can now be built as it was prior to the engine blow-up and subsequent replacement of the wings with a set taken from the F Mk III production line! The kit does correctly now show an F Mk I wing without air brakes and the non-truncated bulges running back from the wheel wells. All other points and facts are identical to the previous unrevised edition mentioned above.

Tamiya 1/48th Meteor F Mk I (Revised Edition)

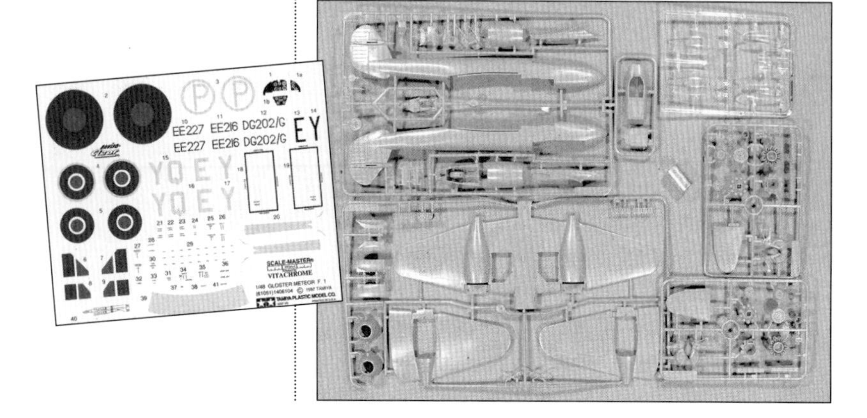

F Mk III

This kit (#61083) was originally released in 2002 and was an update based on the previous F Mk I kit.

The decal options in this kit were as follows:

- 1. EE235, YQ•H of No.616 Squadron, 1945.
- 2. EE239 of No.616 Squadron, flown by Sqn Ldr D. Barry based at Melsbroek, Belgium in March 1945.

The above option is in the overall 'distemper white' scheme and optional extra codes are included for EE240 and EE241 of the same unit.

Verdict

When Tamiya did the F Mk III version, what did they change? Well, not a lot really. The main fuselage is identical to the previous F Mk I version but if you look at the sprues side by side you will see that the cockpit decking and rear armoured bulkhead are off-set to the left on the F Mk I, while the F Mk III features a new sprue off-set to the right containing the revised cockpit decking and bulkhead plus the addition of a ventral fuel tank. The only other difference in the kit from the F Mk I is the clear sprue, which once again has a new section to the left in comparison with the F Mk I version that contains the three-part sliding canopy of this version. The kit does not include the previous F Mk I canopy elements, as that section of the mould has been truncated on the sprues.

One point to note with this kit though is that Tamiya would have you fit the long exhaust associated with the W.2B/23C engine. Now although this is correct for the first fifteen F Mk IIIs (often referred to simply as the F Mk III [Early] in many books), this does not apply to any machine after EE244. Thankfully Tamiya are on the ball here and only offer colour options for EE235 and EE239. If you use any aftermarket decals on this kit though, be aware that you will have to modify part number C9 and dispense with the W.2B/23C engines included as the later machines were powered by the Derwent 1. The Derwent 1's installation would also require the addition of a number of air intakes on the upper cowlings, so there is a bit of work involved in making this kit into anything other than one of the first fifteen airframes. Also note that with the markings for EE239 (in white distemper) [and the alternative EE240 and 241] it is shown with a large 'Q' [or 'R' and 'S'] on the nose wheel door. Photographs exist of EE239 both with and without this nose door code letter, so its application is up to you. The photographs do clearly show that the windscreen framing on EE239 was not painted with the white distemper and therefore retains its original Dark Green colour.

The above tells you what is currently available in 1/72nd and 1/48th. Hopefully the promised NF series kits in 1/48th will soon surface from Classic Airframes but there is still a real need for some modern versions of the Meteor in 1/72nd scale and how about an F Mk 3, 4 or 8 in 1/32nd scale please!

Now that we have a starting point it is time to get a better understanding of the actual aircraft, so read on...

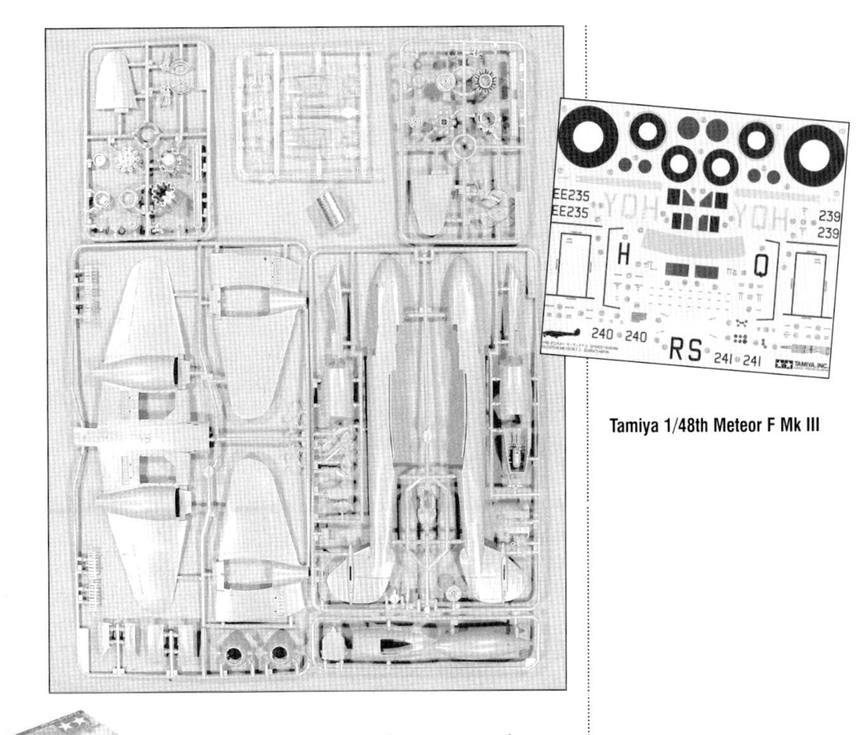

Tamiya 1/48th Meteor F Mk III

Notes: The Meteor Wing

Many of the above kits feature a huge variety in the position of panel lines on the wings. Just about every kit depicts this aspect of the outer wing panels in a different manner. The most consistent though is an additional panel line between the detachable wingtip and the join between the wing and engine nacelle. Most machines have a single panel line in this area, but just about every kit shows two. The NF series actually have three panel lines, due mainly to the extended wingspan and the fact that there are cannon bays in the outer panels. No machine that I have studied in the production of this book (prototype with F Mk III wing, F Mk 4, F Mk 8, T Mk 7, NF Mk 14 and TT Mk 20) has the second panel line present. There are lines of flush rivets, but no break in the skinning to cause this second panel line. I will leave this open to the modeller to decide, but point out that my comments and assessments about the above kits are based on viewing the real machines (where possible) and not published plans, as just about every set of scale plans shows the second panel line as well.

Thanks

Our thanks to Aeroclub, CzechMaster Resin, Hannants (Classic Airframes), Humbrol (Airfix), PJ Productions and Tamiya (The Hobby Company Ltd) for supplying samples for use in this section.

A special word of thanks must also go to Tim Cant and Alex for the loan of certain out-of-production kits for inclusion in this chapter.

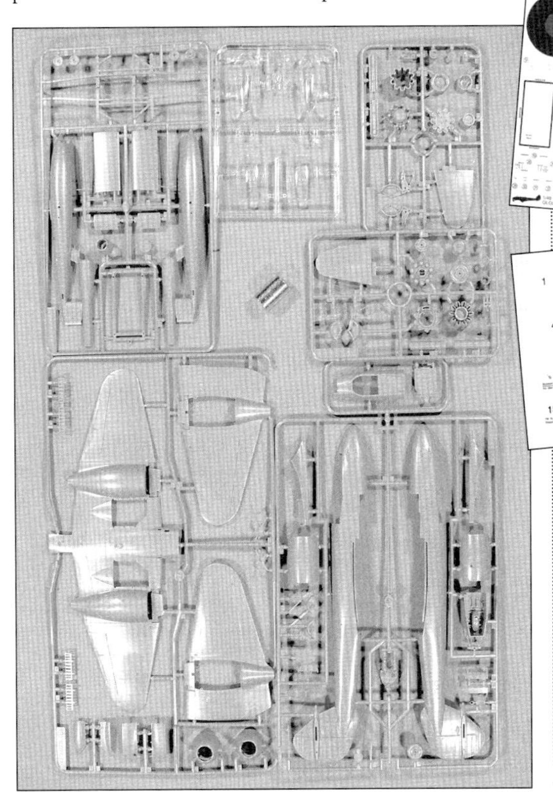

Tamiya 1/48th Meteor F Mk I with Fieseler Fi 103 [V-1] (#61065)

Understanding the Subject

Chapter 7

In this chapter we will take a look at each version of the Meteor, highlighting differences between each version, as well as giving details of how to model them in 1/72nd and 1/48th scale.

The following review has been based on a detailed study of thousands of photographs and close reference to all the official publications for each type. This has been backed up with the information carried in a great number of the titles listed in Appendix IX of this book, along with many a pleasant hour in and around preserved examples here in the UK.

We appreciate that there are many areas of the Meteor which we may highlight in a different manner to that which has been accepted so far, and we also know that we will still miss things, so if anyone reading this has points they would like to raise and has evidence to back them up, we would love to hear from you. Any reprinted examples of this title in the future can therefore incorporate any new information that may be brought to light.

Please note that we have refrained from giving details in relation to 1/32nd & 1/24th scale versions, as (at the time of writing) there was no mainstream injection moulded kit available on which to base these conversions.

NOTE: All items shown are for 1/72nd scale and for 1/48th scale in brackets ().

KEY

K - Item/s included in kit
M - Modify kit component
S - Scratchbuild component

Items that are listed without the above codes following denote items that are omitted, or which can be added if the modeller wishes (e.g. antenna etc)

Gloster Meteor Prototype DG202/G [1st Stage]
Kits
1/72nd Airfix F Mk III
1/48th Tamiya F Mk I (revised edition)

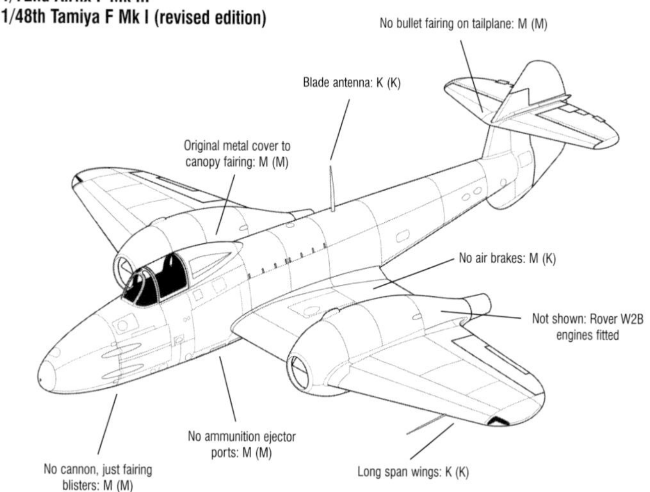

Gloster Meteor Prototype DG202/G [2nd Stage]
Kits
1/72nd Airfix F Mk III
1/48th Tamiya F Mk I (revised edition)

Note
As DG202/G [1st Stage] except:

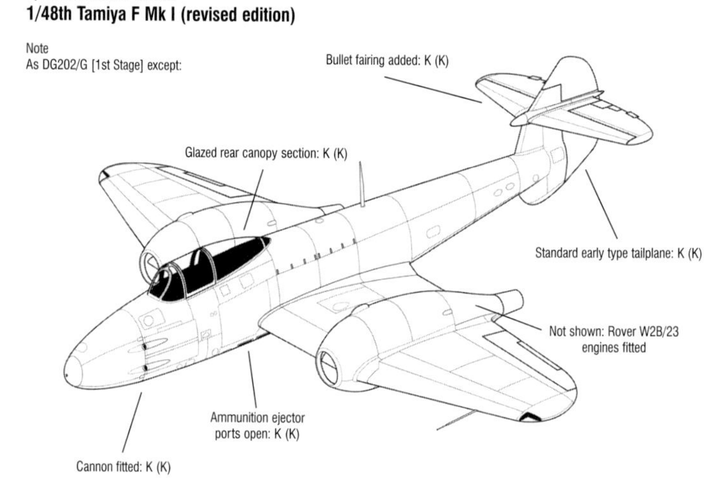

Gloster Meteor Prototype DG204/G [with Vickers F.2 engines]
Kits
1/72nd Airfix F Mk III
1/48th Tamiya F Mk I (revised edition)

Note
As DG202/G [2nd Stage] except:

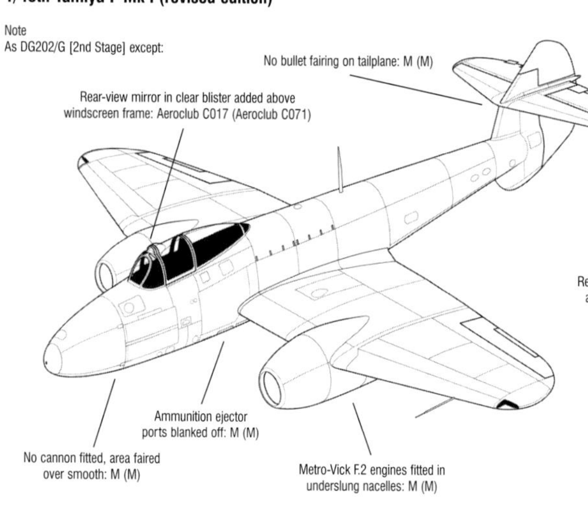

Gloster Meteor Prototype DG205/G [without bullet fairing fin/tailplane]
Kits
1/72nd Airfix F Mk III
1/48th Tamiya F Mk I (revised edition)

Note
As DG202/G [2nd Stage] except:

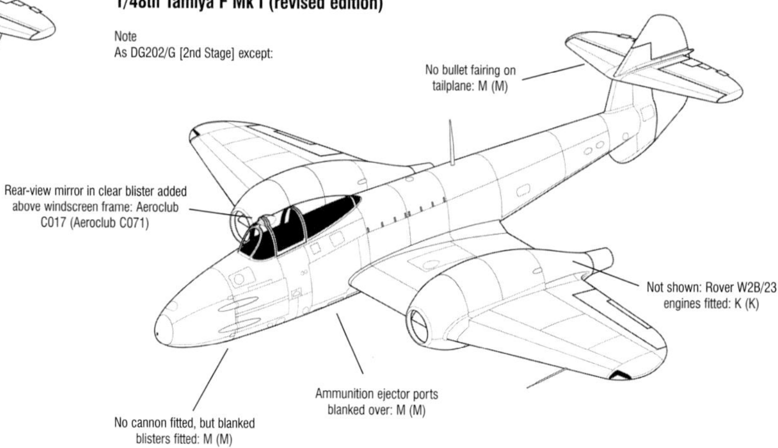

Gloster Meteor Prototype DG206/G [with Halford H.1 engines]

Kits

1/72nd Airfix F Mk III

1/48th Tamiya F Mk I (revised edition)

Note

As DG202/G [with Vickers F.2 engines] except:

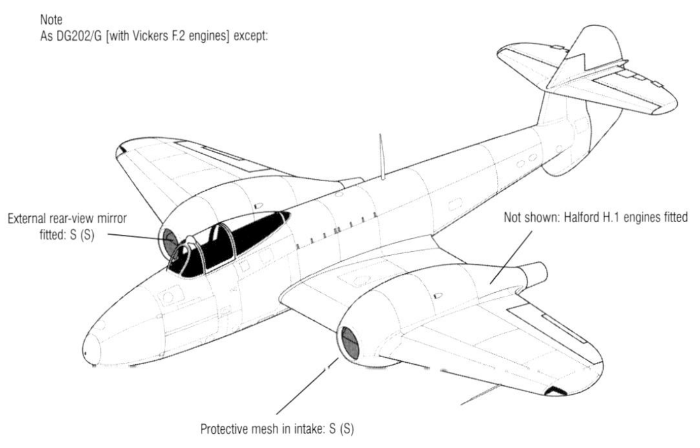

Gloster Meteor Prototype DG208/G [with increased fin area and straight-line fin leading edge]

Kits

1/72nd Airfix F Mk III

1/48th Tamiya F Mk I (revised edition)

Note

As DG202/G [2nd Stage] except:

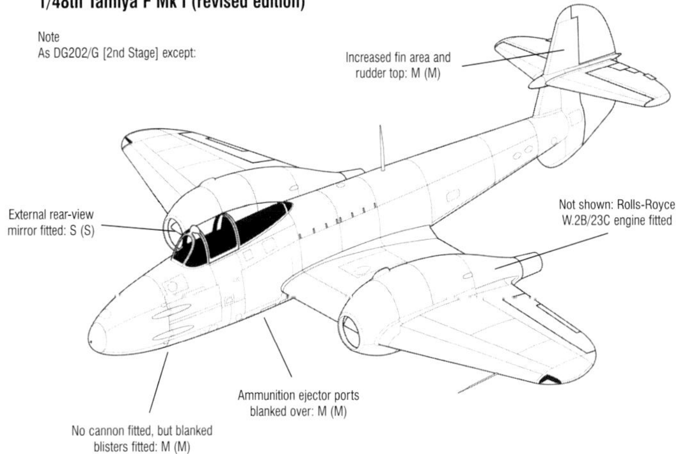

Gloster Meteor F Mk 1 [Production]

Kits

1/72nd Airfix F Mk III

1/48th Tamiya F Mk I (revised edition)

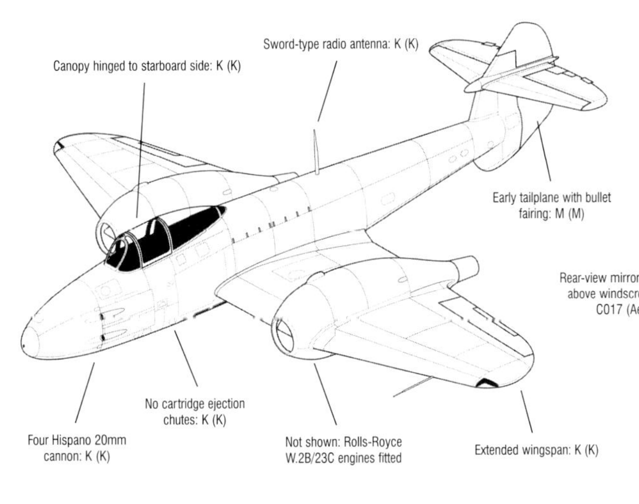

Gloster Meteor F Mk 1 EE223/G

1/72nd Airfix F Mk III

1/48th Tamiya F Mk I (revised edition)

Note

As F Mk 1 [Production] except:

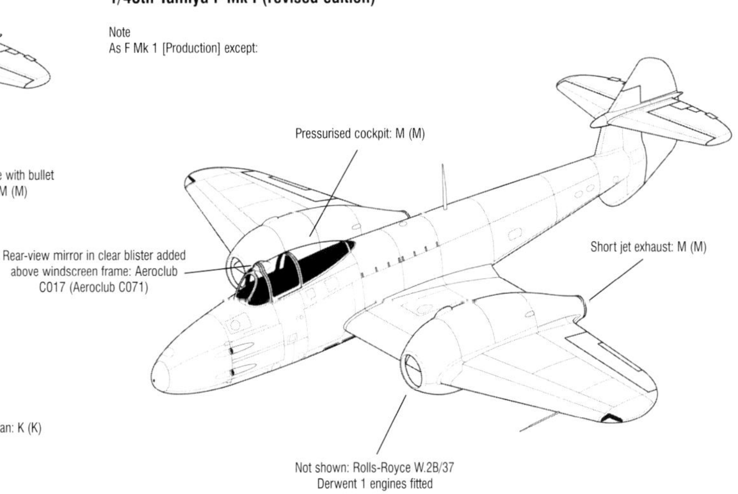

Gloster Meteor F Mk 1 EE227 [without top of fin]

Kits

1/72nd Airfix F Mk III

1/48th Tamiya F Mk I (revised edition)

Note

As F Mk 1 [Production] except:

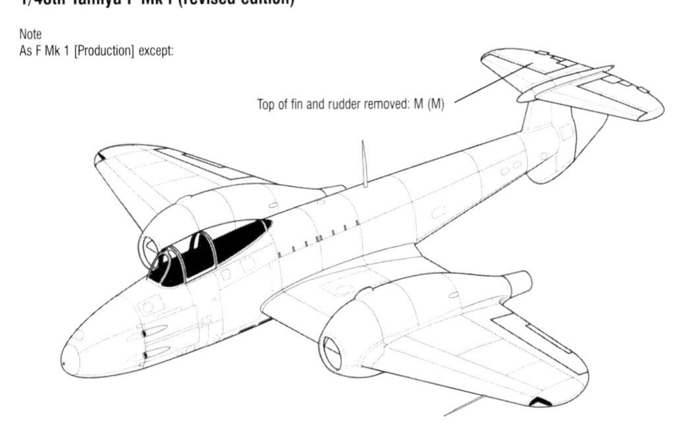

Gloster Meteor F Mk 1 EE227 [turbo-prop 'Trent Meteor']

Kits

1/72nd Airfix F Mk III

1/48th Tamiya F Mk I (revised edition)

Note

As F Mk 1 [Production] except:

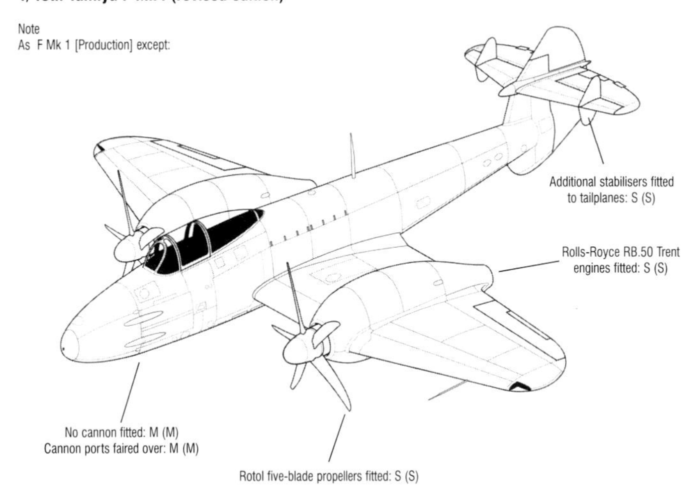

Gloster Meteor F Mk 3 [Production]

Kits
1/72nd Airfix F Mk III
1/48th Tamiya F Mk III

Note
As F Mk 1 [Production] except:

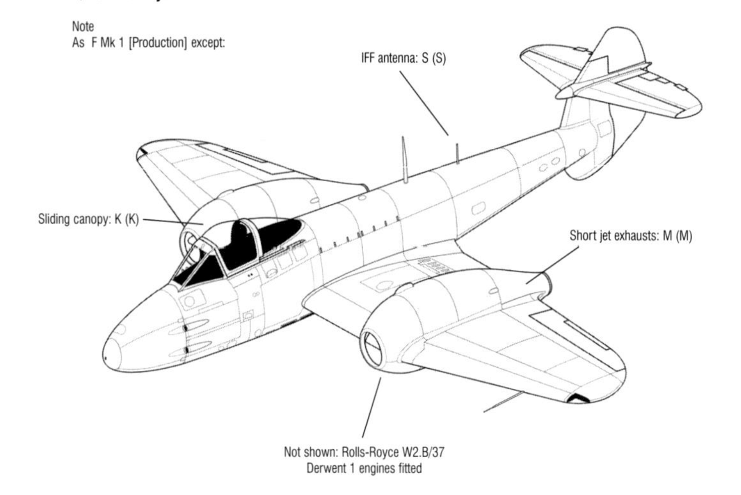

Gloster Meteor F Mk 3 EE445 [Laminar Flow Wing]

Kits
1/72nd Airfix F Mk III
1/48th Tamiya F Mk III

Note
As F Mk 3 [Production] except:

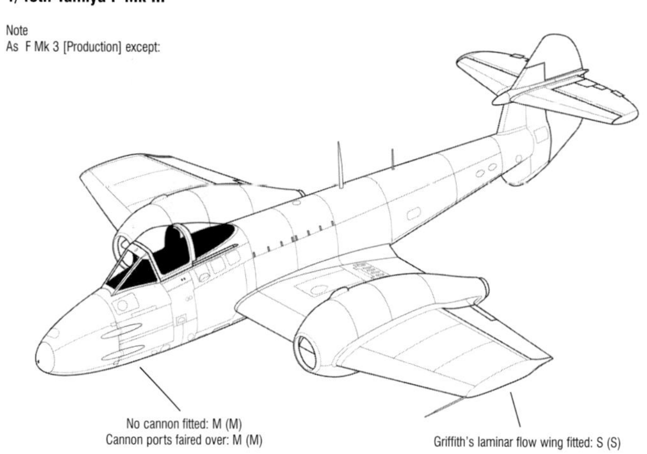

Gloster Meteor F Mk 3 EE387 [Royal Navy]

Kits
1/72nd Airfix F Mk III
1/48th Tamiya F Mk III

Note
As F Mk 3 [Production] except:

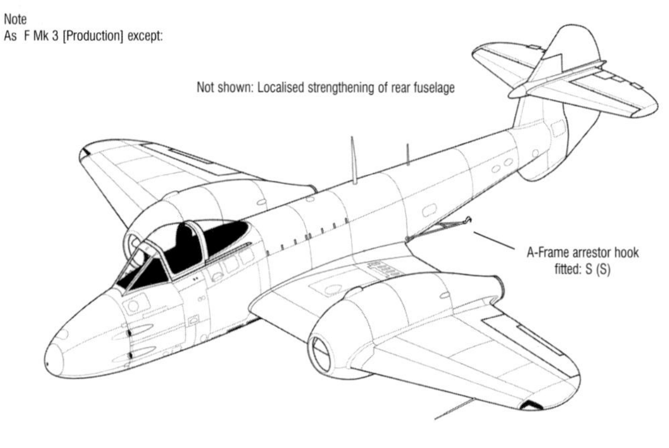

Gloster Meteor F Mk 3 EE389 & EE397 [In-flight Refuelling]

Kits
1/72nd Airfix F Mk III
1/48th Tamiya F Mk III

Note
As F Mk 3 [Production] except:

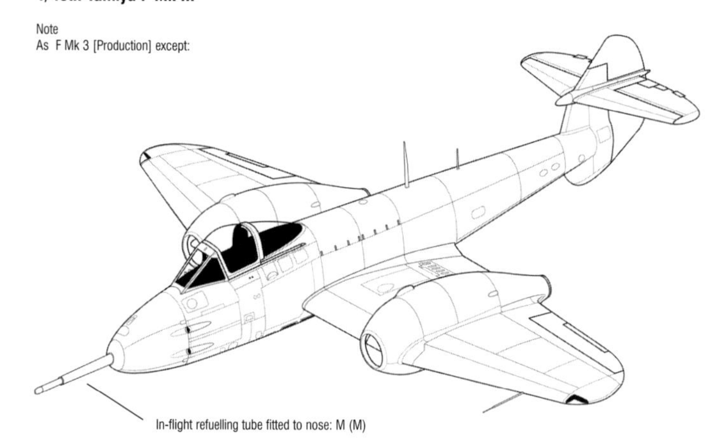

Gloster Meteor F Mk 3 EE454 & EE455 [Air Speed Record]

Kits
1/72nd Airfix F Mk III
1/48th Tamiya F Mk III

Note
As F Mk 3 [Production] except:

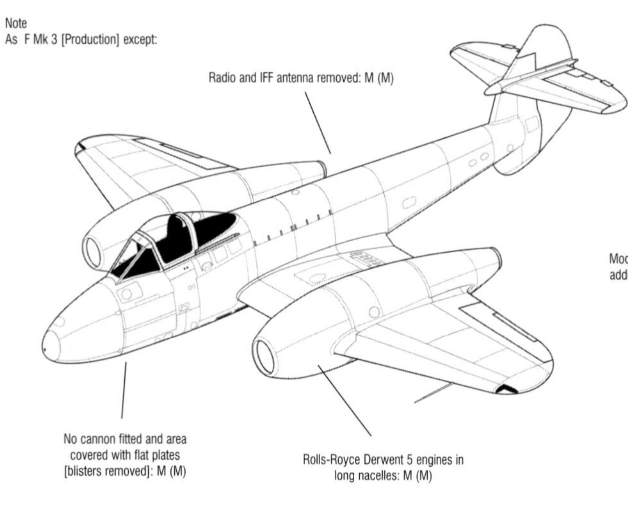

Gloster Meteor F Mk 3 EE416 [used for live ejection trials]

Kits
1/72nd Airfix F Mk III
1/48th Tamiya F Mk III

Note
As F Mk 3 [Production] except:

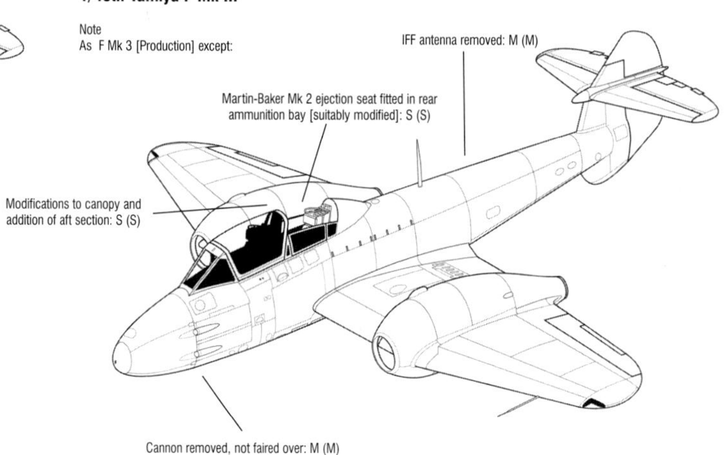

Gloster Meteor F Mk 4 [Early Production]

Kits
1/72nd Airfix F Mk III
1/48th Tamiya F Mk III

Note
As F Mk 3 [Production] except:

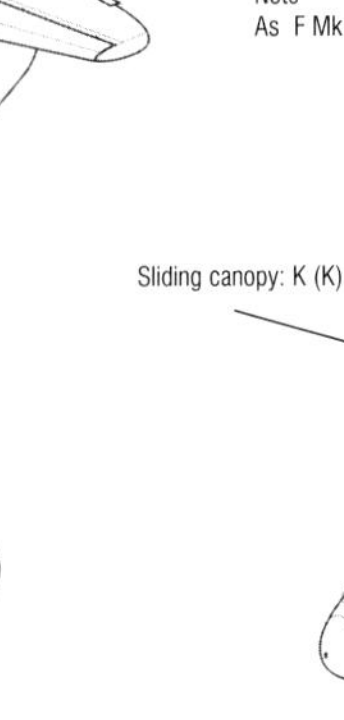

Rolls-Royce Derwent 5 engines in long nacelles: Obtain from F Mk 4 kit (Obtain from F Mk 4 kit)

F Mk 3 long span wing: M (M)

Gloster Meteor F Mk 4 [Production]

Kits
1/72nd Frog Mk 4
1/48th Classic Airframes F Mk 4

Note
As F Mk 3 [Production] except:

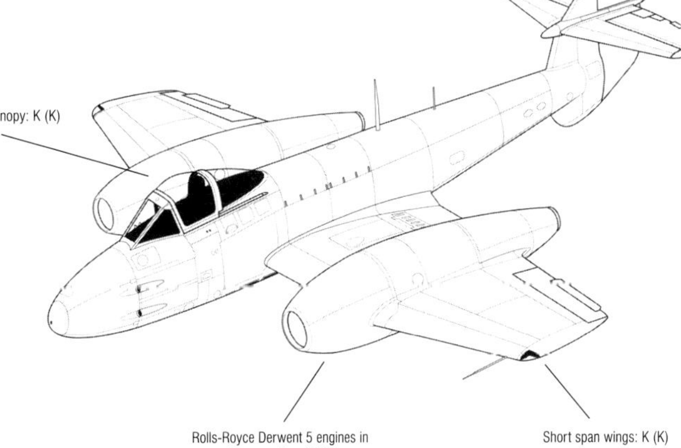

Gloster Meteor F Mk 4 VZ389 [In-flight Refuelling]

Kits
1/72nd Frog Mk 4
1/48th Classic Airframes F Mk 4

Note
As F Mk 4 [Production] except:

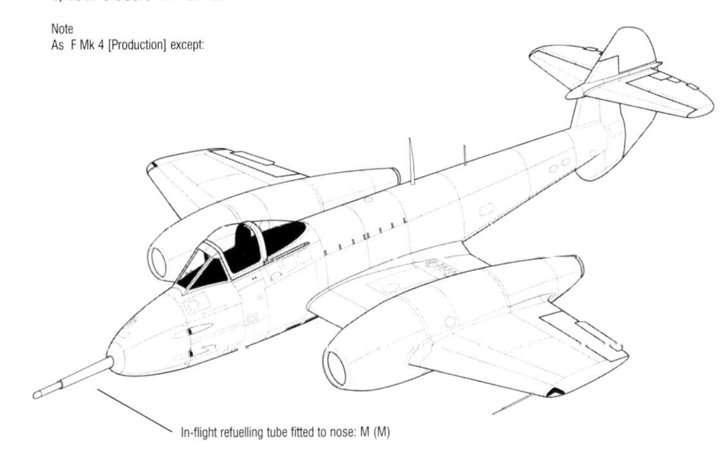

Gloster Meteor F Mk 4 [without cannon, e.g. VW790, G-AIDC]

Kits
1/72nd Frog Mk 4
1/48th Classic Airframes F Mk 4

Note
As F Mk 4 [Production] except:

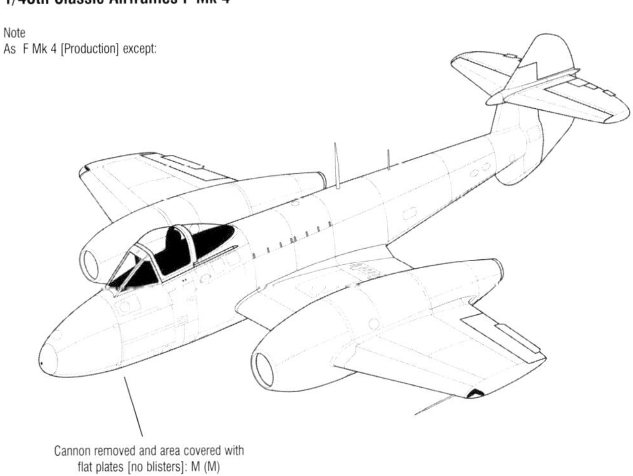

Gloster Meteor F Mk 4 EE549 & EE550

Kits
1/72nd Frog Mk 4
1/48th Classic Airframes F Mk 4

Note
As F Mk 4 [Production] except:

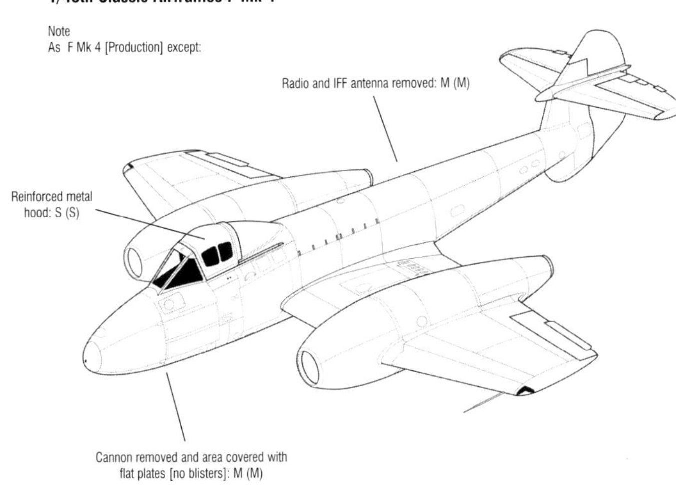

Gloster Meteor F Mk 4 G-AIDC [Demonstrator]

Kits
1/72nd Frog Mk 4
1/48th Classic Airframes F Mk 4

Note
As F Mk 4 [Production] except:

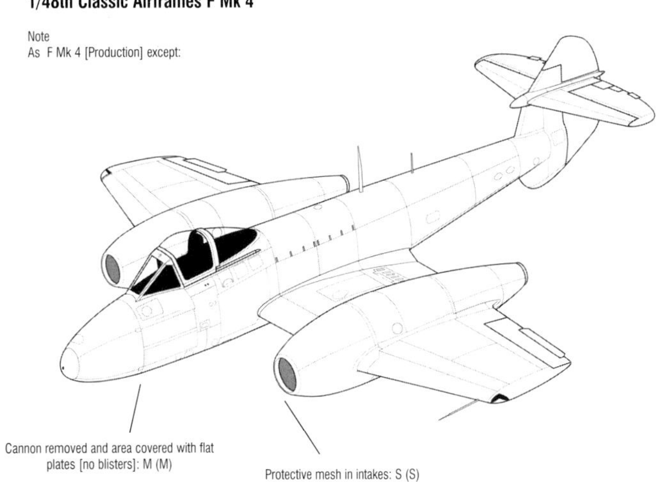

Gloster Meteor F Mk 4 G-AKPK [ex-G-AIDC after conversion to two-seater]

Kits
1/72nd Frog Mk 4
1/48th Classic Airframes F Mk 4

Note
As F Mk 4 [Production] except:

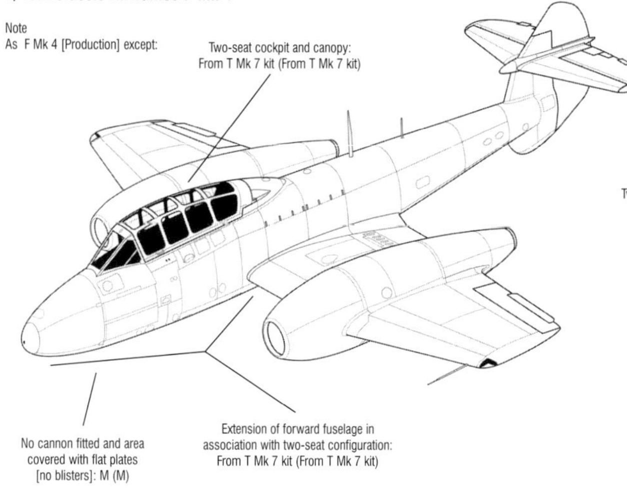

Gloster Meteor F Mk 4 EE573 [with 'Homing Eye' nose cone, TFU Defford]

Kits
1/72nd Frog Mk 4
1/48th Classic Airframes F Mk 4

Note
As F Mk 4 [Production] except:

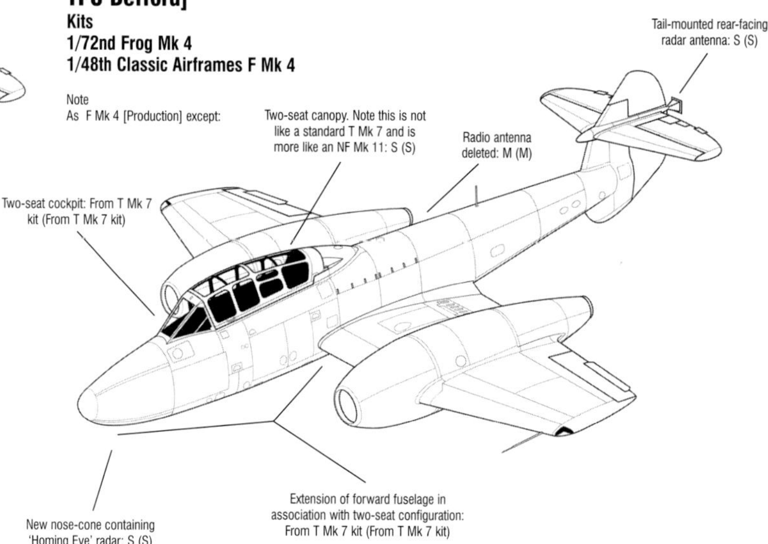

Gloster Meteor F Mk 4 RR435

Kits
1/72nd Frog Mk 4
1/48th Classic Airframes F Mk 4

Note
As F Mk 4 [Production] except:

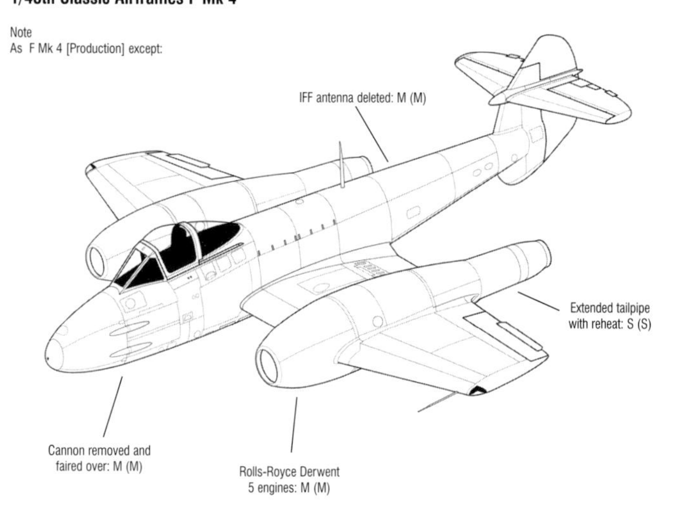

Gloster Meteor F Mk 4 RA490 [with Vickers F.2 engines, 1st Stage]

Kits
1/72nd Frog Mk 4
1/48th Classic Airframes F Mk 4

Note
As F Mk 4 [Production] except:

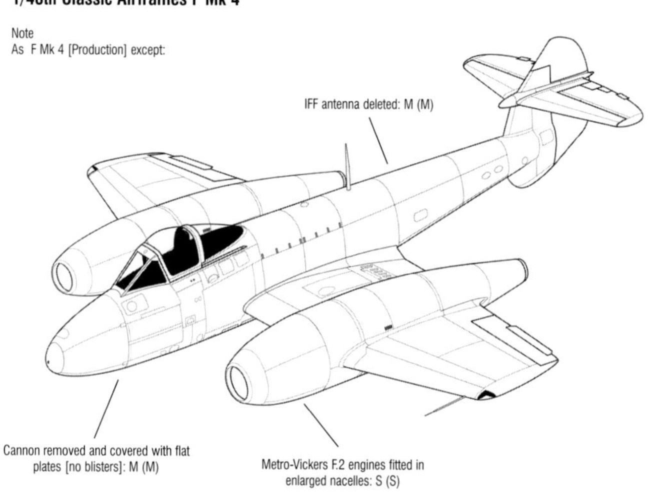

Gloster Meteor F Mk 4 [RA490 with Nene engines, 2nd Stage]

1/72nd Frog Mk 4
1/48th Classic Airframes F Mk 4

Note
As F Mk 4 RA490 [with Vickers F.2 engines, 1st Stage] except:

Whip antenna added to dorsal spine: S (S)
IFF antenna removed: M (M)
Additional stabilisers added to tailplanes: S (S)
F Mk 8 [late] type tail fitted: From F Mk 8 kit (From F Mk 8 kit)
Rolls-Royce Nene engines with jet-deflection system in new nacelles: S (S)

Gloster Meteor F Mk 4 RA491 [1st stage]

Kits
1/72nd Frog Mk 4
1/48th Classic Airframes F Mk 4

Note
As F Mk 4 [Production] except:

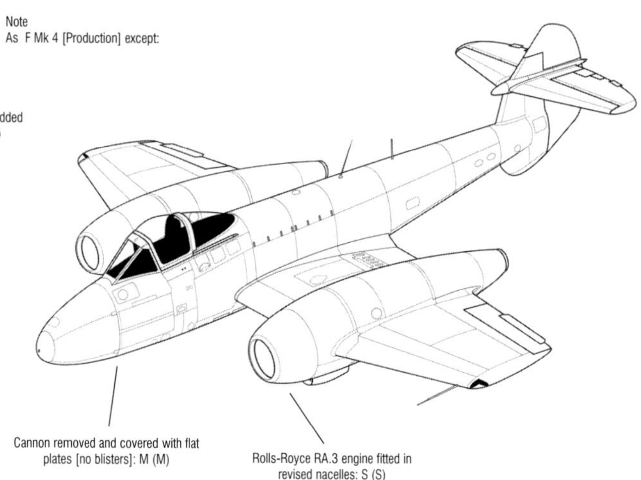

Gloster Meteor F Mk 4 RA491 [2nd stage]

Kits
1/72nd Frog Mk 4
1/48th Classic Airframes F Mk 4

Note
As F Mk 4 [Production] except:

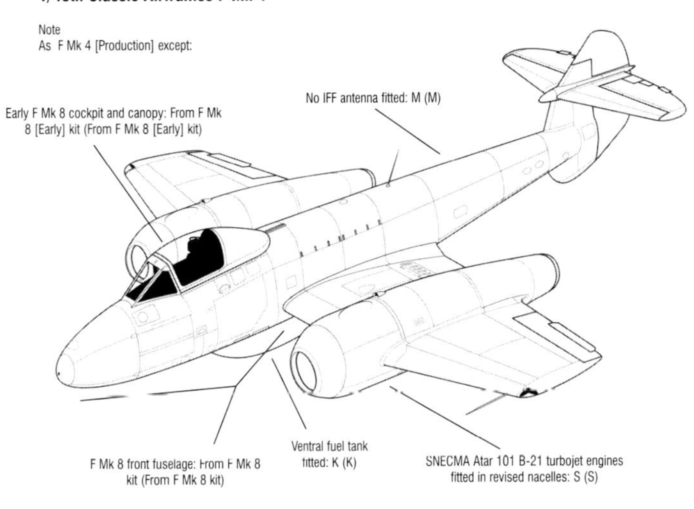

Gloster Meteor F Mk 4 VT196 [1st stage]

Kits
1/72nd Frog Mk 4
1/48th Classic Airframes F Mk 4

Note
As F Mk 4 [Production] except:

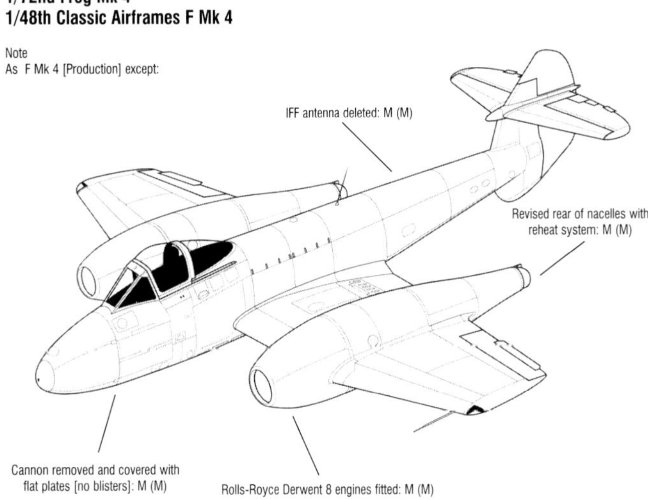

Gloster Meteor F Mk 4 VT196 [2nd stage]

Kits
1/72nd Frog Mk 4
1/48th Classic Airframes F Mk 4

Note
As F Mk 4 VT196 [1st stage] except:

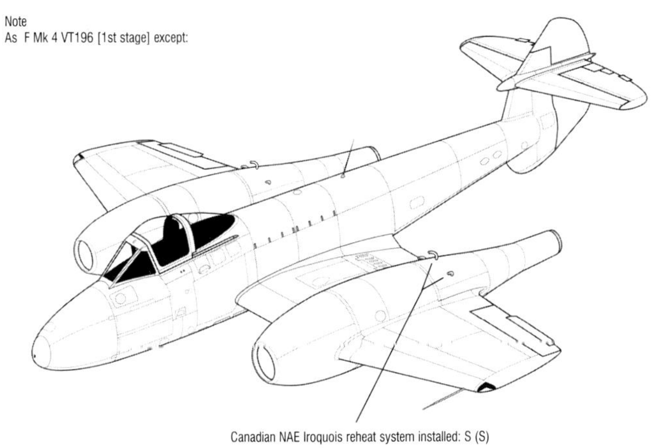

Gloster Meteor F Mk 8 [Early production]

Kits
1/72nd Aeroclub, Frog, PJ Productions or Rareplanes
1/48th Classic Airframes F Mk 8 (Early)

Note
As F Mk 4 [Production] except:

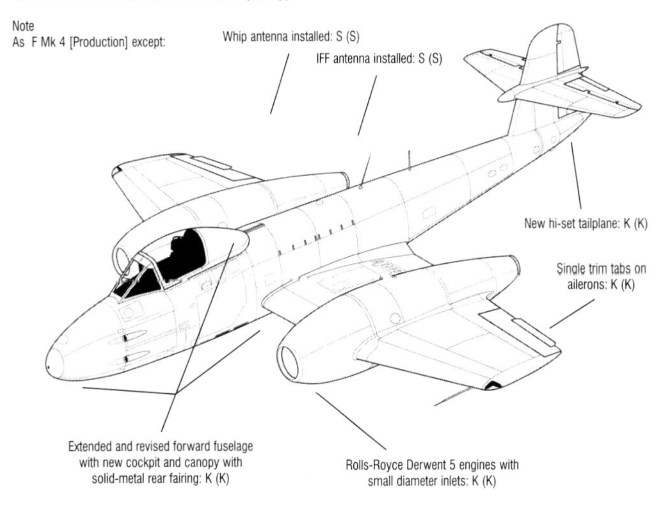

Gloster Meteor F Mk 8 [Mid-production]

Kits
1/72nd Aeroclub, Frog, PJ Productions or Rareplanes
1/48th Classic Airframes F Mk 8 (Early)

Note
As F Mk 8 [Early production] except:

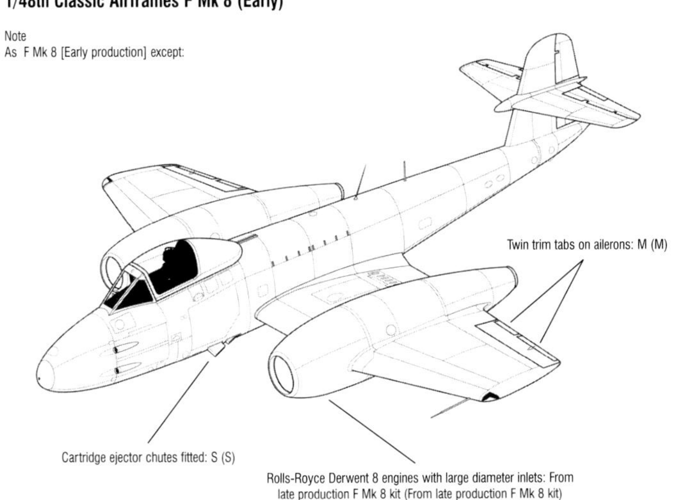

Gloster Meteor F Mk 8 [Late Production]

Kits
1/72nd Aeroclub, Frog, PJ Productions or Rareplanes
1/48th Classic Airframes F Mk 8 (Early)

Note
As F Mk 8 [Mid-production] except:

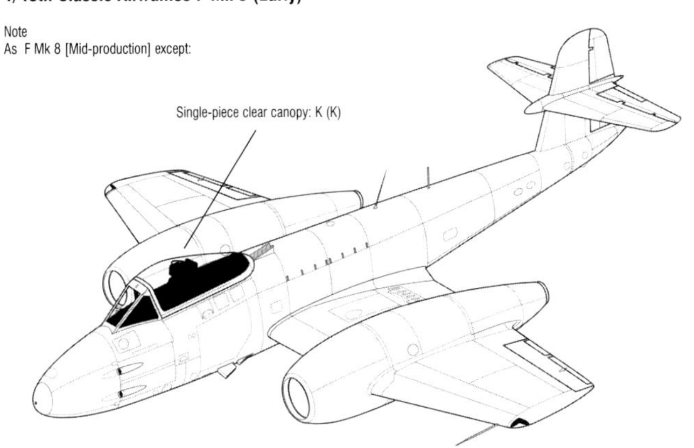

Gloster Meteor F Mk 8 [In-flight Refuelling]
Kits
1/72nd Aeroclub, Frog, PJ Productions or Rareplanes
1/48th Classic Airframes F Mk 8 (Early)

Note
As F Mk 8 [Early production] except:

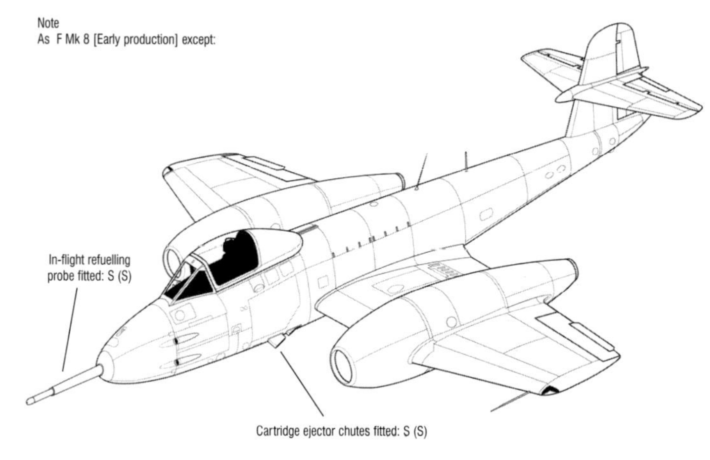

Gloster Meteor F Mk 8 WA982 [with Soar RSr.2 wing tip motors]
Kits
1/72nd Aeroclub, Frog, PJ Productions or Rareplanes
1/48th Classic Airframes F Mk 8 (Early)

Note
As F Mk 8 [Early production] except:

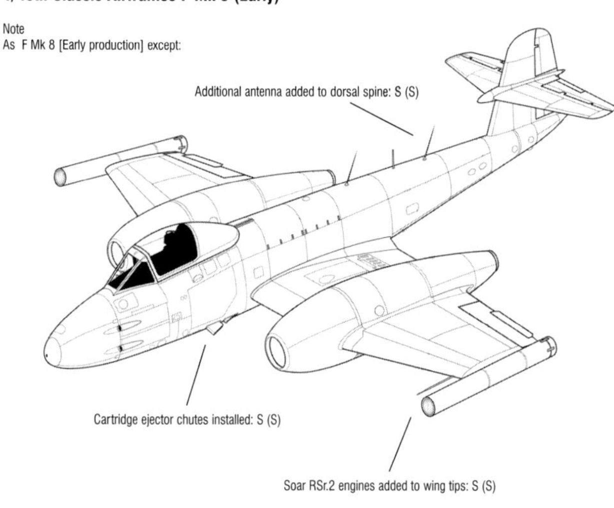

Gloster Meteor F Mk 8 WK935 [with prone pilot cockpit]
Kits
1/72nd Aeroclub, Frog, PJ Productions or Rareplanes
1/48th Classic Airframes F Mk 8 (Early)

Note
As F Mk 8 [Mid-production] except:

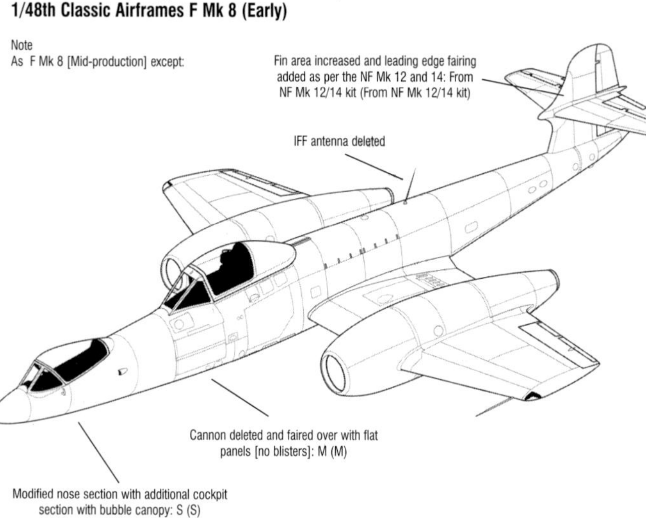

Gloster Meteor F Mk 8 WA820 [with Sapphire Sa.2 engines]
Kits
1/72nd Aeroclub, Frog, PJ Productions or Rareplanes
1/48th Classic Airframes F Mk 8 (Early)

Note
As F Mk 8 [Mid-production] except:

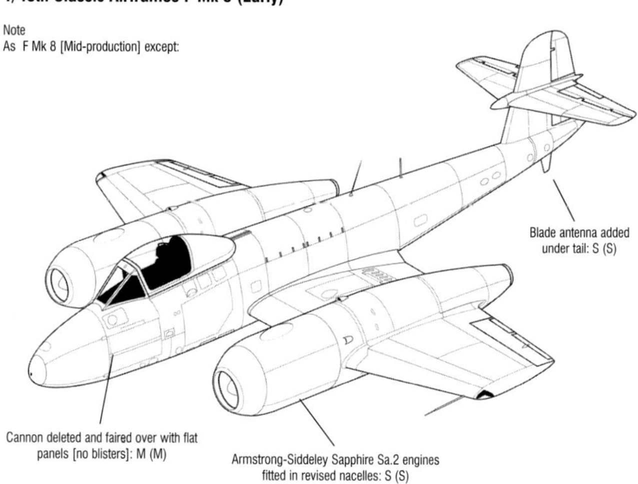

Gloster Meteor F Mk 8 VZ517 [with Screamer rocket motor]
Kits
1/72nd Aeroclub, Frog, PJ Productions or Rareplanes
1/48th Classic Airframes F Mk 8 (Early)

Note
As F Mk 8 [Mid-production] except:

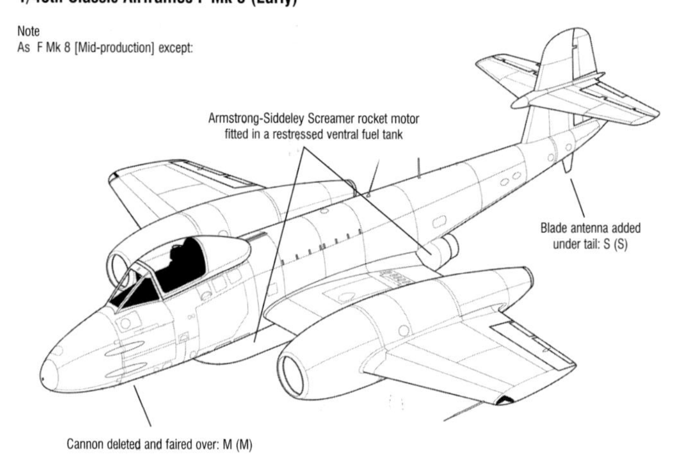

Ground Attack

Gloster Meteor F Mk 8 G-AMCJ/G.7-1 [ground-attack version]
Kits
1/72nd Aeroclub, Frog, PJ Productions or Rareplanes
1/48th Classic Airframes F Mk 8 (Early)

Note
As F Mk 8 [Early-production] except:

Drop tanks fitted on wingtips: S (S)

Cartridge ejector chutes fitted: S (S)

Additional strengthening of wing to take combinations of weapon loads:
2x 1000lb bombs with ventral pack containing 2x cannon, plus wingtip tanks
4x 1000lb bombs and tip tanks
24x 95lb rockets and tip tanks
16x 95lb rockets, ventral pack with 2x cannon plus tip tanks
580 Imp. Gal. ventral fuel tank, plus underwing and tip tanks for ferry flights (1,500 mile range)

Fighter Reconnaissance & Photo-Reconnaissance

Gloster Meteor FR Mk 5 VT347 [Prototype]
Kits
1/72nd Frog Mk 4
1/48th Classic Airframes F Mk 4

Note
As F Mk 4 [Production] except:

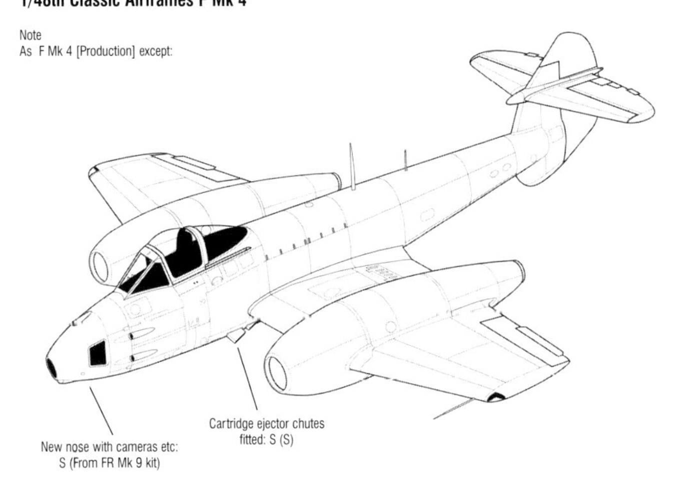

Gloster Meteor FR Mk 9 [Early production]
Kits
1/72nd CzechMaster F Mk 8/FR Mk 9
1/48th Classic Airframes FR Mk 9

Note
As F Mk 8 [Early production] except:

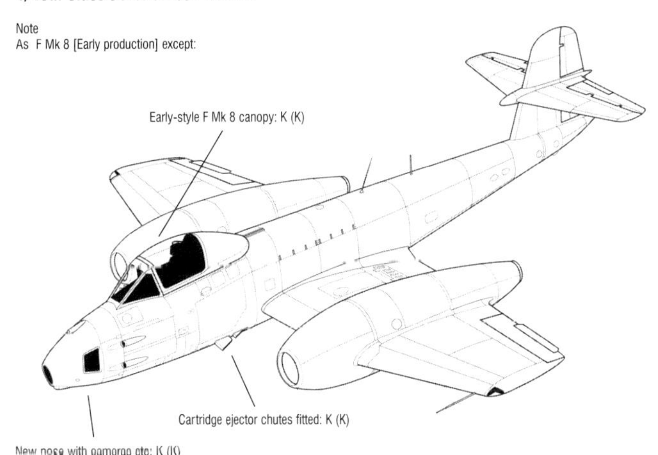

Gloster Meteor FR Mk 9 [Mid-production]
Kits
1/72nd CzechMaster F Mk 8/FR Mk 9
1/48th Classic Airframes FR Mk 9

Note
As F Mk 8 [Mid-production] except:

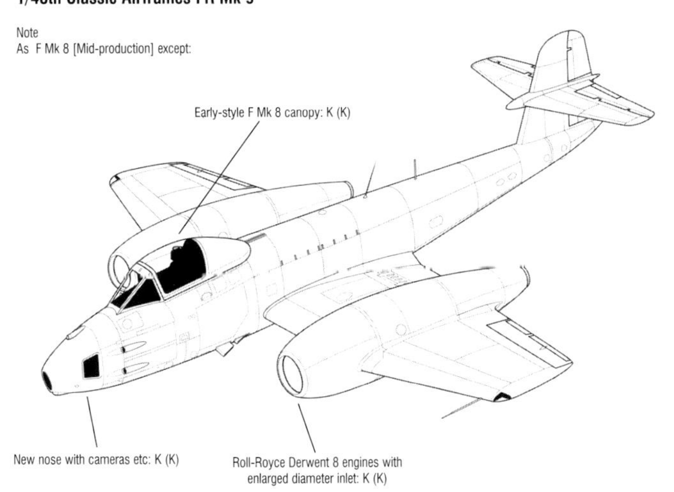

Gloster Meteor FR Mk 9 [Late production]
Kits
1/72nd CzechMaster F Mk 8/FR Mk 9
1/48th Classic Airframes FR Mk 9

Note
As F Mk 8 [Late production] except:

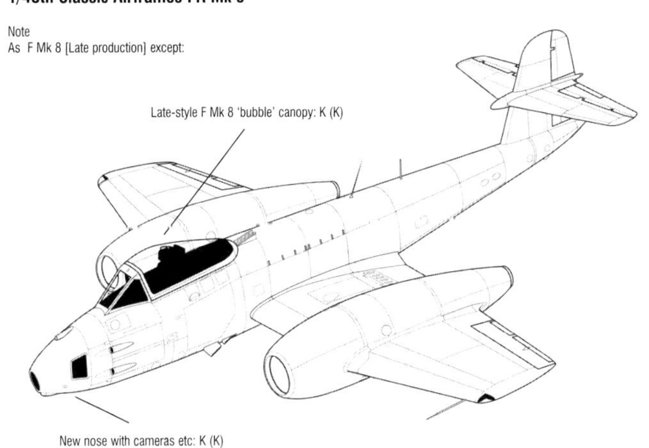

Gloster Meteor FR Mk 9 VZ608 [with RB.108 lift engine]
Kits
1/72nd CzechMaster F Mk 8/FR Mk 9
1/48th Classic Airframes FR Mk 9

Note
As FR Mk 9 [Late production] except:

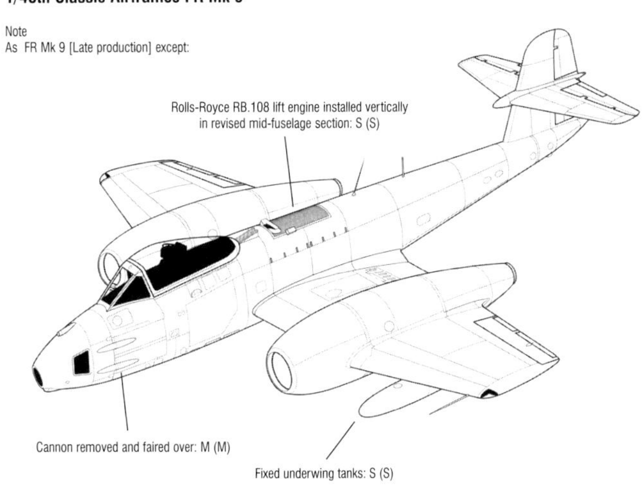

Gloster Meteor PR Mk 10 [Early production]
Kits
1/72nd CzechMaster F Mk 8/FR Mk 9
1/48th Classic Airframes FR Mk 9

Note
As F Mk 8 [Early production] except:

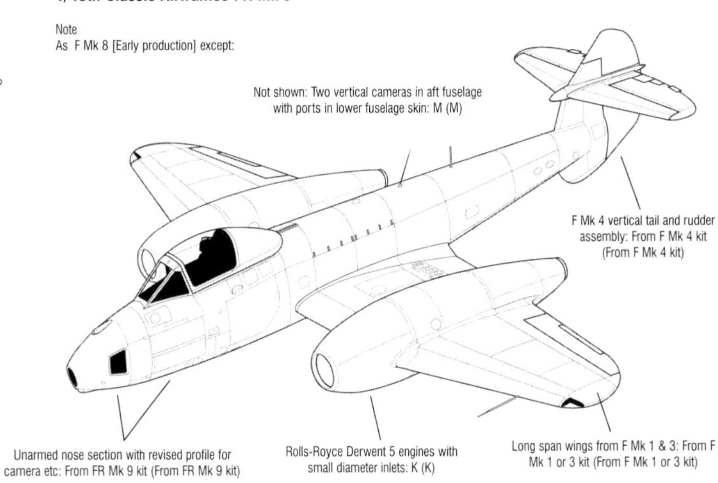

Gloster Meteor PR Mk 10 [Mid-production]
Kits
1/72nd CzechMaster F Mk 8/FR Mk 9
1/48th Classic Airframes FR Mk 9

Note
As PR Mk 10 [Early production] except:

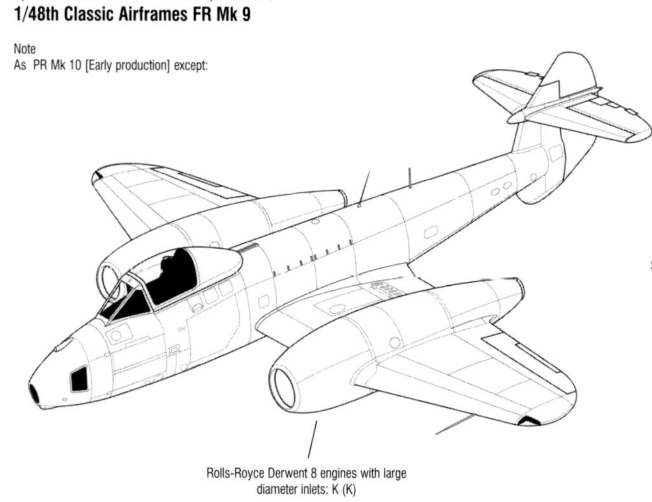

Gloster Meteor PR Mk 10 [Late production]
Kits
1/72nd CzechMaster F Mk 8/FR Mk 9
1/48th Classic Airframes FR Mk 9

Note
As PR Mk 10 [Mid-production] except:

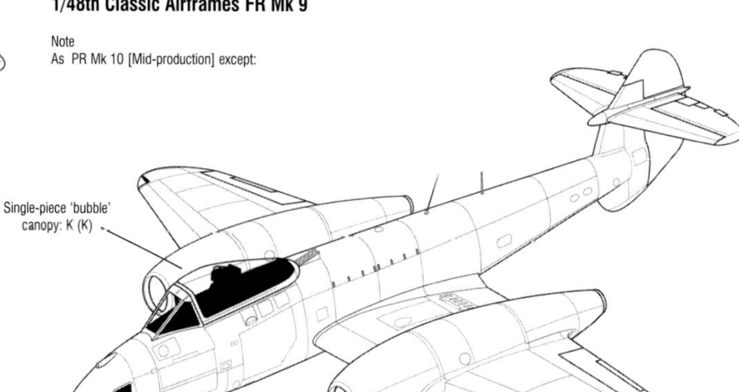

Trainers

Gloster Meteor T Mk 7 [Early produotion]
Kits
1/72nd Aeroclub T Mk 7
1/48th Classic Airframes T Mk 7

Note
As F Mk 4 [Production] except:

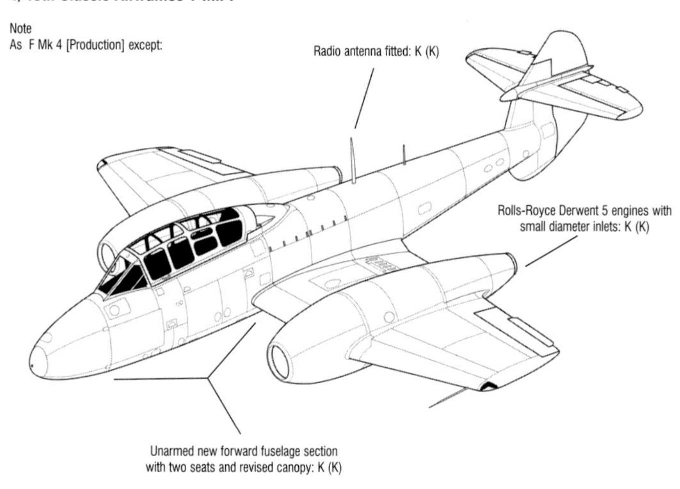

Gloster Meteor T Mk 7 [Production]
Kits
1/72nd Aeroclub T Mk 7
1/48th Classic Airframes T Mk 7

Note
As F Mk 7 [Early production] except:

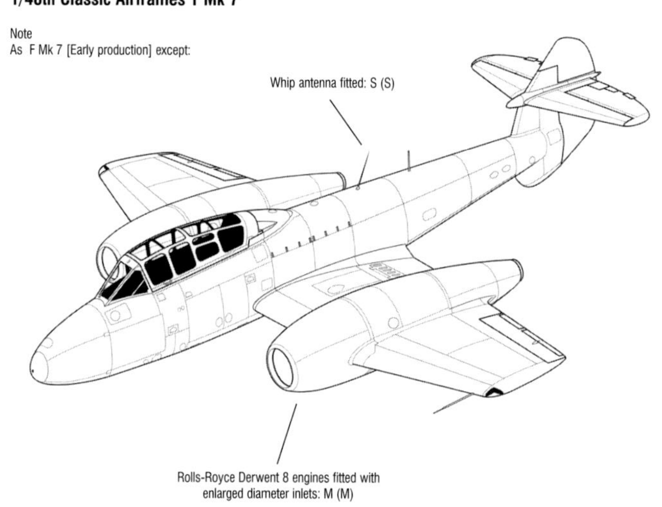

Gloster Meteor T Mk 7 G-ANSO
Kits
1/72nd Aeroclub T Mk 7
1/48th Classic Airframes T Mk 7

Note
As F Mk 7 [Early production] except:

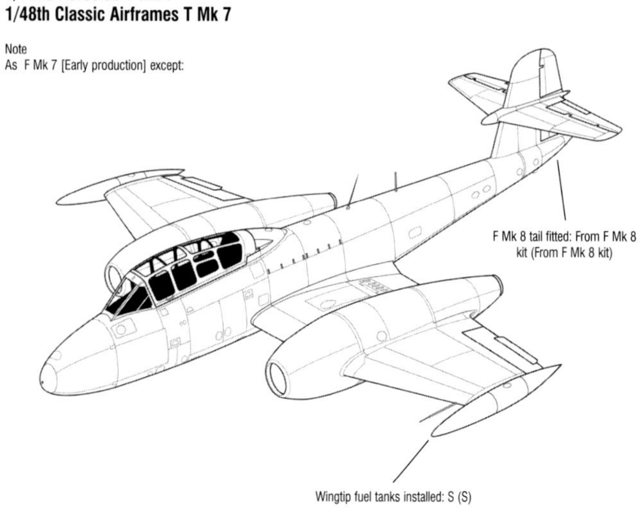

Gloster Meteor T Mk 7 VW413 [prototype for NF Mk 11]
Kits
1/72nd Aeroclub T Mk 7
1/48th Classic Airframes T Mk 7

Note
As F Mk 7 [Early production] except:

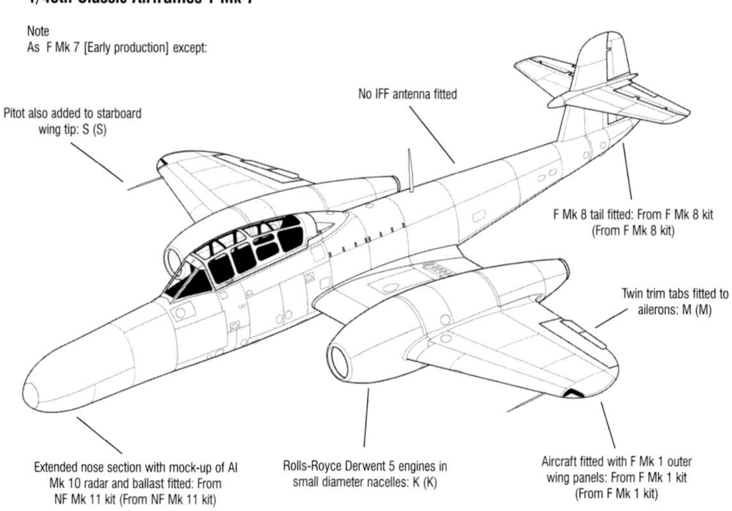

Gloster Meteor T Mk 7 VW411 [Hybrid]

Kits
1/72nd Aeroclub T Mk 7
1/48th Classic Airframes T Mk 7

Note
As F Mk 7 [Early production] except:

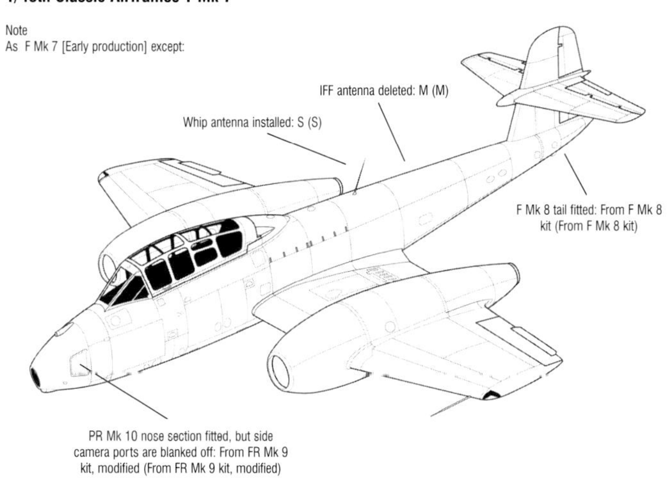

Gloster Meteor T Mk 7 VW443 ['Blue Jay' radar]

Kits
1/72nd Aeroclub T Mk 7
1/48th Classic Airframes T Mk 7

Note
As F Mk 7 [Late production] except:

Gloster Meteor T Mk 7 WA634 [1st Stage]

Kits
1/72nd Aeroclub T Mk 7
1/48th Classic Airframes T Mk 7

Note
As F Mk 7 [Early production] except:

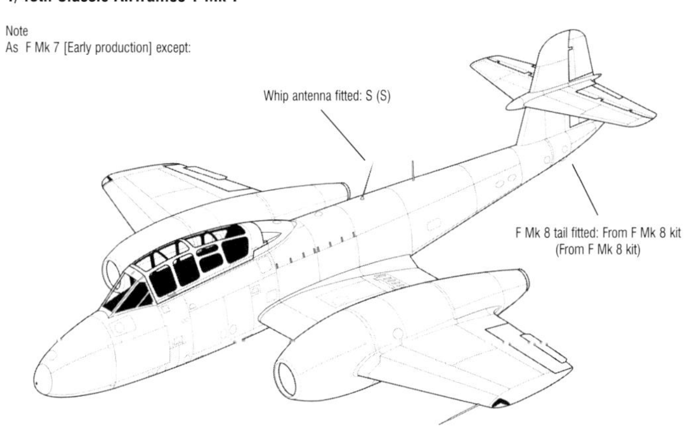

Gloster Meteor T Mk 7 WA634 [2nd Stage]

Kits
1/72nd Aeroclub T Mk 7
1/48th Classic Airframes T Mk 7

Note
As T Mk 7 [WA634, 1st Stage] except:

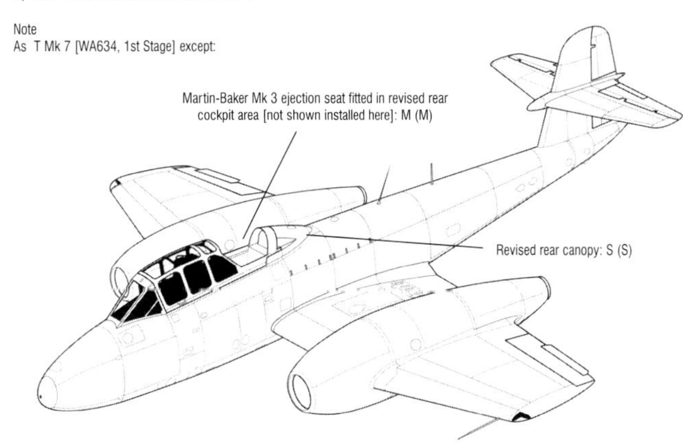

Gloster Meteor T Mk 7 WA634 [3rd Stage]

Kits
1/72nd Aeroclub T Mk 7
1/48th Classic Airframes T Mk 7

Note
As T Mk 7 WA634 [1st Stage] except:

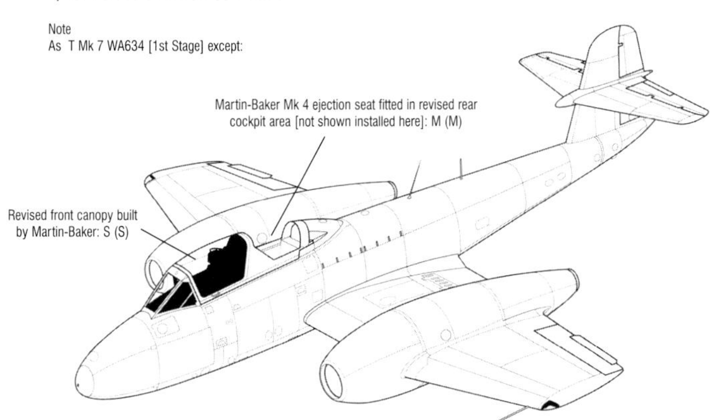

Gloster Meteor T Mk 7 VF877

Kits
1/72nd Aeroclub T Mk 7
1/48th Classic Airframes T Mk 7

Note
As F Mk 7 [Early production] except:

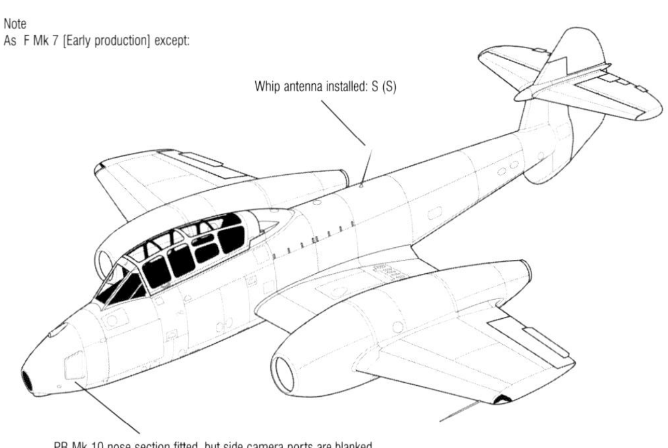

Gloster Meteor T Mk 7 WL419 [ejection seat trials]

Kits
1/72nd Aeroclub T Mk 7
1/48th Classic Airframes T Mk 7

Note
As F Mk 7 [Early production] except:

Blade antenna fitted: S (S)

Martin-Baker ejection seats fitted in revised rear cockpit area [not shown installed here]: M (M)

Revised canopy built by Martin-Baker: S (S)

F Mk 8 tail fitted: From F Mk 8 kit (From F Mk 8 kit)

Night Fighters

Armstrong-Whitworth Meteor NF Mk 11 [Prototypes]

Kits
1/72nd Matchbox NF Mk 11/12/14
1/48th Classic Airframes NF series (when released)

Note
As T Mk 7 [Production] except:

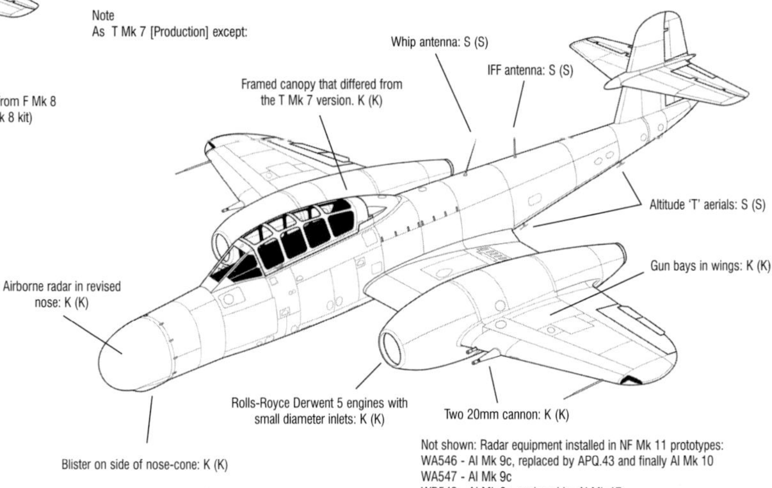

Armstrong-Whitworth Meteor NF. Mk 11 [Early production]

Kits
1/72nd Matchbox NF Mk 11/12/14
1/48th Classic Airframes NF series (when released)

Note
As T Mk 7 [Production] except:

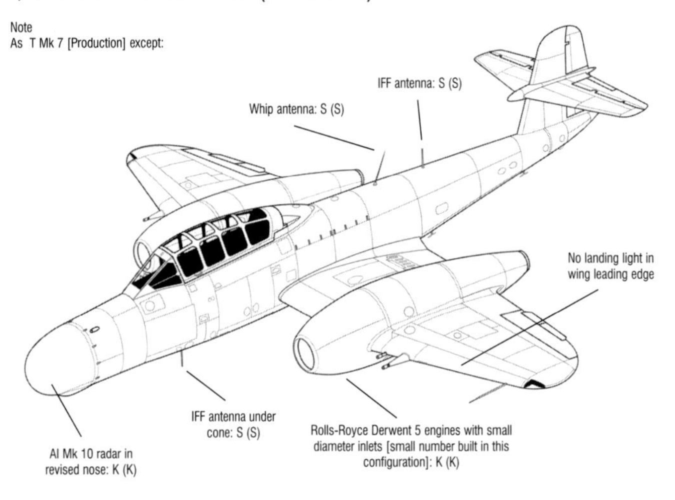

Armstrong-Whitworth Meteor NF. Mk 11 [Mid & Late production]

Kits
1/72nd Matchbox NF Mk 11/12/14
1/48th Classic Airframes NF series (when released)

Note
As NF Mk 11 [Early production] except:

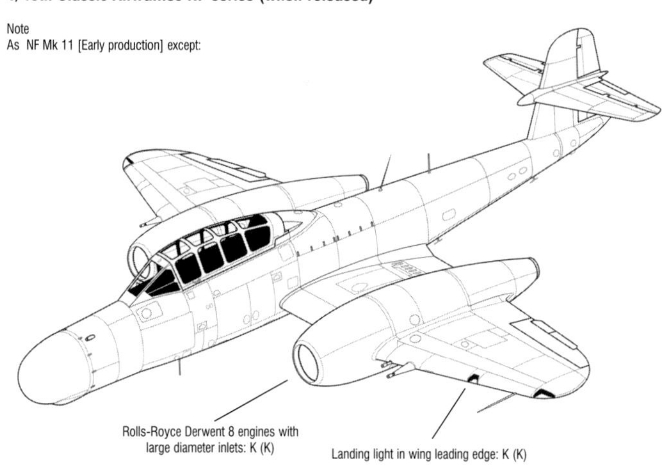

Armstrong-Whitworth Meteor NF Mk 11 WD604

Kits
1/72nd Matchbox NF Mk 11/12/14
1/48th Classic Airframes NF series (when released)

Note
As NF Mk 11 [Mid & late production] except:

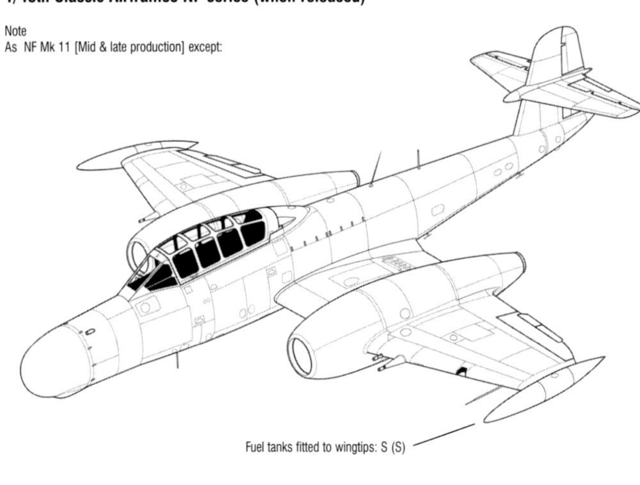

Armstrong-Whitworth Meteor NF Mk 11 [French electronics]

Kits
1/72nd Matchbox NF Mk 11/12/14
1/48th Classic Airframes NF series (when released)

Note
As NF Mk 11 [Mid & late production] except:

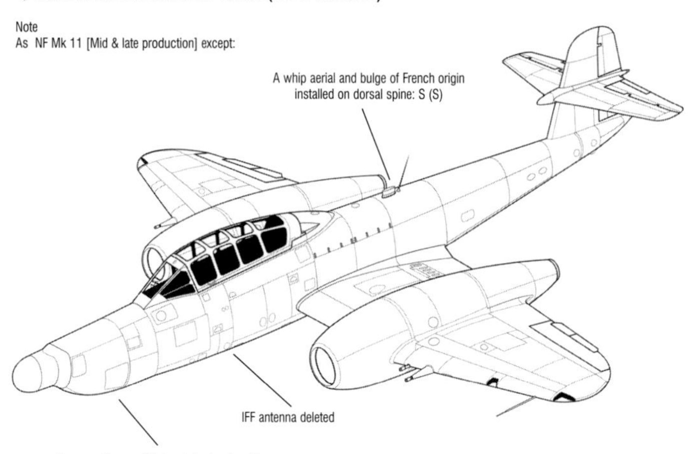

Armstrong-Whitworth Meteor NF Mk 11 WD790 [1st Stage]

Kits

1/72nd Matchbox NF Mk 11/12/14

1/48th Classic Airframes NF series (when released)

Note
As NF Mk 11 [Mid & late production] except:

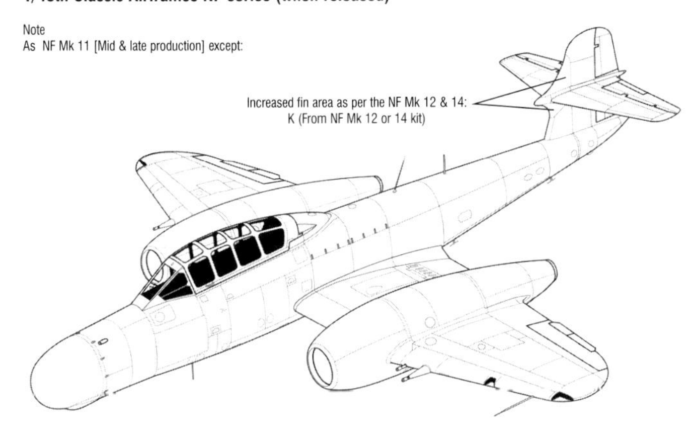

Armstrong-Whitworth Meteor NF Mk 11 WD790 [2nd Stage]

Kits

1/72nd Matchbox NF Mk 11/12/14

1/48th Classic Airframes NF series (when released)

Note
As NF Mk 11 [WD790 1st Stage] except:

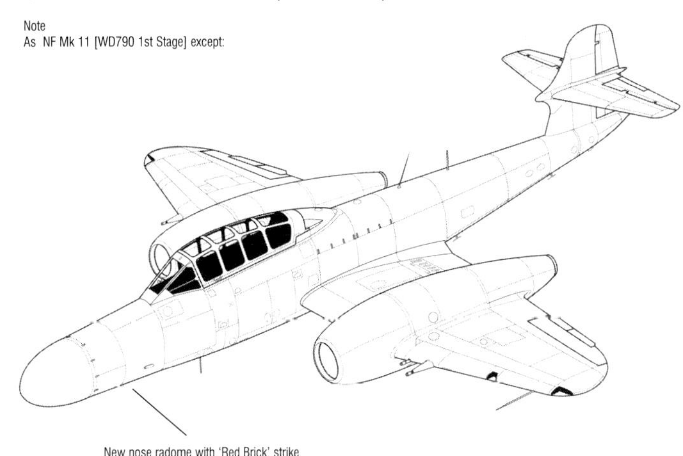

Armstrong-Whitworth Meteor NF Mk 11 WD790 [3rd Stage]

Kits

1/72nd Matchbox NF Mk 11/12/14

1/48th Classic Airframes NF series (when released)

Note
As NF Mk 11 WD790 [1st Stage] except:

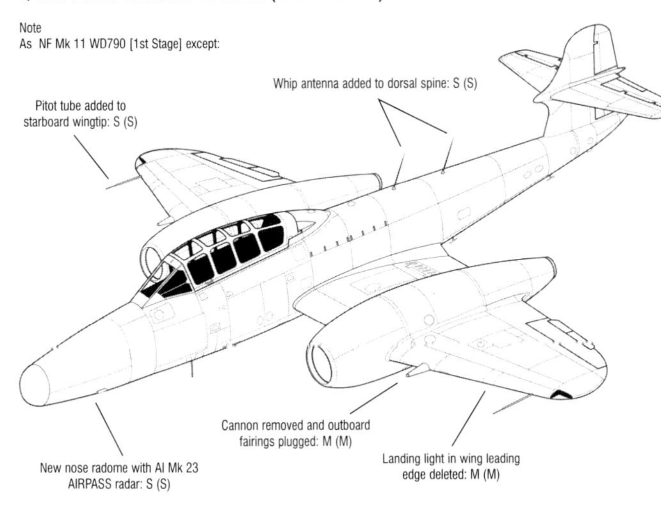

Armstrong-Whitworth Meteor NF Mk 11 WD790 [Final Stage]

Kits

1/72nd Matchbox NF Mk 11/12/14

1/48th Classic Airframes NF series (when released)

Note
As NF Mk 11 WD790 [3rd Stage] except:

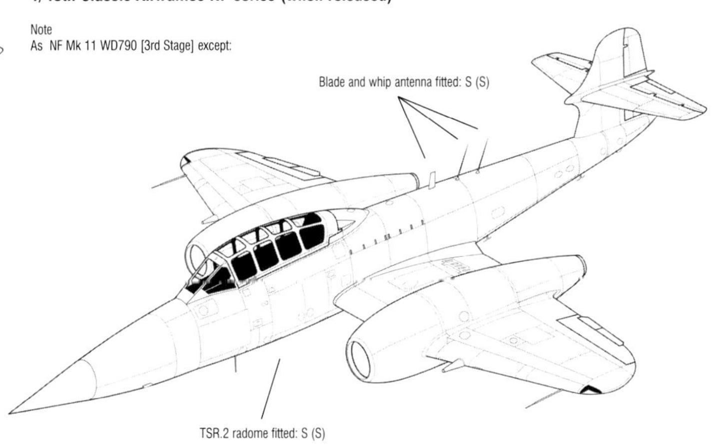

Armstrong-Whitworth Meteor NF Mk 11 WM180

Kits

1/72nd Matchbox NF Mk 11/12/14

1/48th Classic Airframes NF series (when released)

Note
As NF Mk 11 [Mid & late production] except:

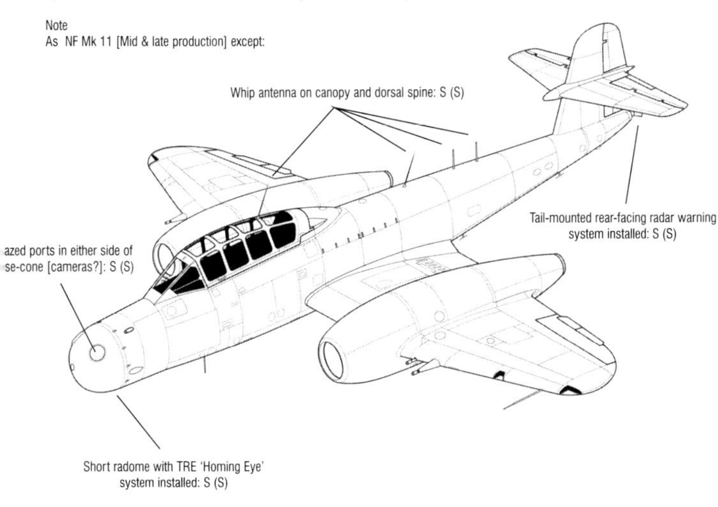

Armstrong-Whitworth Meteor NF Mk 11 WM262

Kits

1/72nd Matchbox NF Mk 11/12/14

1/48th Classic Airframes NF series (when released)

Note
As NF Mk 11 [Mid & late production] except:

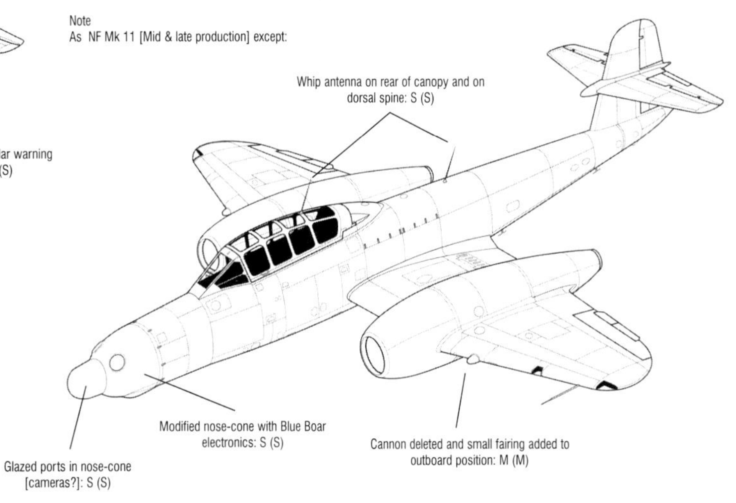

Armstrong-Whitworth Meteor NF Mk 11 WM372, 373 & 374 and WD743, 744 & 755

Kits
1/72nd Matchbox NF Mk 11/12/14
1/48th Classic Airframes NF series (when released)

Note
As NF Mk 11 WM262 except:

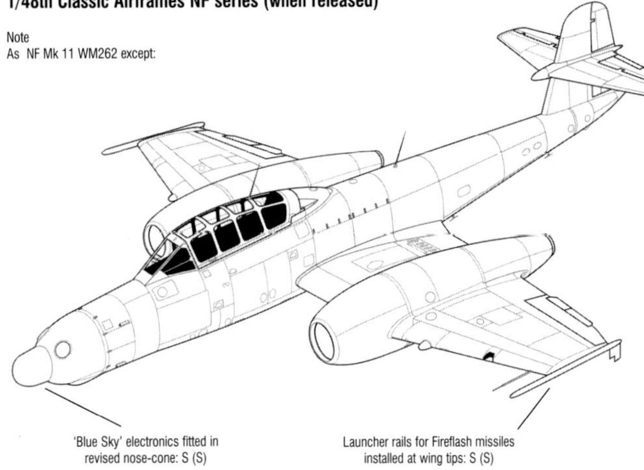

Armstrong-Whitworth Meteor NF Mk 12 [Production]

Kits
1/72nd Matchbox NF Mk 11/12/14
1/48th Classic Airframes NF series (when released)

Note
As NF Mk 11 WD670 [2nd Stage] except:

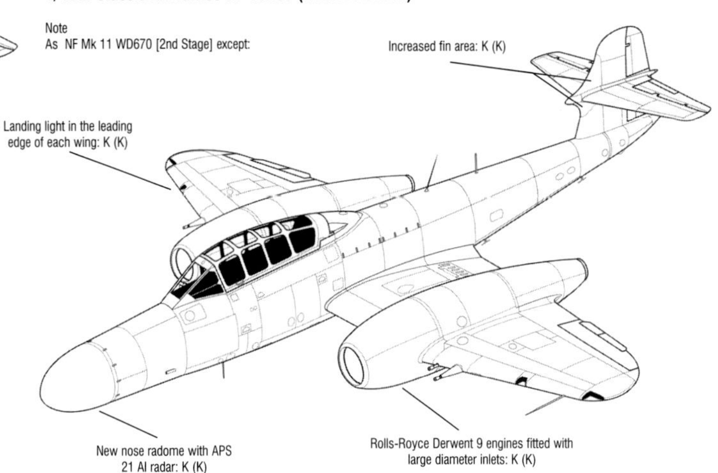

Armstrong-Whitworth Meteor NF Mk 13 [Production]

Kits
1/72nd Matchbox NF Mk 11/12/14
1/48th Classic Airframes NF series (when released)

Note
As NF Mk 11 [Mid & Late Production] except:

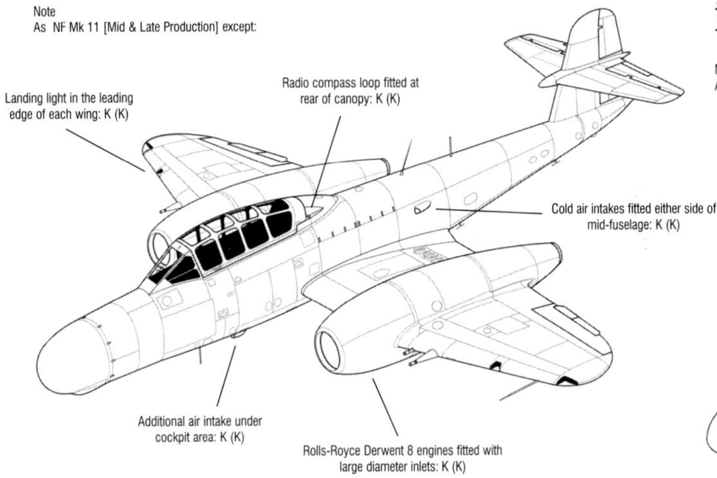

Armstrong-Whitworth Meteor NF Mk 14 [Production] and NF (T) Mk 14

Kits
1/72nd Matchbox NF Mk 11/12/14
1/48th Classic Airframes NF series (when released)

Note
As NF Mk 12 [Production] except:

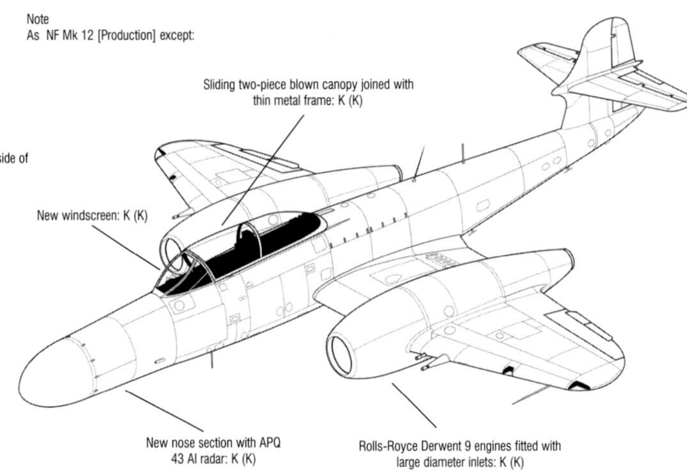

Armstrong-Whitworth Meteor NF Mk 14 WM261/G-ARCX

Kits
1/72nd Matchbox NF Mk 11/12/14
1/48th Classic Airframes NF series (when released)

Note
As NF Mk 14 [Production] except:

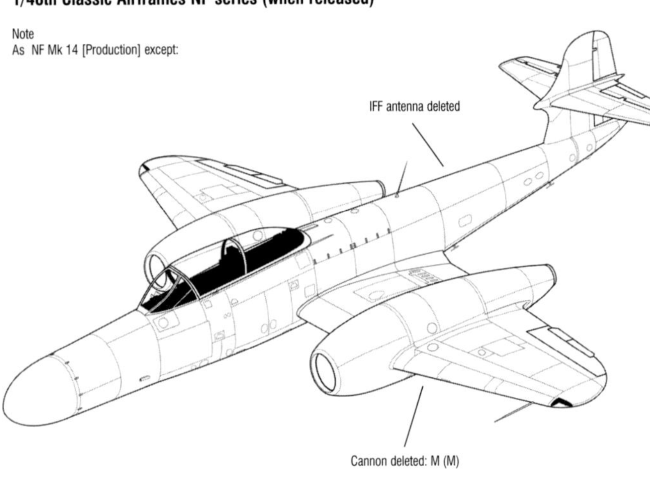

Target Tugs

Gloster Meteor F (TT) Mk 8

Kits
1/72nd Aeroclub, Frog, PJ Productions or Rareplanes
1/48th Classic Airframes F Mk 8 (Early)

Note
As F Mk 8 [Mid-production] except:

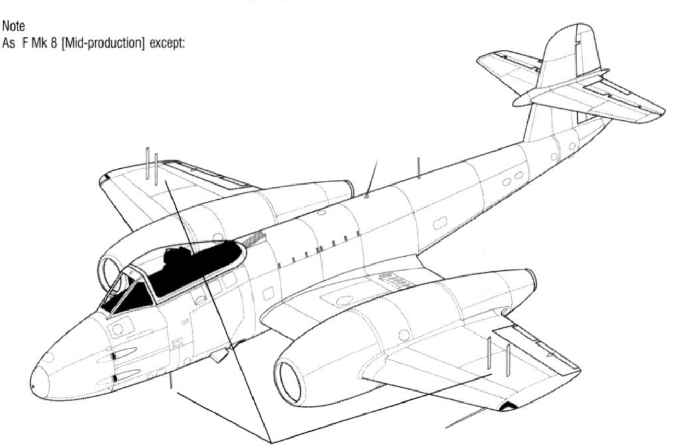

Armstrong-Whitworth Meteor TT Mk 20

Kits
1/72nd Matchbox NF Mk 11/12/14
1/48th Classic Airframes NF series (when released)

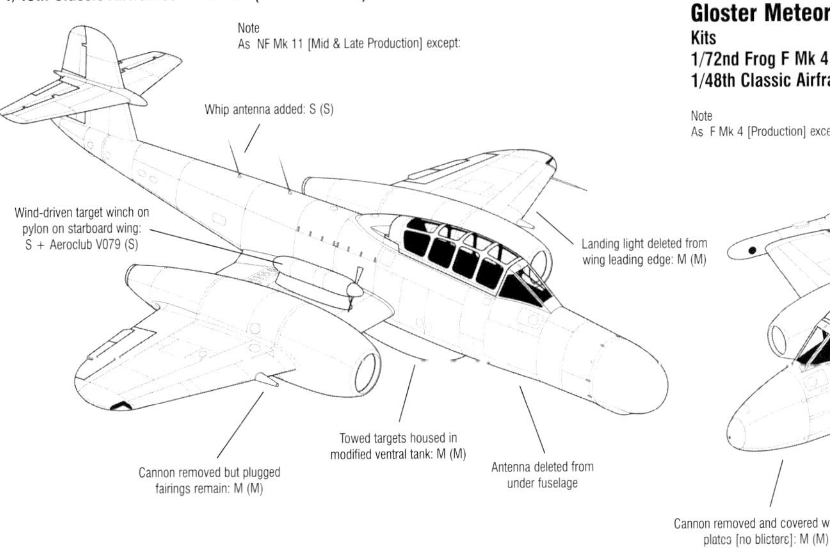

Gloster Meteor F Mk 8 converted to U Mk 16 standard

Kits
1/72nd Aeroclub, Frog, PJ Productions or Rareplanes
1/48th Classic Airframes F Mk 8 (Early)

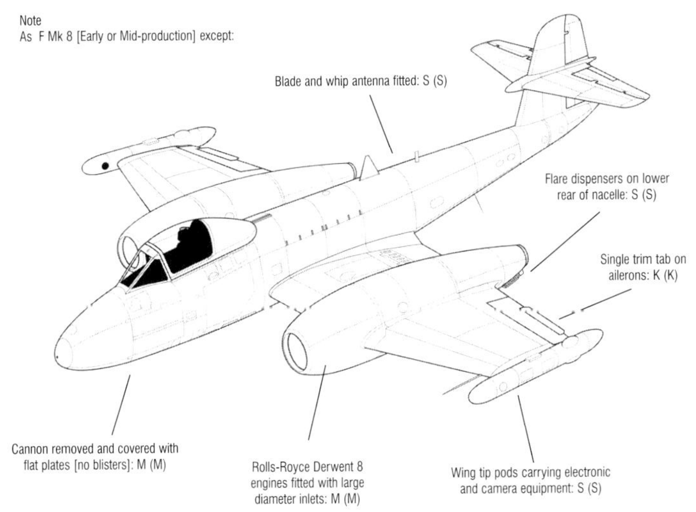

Drones

Gloster Meteor F Mk 4 converted to U Mk 15 standard

Kits
1/72nd Frog F Mk 4
1/48th Classic Airframes F Mk 4

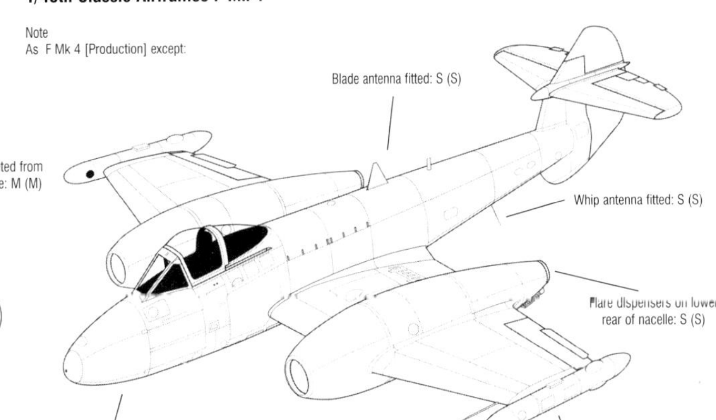

Gloster Meteor F Mk 8 converted to U Mk 21 standard

Kits
1/72nd Aeroclub, Frog, PJ Productions or Rareplanes
1/48th Classic Airframes F Mk 8 (Early)

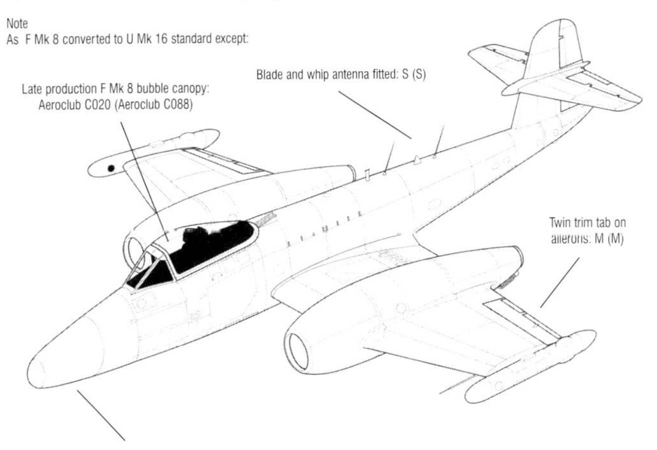

WA982 was fitted with Rolls-Royce Soar expendable engines which were fueled via the wings from the ventral tank

Detailing

Chapter 8

One of the most complex areas to deal with in any modelling project is that of interior (and exterior) detail. What precisely is in the cockpit? What do the interior of the wheel wells look like? etc are all questions which modellers ask. It can be a time-consuming process gathering all the information you need to attempt to detail any subject, so what we are offering in this chapter is a concise (ish!) section dealing with all those areas of the subject that you will be wanting to know about.

Cockpit • 1

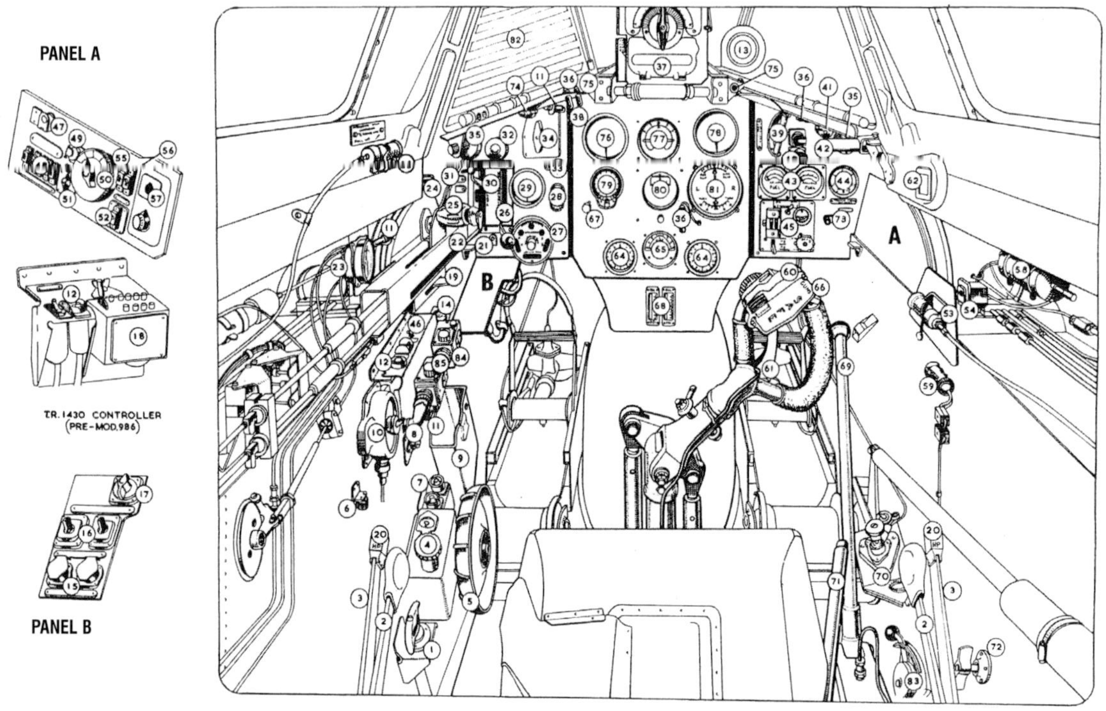

F Mk 4 (EE531) Cockpit layout
(©Crown Copyright)

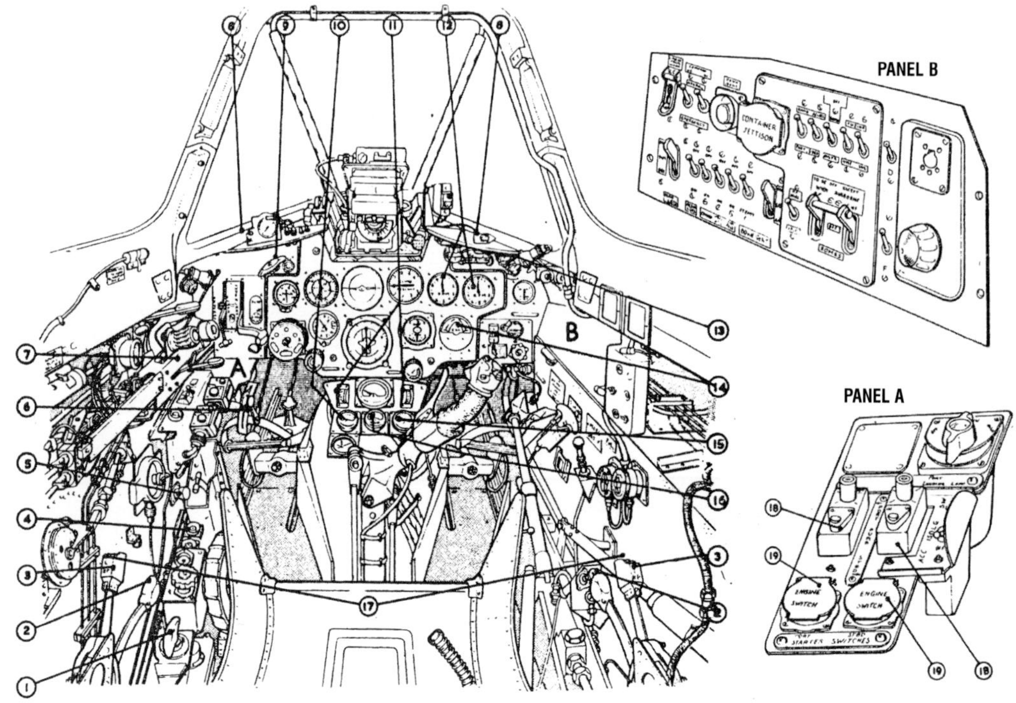

F Mk 8
Diagram showing the engine controls and instruments
(©Crown Copyright)

1. Fuel balance cock control
2. Low pressure fuel cock control
3. High pressure fuel cock control
4. Tank pump test push buttons
5. Tank pump test socket
6. Bomb and wing tank jettison lever
7. Throttle controls
8. Engine fire warning lamps
9. Ventral tank jettison control
10. Fuel contents gauges
11. Oil pressure gauges
12. Tachometers
13. Engine fire extinguisher push buttons
14. Dual exhaust temperature gauges
15. Fuel contents gauges (main tank, rear compartment)
16. Fuel contents gauges (front tank)
17. Relighting switches
18. Tank pump circuit breakers
19. Start push buttons

Cockpit • 2

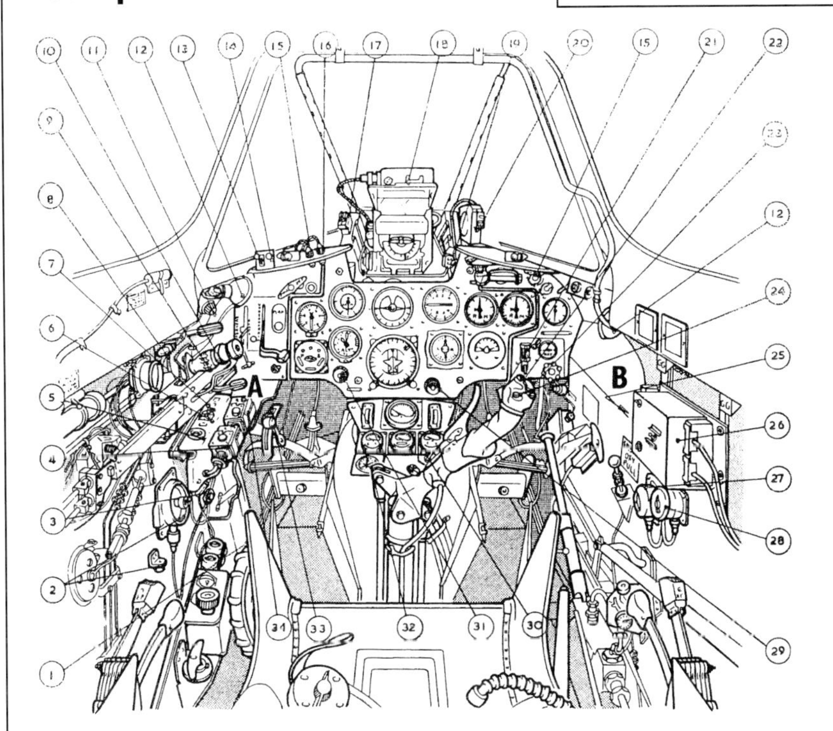

FR Mk 9
Diagram showing the operational and miscellaneous equipment
(©Crown Copyright)

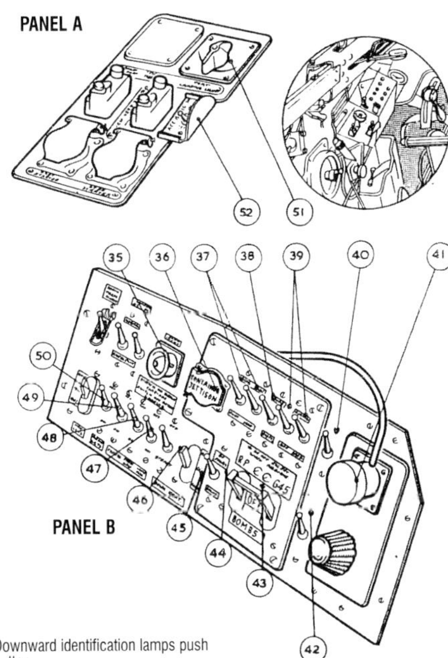

1. Map case
2. Camera footage indicator
3. Trimmer lamp
4. No.2 VHF radio controller
5. 'G Auto' switch
6. 'G Manual' switch
7. Set selector switch
8. Brake gauge lamp
9. Gyro gunsight range control
10. Press-to-speak switch
11. Ancillary lamps dimmer switch
12. Ultra-violet flood lamps
13. Nose camera switch
14. Nose camera warning lamp
15. Instrument panel lamps
16. Emergency lamps
17. Gyro gunsight control switch
18. Retractable gyro gunsight
19. Gunsight emergency retraction control
20. Gunsight master circuit breaker
21. Gun firing trigger
22. Gun firing safety catch
23. Bomb or rocket firing switch
24. Cine camera switch
25. Emergency lamp switch
26. Nose camera controller
27. Gunsight selector dimmer
28. Gunsight 'rocket/guns' switch
29. Instrument panel lamps dimmer switch
30. Generator failure warning lamp
31. Ultra-violet lamps dimmer switch
32. Clock
33. Bomb or tank manual jettison lever
34. No.1 VHF radio controller
35. Downward identification lamps push button
36. Bomb container jettison push button
37. Bomb selector switches
38. Bomb distributor switch
39. Bomb fusing switches
40. IFF on/off switch
41. IFF controller
42. IFF distress switch
43. Bomb and rocket firing selector switch
44. Rocket pair/salvo selector switch
45. Downward identification lamps selector switch
46. Downward identification lamps steady switch
47. Pressure head heater switch
48. Camera and pressure head heater switch
49. Recognition lamp switch
50. Navigation lamps switch
51. Landing lamp switch
52. Accumulator isolating switch

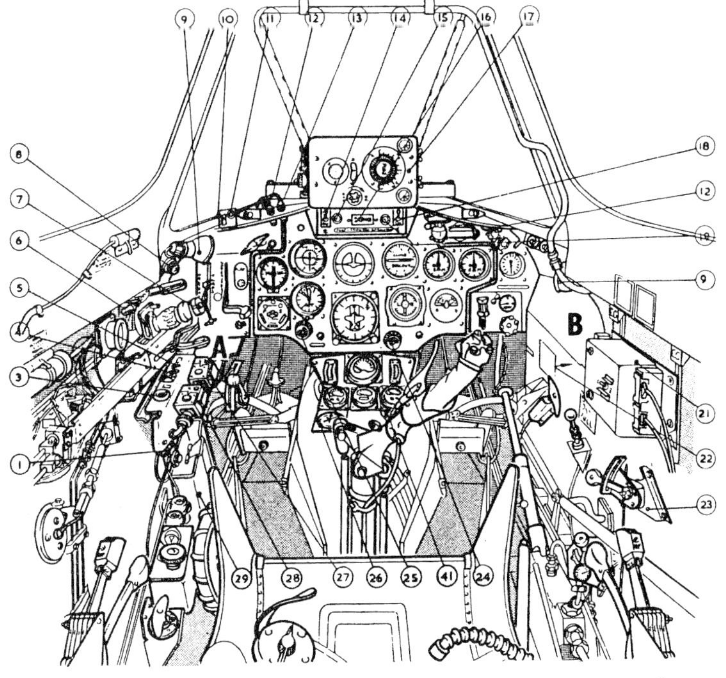

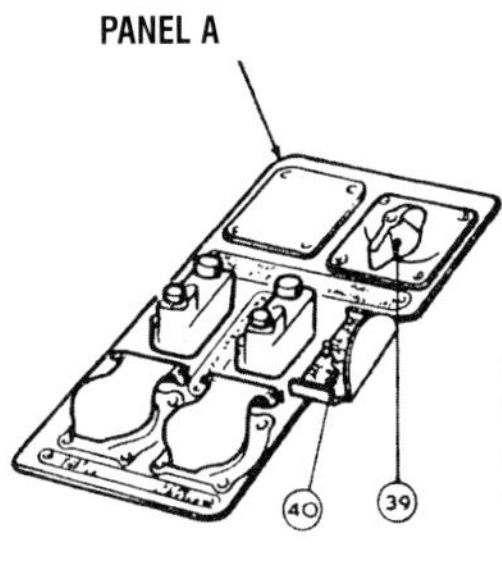

PR Mk 10
Diagram showing the operational and miscellaneous equipment
(©Crown Copyright)

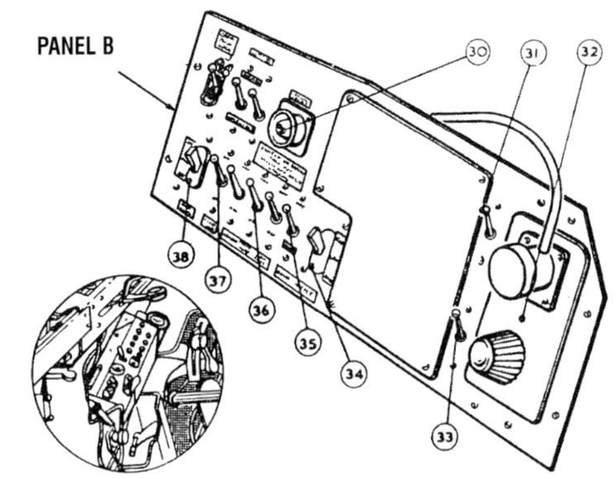

1. Trimmer lamp
2. N/A
3. 'G Manual' switch
4. 'G Auto' switch
5. Radio change-over switch
6. Brake gauge lamp
7. Press-to-speak switch
8. Ancillary lamps dimmer switch
9. Ultra-violet flood lamps
10. Nose camera switch
11. Nose camera warning lamp
12. Instrument panel lamps
13. Emergency lamps
14. Port camera switch
15. Port camera warning lamp
16. Counter switch
17. Rear cameras controller
18. Starboard camera switch
19. Starboard camera warning lamp
20. N/A
21. Nose camera controller
22. Emergency lamp switch
23. Camera shutter jettison
24. Instrument panel lamps dimmer switch
25. Ultra-violet lamps dimmer switch
26. Clock
27. Radio controller (No.1 set)
28. Radio controller (No.2 set)
29. Map case
30. Downward identification lamps push button
31. IFF distress switch
32. IFF controller
33. IFF on/off switch
34. Downward identification lamps selector switch
35. Downward identification lamps steady switch
36. Pressure head heater switch
37. Recognition lamp switch
38. Navigation lamps switch
39. Landing lamp switch
40. Accumulator isolating switch
41. Generator failure warning lamp

Cockpit • 3

NF Mk 11
Diagram showing the operational and miscellaneous equipment in the front cockpit area
(©Crown Copyright)

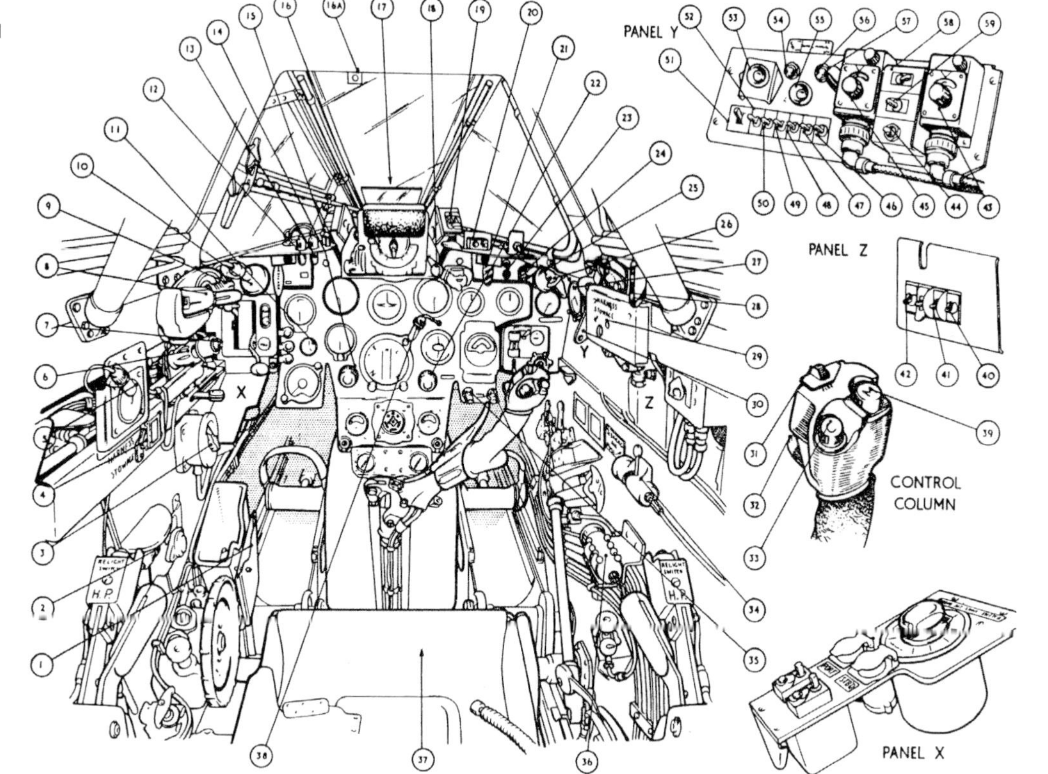

1. Pilot's notes and map case
2. Trimmer lamp
3. Selector dimmer control
4. Harness stowage
5. Brake pressure gauge lamp
6. Range control
7. Press-to-transmit switch
8. Hood opening handle
9. Ancillary lamps dimmer switch
10. Ultra-violet lamps
11. Clock
12. Instrument panel lamps
13. Emergency lamps
14. Ultra-violet lamps dimmer switch
15. Gunsight spare bulbs
16. Gyro gunsight
17. Gunsight recorder camera
18. Gunsight emergency retraction control
19. Gunsight retractor frame switch
20. Gunsight master circuit breaker
21. Hood jettison handle
22. Instrument panel lamps dimmer switch
23. Telebriefing switch and lamp
24. Instrument panel lamps
25. Ultra-violet lamps
26. Time-of-flight clock lamp
27. Time-of-flight clock
28. Canopy emergency release, rear hooks
29. Canopy hood starboard catches indicator
30. Harness stowage
31. Gun firing safety catch
32. Gun firing trigger
33. Cine camera push button
34. Harness release lever
35. Generator failure warning lamp
36. Tel/mic socket
37. Stowage for gunsight recorder camera
38. Compass lamp
39. Press-to-mute switch
40. Emergency lighting switch
41. Battery isolating switch
42. Night gunnery training lamps switch (pre-MOD.5221)
43. VHF frequency controller
44. Intercom emergency switch
45. VHF frequency controller
46. Taxi lamps switch
47. Pressure head heater switch
48. Navigation lamps switch
49. Cine camera sunny/cloudy switch
50. Cine camera master switch
51. Downward identification lamps selector switch
52. Downward identification lamps steady switch
53. Downward identification lamps push button
54. IFF distress switch
55. 'G Auto' switch
56. 'G Manual' switch
57. Switch panel lamp
58. VHF change-over switch

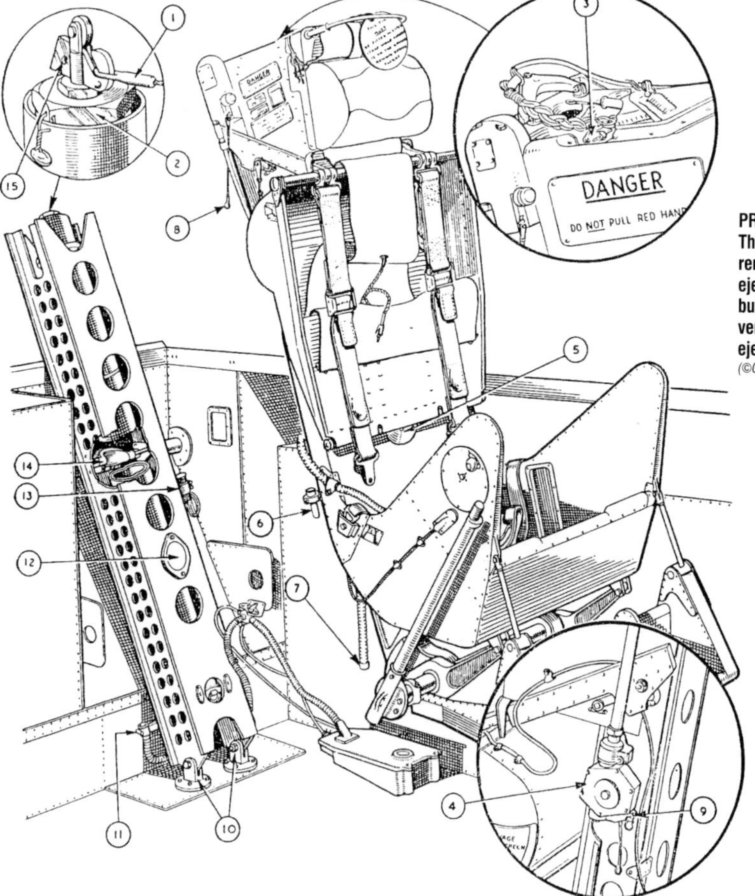

PR Mk 10
This diagram shows the removal procedure for the ejection seat in the PR Mk 10, but it also applied to all versions of the Meteor with an ejection seat
(©Crown Copyright)

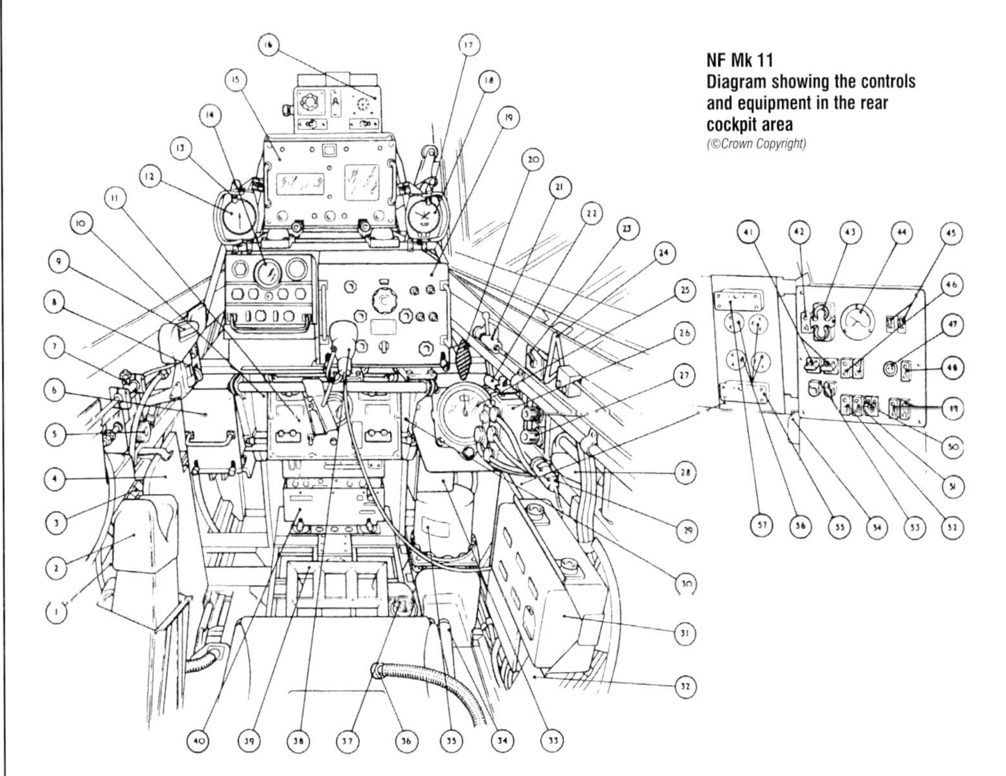

NF Mk 11
Diagram showing the controls and equipment in the rear cockpit area
(©Crown Copyright)

1. Junction box (SCR.720 & SCR.729)
2. Visor (stowed) (SCR.720 & SCR.729)
3. Protractor stowage
4. Chart board (stowed)
5. Dimmer switch for ASI and altimeter flood lamps (post-MOD.5381)
6. Rectifier Type 88 (SCR.720)
7. Hood seal pressure test connection
8. Oxygen supply regulator
9. Hood opening handle
10. Receiver (Gee)
11. Control box (SCR.720)
12. Airspeed indicator (post-MOD.5381)
13. ASI flood lamp (post-MOD.5381)
14. Indicator (Gee)
15. Indicator (SCR.720 & SCR.729)
16. Control box (SCR.729)
17. Altimeter flood lamp (post-MOD.5381)
18. Altimeter (post-MOD.5381)
19. Synchroniser (SCR.720 & SCR.729)
20. Hood jettison handle
21. Harness release
22. Compass master indicator flood lamp
23. Intercom emergency switch
24. Hood emergency release, rear hooks
25. Master indicator, gyro-magnetic compass Mk 4B
26. Control box Type 89 and 90 (IFF)
27. Dimmer switch (post-MOD.5103) for chart lamp and compass master indicator flood lamp
28. Asbestos gloves
29. Mic/tel socket
30. Wave-form generator (Gee)
31. Amplifier (compass)
32. Control box, three-phase AC supply
33. Power unit (SCR.720)
34. Seat adjuster lever
35. Rectifier Type 90 (SCR.720)
36. Oxygen mask socket
37. Press-to-mute switch (foot-operated)
38. Chart lamp
39. Footrest
40. Transmitter/receiver SCR.729
41. Generator reset switches
42. Gee AC circuit breaker
43. Radar AC supply push button
44. Phase-failure indicator, three-phase AC supply
45. Flight instruments emergency switches, three-phase AC supply
46. Generator field circuit breakers
47. Chart lamp supply socket
48. SCR.720 DC circuit breaker
49. VHF circuit breakers
50. Gee AC and DC switches
51. SCR.720 AC circuit breaker
52. SCR.729 AC circuit breaker
53. Generator failure warning lamps
54. IFF supply socket
55. Generator test panel trimmer
56. Generator test panel test sockets (volts and amps)
57. Generator test panel trimmer

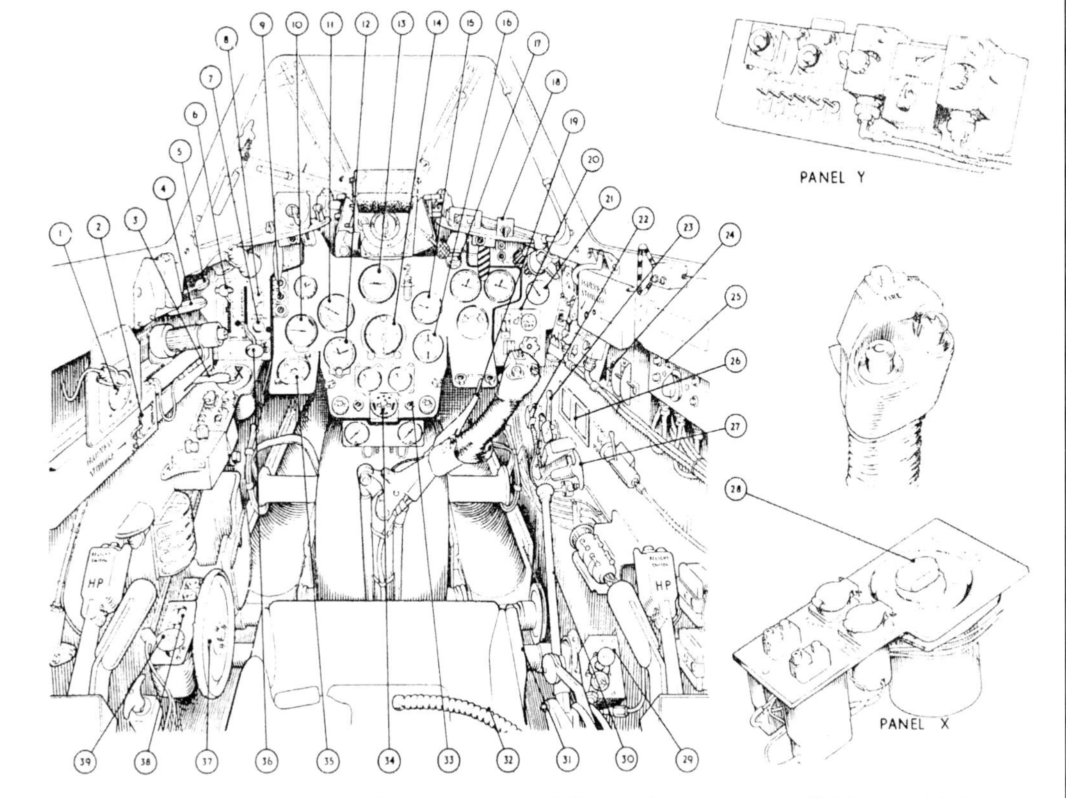

NF Mk 12
Diagram showing the flying controls and instruments in the front cockpit area
(©Crown Copyright)

1. Wheel brake pressure gauge
2. ASI deviation card holder
3. N/A
4. Cabin refrigeration control (MOD.5161 only)
5. Cabin pressurising and ventilation control
6. Flap selector lever (up-neutral-down)
7. Rudder pedal adjuster release
8. Flap position indicator
9. Altimeter limit indicator
10. Machmeter
11. Airspeed indicator
12. Altimeter
13. Artificial horizon
14. Gyro unit, gyro-magnetic compass Mk 4B
15. Rate-of-climb indicator
16. Turn-and-slip indicator
17. Standby compass, Type E2A
18. Windscreen heater switch
19. Wheel brake lever
20. Oxygen supply regulator
21. Cabin air pressure altimeter
22. Cabin heating control
23. De-misting lever
24. Cabin air pressure warning horn switch
25. Compass control panel
26. Compass deviation card holders
27. Undercarriage emergency lowering control
28. Altitude limit switch
29. Windscreen de-icing pump
30. Undercarriage hydraulic handpump
31. Seat adjuster lever
32. Oxygen mask socket
33. Undercarriage warning lamp
34. Undercarriage position indicator
35. Radio altimeter altitude indicator
36. Undercarriage selector lever
37. Elevator trimmer handwheel
38. Elevator rudder and trim indicator
39. Rudder trimmer handwheel

NF Mk 12
Diagram showing the controls and equipment in the rear cockpit area
(©Crown Copyright)

CONTROL PANEL AND GENERATOR TEST PANEL

1. Dimmer switch, controls console lamps
2. Hood seal pressure test connection
3. Control box, Type 89 (IFF)
4. Oxygen supply regulator
5. Hood opening handle
6. Indicator (Gee)
7. Console, radar
8. Airspeed indicator
9. ASI and altimeter flood lamp
10. Altimeter
11. Chart lamp
12. Master indicator, gyro-magnetic compass Mk 4B
13. Hood jettison handle
14. Dimmer switch for ASI and altimeter flood lamp
15. Compass deviation card holder
16. Harness release
17. Compass master indicator flood lamp
18. Control box (SCR.729)
19. Intercom emergency switch
20. Hood emergency release, rear hooks
21. Dimmer switch for compass master indicator flood lamp
22. Chart lamp dimmer switch
23. Harness stowage
24. Generator field circuit breakers
25. Generator reset switches
26. Generator test panel trimmer
27. Generator test panel test sockets (volts and amps)
28. Generator test panel test sockets (volts and amps)
29. Generator test panel trimmer
30. Warning lamp, generator failure
31. Chart lamp supply socket
32. Radar AC supply - Inverter Type DI
33. Phase failure indicator, three-phase AC supply
34. Emergency switches, flight instruments, three-phase AC supply
35. Circuit breaker AC supply, SCR.729
36. Circuit breaker DC supply, SCR.729
37. Circuit breaker DC supply, VHF Set No.1
38. Circuit breaker DC supply, VHF Set No.2
39. Gee AC and DC supply switches
40. Circuit breaker DC supply, Inverter Type 200
41. IFF supply socket
42. First-aid outfit
43. Asbestos gloves
44. Mic/tel socket
45. Amplifier (compass)
46. Control box, three-phase AC supply
47. Seat adjuster lever
48. Oxygen mask socket
49. Press-to-mute switch (foot-operated)
50. Footrest
51. Transmitter/receiver SCR.729
52. Control unit, gyro gunsight
53. Protractor stowage
54. Control unit, gyro gunsight
55. Visor (stowed)
56. Control box, Type 90 (IFF)
57. Harness stowage
58. Chart board (stowed)

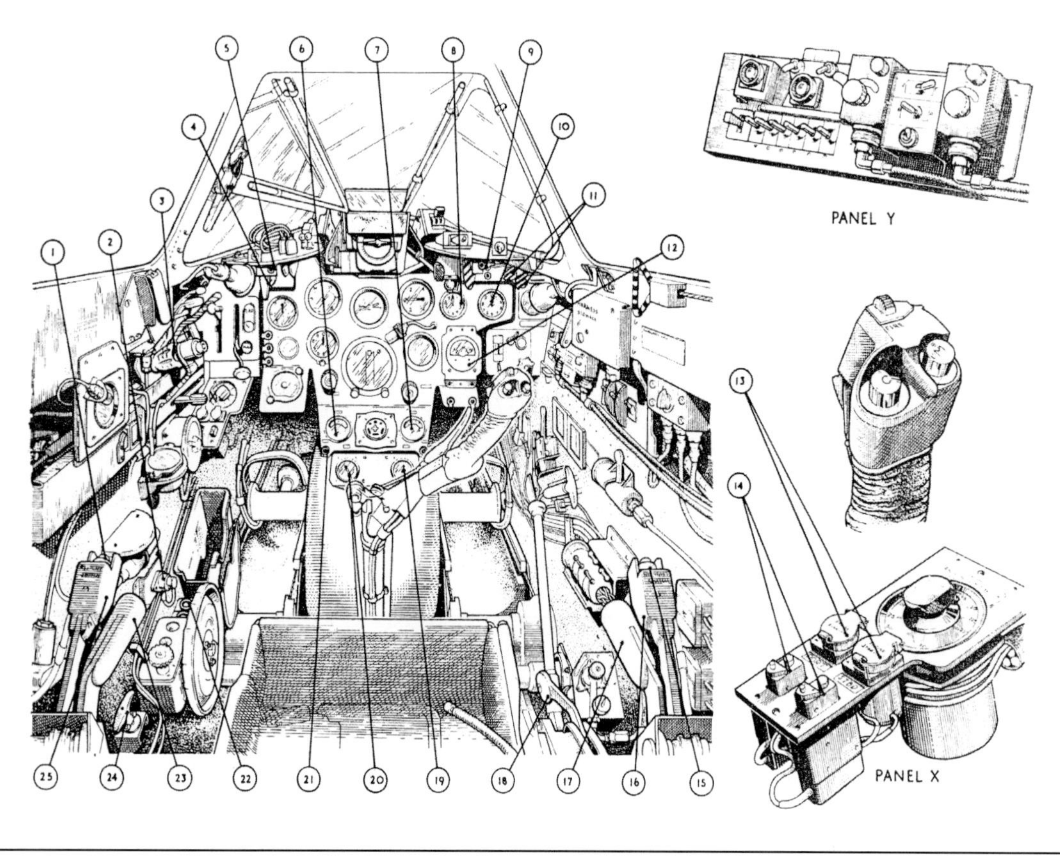

NF Mk 13
Diagram showing the engine controls and equipment in the front cockpit area
(©Crown Copyright)

1. Relight switch
2. Tank pump test socket
3. Throttle controls
4. Drop tank air control and ventral tank jettison control
5. Engine fire warning lamp
6. Fuel contents gauge
7. Fuel contents gauge
8. Tachometer
9. Engine fire warning lamp
10. Tachometer
11. Engine fire extinguisher push buttons
12. Dual exhaust temperature gauge
13. Engine start push buttons
14. Tank pump circuit breakers
15. Relight switch
16. High pressure fuel cock control
17. Low pressure fuel cock control
18. Wing drop tanks jettison control
19. Oil pressure gauge
20. Oil pressure gauge
21. Fuel pressure warning lamp
22. Tank pump test switches
23. Low pressure fuel cock control
24. Fuel balance cock control
25. High pressure fuel cock control

NF Mk 13
Diagram showing the controls and equipment in the rear cockpit area
(©Crown Copyright)

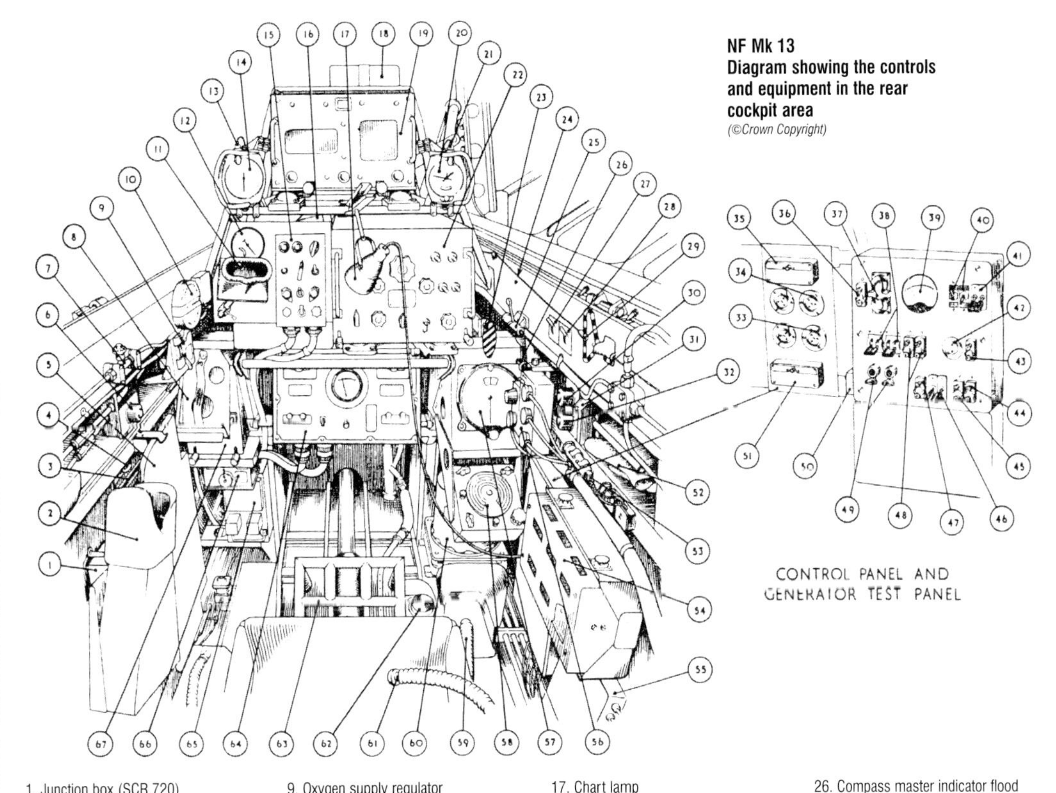

1. Junction box (SCR.720)
2. Visor (stowed) (SCR.720)
3. Protractor stowage
4. Harness stowage
5. Chart board (stowed)
6. Dimmer switch for ASI and altimeter flood lamps
7. Hood seal pressure test connectors
8. Stowage for Rebecca visor
9. Oxygen supply regulator
10. Hood opening handle
11. Rebecca indicator and visor
12. Radio compass indicator
13. ASI flood lamp
14. Airspeed indicator
15. Rebecca control unit
16. Transformer and regulator (radio compass)
17. Chart lamp
18. First-aid outfit
19. Indicator (SCR.720)
20. Altimeter
21. Altimeter flood lamp
22. Synchroniser (SCR.720)
23. Hood jettison handle
24. Holder compass deviation card
25. Harness release
26. Compass master indicator flood lamp
27. I/C switch (radio compass)
28. Intercom emergency switch
29. Hood emergency release, rear hooks
30. Compass flood light dimmer switch
31. Harness stowage
32. Chart lamp dimmer switch
33. Generator test panel, test sockets (volts and amps)
34. Generator test panel, test sockets (volts and amps)
35. Generator test panel trimmer
36. M.G.7 supply circuit breaker (Rebecca)
37. Radar AC supply push buttons
38. Generator reset switch
39. Phase failure indicator, three-phase AC supply
40. Flight instrument emergency switches, three-phase AC supply
41. Radio compass supply switches
42. Chart lamp supply socket
43. SCR.720 DC circuit breaker
44. VHF supply circuit breaker
45. VHF supply circuit breaker
46. Rebecca AC and DC supply switches
47. SCR.720 AC circuit breaker
48. Generator field circuit breakers
49. Generator failure warning lamps
50. IFF supply socket
51. Generator test panel trimmer
52. Asbestos gloves
53. Mic/tel socket
54. Amplifier (compass)
55. Control box, three-phase AC supply
56. Control box Type 89 & 90 (IFF)
57. Master indicator, gyro-magnetic compass Mk 4B
58. Receiver controller (radio compass)
59. Seat adjuster lever
60. Rectifier Type 90 (SCR.720)
61. Oxygen mask socket
62. Press-to-mute switch (foot-operated)
63. Footrest
64. Control box (SCR.720)
65. Receiver (radio compass)
66. Loop aerial test plug (radio compass)
67. Rectifier, Type 88 (SCR.720)

TT Mk 20
Note: The front cockpit area of the TT Mk 20 is very similar to the NF Mk 11 on which it was based.
Diagram showing the controls and equipment in the rear cockpit area
(©Crown Copyright)

1. ARI.23007 cable test unit (TT equipment)
2. Terminal block T.T.9 (TT equipment)
3. Terminal block T.T.1 (TT equipment)
4. Chart board (stowed)
5. Protractor stowage
6. Target release switches (TT equipment)
7. Dimmer switch
8. ARI.23007 cable test unit floodlight
9. Oxygen supply regulator
10. Hood seal pressure test connection
11. Hood opening handle
12. Interlock reset (TT equipment)
13. Electro-magnetic indicators (TT equipment)
14. Pay-out over-ride switch (TT equipment)
15. Cable cutter control handle [emergency] (TT equipment)
16. Windmill tachometer (TT equipment)
17. Windmill tachometer flood lamp
18. ARI.23007 recorder flood lamp
19. Indicator lights (TT equipment)
20. ARI.23007 recorder (TT equipment)
21. Footage indicator flood lamp
22. In over-ride switch button (TT equipment)
23. Footage indicator (TT equipment)
24. Reset footage indicator (TT equipment)
25. Emergency brake switch (TT equipment)
26. Hood jettison handle
27. Harness release
28. Hood emergency release, rear hooks
29. R.T./beacon switch
30. Intercom emergency switch
31. Inching switch (TT equipment)
31A. Compass master indicator flood lamp
32. Master indicator, gyro-magnetic compass Mk 4B
33. Dimmer switch
34. Haul-in/Payout selector switch (TT equipment)
35. Asbestos gloves
36. Mic/tel socket
37. Dimmer switch
38. Master circuit breaker (TT equipment)
39. Amplifier (compass)
40. ASI
41. Control box, three-phase AC supply
42. Altimeter
42. ARI.5307 receiver
44. Seat adjuster lever
45. Oxygen mask socket
46. Press-to-mute switch (foot-operated)
47. ARI.23007 battery box (TT equipment)
48. Footrest
49. Chart lamp
50. Generator test panel trimmers
51. Generator test panel test sockets (volts and amps)
52. Generator reset switches
53. Phase failure indicator, three-phase AC supply
54. Chart lamp supply socket
55. Flight instrument emergency switches
56. VHF circuit breakers
57. Generator field circuit breakers
58. Generator failure warning lamps
59. Generator test panel trimmers

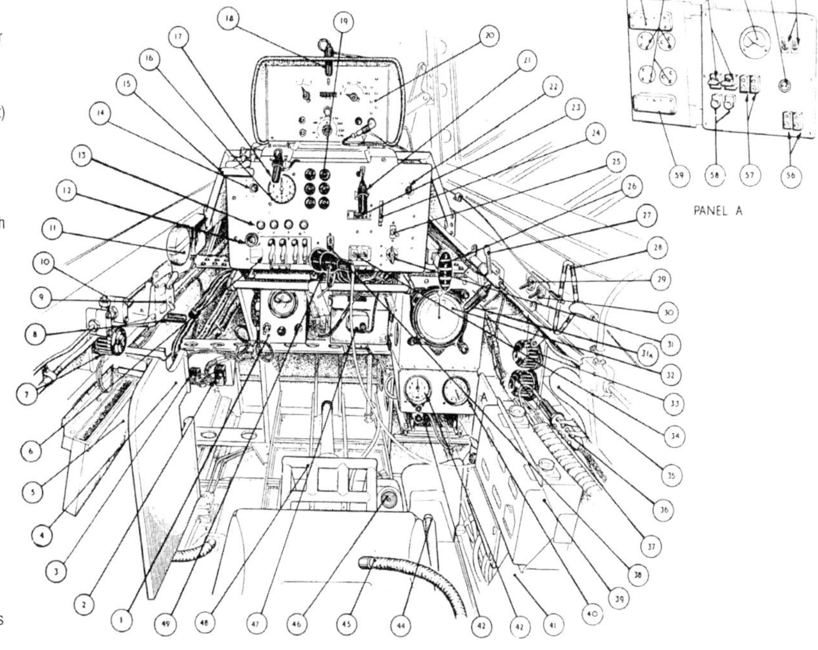

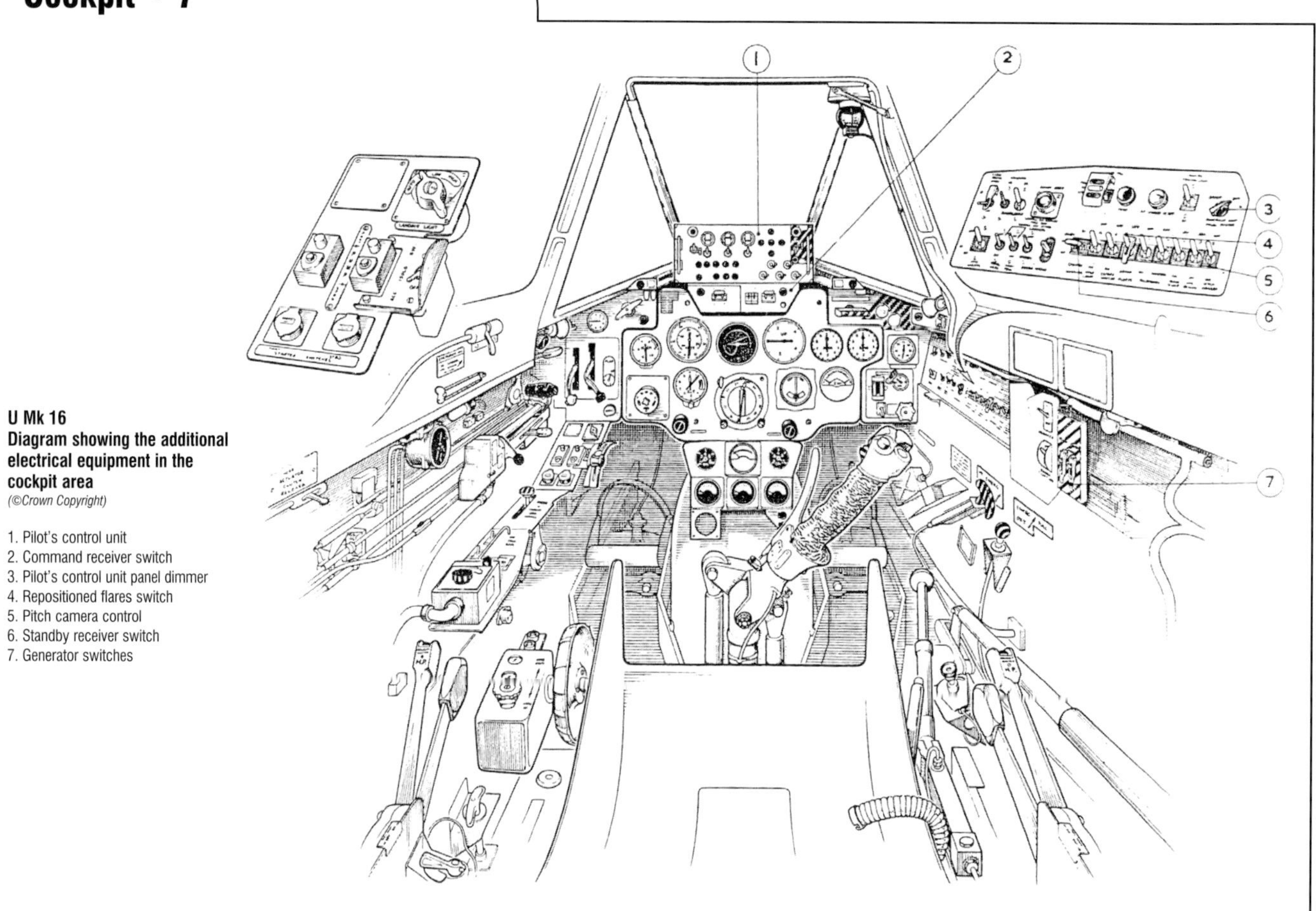

U Mk 16
Diagram showing the additional electrical equipment in the cockpit area
(©Crown Copyright)

1. Pilot's control unit
2. Command receiver switch
3. Pilot's control unit panel dimmer
4. Repositioned flares switch
5. Pitch camera control
6. Standby receiver switch
7. Generator switches

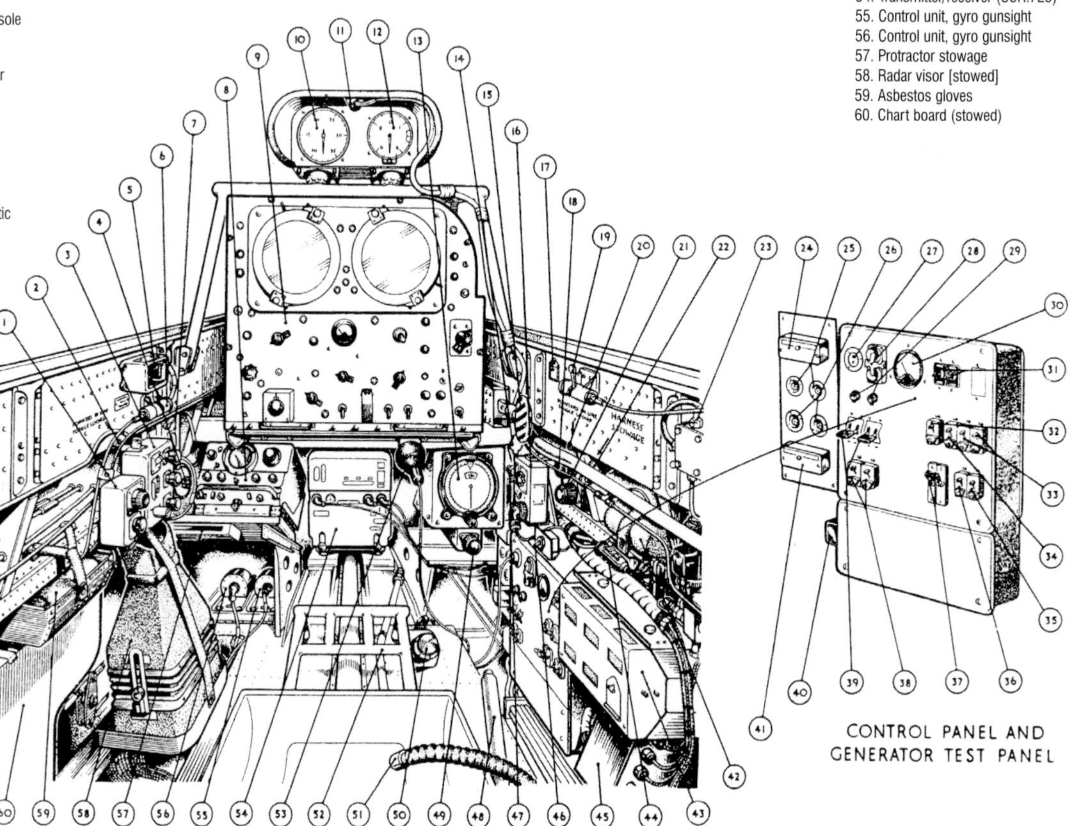

NF Mk 14
Diagram of the rear cockpit layout
(©Crown Copyright)

1. Control unit Type 89 (IFF)
2. Hood jettison mechanical lock indicators
3. Control unit Type 90 (IFF)
4. Dimmer switch for control console lamps
5. Hood opening switch
6. Hood actuator declutching lever
7. Oxygen system regulator
8. Stowage for Rebecca visor
9. Radar console
10. Air speed indicator
11. ASI and altimeter flood lamp
12. Altimeter
13. Master indicator, gyro-magnetic compass Mk 4B
14. Press-to-transmit switch (post-MOD.5755)
15. Hood jettison handle
16. Control box (SCR.729)
17. Compass deviation card holder
18. Dimmer switch for compass master indicator flood lamp
19. Harness release
20. Altimeter
21. Chart lamp dimmer switch
22. Harness stowage
23. Hood seal pressure test connectors
24. Generator test panel trimmer
25. Generator test panel, test sockets (volts and amps)
26. Generator test panel, test sockets (volts and amps)
27. Chart lamp supply socket
28. Radar AC supply, inverter Type DI
29. Generator failure-warning lamps
30. Phase failure indicator, three-phase AC supply
31. Flight instrument emergency switches, three-phase AC supply
32. Circuit breaker DC supply, inverter Type 200
33. Circuit breaker AC supply, SCR.729
34. Circuit breaker DC supply, SCR.729
35. Circuit breaker DC supply, VHF Set No.1
36. Circuit breaker DC supply, VHF Set No.2
37. Radar AC supply push buttons
38. Generator field circuit breakers
39. Generator reset switch
40. IFF supply socket
41. Generator test panel trimmer
42. First-aid outfit
43. Amplifier (compass)
44. Mic/tel socket
45. Control box, three-phase AC supply
46. Intercom. emergency switch
47. Compass master indicator flood lamp
48. Seat adjuster lever
49. Dimmer switch for ASI and altimeter flood lamp
50. Press-to-mute switch (foot operated)
51. Oxygen mask socket
52. Footrest
53. Chart lamp
54. Transmitter/receiver (SCR.729)
55. Control unit, gyro gunsight
56. Control unit, gyro gunsight
57. Protractor stowage
58. Radar visor [stowed]
59. Asbestos gloves
60. Chart board (stowed)

Fuselage & Canopy • 1

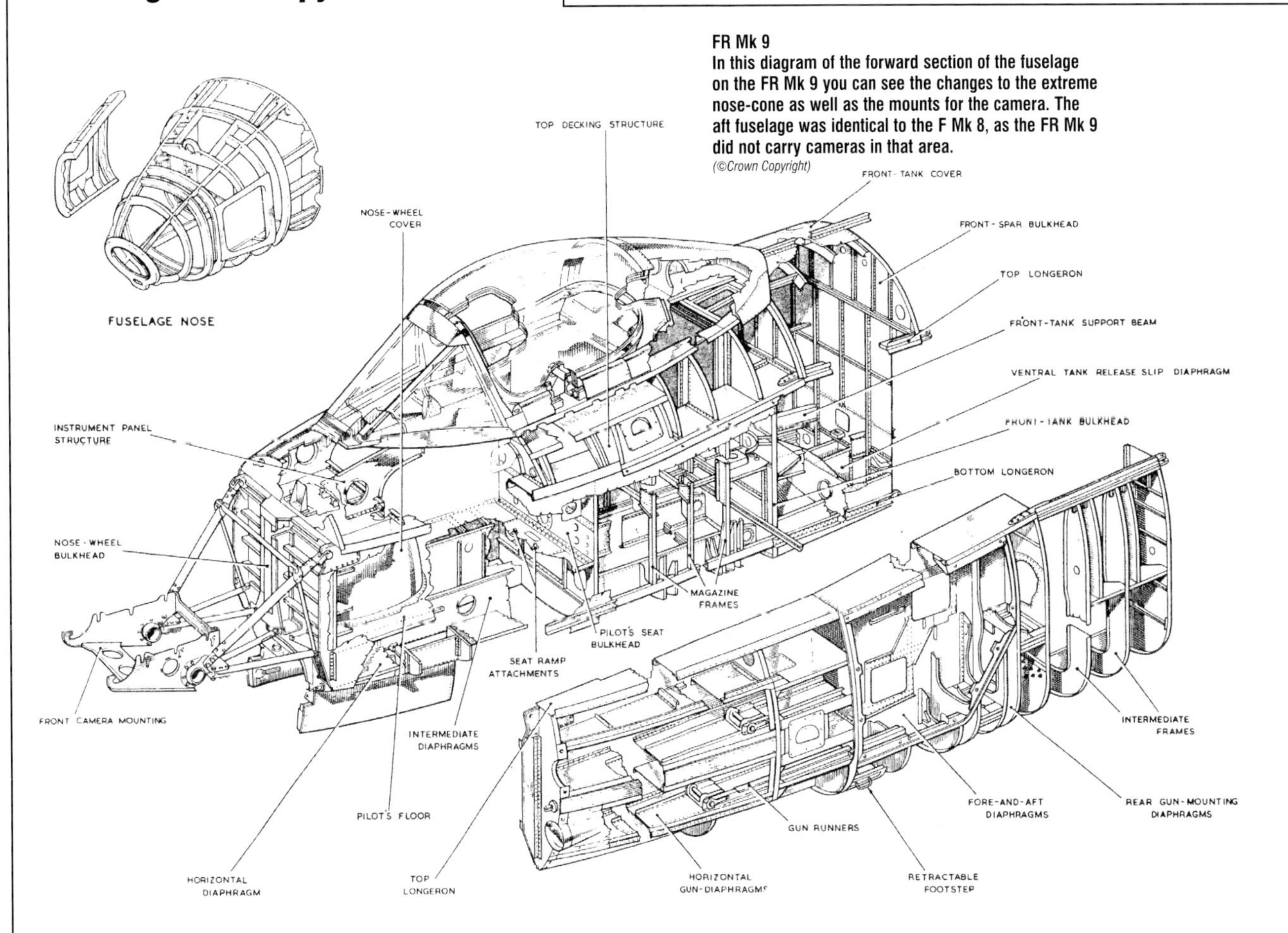

FR Mk 9
In this diagram of the forward section of the fuselage on the FR Mk 9 you can see the changes to the extreme nose-cone as well as the mounts for the camera. The aft fuselage was identical to the F Mk 8, as the FR Mk 9 did not carry cameras in that area.
(©Crown Copyright)

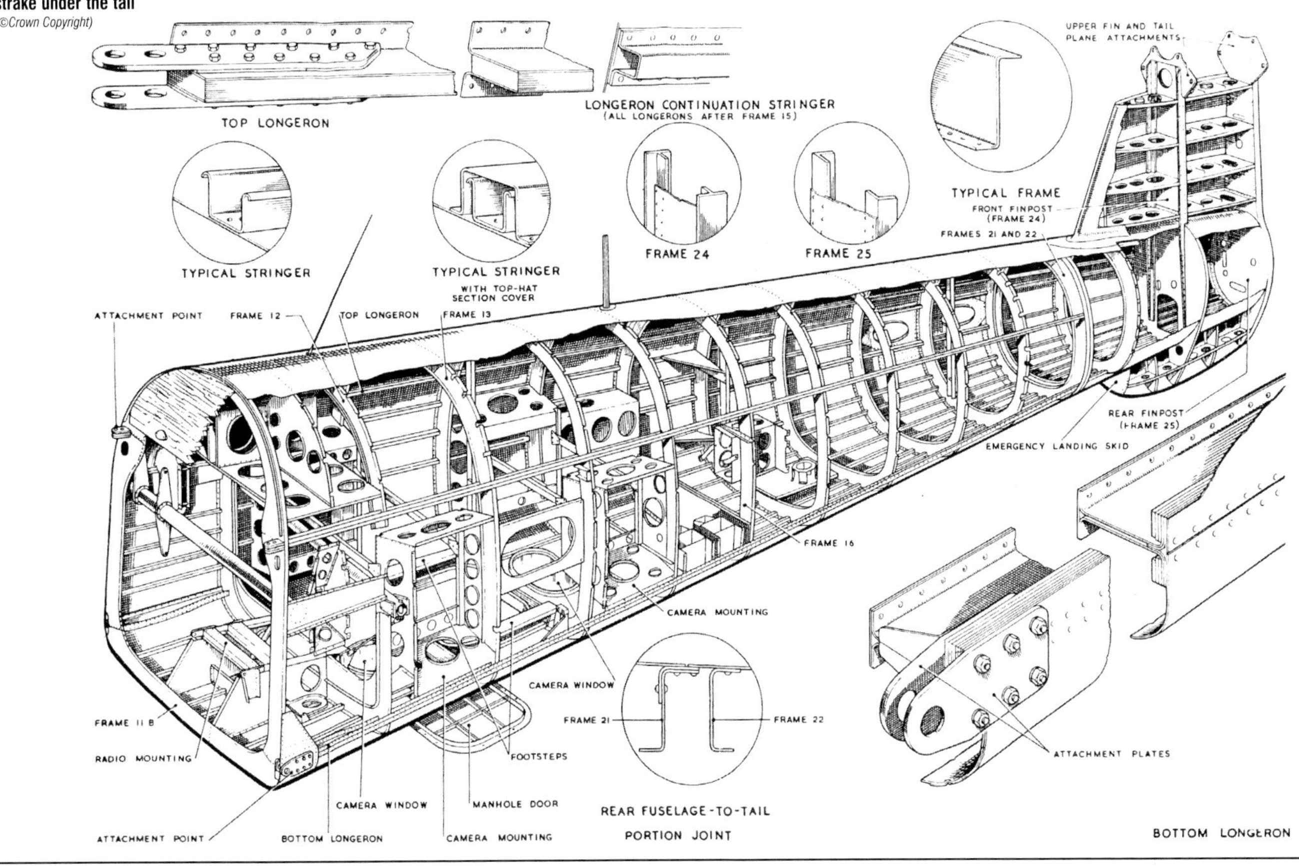

PR Mk 10
The FR Mk 9 and PR Mk 10 are identical with regard to the forward fuselage, the difference is in the rear section. As you can see here provision for the vertical camera in the aft fuselage has led to a lot of additional brackets and frames. Note also the return of the ventral strake under the tail
(©Crown Copyright)

Fuselage & Canopy • 2

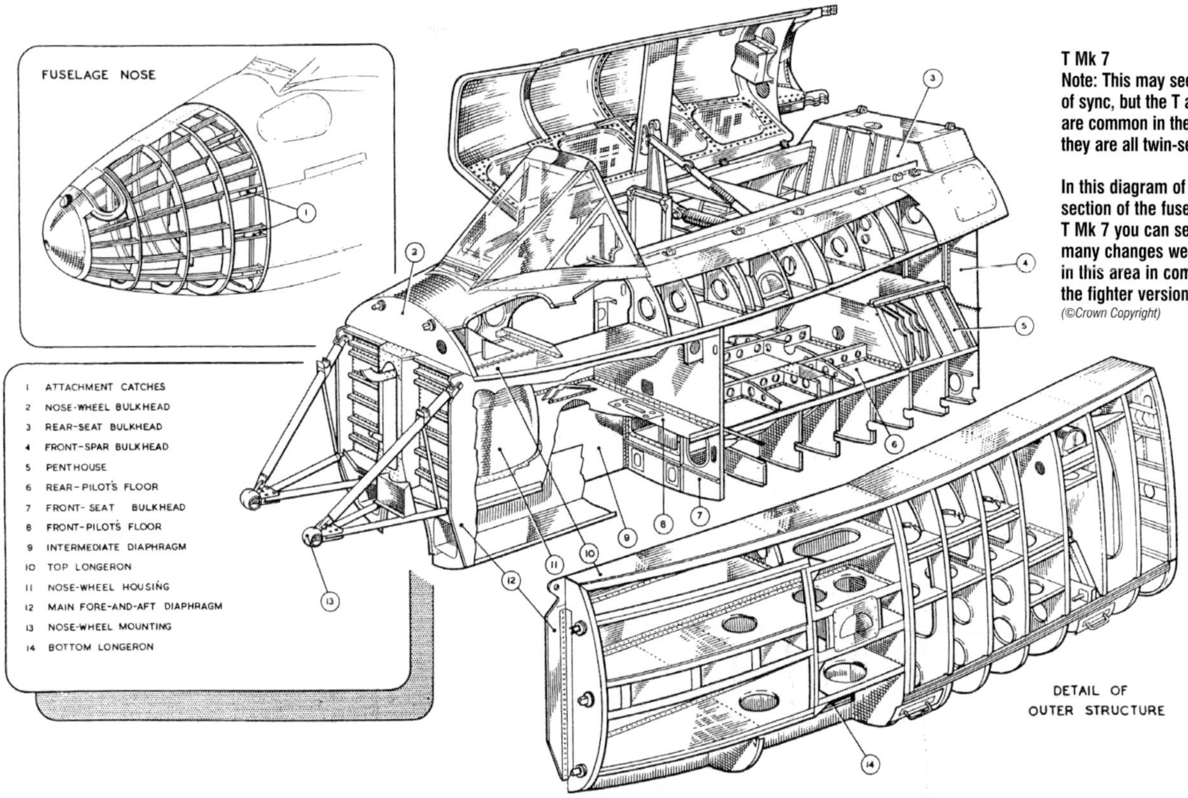

FUSELAGE NOSE
1 ATTACHMENT CATCHES
2 NOSE-WHEEL BULKHEAD
3 REAR-SEAT BULKHEAD
4 FRONT-SPAR BULKHEAD
5 PENTHOUSE
6 REAR-PILOT'S FLOOR
7 FRONT-SEAT BULKHEAD
8 FRONT-PILOT'S FLOOR
9 INTERMEDIATE DIAPHRAGM
10 TOP LONGERON
11 NOSE-WHEEL HOUSING
12 MAIN FORE-AND-AFT DIAPHRAGM
13 NOSE-WHEEL MOUNTING
14 BOTTOM LONGERON
DETAIL OF
OUTER STRUCTURE

T Mk 7
Note: This may seem a bit out of sync, but the T and NF series are common in the sense that they are all twin-seaters.

In this diagram of the forward section of the fuselage on the T Mk 7 you can see just how many changes were effected in this area in comparison with the fighter versions
(©Crown Copyright)

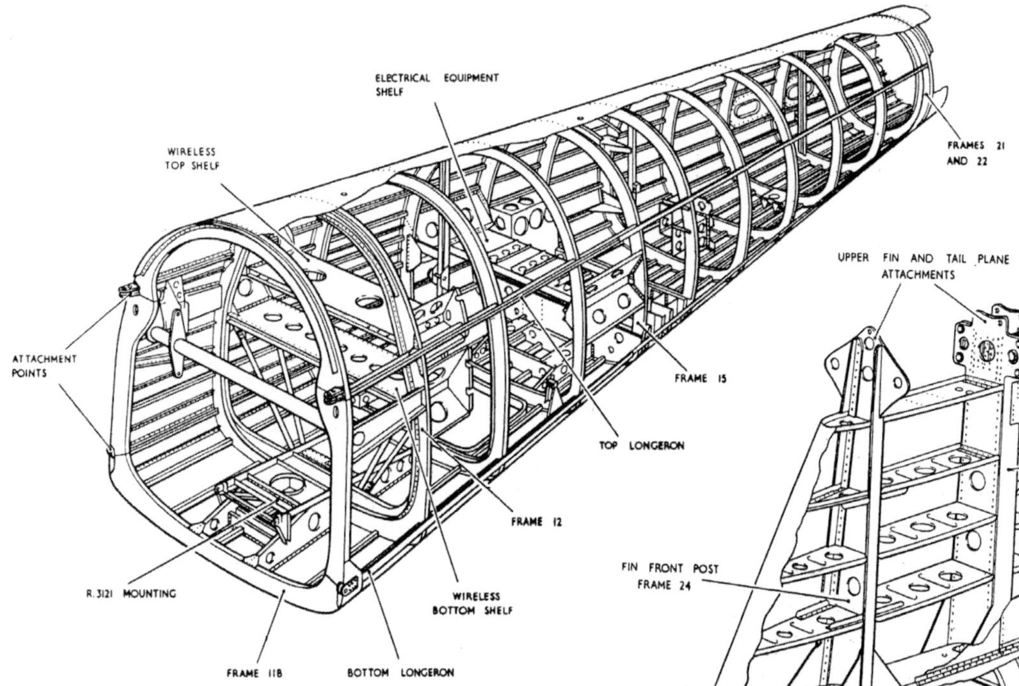

ELECTRICAL EQUIPMENT
SHELF
WIRELESS
TOP SHELF
FRAMES 21
AND 22
ATTACHMENT
POINTS
FRAME 15
TOP LONGERON
FRAME 12
R.3121 MOUNTING
WIRELESS
BOTTOM SHELF
FRAME 11B
BOTTOM LONGERON

NF Mk 11
The aft section on the NF Mk 11 is a very different beast; as you can see it is truncated at frame 21/22 for the fitment of the later hi-tail
(©Crown Copyright)

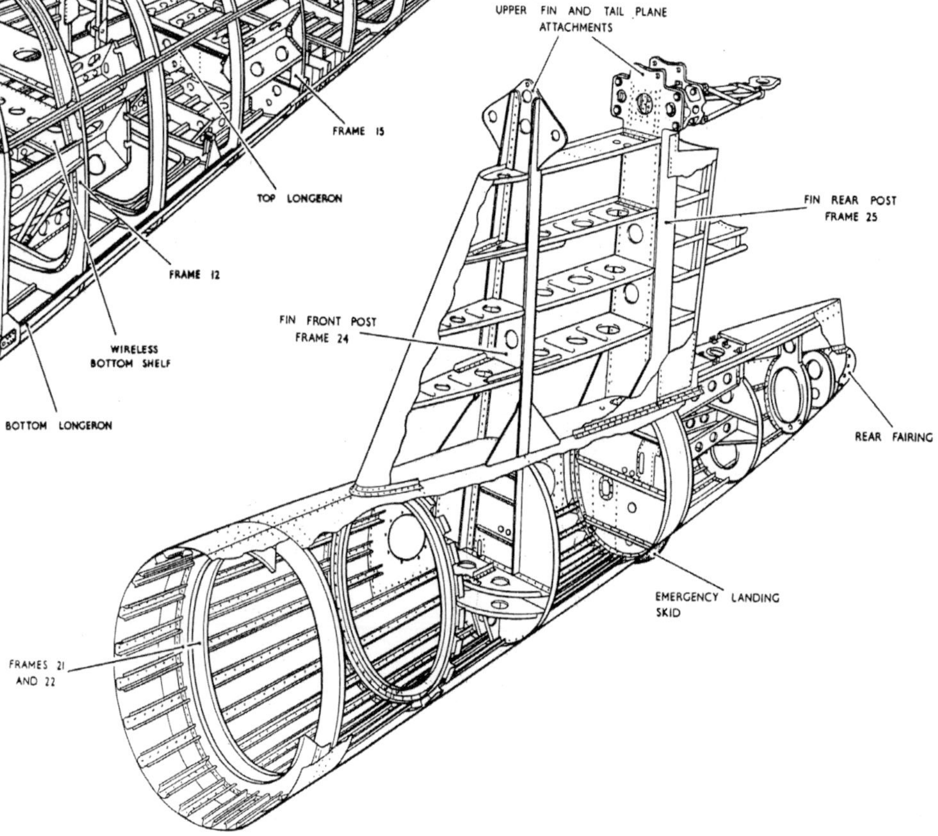

UPPER FIN AND TAIL PLANE
ATTACHMENTS
FIN REAR POST
FRAME 25
FIN FRONT POST
FRAME 24
REAR FAIRING
EMERGENCY LANDING
SKID
FRAMES 21
AND 22

F Mk 8
This diagram shows the construction of the aft section of the fuselage for the F Mk 8. Note the revised vertical fin and lack of ventral strake
(©Crown Copyright)

Fuselage & Canopy • 3

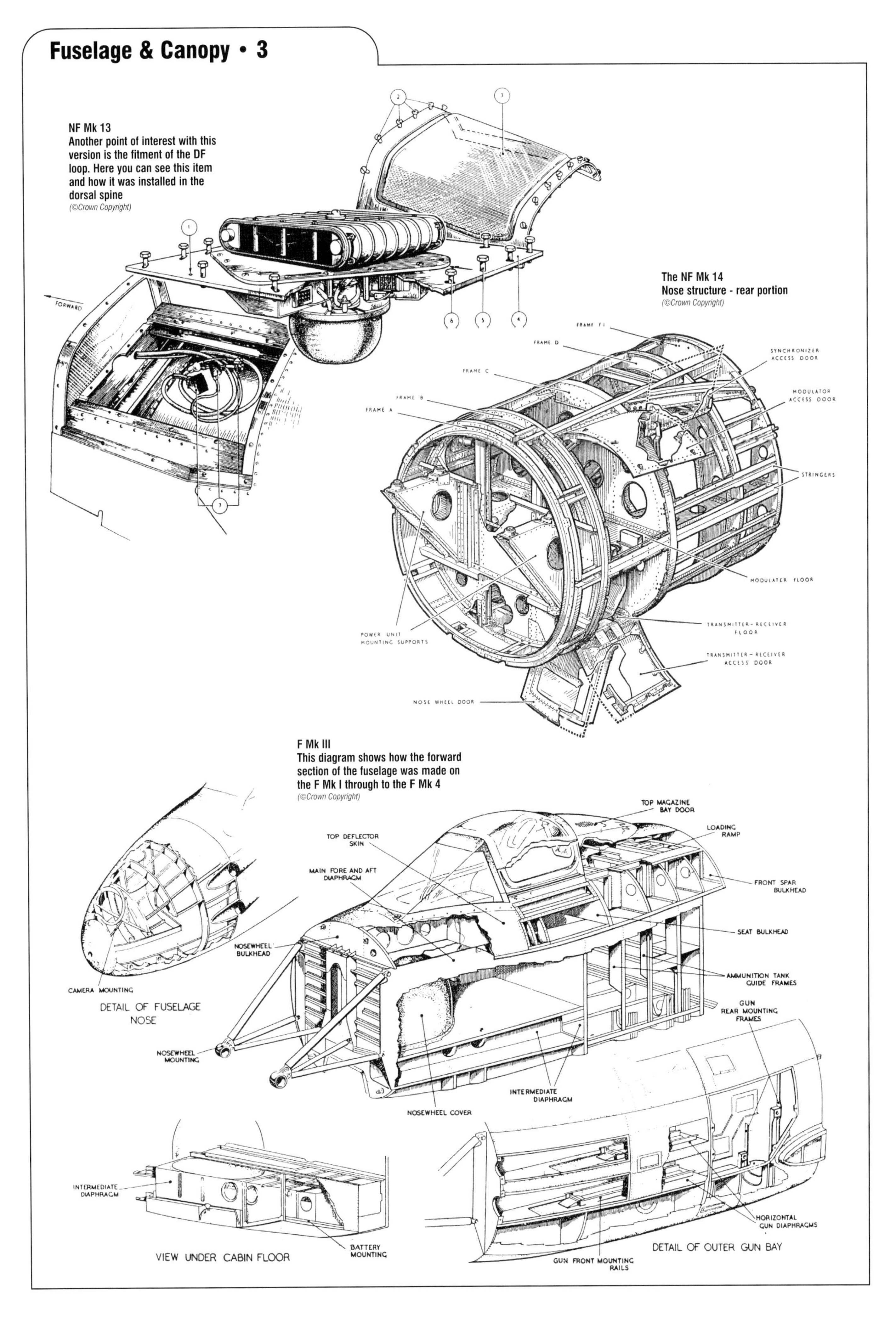

NF Mk 13
Another point of interest with this version is the fitment of the DF loop. Here you can see this item and how it was installed in the dorsal spine
(©Crown Copyright)

The NF Mk 14
Nose structure - rear portion
(©Crown Copyright)

F Mk III
This diagram shows how the forward section of the fuselage was made on the F Mk I through to the F Mk 4
(©Crown Copyright)

Wings

F Mk III
This is actually a diagram from the PR Mk 10 manual, but this shows the long-span wings that were also fitted to the F Mk I and F Mk III
(© Crown Copyright)

F Mk 4 & T Mk 7 (F Mk 8 and FR Mk 9)
This is a diagram of the construction of the short-span wing of the F Mk 4 series
(© Crown Copyright)

NF Series
This is the outer wing panel of the NF Mk 11, which is the same for all NF series machines
(© Crown Copyright)

Centre Sections & Engines

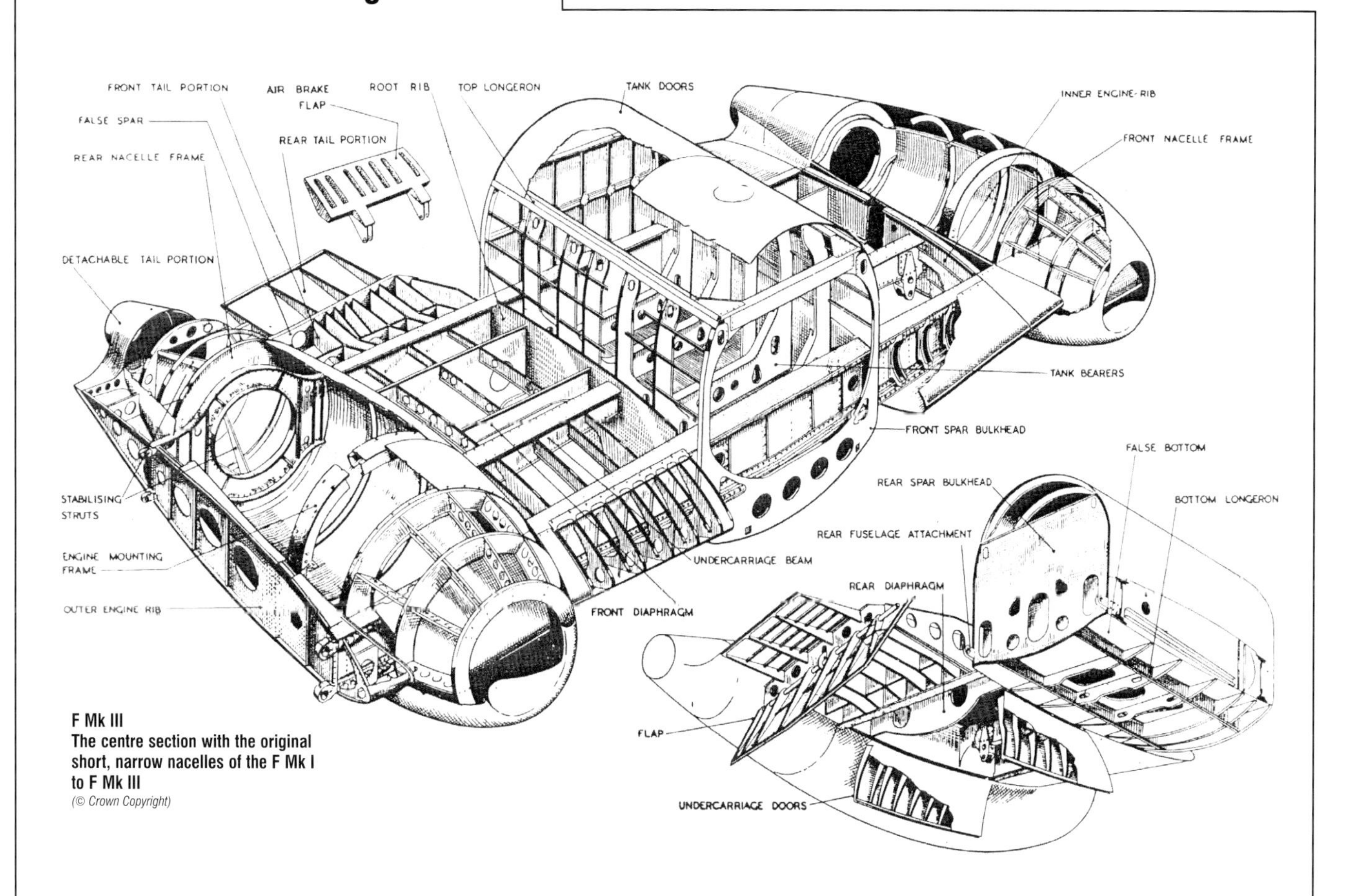

F Mk III
The centre section with the original short, narrow nacelles of the F Mk I to F Mk III
(© Crown Copyright)

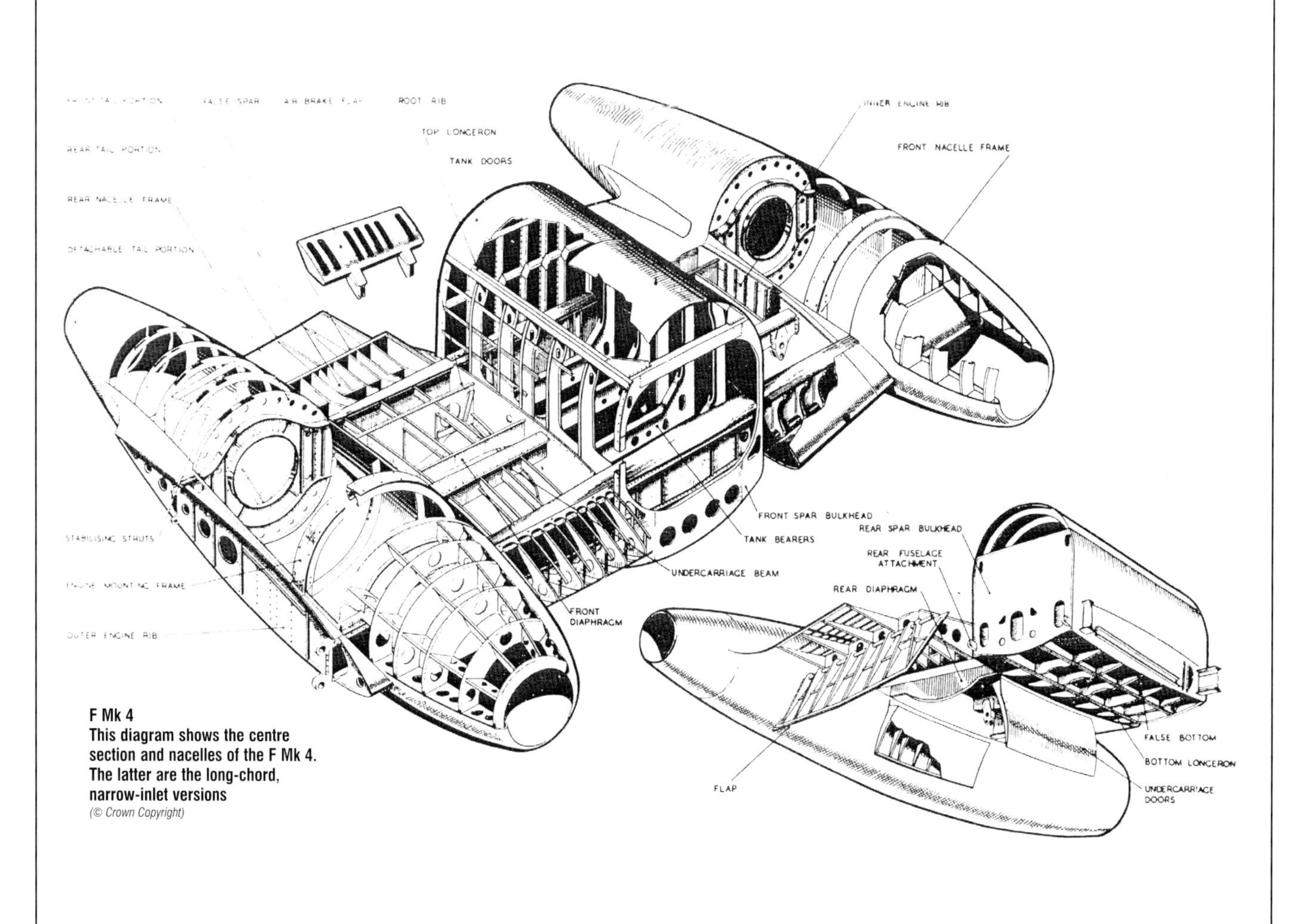

F Mk 4
This diagram shows the centre section and nacelles of the F Mk 4. The latter are the long-chord, narrow-inlet versions
(© Crown Copyright)

Armament & Fuel Tanks

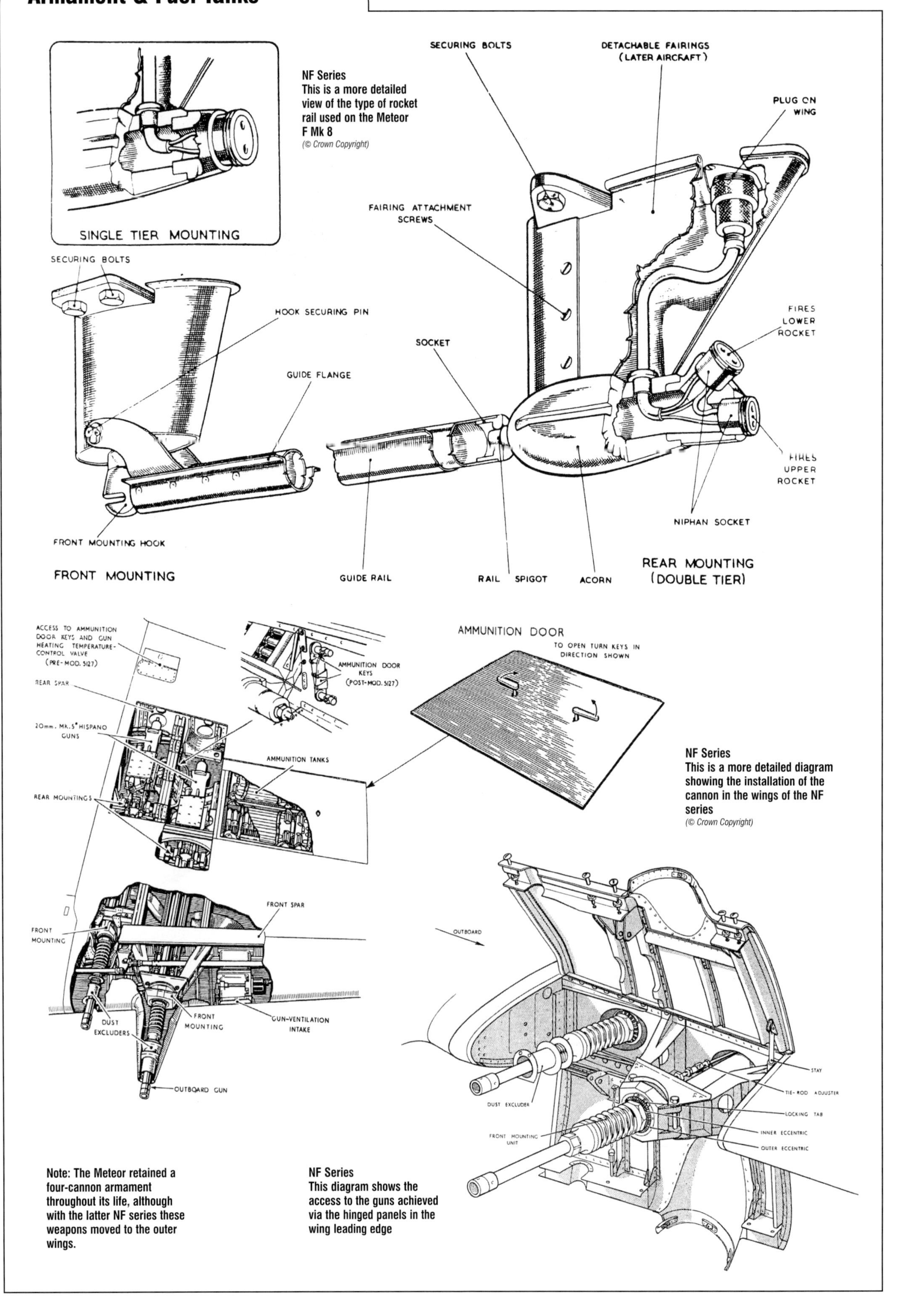

NF Series
This is a more detailed view of the type of rocket rail used on the Meteor F Mk 8
(© Crown Copyright)

NF Series
This is a more detailed diagram showing the installation of the cannon in the wings of the NF series
(© Crown Copyright)

Note: The Meteor retained a four-cannon armament throughout its life, although with the latter NF series these weapons moved to the outer wings.

NF Series
This diagram shows the access to the guns achieved via the hinged panels in the wing leading edge

Undercarriage

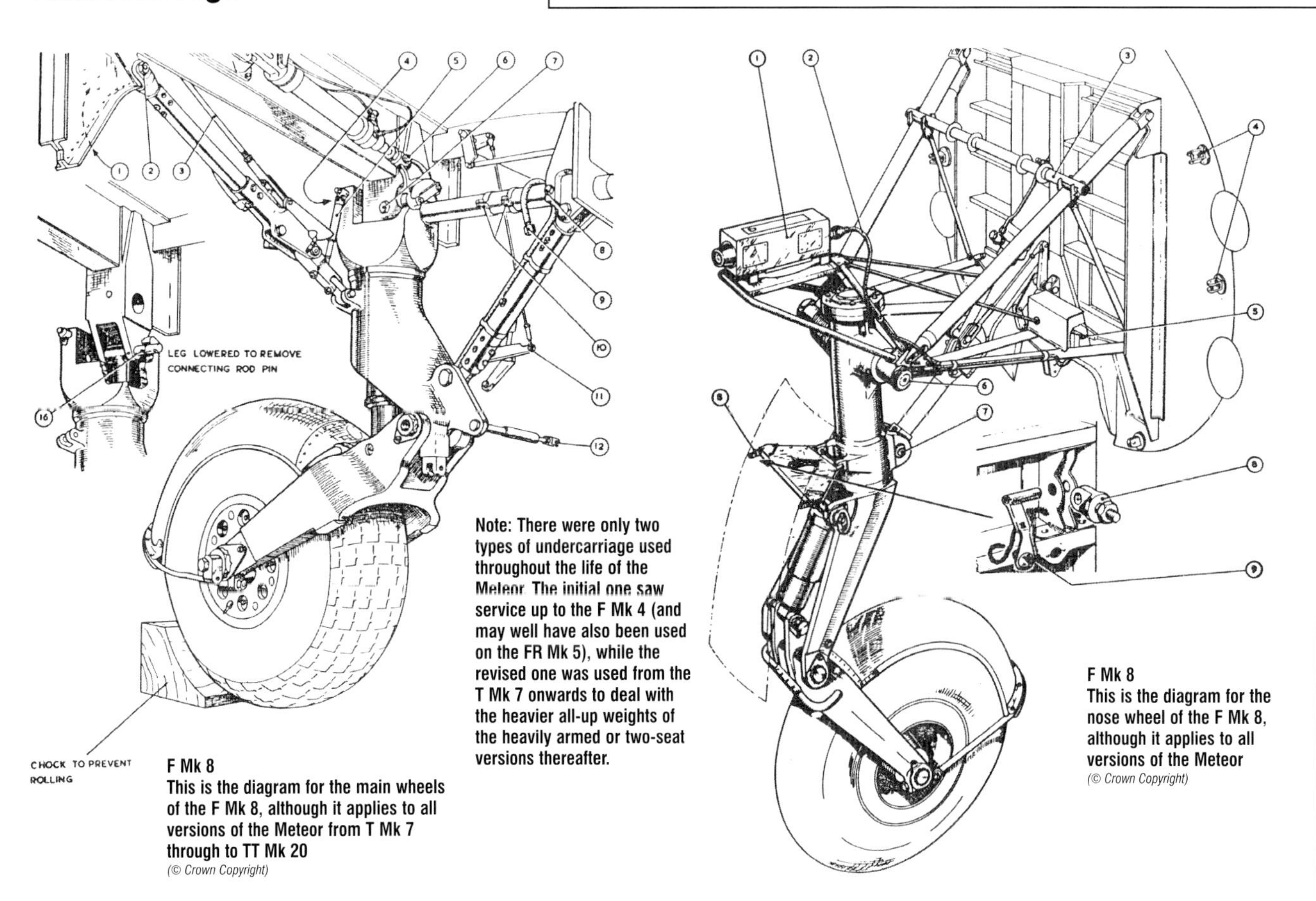

F Mk 8
This is the diagram for the main wheels of the F Mk 8, although it applies to all versions of the Meteor from T Mk 7 through to TT Mk 20
(© Crown Copyright)

Note: There were only two types of undercarriage used throughout the life of the Meteor. The initial one saw service up to the F Mk 4 (and may well have also been used on the FR Mk 5), while the revised one was used from the T Mk 7 onwards to deal with the heavier all-up weights of the heavily armed or two-seat versions thereafter.

F Mk 8
This is the diagram for the nose wheel of the F Mk 8, although it applies to all versions of the Meteor
(© Crown Copyright)

Radar Equipment

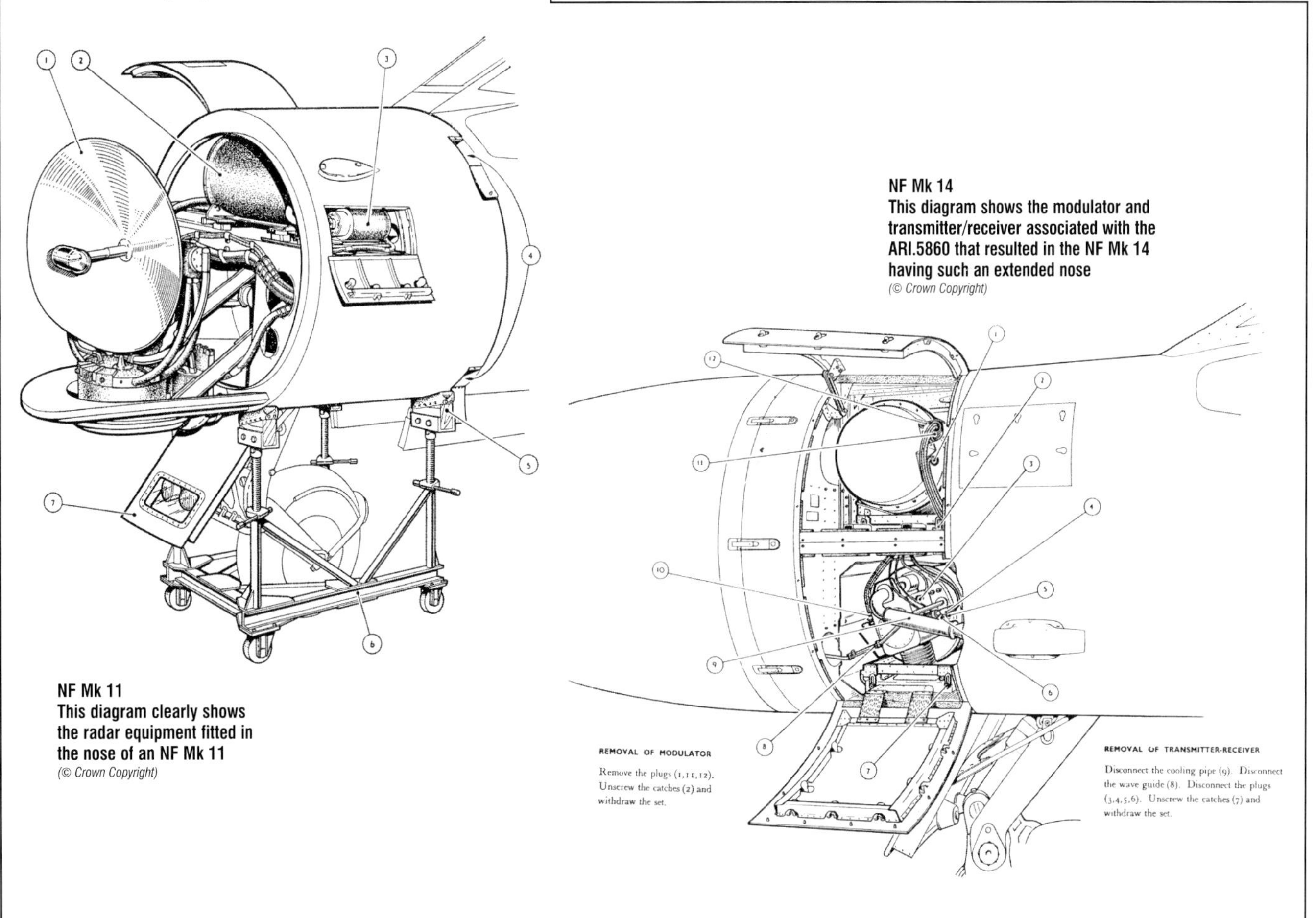

NF Mk 11
This diagram clearly shows the radar equipment fitted in the nose of an NF Mk 11
(© Crown Copyright)

NF Mk 14
This diagram shows the modulator and transmitter/receiver associated with the ARI.5860 that resulted in the NF Mk 14 having such an extended nose
(© Crown Copyright)

Photographic Equipment

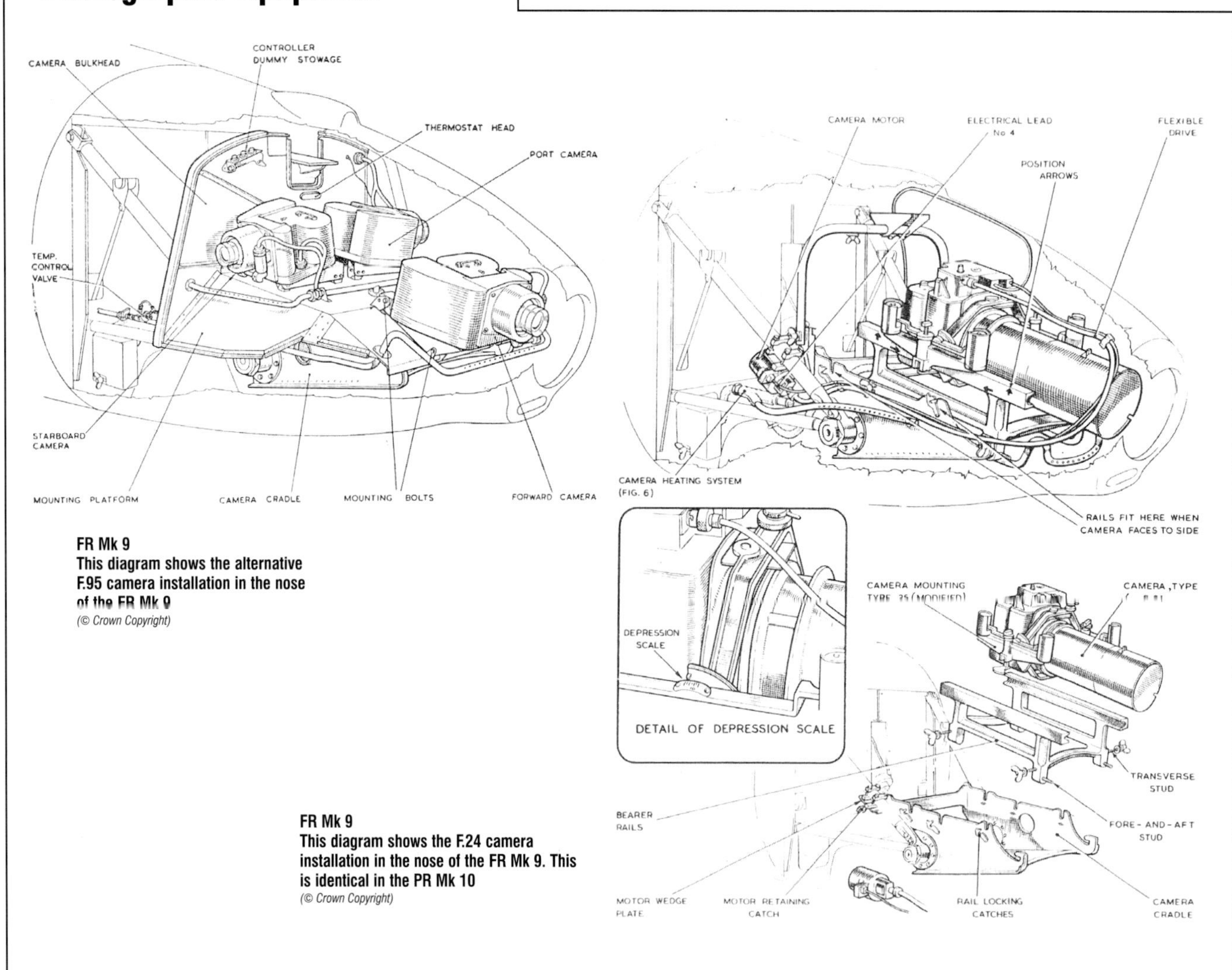

FR Mk 9
This diagram shows the alternative F.95 camera installation in the nose of the FR Mk 9
(© Crown Copyright)

FR Mk 9
This diagram shows the F.24 camera installation in the nose of the FR Mk 9. This is identical in the PR Mk 10
(© Crown Copyright)

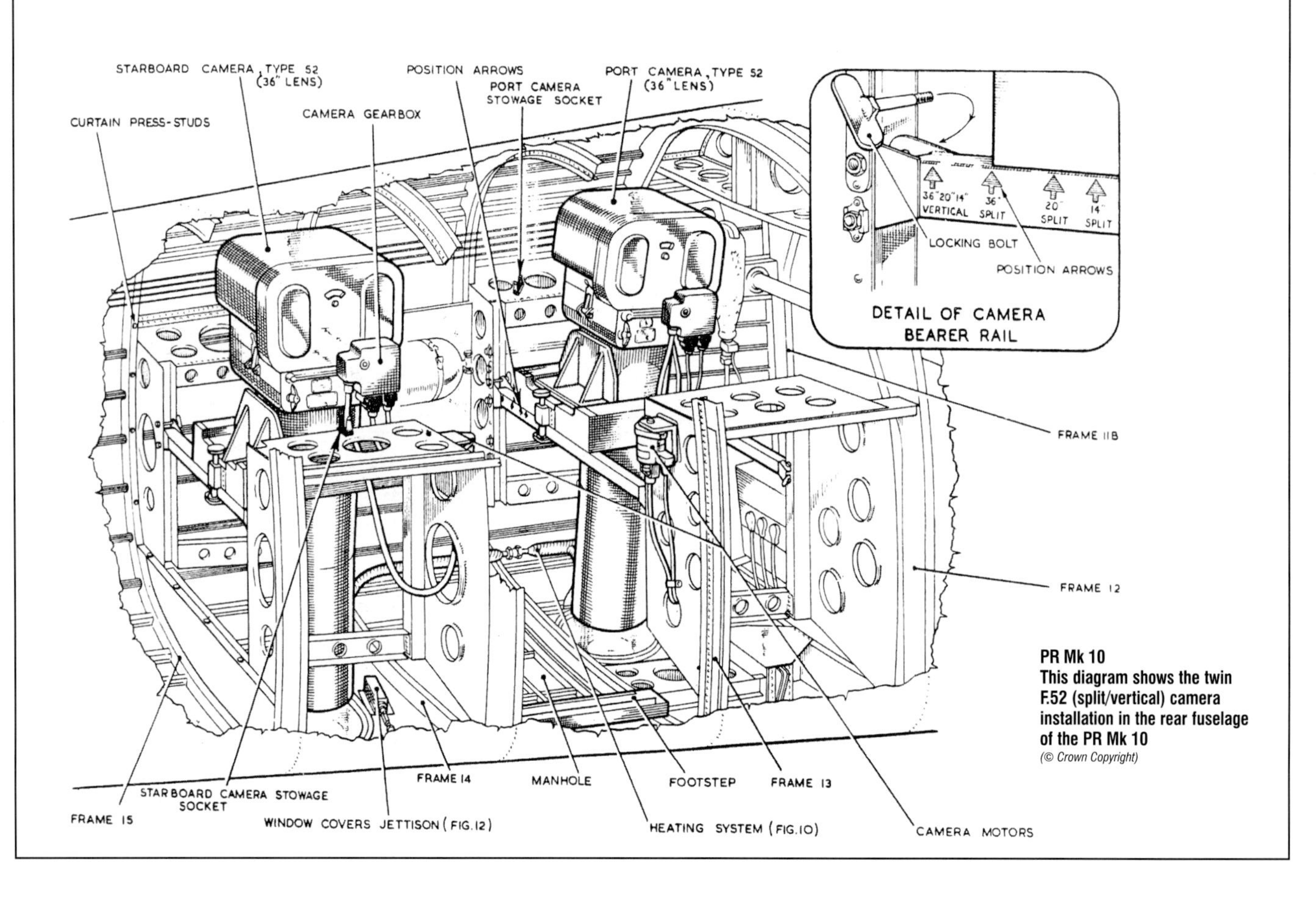

PR Mk 10
This diagram shows the twin F.52 (split/vertical) camera installation in the rear fuselage of the PR Mk 10
(© Crown Copyright)

Miscellaneous • 1

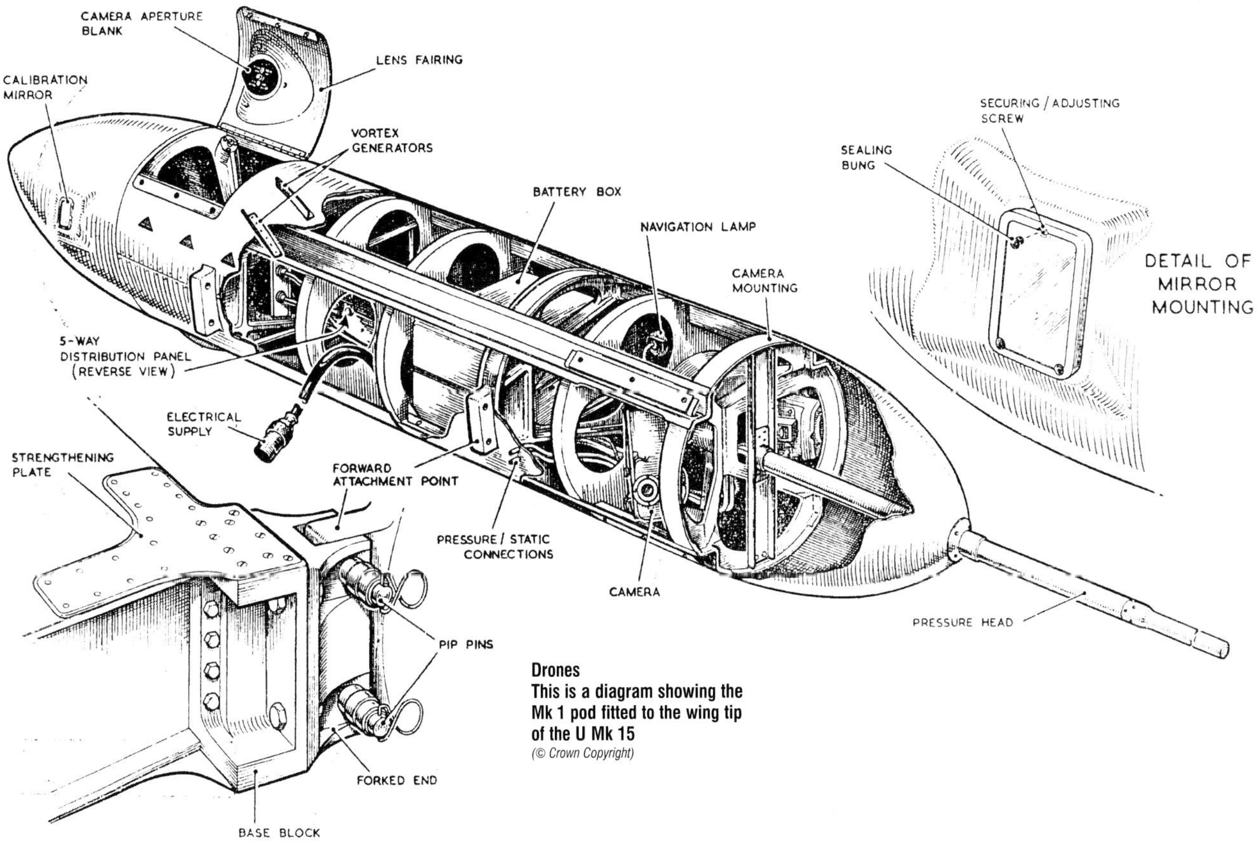

CAMERA APERTURE BLANK
CALIBRATION MIRROR
LENS FAIRING
VORTEX GENERATORS
BATTERY BOX
NAVIGATION LAMP
CAMERA MOUNTING
SECURING / ADJUSTING SCREW
SEALING BUNG
DETAIL OF MIRROR MOUNTING
5-WAY DISTRIBUTION PANEL (REVERSE VIEW)
ELECTRICAL SUPPLY
STRENGTHENING PLATE
FORWARD ATTACHMENT POINT
PRESSURE / STATIC CONNECTIONS
CAMERA
PRESSURE HEAD
PIP PINS
FORKED END
BASE BLOCK

Drones
This is a diagram showing the Mk 1 pod fitted to the wing tip of the U Mk 15
(© Crown Copyright)

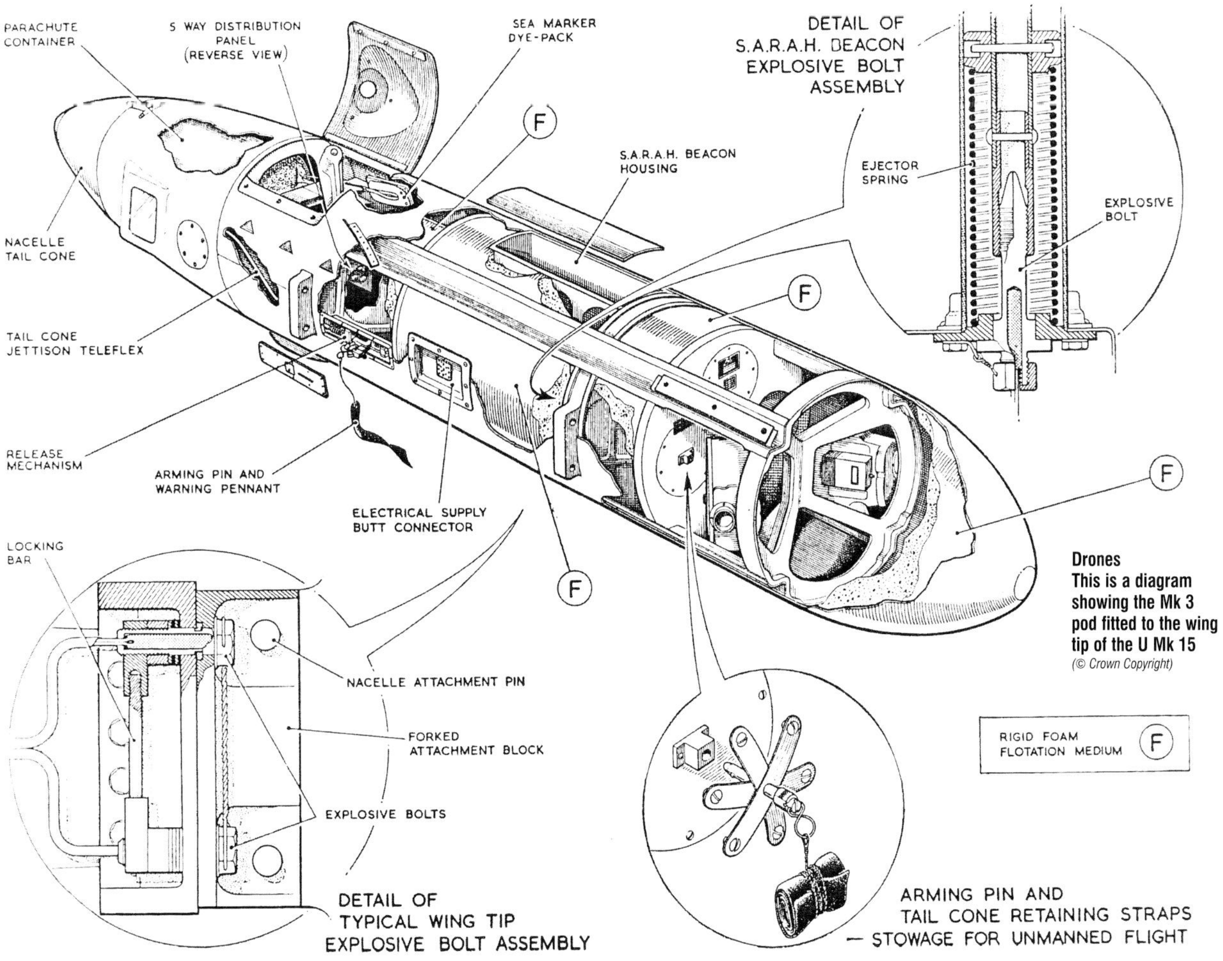

PARACHUTE CONTAINER
5 WAY DISTRIBUTION PANEL (REVERSE VIEW)
SEA MARKER DYE-PACK
DETAIL OF S.A.R.A.H. BEACON EXPLOSIVE BOLT ASSEMBLY
S.A.R.A.H. BEACON HOUSING
EJECTOR SPRING
EXPLOSIVE BOLT
NACELLE TAIL CONE
TAIL CONE JETTISON TELEFLEX
RELEASE MECHANISM
ARMING PIN AND WARNING PENNANT
ELECTRICAL SUPPLY BUTT CONNECTOR
LOCKING BAR
NACELLE ATTACHMENT PIN
FORKED ATTACHMENT BLOCK
EXPLOSIVE BOLTS
DETAIL OF TYPICAL WING TIP EXPLOSIVE BOLT ASSEMBLY
RIGID FOAM FLOTATION MEDIUM (F)
ARMING PIN AND TAIL CONE RETAINING STRAPS — STOWAGE FOR UNMANNED FLIGHT

Drones
This is a diagram showing the Mk 3 pod fitted to the wing tip of the U Mk 15
(© Crown Copyright)

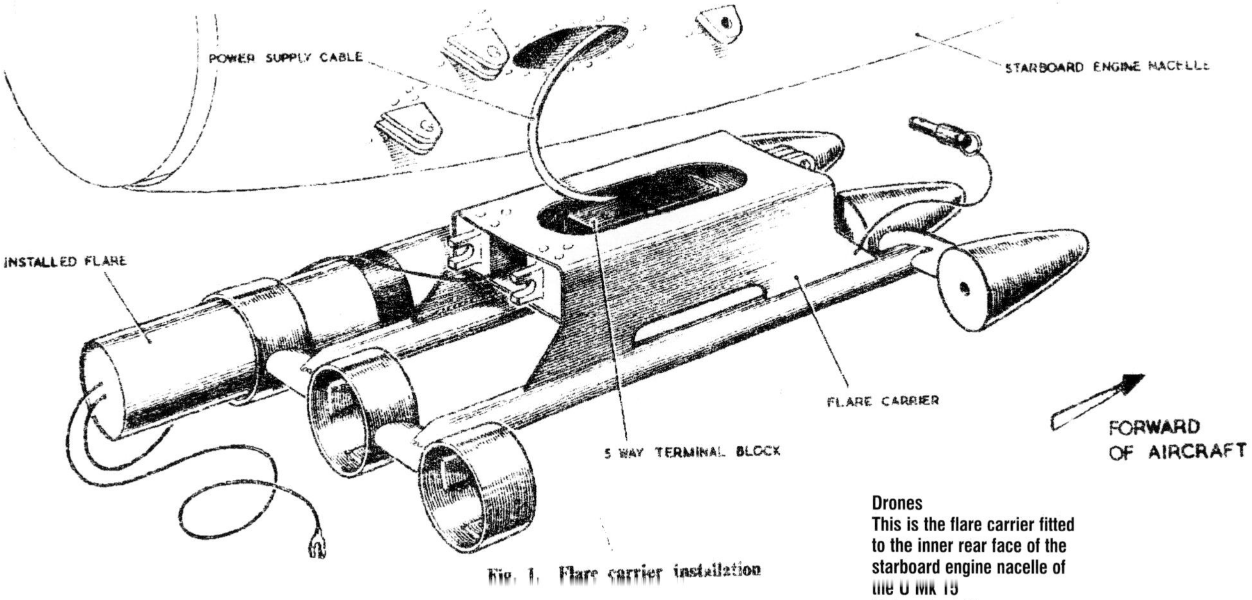

Fig. 1. Flare carrier installation

Drones
This is the flare carrier fitted to the inner rear face of the starboard engine nacelle of the U Mk 15
(© Crown Copyright)

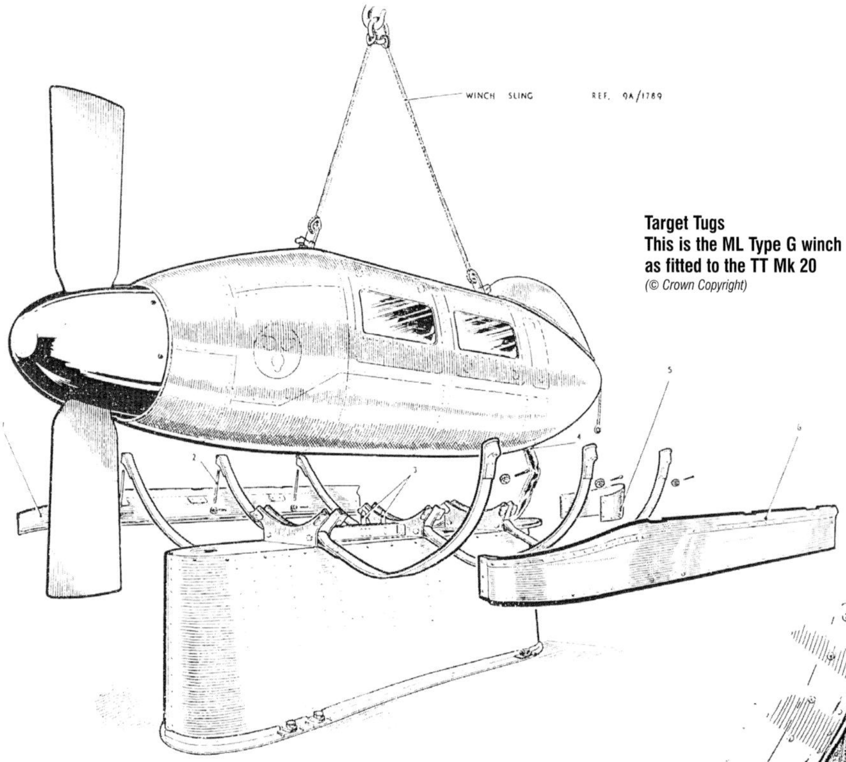

Target Tugs
This is the ML Type G winch as fitted to the TT Mk 20
(© Crown Copyright)

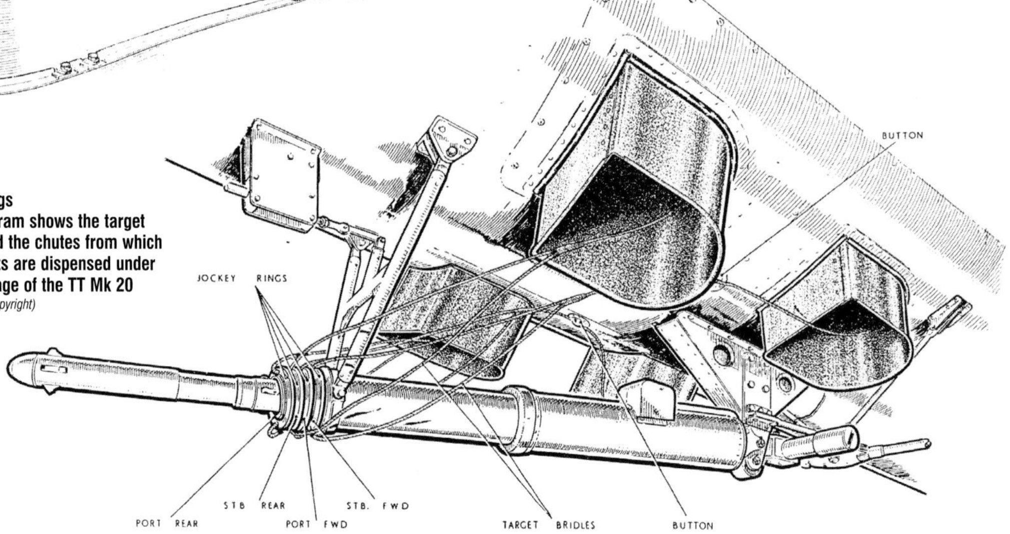

Target Tugs
This diagram shows the target bridle and the chutes from which the targets are dispensed under the fuselage of the TT Mk 20
(© Crown Copyright)

Cockpit Interior Artwork • 1

Meteor F Mk III Instrument Panel

Key to illustration
- 1. Undercarriage indicator
- 2. Flaps indicator
- 3. DR compass indicator
- 4. Instrument flying panel
- 5. Gunsight
- 6. Instrument panel lights
- 7. Hood jettisoning control
- 8. Tank contents gauges
- 9. Oxygen regulator

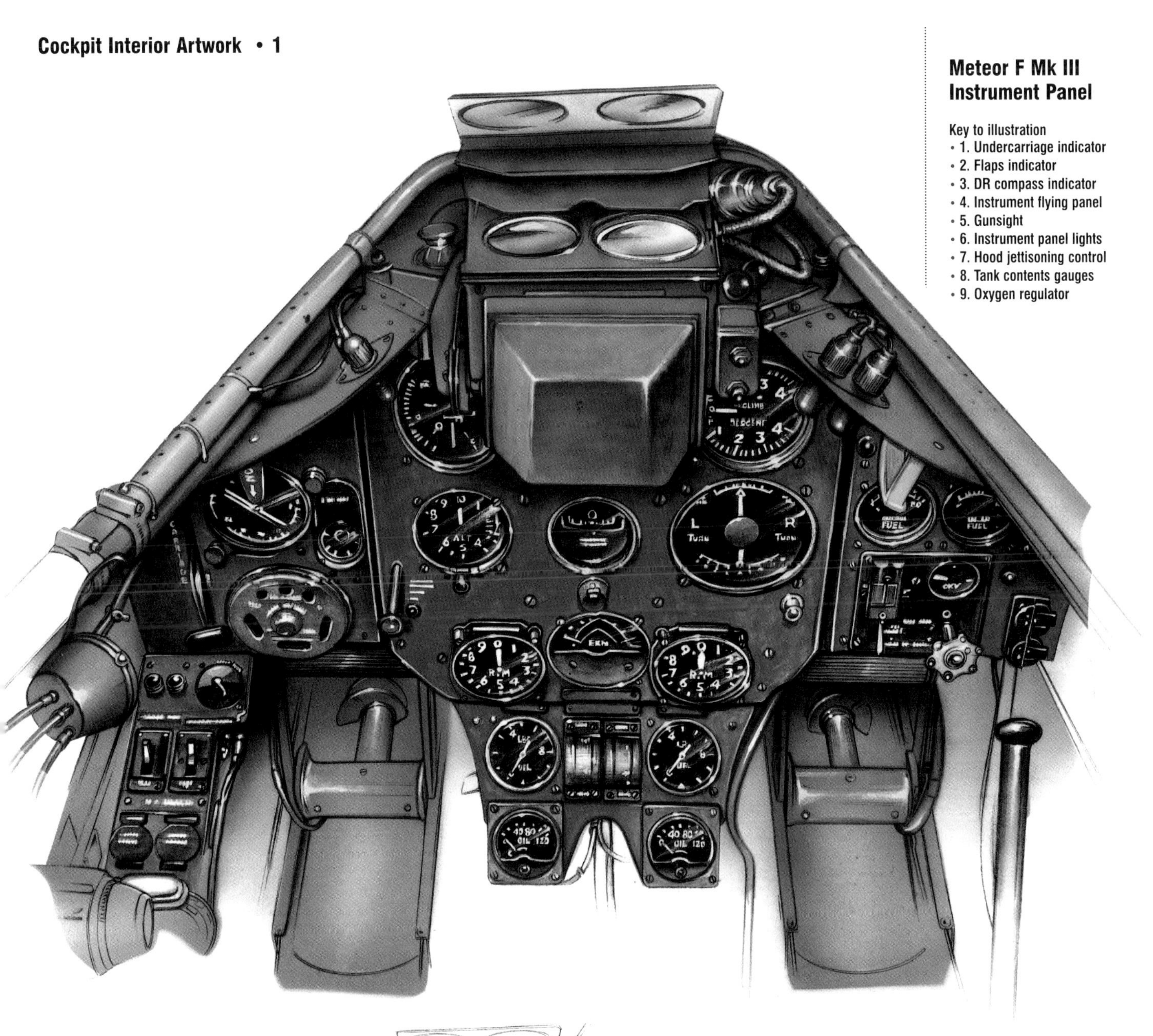

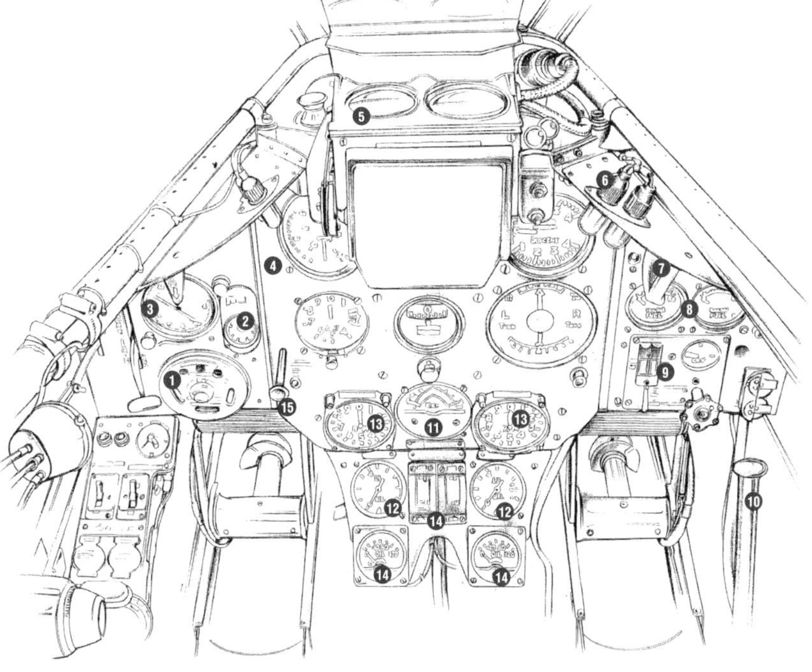

- 10. Hydraulic handpump
- 11. Twin jet pipe temperature gauge
- 12. Burner pressure gauges
- 13. RPM indicator
- 14. Oil pressure and temperature gauges
- 15. Rudder pedal adjuster release

Cockpit Interior Artwork • 2

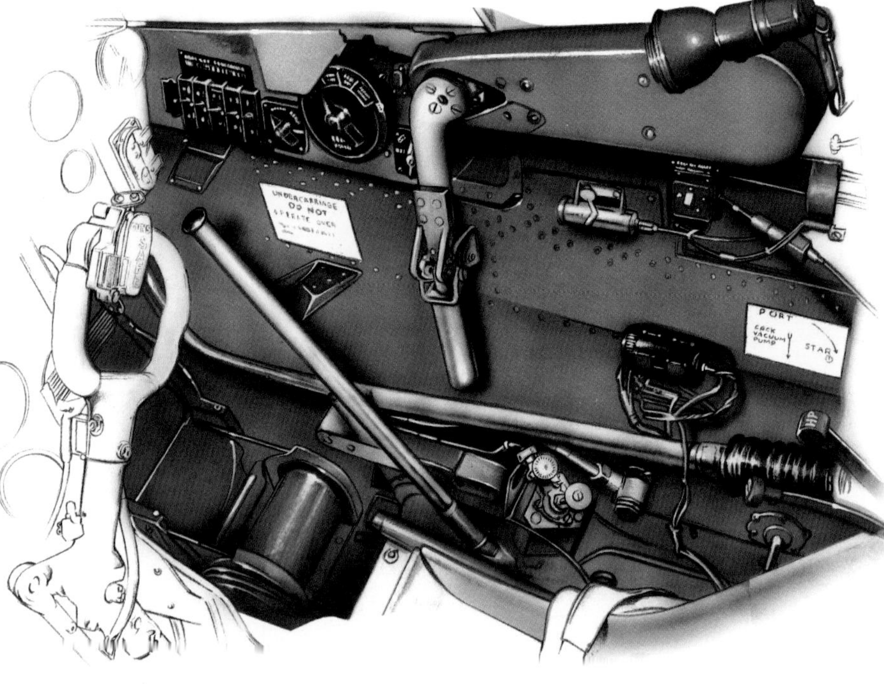

Starboard Sidewall

Key to illustration
- 1. Wheel brake levers
- 2. Gun and camera firing switches
- 3. IFF demolition switches
- 4. Clock
- 5. Navigation, resin and compass light switches, pressure head heater switch
- 6. Identification light swltch
- 7. Gyro gunsight switches
- 8. Hood winding handle
- 9. Harness release
- 10. Emergency lights switch
- 11. Starboard engine H.P. cock control
- 12. Starboard engine L.P. cock control
- 13. Vacuum pump selector cock
- 14. Windscreen de-icer handpump
- 15. Seat adjusting lever

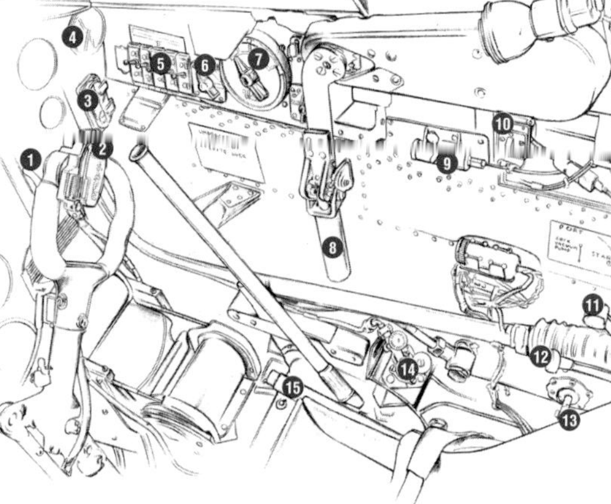

Port Sidewall

Key to illustration
- 1. Port engine L.P. cock control
- 2. Port engine H.P cock control
- 3. 'G' switch
- 4. Triple air pressure gauge
- 5. Throttle lever
- 6. Flood light
- 7. Air brake control
- 8. Flap selector lever
- 9. Undercarriage selector lever
- 10. Relighting switches
- 11. Landing lamp switch
- 12. Low pressure pump switches
- 13. Starter switches
- 14. Air brake position indicator
- 15. T.R.1143 controller
- 16. Low pressure test push buttons
- 17. Trim indicator
- 18. Elevator trim control
- 19. Rudder trim control
- 20. Fuel tank balance cock control

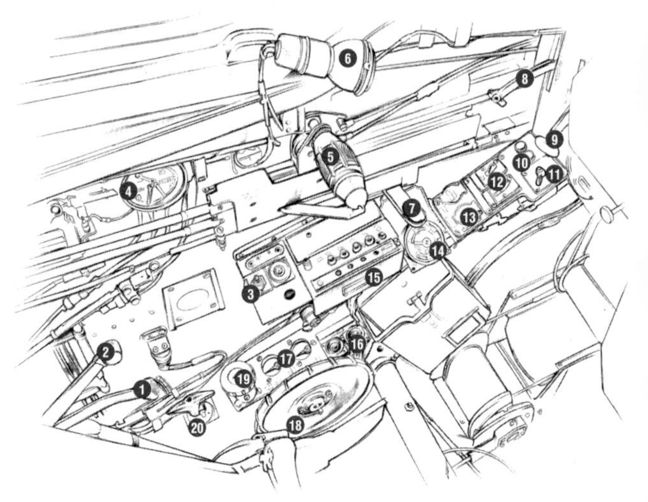

Meteor T Mk 7 Front Instrument panel

Key to illustration

- 1. Engine starter push buttons (2)
- 2. Engine relight push buttons (2)
- 3. Undercarriage selector lever
- 4. Flaps selector lever
- 5. Access hole for adjusting voltage regulator
- 6. Direct vision panel control handwheel

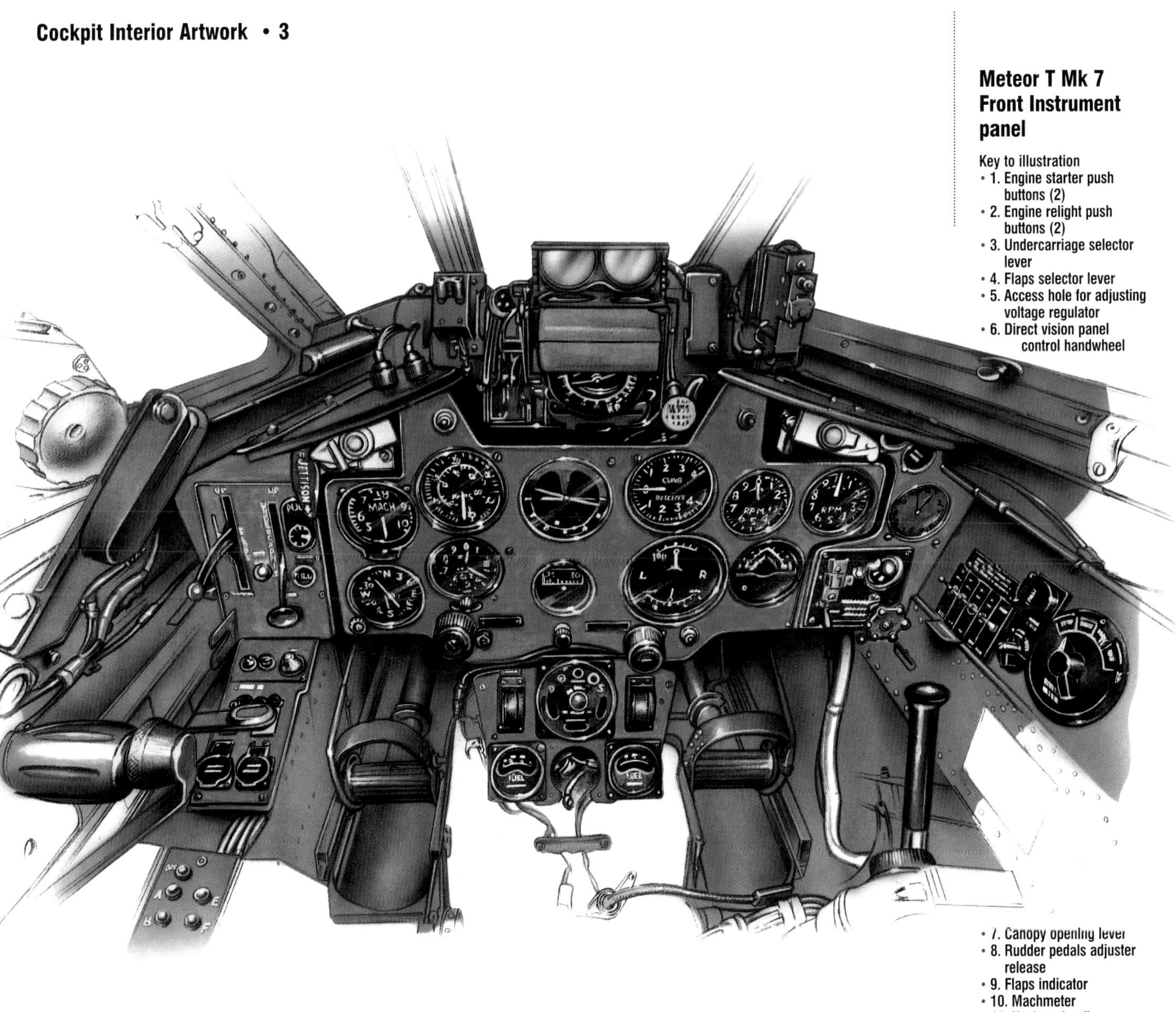

- 7. Canopy opening lever
- 8. Rudder pedals adjuster release
- 9. Flaps indicator
- 10. Machmeter
- 11. No.1 engine fire warning light
- 12. Cockpit emergency light
- 13. Cockpit red floodlight
- 14. Gunsight retraction control
- 15. Retractable gunsight
- 16. Gunsight emergency retraction control
- 17. Gunsight master circuit-breaker control
- 18. No.2 engine fire warning light
- 19. Engine fire extinguisher push buttons (2)
- 20. Canopy jettison handle
- 21. Clock
- 22. Engine speed indicators (2)
- 23. Oxygen regulator
- 24. Hydraulic emergency handpump
- 25. Press-to-speak switch
- 26. Dual jet pipe temperature gauge
- 27. Cockpit lighting dimmer switch
- 28. No.2 engine oil pressure gauge
- 29. Fuel contents gauge (rear compartment)
- 30. Undercarriage indicator
- 31. Fuel contents gauge (front compartment)
- 32. No.1 engine oil pressure gauge
- 33. U/V lighting dimmer switch
- 34. R.I. compass repeater

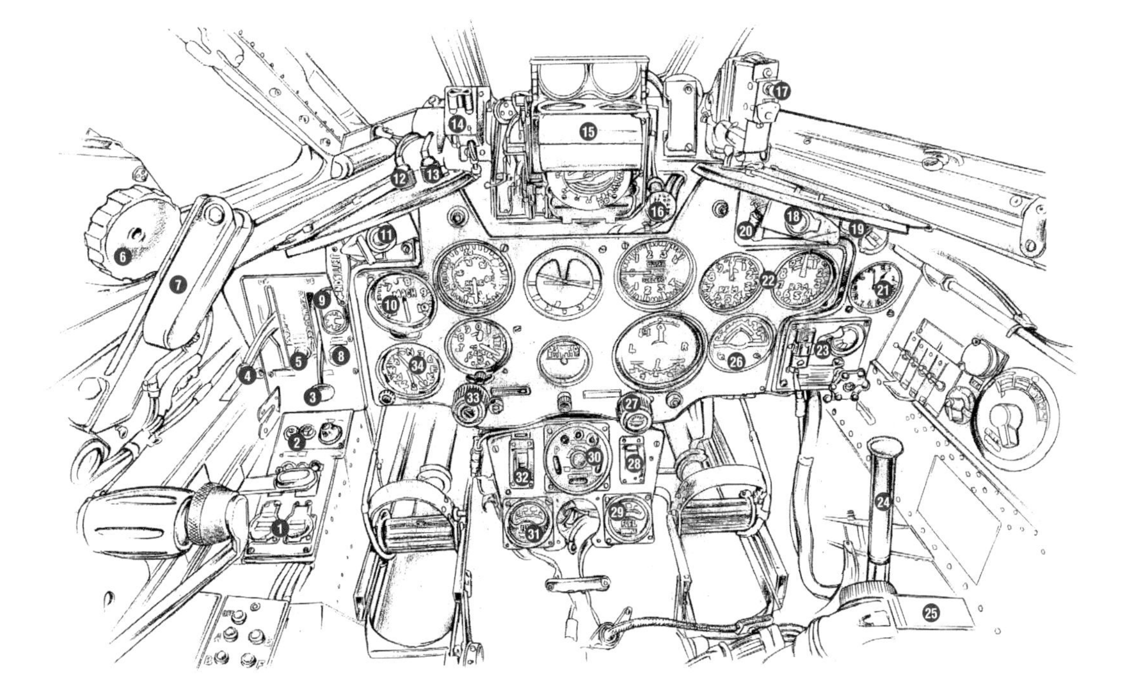

Cockpit Interior Artwork • 4

Port sidewall (Front)

Key to illustration
- 1. Crowbar
- 2. No.1 engine L.P. cock
- 3. No.1 engine H.P. cock
- 4. Mounting for camera footage indicator
- 5. Micro-switch for operating undercarriage warning light
- 6. Micro-switch in starting circuit to ensure throttle closed
- 7. Pneumatic supply and brake pressure gauge
- 8. 'G' switches
- 9. VHF eight-channel radio controller
- 10. Throttle levers (2)
- 11. Cockpit ventilating control
- 12. Cockpit lighting dimmer switch
- 13. Air brakes control lever
- 14. Drop tanks warning light
- 15. Drop tanks control cock and ventral drop tank jettison handle
- 16. Landing light switch
- 17. Low pressure pumps circuit breaker switches (2)
- 18. Low pressure pumps ammeter test socket
- 19. Port rudder pedal
- 20. Map case
- 21. Low pressure pumps test push buttons (2)
- 22. Elevator trimming tab control
- 23. Elevator trimming tab indicator
- 24. Pilot's safety harness release box
- 25. Rudder trimming tab indicator
- 26. Rudder trimming tab control
- 27. Fuel balance cock

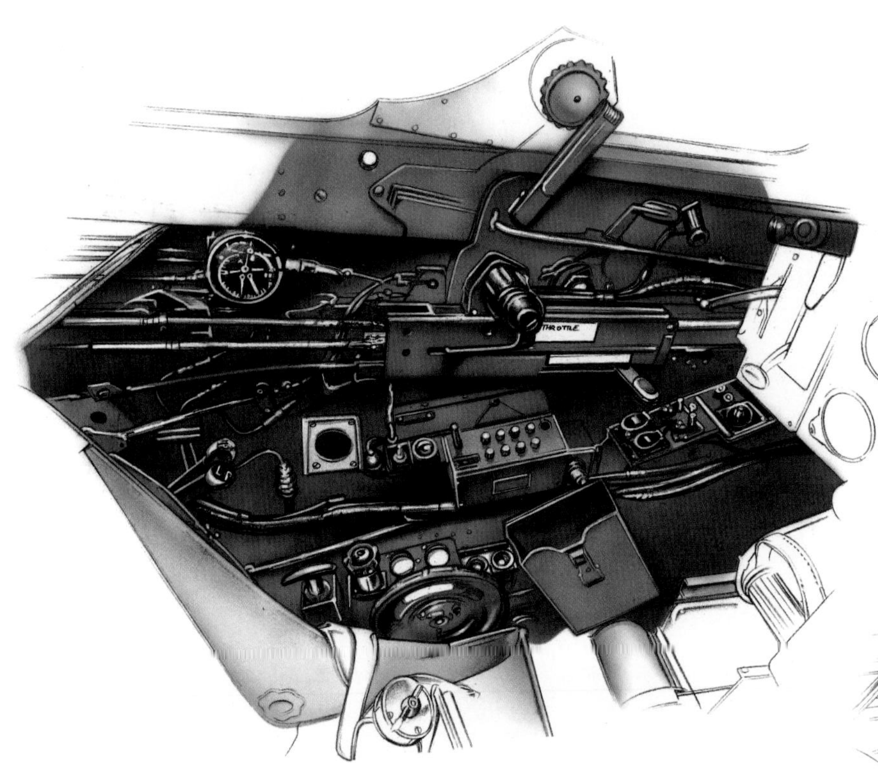

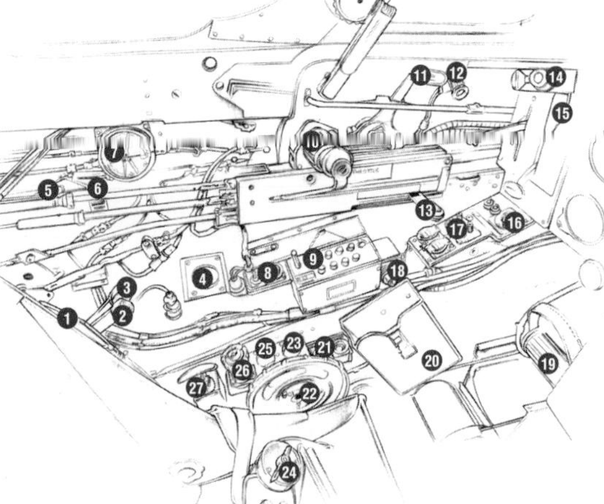

Starboard sidewall (Front)

Key to illustration
- 1. Starboard rudder pedal
- 2. Control column
- 3. Cine camera master switch
- 4. Navigation lights switch
- 5. Pressure head heater switch
- 6. Resin lights switch
- 7. R.I. compass switch
- 8. Identification light push button
- 9. Identification light selector switch
- 10. Gyro gunsight dimmer selector control
- 11. IFF 'D' switch
- 12. IFF 'F' switch
- 13. IFF controller
- 14. Cockpit heating control
- 15. Canopy jettison toggle indicator
- 16. Pilot's safety harness release
- 17. Cockpit emergency light switch
- 18. R.I. compass card holder
- 19. Stand-by compass card holder
- 20. Pilot's mic/tel socket
- 21. No.2 engine H.P. cock
- 22. No.2 engine L.P. cock
- 23. Windscreen de-icing handpump
- 24. Pilot's oxygen pipe
- 25. Wing drop tanks jettison lever
- 26. Seat adjusting lever
- 27. Bracket for controls locking rod

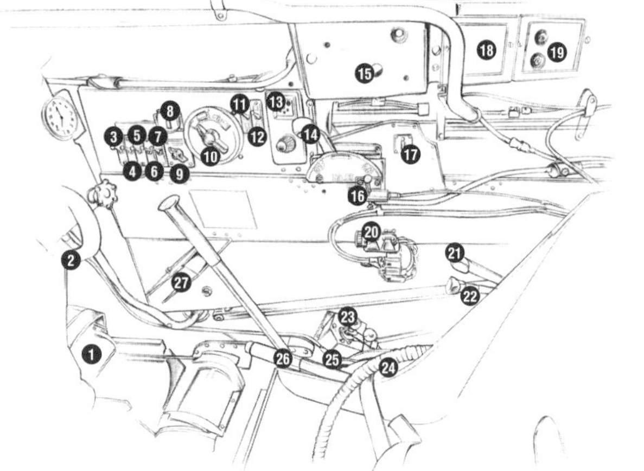

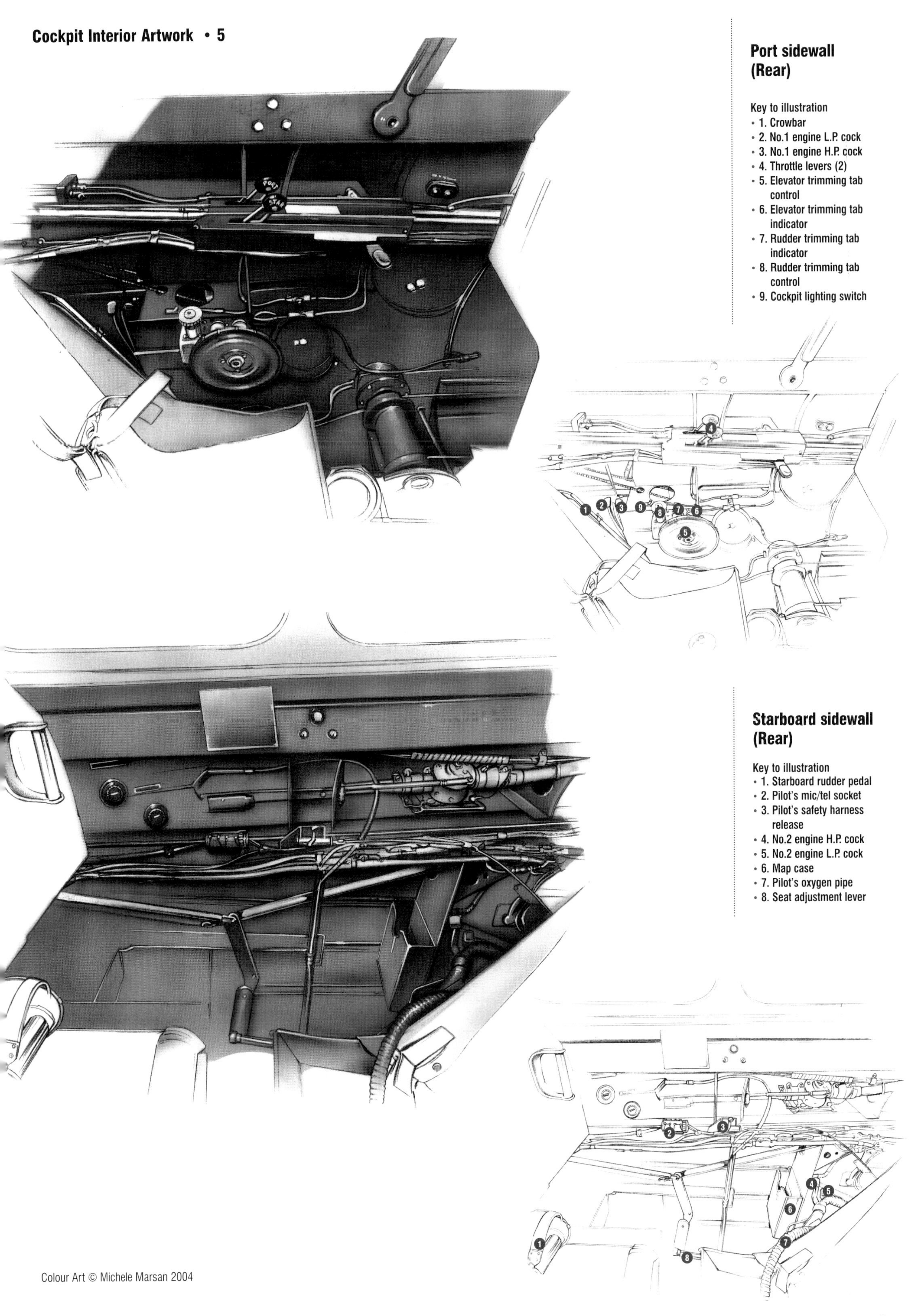

Port sidewall (Rear)

Key to illustration

- 1. Crowbar
- 2. No.1 engine L.P. cock
- 3. No.1 engine H.P. cock
- 4. Throttle levers (2)
- 5. Elevator trimming tab control
- 6. Elevator trimming tab indicator
- 7. Rudder trimming tab indicator
- 8. Rudder trimming tab control
- 9. Cockpit lighting switch

Starboard sidewall (Rear)

Key to illustration

- 1. Starboard rudder pedal
- 2. Pilot's mic/tel socket
- 3. Pilot's safety harness release
- 4. No.2 engine H.P. cock
- 5. No.2 engine L.P. cock
- 6. Map case
- 7. Pilot's oxygen pipe
- 8. Seat adjustment lever

Cockpit • 1

Prototype DG202/G

•**1** Overall view of the cockpit showing the instrument panel and control column

•**2** Overall view of the starboard sidewall

•**3** A look down at the port sidewall

Note: For F Mk III cockpit interior see the Cockpit Interior Artwork elsewhere in this title.

F Mk 4 (EE531)

•**4** Overall view of the rather spartan instrument panel in this example. See the diagrams elsewhere for a more representative F Mk 4 instrument panel

•**5** The starboard sidewall. It really is that bare, there are just a few brackets missing (see diagrams elsewhere), that is all

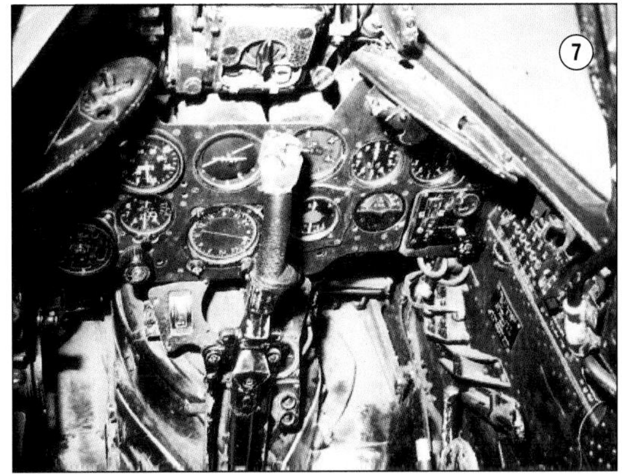

F Mk 4 (EE531)

• **6** The rear bulkhead area. The bracket and bar unit is where the pilot's seat harness would usually come up through and over his shoulders

F Mk 8

• **7** Lower section of the instrument panel and control column

• **8** The starboard sidewall

• **9** The port sidewall

• **10** A look down onto the top of the ejection seat

NF Mk 14

• **11** The starboard sidewall of WS838

• **12** The port sidewall of WS838

• **13** The rear seat and bulkhead of WS838

Fuselage & Canopy • 1

Note: The F Mk 1 through to the F Mk 4 shared a common fuselage structure. The T Mk 7, NF series and TT Mk 20 also shared common fuselage elements while the F Mk 8 and FR Mk 9 had the revised tail

Prototype DG202/G

• **1** Close-up of the nose-cone area. The hole is a venturi, the plugged one above it is where a camera gun would be. Note the oval panel above this that allows access to the camera

• **2** The port side of the nose. Note the separate nose-cone, the access doors for the cannon, the access panel forward of the windscreen and the footstep below the cockpit

• **3** Overall view of the starboard side of the nose. Note the large panel aft of the cockpit, which is for access to the cannon ammunition bays

• **4** The port side of the canopy. Note the handle to release it from outside and the hinged panel in the windscreen side panel

• **5** The footstep and handhold in the port side

• **6** The upper decking of the mid-fuselage section comes off to allow access to the fuel tank within. Note the catches all along the join line

• **7** The aft port fuselage. Here you can see the two access panels, one for the elevator and the other for the rudder control cables. These are repeated on the starboard side

Fuselage & Canopy • 2

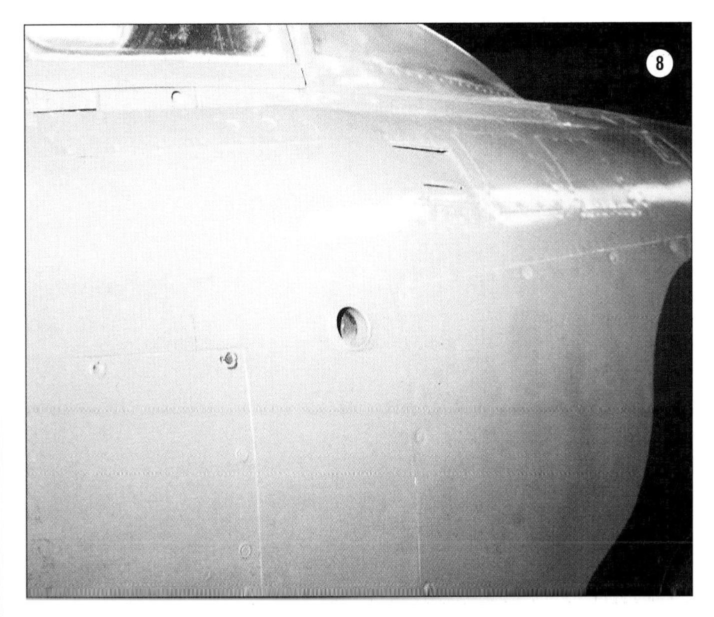

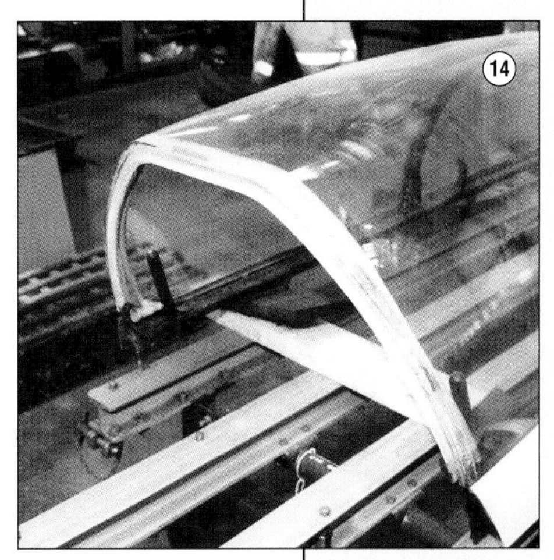

F Mk 4 (EE531)

• **8** The prominent hole in the port side of the fuselage is an air outlet that relates to the cockpit ventilation system in the Meteor and nearly all marks have it

• **9** In this shot of the windscreen area you can see the access panel in this area

• **10** Here you can see the rails and the clear aft section of the canopy

• **11** The ventral strake below the tail was on all versions that used the initial tail design until the high tail (E.1/44) fitted to the F Mk 8 arrived

F Mk 8

• **12** Here is a view of the canopy sill and cockpit rails

• **13** This earlier style F Mk 8 (actually the prone pilot version), shows the solid rear section of the canopy well

NF Mk 14

• **14 - 16** Three views of the blown canopy from an NF Mk 14, in this case the RAF Museum example undergoing restoration in 2004

• **17** I think this shot of the nose of the Midland Air Museum's NF Mk 14 just goes to show how long this area of the type was

Tail & Tailplanes

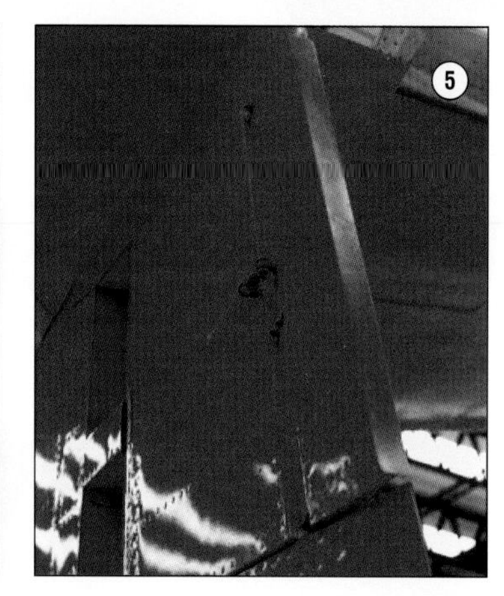

Prototype DG202/G

- **1** Overall view of the port side of the tail unit. Note the acorn at the leading edge by the tailplane junction
- **2** A view of the trailing edge of the rudder. Note the trim tab and linkage and formation light
- **3** Close-up of the formation light on the tail

F Mk 4 (T Mk 7 identical)

Note: The later T Mk 7s flown in Israel and the two currently used by Martin-Baker all have the (E.1/44) F Mk 8 tail unit.

- **4** A close-up of the lower section of the rudder

F Mk 8 (FR Mk 9, NF Mk 11 and 13 and U Mk 16 & 21)

- **5** This is the rudder fitted to the Martin-Baker T Mk 7 and as you can see this F Mk 8 unit includes the flange on the trim tab
- **6** This is the tailplane of the Martin-Baker T Mk 7, the unpainted trim tab is useful to highlight its shape and hinge positions
- **7** Details of the lower section of the tailcone and lower hinge on the prone-pilot F Mk 8
- **8** Overall view of the rudder on the prone-pilot F Mk 8
- **9** Overall view of the revised vertical fin with its increased area

Wings

F Mk III

• **1** This is actually the prototype DG202/G but it has an F Mk III wing fitted as borne out by the installation of air brakes

• **2** View of the flaps

F Mk 4 & T Mk 7 (F Mk 8 and FR Mk 9)

• **3** While this is the outboard section of the aileron on the same wing

• **4** ... and this is the light in the trailing edge of the port wingtip

• **5** This shot shows the fillet between the engine nacelle and the inboard wing section

NF Series

• **6** It is unusual to look up inside the inboard flap area, but with this machine being restored by the RAFM I was able to get this shot

• **7** Here is the outboard flap on the starboard wing

• **8** This shot shows the port cannon. Note that the inboard one has been removed and the hole plugged

Centre Section & Engines • 1

F Mk III

• **1** This is actually the prototype, although it has Mk III wings fitted, but you can see the short nacelles fitted to the early marks

• **2** This view from the side clearly shows the short nacelle front

• **3** The W.2B engines meant that the exhaust pipe extended past the rear of the nacelle, as can be seen here. The prototypes, F Mk Is and first fifteen F Mk IIIs all had this type of exhaust

F Mk 4

• **4** This shot shows the outline and profile of the bulge

• **5** This view underneath the inboard wing section shows the truncated bulge from the rear of the wheel well, as well as the air brake. Note the spacing of the slots in the air brake (2, 4, 3) and that they are not equally spaced. The upper air brake has only seven slots, unequally spaced 2, 3, 2

T Mk 7

• **6** Thanks to the generosity of the staff at Martin-Baker I was able to get a good selection of images of the Derwent 8 engines fitted to their T Mk 7s. Here is an overall shot of the starboard engine

• **7** This is the rear bulkhead. Note the lagged hot air pipes going into each side of the upper part of the bulkhead

• **8** This is the front section of the engine with all the ancillary equipment visible

• **9** You cannot get a better visual reference from the difference between large and small intakes than this. This is the small diameter unit...

• **10** ...while these are the big diameter ones. The fitment of the blanking plate does, in this instance, help you see the difference clearly in the size of the inlet

Centre Section & Engines • 2

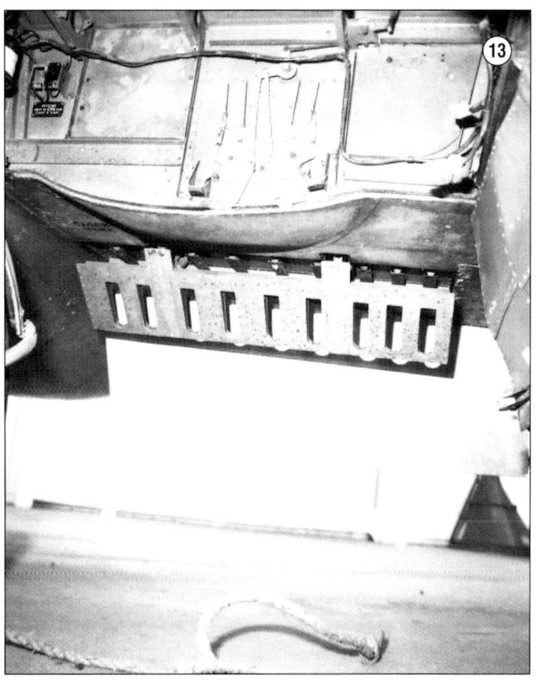

F Mk 8 (FR Mk 9 & PR Mk 10)

•**12** It is quite a way into the intakes of an F Mk 8, as can be seen here. The splitter going across the front of the engine is actually the forward wing spar

•**13** Although this also shows a bit of the undercarriage area, this does show the shape and slots in the ventral air brakes on the F Mk 8. As you can see they are not equally spaced on the surface of the skin, being set 2, 4, 3.

•**14** Here is a nice shot of the upper air brakes. Note the 2, 3, 2 spread of the slots

•**15** All Meteors have it, so I thought I would show it here. This is the joining strip that runs along both upper and lower wings just outboard of the engine nacelles. It covers the transit joint for the outer wing panels

•**16** This is the long tail end of the F Mk 8 nacelle. Note that the exhaust cone does not protrude past the back of the nacelle by much, unlike the W.2B-powered F Mk I and early F Mk IIIs

•**17** This is a good side profile of the long forward section of the engine nacelle on the F Mk 8. This is the large diameter inlet size

Centre Section & Engines • 3

NF Series

• **18 - 20** These three shots give a nice set of walk-around images of a Derwent 9, as fitted to the NF Mk 14. The previous Derwent 8 is virtually identical

• **21** Although it is a jet, the Meteor still had wood used in its construction, as seen here on the intake lips

• **22** It looks identical to me, but this is the bulge over the wheel well on the upper skin of the inboard wing section of an NF Mk 14

Undercarriage • 1

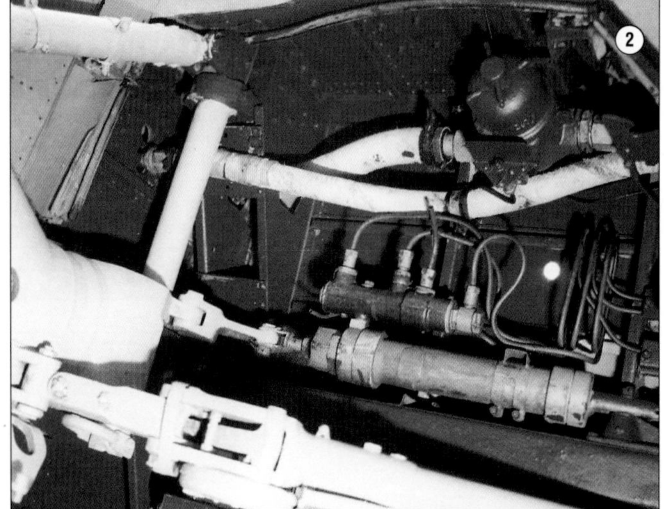

Note: There were only two types of undercarriage used throughout the life of the Meteor. The initial one saw service up to the F Mk 4 (and may well have also been used on the FR Mk 5), while the revised one was used from the T Mk 7 onwards to deal with the heavier all-up weights of the heavily armed or two-seat versions thereafter.

F Mk III & F Mk 4

• **1** This is the nose wheel from the starboard side

• **2** You are looking directly upwards into the wheel well alongside the main strut and here can be seen the linkage and hydraulics associated with the leg's retraction. The lagged pipes running from side to side are hot air pipes that bleed air off the exhaust to warm the cannon bays

• **3** This is an F Mk 4 main wheel, viewed from the rear

• **4** This is the outer main door of the port wheel of an F Mk 4. Note the curve that creates the bulge over the wheel well area to accommodate the oleo and wheel once retracted

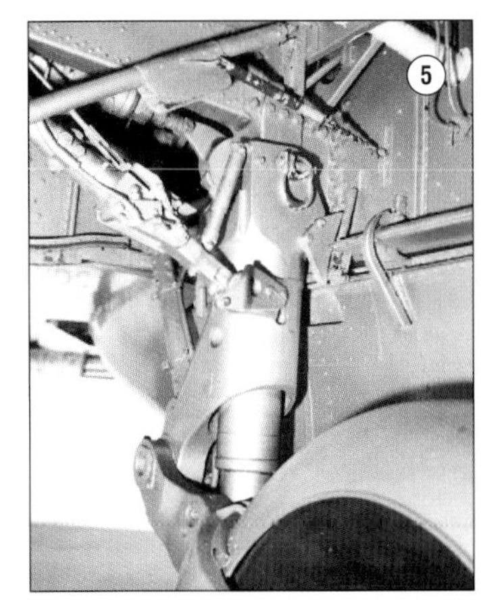

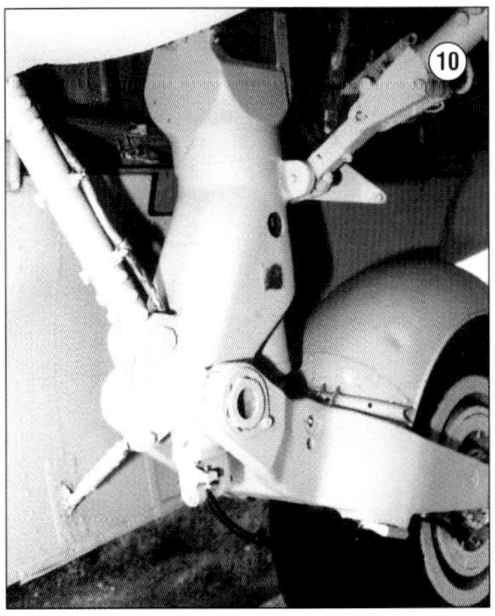

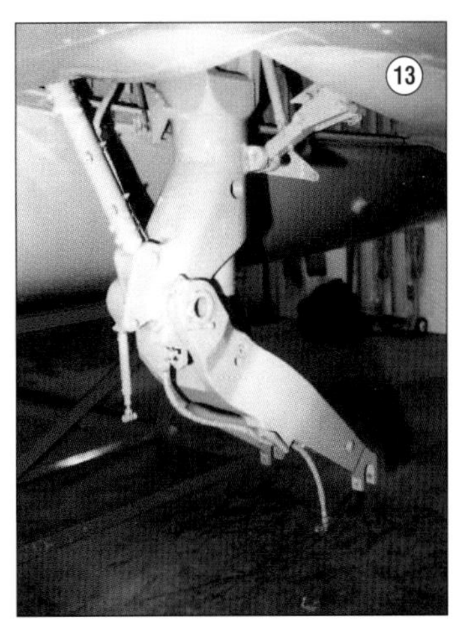

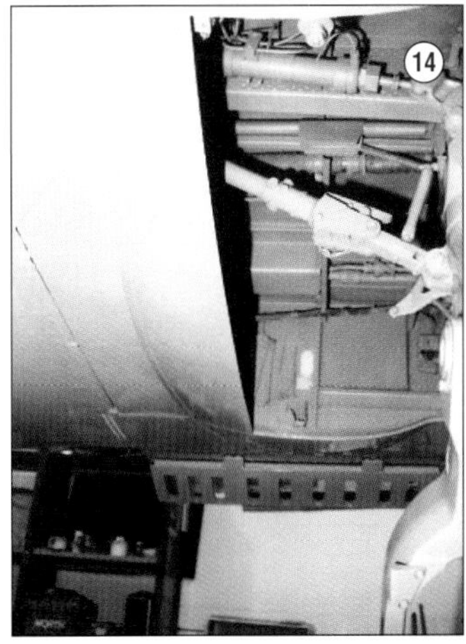

F Mk 8

•**5** This is the wheel well of the prone-pilot F Mk 8 and it shows the anchor point of the main oleo leg

•**6** This is mid section of the wheel well of the prone-pilot F Mk 8

•**7** This is the extreme forward section of the wheel well of the prone-pilot F Mk 8, looking forward

•**8** A useful overall shot of the starboard main wheel of the prone-pilot F Mk 8, looking outboard

T Mk 7

•**9** As the T Mk 7 undercarriage is identical to the F Mk 8, I will concentrate on images of the former here. This is the nose wheel area of a T Mk 7, looking forward

NF Series

As the NF series share the same common undercarriage with those marks after the T Mk 7, all I will show here are a few additional images.

•**10** This is an overall view of the starboard undercarriage leg of an NF Mk 14, looking outboard. It does look more substantial than the earlier versions in this shot, doesn't it?

•**11** This is the outer face of the main wheel hub on an NF Mk 14

•**12** As you can see, the NF Mk 14 has a clear window in the nose wheel door

•**13** You rarely get to see an NF Mk 14 in bits, so this shot of the RAF Museum example during painting show some aspects not usually visible on an assembled airframe

•**14** I took the opportunity to take this image, as it shows the outer door of the main undercarriage closed, which in turn shows the bulge over the wheel well very well indeed. This is an NF Mk 14

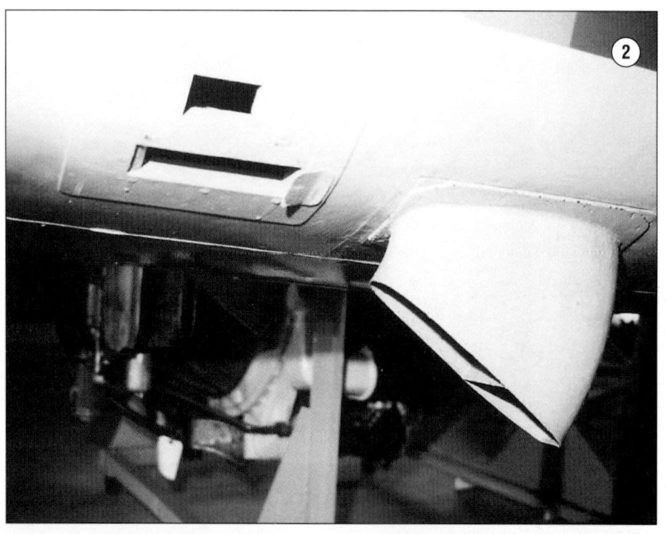

Note: The Meteor retained a four-cannon armament throughout its life, although with the latter NF series these weapons moved to the outer wings.

•**1** A close-up look into the cannon ports on the prototype

•**2** This is a shot of the spent cartridge ejector chute on the F Mk 4. You can see that the rear cannon ejection port had no chute attached to it

•**3** An overall shot of the ventral tank fitted to the Meteor, this is one used on a T Mk 7

•**4** These are the twin ejector chutes of the F Mk 8

•**5** The forward section of the tank is just an aerodynamic fairing

•**6** The rear includes the feed and pressurisation pipes

•**7** Here you can see the vents in the rear, port side, there is another in the other side as well

Armament & Fuel Tanks • 2

• **8** Looking aft along the underside of the fuselage you can see the two pipes associated with the ventral tank

• **9** This is a drop tank from an NF-series airframe, viewed from the back looking forward. Note the sway brace at the rear

• **10** This is a detailed look at the rear of the tank. Note the blunt profile and drain plug

• **11** This is a shot of a drop tank installed under the wing of an NF Mk 14 but without the aerodynamic fairing covering it

Miscellaneous • 1

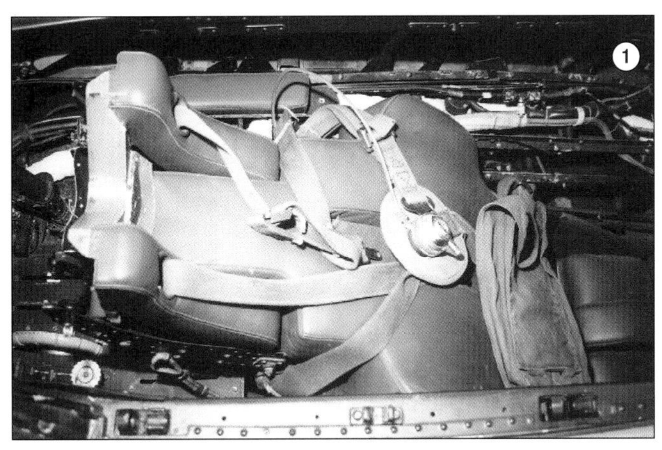

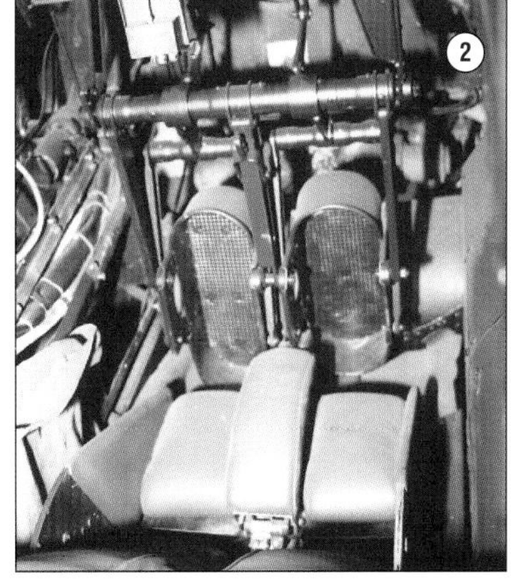

Prone Pilot Meteor

• **1** This is the 'couch' for the prone pilot position

• **2** These are the rudder pedals behind the seat in the prone-pilot Meteor

• **3** This is the small instrument panel for the prone pilot

• **4** This is a view down onto the control column and trim wheel mounted ahead of the seat in the prone-pilot Meteor

Prone Pilot Meteor

• **5** This overall shot shows the canopy fitted to the prone-pilot Meteor. It was a Sea Hawk unit!

• **6** This is the extension added to the nose of the prone-pilot Meteor. It goes from the forward bulkhead where the nose oleo attached and is a constant diameter until it tapers to the nose-cone from a point below the rear edge of the windscreen of the forward cockpit

Martin-Baker F Mk III

Only the nose of this machine exists and the front cockpit is a standard F Mk III. The back 'cockpit' was just the ammunition bay modified to squeeze a seat into. It was a real tight squeeze and as a result, even with the seat removed, it was almost impossible to photograph inside. Here are a few images anyway.

• **7** This shot shows the revised rear section of the canopy. The side panels hinge downwards

The following photographs show the T Mk 7 that is now on show at the RAF Museum, Cosford.

• **8** The rear section of the canopy is cut away as seen here

• **9** While this is a heavily modified rear section

• **10** This is the aft section

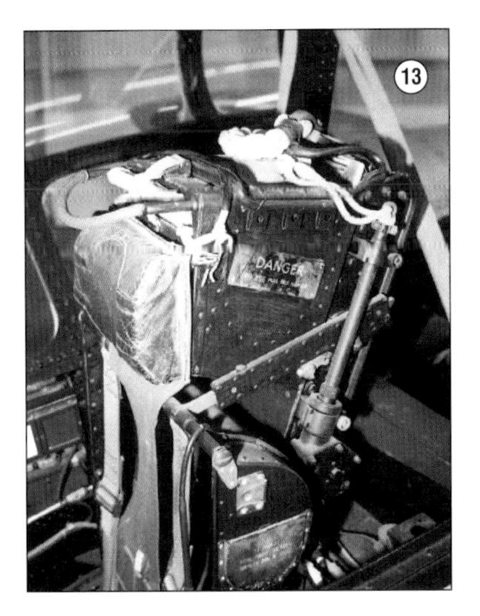

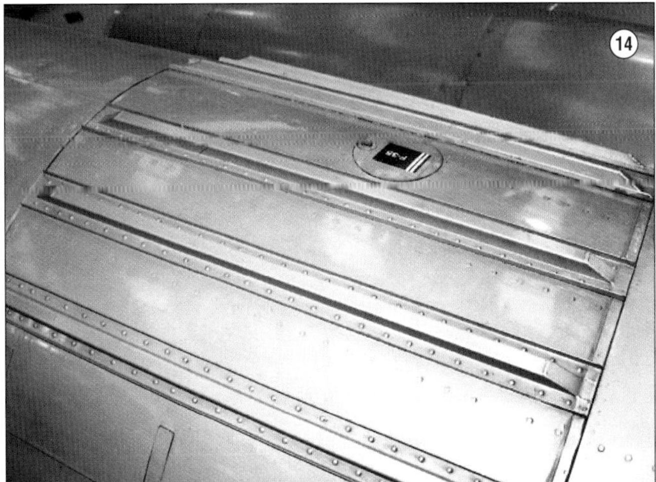

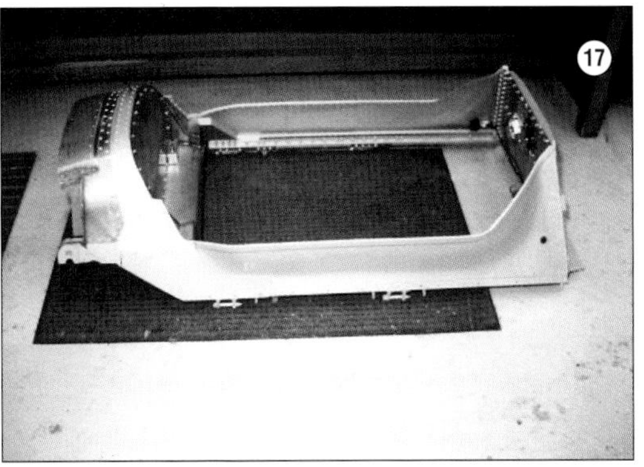

•**11** This shot shows the rear bulkhead in the back seat position. You may be able to make out the four holes in the ridge across the bulkhead where the seat rails were attached

•**12** With no rear seat fitted, this is the rather bare floor area and lower section of the rear bulkhead

•**13** An upper view of the Mk 2 seat fitted in the front cockpit

The following photographs show the T Mk 7 that is owned and operated by Martin-Baker Plc (WL419).

•**14** These are the reinforcing ribs added to the fuel tank cover on the dorsal spine of the fuselage. They stop the cover buckling during seat firing

•**15 - 16** Two shots of the interior of WL419 showing just how modern this machine now is. The seat fitted at the time of my visit was a Mk 10ME (the 'ME' being for Meteor as it is specially modified by Martin--Baker for use in their Meteor)

•**17** The forward canopy of WL419 is sort of standard, although there are ribs and other modifications that have been added by Martin-Baker. The rear section is hand-made though. This shot show the entire unit off the airframe and I rather like the stainless steel rear bulkhead area on it. Obviously this is there to resist the effects of the rocket exhaust from multiple ejection seat firings

Meteor Camouflage and Markings

TT Mk 20 WM159 was a converted NF Mk 11 and was operated by the FRU before being scrapped on the 20th July 1970. It is seen here during a visit to Malta, on Hal Far airfield
(© R.J. Caruana)

Early Gloster Meteors were finished in the contemporary standard Day Fighter Scheme. The upper surfaces wore a disruptive pattern of Dark Green and Ocean Grey (MAP Shade) to a standard pattern laid out in MAP Pattern No. 2, which varied very little from one aircraft to another, on both F Mk I and F Mk III examples.

The eight F.9/40 prototypes had Yellow applied to all undersides and usually carried the identification marking of a circle enclosing a 'P', both in Yellow, in its centre. This was specified to be 32in (81cm) diameter and was carried just aft of the fuselage roundel. All other markings were also to contemporary standard, consisting of 'C1' type roundels of 35in (90cm) diameter on the fuselage sides, 'B' type roundels of 53in (137cm) diameter on the upper surfaces of the outer wing panels, and 'C' type roundels of 32in (81cm) diameter under the outer wing panels. With the exception of DG204/G and DG209/G, they all carried the 18in (46cm) wide Sky band around the rear fuselage. The specified 24in (61cm) fin flash, positioned on the top section of the tailplane, overlapped onto the movable front tip of the rudder. This was discountinued on aircraft that appeared after DG205/G, and the fin flash was shortened to suit the height of the fin. Serial numbers were carried on both sides of the rear fuselage in 8in (20cm) high digits, painted with a 1in (2.5cm) stroke in Night.

Production F Mk Is were practically identically finished with the exception that the undersurfaces were changed from (prototype) Yellow to Medium Sea Grey (33B/679). The Sky fuselage band was retained as standard, positioned immediately in front of the fin-to-fuselage joint. It is interesting to note that the first two F Mk Is delivered (EE213 and EE214) retained the yellow bellies for quite some time after delivery to No. 616 Squadron. Aircraft of this squadron carried the code 'YQ' in 20in (51cm) high letters in Sky. Another marking not carried by the prototypes was a yellow stripe, 6in (15.2cm) high and 69in (175cm) long around the wing leading edges, the height being equally divided between upper and lower surfaces.

The only F Mk II (DG207) was finished in a similar manner to the F.9/40 prototypes. The F Mk III continued with the standard operational F Mk I scheme. However, some of these aircraft with No. 616 Squadron received an overall coat of white distemper paint during early 1945 whilst based at Melsbroek, in Belgium (e.g. EE239). It has never been clearly stated whether this was a temporary winter camouflage scheme or whether it was to serve as a quick recognition aid, seeing that on some occasions the Meteors were jumped on by 'friendly' aircraft that had mistaken them for Me 262s. All squadron codes were overpainted by the white distemper, leaving only the national markings and a rectangular patch around the serial numbers uncovered.

The first major change came in March 1945 when the 'B' type roundels above the wings were changed to 'C' type by the simple addition of a white circle between the red and blue areas. This, however, did not always result in perfect proportions between

This is the F Mk 8 flown by the CO of No.616 Squadron and this photograph shows this machine during one of the squadron's Summer Camps to Ta'Qali. Note the soot around the gun ports
(© R.J. Caruana)

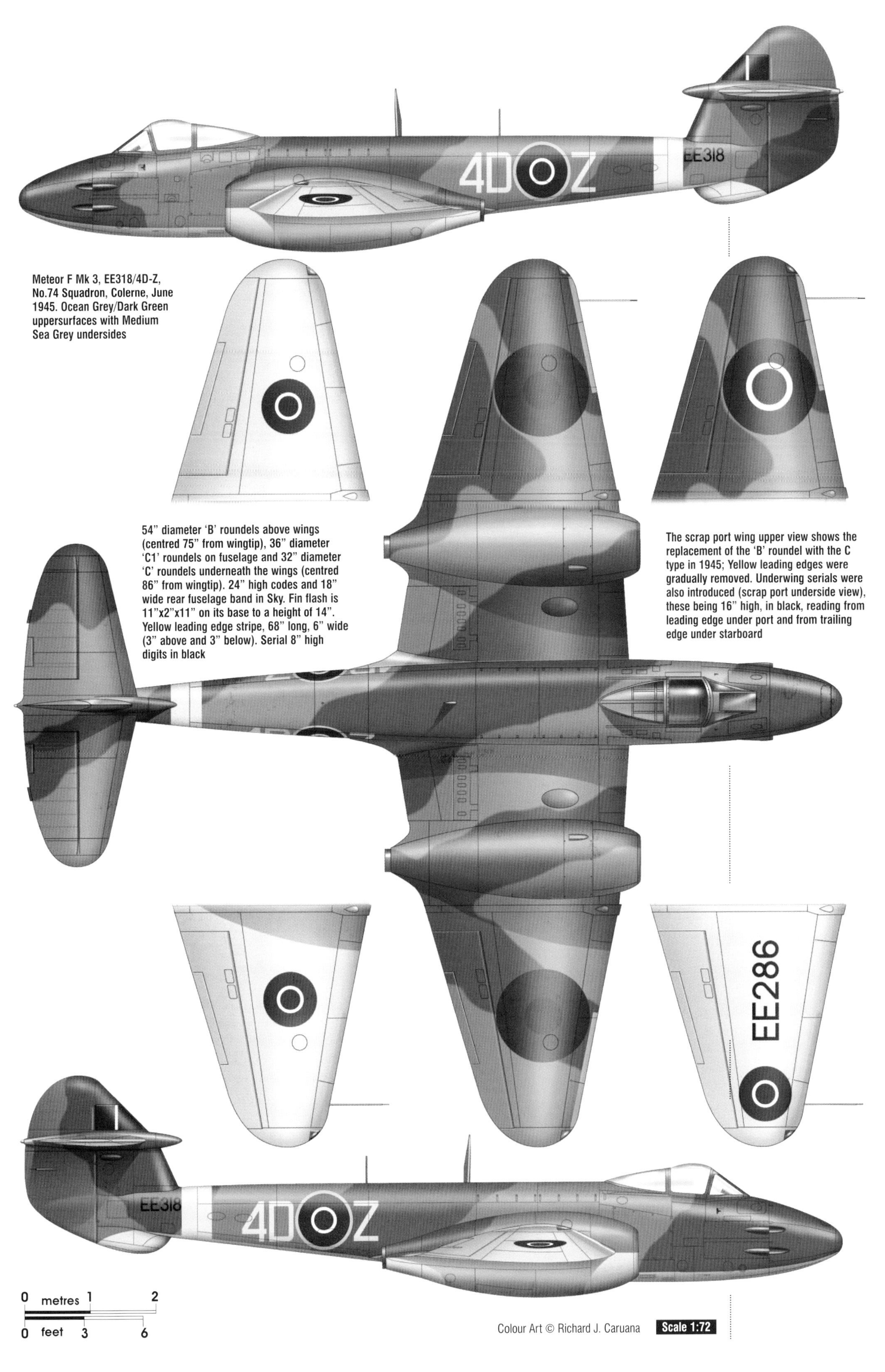

Meteor F Mk 3, EE318/4D-Z, No.74 Squadron, Colerne, June 1945. Ocean Grey/Dark Green uppersurfaces with Medium Sea Grey undersides

54" diameter 'B' roundels above wings (centred 75" from wingtip), 36" diameter 'C1' roundels on fuselage and 32" diameter 'C' roundels underneath the wings (centred 86" from wingtip). 24" high codes and 18" wide rear fuselage band in Sky. Fin flash is 11"x2"x11" on its base to a height of 14". Yellow leading edge stripe, 68" long, 6" wide (3" above and 3" below). Serial 8" high digits in black

The scrap port wing upper view shows the replacement of the 'B' roundel with the C type in 1945; Yellow leading edges were gradually removed. Underwing serials were also introduced (scrap port underside view), these being 16" high, in black, reading from leading edge under port and from trailing edge under starboard

Colour Art © Richard J. Caruana **Scale 1:72**

Ex-Nos.609 and 85 Squadron F Mk 8 WH301 was allocated Inst. Airframe number 7930M and allocated to the RAF Museum, where it is seen at their old store at Henlow in the 1970s during one of their open days [note Sycamore in background]
(© R.J. Caruana)

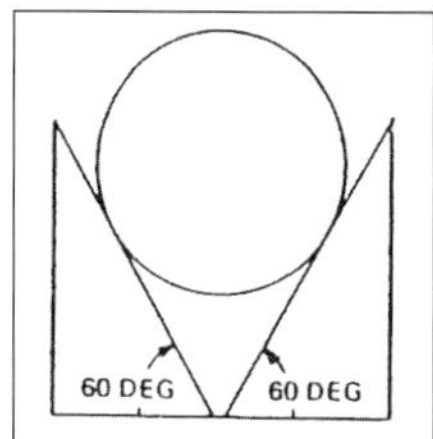

the areas of colour and a number of variations can be noted from photographs of the period. New-build Meteors on the production line were given the new 'C' type upper roundels before delivery, the overall diameter remaining unchanged.

Towards the end of 1945 Meteors began to leave the production line in a high-gloss finish on the upper surfaces, although the colours remained the same. In early 1946 underwing serial numbers were reintroduced on most RAF aircraft. This meant that the underwing roundel had to be moved further towards the wing tip to accommodate the serials that were 16in (40cm) high in Night, having a 2.75in (7cm) stroke. These read from the leading edge under the port wing and from the trailing edge under the starboard.

By 1948, when the Meteor F Mk 4 had taken over the task of Home Defence, camouflage had been abolished and the aircraft were finished in silver dope overall (Aluminium 33B/317 516 Type C - Cellulose) and this included the inside of wheel wells and engine air intakes. Upper wing markings were slightly reduced in diameter to 48in (122cm) whilst those under the wings were 36in (91cm). Codes were invariably painted in Night, although their height varied from squadron to squadron.

A major change in national markings took place with the issue of IMO A.413/47 in May 1947, stipulating the introduction of a 1-2-3 proportioned roundel in all positions in bright colours, generally referred to in modelling circles as 'D' type.

Camouflage was reintroduced in December 1953 using Gloss Dark Green (BS381C: 641) and Gloss Dark Sea Grey (BS381C: 638). Undersides remained in Aluminium. Most F Mk 8 Meteors carried this scheme in service. FR Mk 9s were similarly finished with the exception that their undersides were finished in PRU Blue (BS318C: 636). PR Mk 10s were finished in Aluminium overall, although there are photographs of late production airframes in overall camouflage. The taller part of the upper fin of the F Mk 8 (and all those that carried the E.1/44 tail) permitted the use of a 30in (76cm) high flash, with a width of 24in (61cm).

This was a time when squadron colours, in the form of multi-coloured bars flanking the fuselage roundels, came into widespread use among RAF squadrons. This Meteor variant is

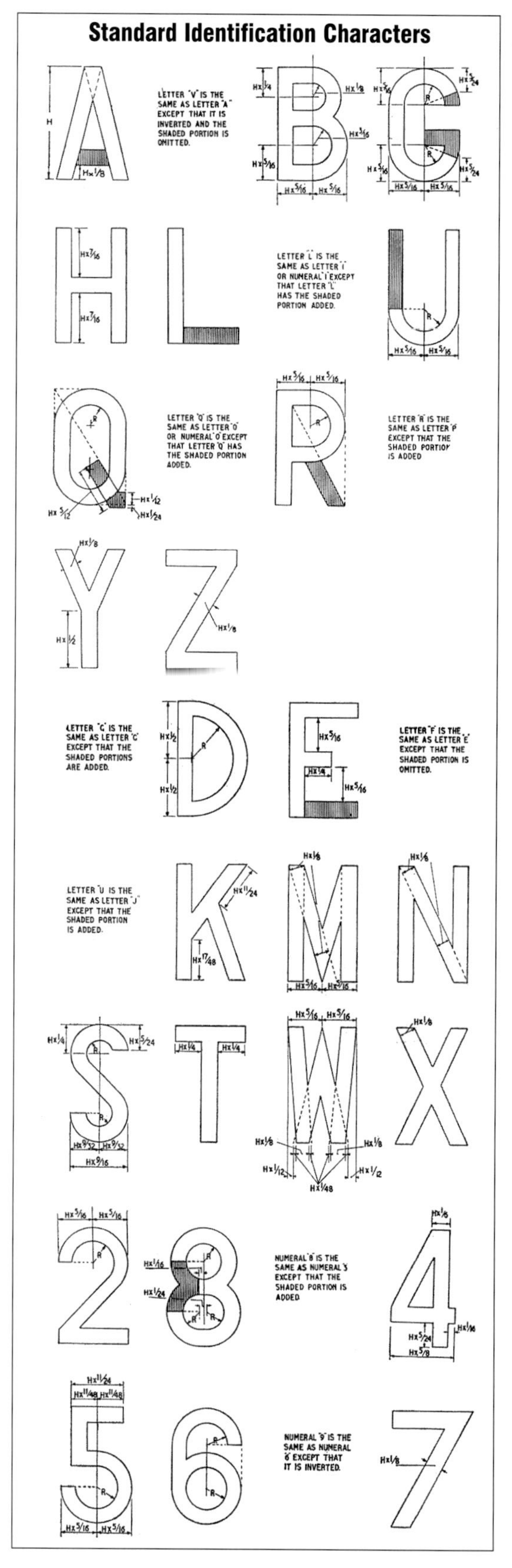

Meteor F Mk 4, EG-39, SV•B of No.4 Squadron, 1 Wing in June 1952 at Koksyde. This aircraft is returning from an air firing practice session as denoted by the soot around the gun ports
(©via Rudy Binnemans)

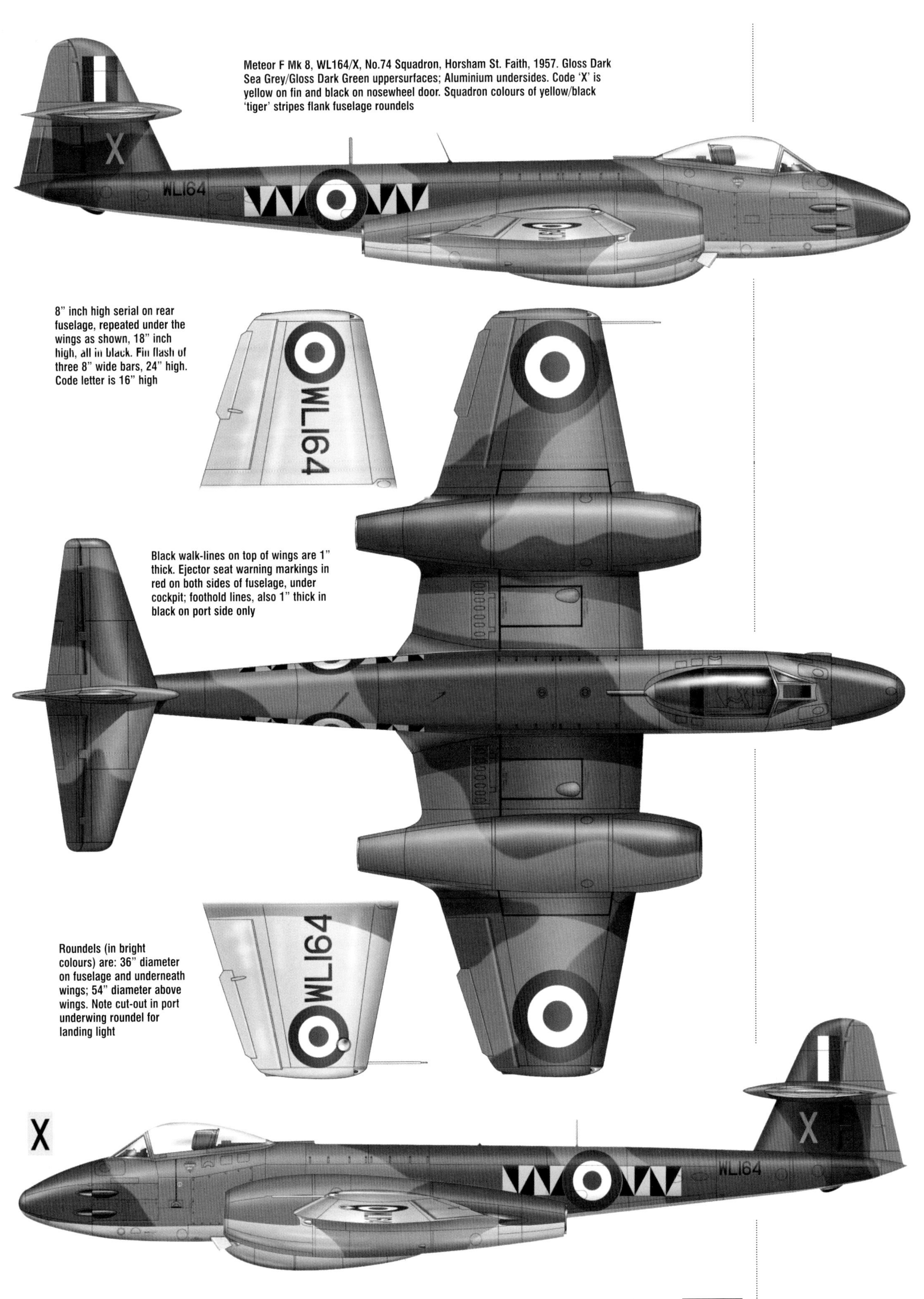

Meteor F Mk 8, WL164/X, No.74 Squadron, Horsham St. Faith, 1957. Gloss Dark Sea Grey/Gloss Dark Green uppersurfaces; Aluminium undersides. Code 'X' is yellow on fin and black on nosewheel door. Squadron colours of yellow/black 'tiger' stripes flank fuselage roundels

8" inch high serial on rear fuselage, repeated under the wings as shown, 18" inch high, all in black. Fin flash of three 8" wide bars, 24" high. Code letter is 16" high

Black walk-lines on top of wings are 1" thick. Ejector seat warning markings in red on both sides of fuselage, under cockpit; foothold lines, also 1" thick in black on port side only

Roundels (in bright colours) are: 36" diameter on fuselage and underneath wings; 54" diameter above wings. Note cut-out in port underwing roundel for landing light

 Scale 1:72

Royal Air Force Meteor Squadron Markings

No.2 Squadron

No.5 Squadron

No.8 Squadron

No.11 Squadron

No.19 Squadron

No.25 Squadron

No.29 Squadron

No.33 Squadron

No.39 Squadron

No.41 Squadron

No.43 Squadron

No.46 Squadron

No.54 Squadron

No.60 Squadron

No.63 Squadron

No.64 Squadron

No.65 Squadron

Note: These markings do not cover all markings carried by T Mk 7s operating in the secondary role with other squadrons

No.66 Squadron (early version)

No.66 Squadron (late version)

No.68 Squadron

No.72 Squadron

No.74 Squadron

No.85 Squadron

No.87 Squadron

No.92 Squadron

No.96 Squadron

Royal Air Force Meteor Squadron Markings

No.111 Squadron

No.256 Squadron

No.604 Squadron

No.141 Squadron

No.257 Squadron

No.608 Squadron

No.125 Squadron

No.263 Squadron

No.609 Squadron

No.151 Squadron

No.264 Squadron

No.610 Squadron

No.152 Squadron

No.500 Squadron

No.611 Squadron

No.153 Squadron

No.504 Squadron

No.615 Squadron

No.208 Squadron

No.600 Squadron

No.616 Squadron

No.219 Squadron

No.601 Squadron

No.2 Air Navigation School

No.245 Squadron

Note: These markings do not cover all markings carried by T Mk 7s operating in the secondary role with other squadrons

No.2 Armament Practice School

Modeller's Cross-reference Colour Chart

COLOUR	FS 595A	BS or RAL	USE	AVAILABLE PAINTS
Royal Air Force				
Dark Green	~4079		Topside Camouflage	AeroMaster Warbird Enamel: 9111, Dark Green
			with Ocean Grey or	AeroMaster Warbird Acrylic: 1111, Dark Green
			Dark Sea Grey	Aster: 310, Dark Green
				Compucolor: CAC2, Forest Green
	~4079			Floquil: M196, Dark Green 34079
	~4079			Floquil: 3143, British Dark Green 34079
				Humbrol Authentic: HG02, Dark Green RLM71
	~4079			Humbrol Authentic: HU07, Green 34079
	~4079			Lifecolor: UA001, Dark Green
	~4079			MisterKit: RAF04, Dark Green
				ModelMaster: 1710, Dark Green
	~4079			Mr Color: 309, Dark Green FS34079
				Pactra: M5
	~4079			Pactra Acrylics: A29, Jungle Green FS34079
				Polly-S: 835, Forest Green
				Polly-S: 814 Dark Green
	~4079			Polly-S Acrylic: Dark Green 34079
	~4079			Polly-S Enamel: Dark Green 34079
				Revell: 68, Dark Green
				Tamiya: XF58, Olive Green
				Vallejo Model Air: 012, Dark Green
	~4079			Xtracolor: X110, Forest Green FS14079
		451		Xtracolor: X1 Dark Green (BS451)
Sky			Undersurfaces, Codes	AeroMaster Warbird Enamel: 9114
			and Fuselage Bands	AeroMaster Warbird Acrylic: 1114
				Aster: 332, Sky Type S
	~4424			Compucolor: CAS10, Light Grey Green
	~4424			Gunze Sangyo Acrylic: H074, Sky
		210		Humbrol Authentic: HB05, Sky Type S
	~4424			Lifecolor: UA095, Sky
	~4424			MisterKit: RAF17, Sky
	~4424			Monogram-Promodeler Acrylic: 88-0038
	~4424			Polly Scale Acrylic: 505254
	~4424			Polly-S Acrylic: 500108
				Revell: 59 Sky
	~4454			Tamiya: XF21, Sky
				Vallejo Model Air: 009, Duck Egg Green
		210		Xtracolor: X7, Sky
Medium Sea			Undersurface & Code Letters	AeroMaster Warbird Enamel: 9113
Grey				AeroMaster Warbird Acrylic: 1113
				Aster: 317 Medium Grey
	~6270			Compucolor: CAC28, Neutral Grey
	~6270			Floquil: M206, Neutral Grey
	~6270			Floquil Enamel: 3151, Sea Grey, Medium
		640		Gunze Sangyo Acrylic: Medium Sea Grey
	~6270			Gunze Sangyo Acrylic: Grey
	~6270			Humbrol Authentic: HF04, Gris Bleu Clair
	~6440			Humbrol Authentic: HB06, Sea Grey Medium
	~6270			Humbrol Authentic: USN2, Medium Grey
		637		Humbrol Super Enamel: No.165, Medium Sea Grey
	~6270			Lifecolor: UA094, Medium Sea Grey
	~6270			MisterKit: RAF03, Medium Sea Grey
				ModelMaster: 1725, Neutral Grey
	~6293			Polly Scale: 505258, Sea Grey, Medium
	~6293			Polly-S Acrylic: British Sea Grey, Medium
	~6270			Replicolor: Grey
				Revell: 73, Medium Sea Grey
	~6424			Tamiya: XF20, Medium Grey
	~6375			Vallejo Model Air: 050, Light Grey
	~6270			Xtracolor: X133, Neutral Grey (FS 16270)
		637		Xtracolor: X3, Medium Sea Grey
Ocean Grey			Uppersurface camouflage	AeroMaster Warbird Enamel: 9112, Ocean Grey
			with Dark Green	AeroMaster Warbird Acrylic: 1112, Ocean Grey
	~6152			Floquil: 3149, Ocean Grey
	~6152			Humbrol Authentic: HN02, Dark Grey
				Humbrol Super Enamels: No.106, Ocean Grey
	~6187			Lifecolor: UA093 Ocean Grey
	~6187			Polly-S: 823, Ocean Grey
	~5237			Polly-S: 5256, Ocean Grey
				Revell: 72, Ocean Grey
				Xtracolor: X6, Ocean Grey
Dark Sea Grey			Uppersurface camouflage	AeroMaster Warbird Enamel: 9122
			with Dark Green	AeroMaster Warbird Acrylic: 1122
				Aster: 316, Sea Grey
				Aster (Acrylic): 613, Matt Sea Grey
				Gunze Sangyo: H75
				Humbrol: 164, Dark Sea Grey
				LifeColor: UA108, Dark Sea Grey
				ModelMaster (Acrylic): 50125, RAF Dark Sea Grey
				ModelMaster (Enamel): 2059, RAF Dark Sea Grey
				Polly Scale (Acrylic): 505264
	~6176			Vallejo Model Air: 048, Dark Sea Grey
				Xtracolor: X4, Dark Sea Grey
Light Aircraft	~6440		Post-1966 in place of	AeroMaster Warbird Color: 9056, Gull Grey
Grey	~6440		Aluminium overall	AeroMaster Warbird Acrylic: 1056, Gull Grey
	~6440			Humbrol: 129, US Gull Grey
	~6440			Gunze Sangyo Aqueous: H325, Grey FS26440
	~6440			ModelMaster Acrylic: 50130, Gull Grey (ANA602)
	~6440			ModelMaster: 1730, Gull Grey (ANA602)
	~6440			Monogram ProModeler Acrylic: 88-0033
	~6440			Pactra Acrylics: A43, Gull Grey
	~6440			Polly S: 500825, Gull Grey (ANA602)
	~6440			Polly Scale: 505090, Gull Grey (ANA602)
	~6440			Tamiya: XF20, Medium Grey
	~6440			Vallejo Model Air: 045, US Light Grey
		BS627		Xtracolor: X015, Light Aircraft Grey
Extra Dark			Uppersurfaces over Sky	AeroMaster Warbird Acrylic: 1118
Sea Grey	~6118			Compucolor: CAC16, Gunship Grey
	~6118			Floquil: M204, Sea Grey
	~6118			Floquil Classic: 3157, Extra Dark Sea Grey
	~6118			Gunze Sangyo Acrylic: H032, Field Grey
	~6118			Gunze Sangyo Acrylic: H072, Dark Sea Grey
	~6118			Gunze Sangyo Acrylic: H305, Grey
	~6118	638		Gunze Sangyo Acrylic: H331, Dark Sea Grey
	~6118			Humbrol Authentic: HF05, Gris Blue Fonce
	~6118			Humbrol Authentic: HM04, German Panzer Grey
	~6118			Humbrol Authentic: HU03, Neutral Grey
	~6118			Humbrol Authentic: HU22, Blue Grey ANA 603
	~6118			Humbrol Authentic: USN1, Dark Grey
		638		Humbrol Super Enamel: No.123, Extra Dark Sea Grey
	~6118			Lifecolor: UA0022, Dark Grey
	~6118			ModelMaster: 1723, Gunship Grey
	~6118			Mr Color: 305, Grey
	~6118			Polly-S: 822, Sea Grey
	~6118			Polly-S Acrylic: 5264, Extra Dark Sea Grey
	~6118			Vallejo Model Air: 053, Dark Sea Grey
	~6118			Xtracolor: X130, Gunship Grey
Night	~7038		Codes & Serial Numbers	AeroMaster Warbird Enamel: 9001, Black
			Target Tug undersides	Aster: 322 Black
			with Yellow	Aster (Acrylic): 616 Black
	~7038			Floquil Classic: 3010, Black
	~7038			Gunze Sangyo Acrylic: H002, Black
	~7038			Gunze Sangyo Acrylic; H012, Flat Black
	~7038			Humbrol Authentic: HB1, Night Black
	~7038			Humbrol Authentic: HU12, Night Black
		624		Humbrol Super Enamels: No.33, Black
	~7038			Lifecolor: LC02 Matt Black
	~7038			MisterKit: RAF25 Night
	~7038			ModelMaster: 1747, Gloss Black
	~7038			ModelMaster: 1749, Flat Black
	~7038			Pactra: MG61, Ebony Black
	~7038			Acrylic: A46, Black
	~7038			Polly-S: PF-10, Black
	~7038			Polly-S: 5214, Night Black
		RAL 9005		Revell: 07, Black
		RAL 9011		Revell: 08, Black
	~7038			Tamiya: X01, Black
	~7038			Tamiya: X18, Semi-gloss Black
	~7038			Tamiya: XF01, Flat Black
	~7038			Testors: 1749, Black
	~7038			Testors: 1747, Black
	7000			Vallejo Model Air: 067, Black
		624		Xtracolor: X12, Night Black
Identification	~5044		Roundels	Gunze Sangyo Acrylic: H326, Blue
Blue (Dull)		~5044		ModelMaster: 1719, Insignia Blue
	~5044			Mr Color: 326, Blue
	~5044			Tamiya: XF17, Sea Blue
	~5044			Xtracolor: X122, Insignia Blue
		110		Xtracolor: X30, RAF Roundel Blue
Identification	~5056		Post-war Roundels	Compucolor: CIS7, Insignia Blue
Blue (Bright)	~			Vallejo Model Air: 004, Blue
Identification Red (Dull)	~0109		Roundels	N/A
Identification	~7875		Roundels	AeroMaster Warbird Enamel: 9002, White
White	~7875		Post-war codes	Compucolor: CAC12, White
	~7875			Humbrol Super Enamel: No.22, White
	~7875			Humbrol Super Enamel: No.34, Matt White
	~7925			Lifecolor: LC01, Matt White
	~7778			Gunze Sangyo Acrylic: H021, Off-White
	~7875			Gunze Sangyo Acrylic: H001, White
	~7875			Gunze Sangyo Acrylic: H011, Flat White
	~7875			Humbrol Authentic: USN6, White
	~7875			ModelMaster: 1745, Insignia White
	~7875			ModelMaster: 1768, Flat White
	~7875			Mr Color: 316, White
	~7875			Pactra: MG52, Alpine White
	~7875			Pactra Acrylic: A47, White
	~7875			Polly-S: PG-10, White
	~7875			Polly-S: II-33, White
	~7875			Polly-S: PF-11, White
	~7875			Tamiya: X02, White
	~7875			Tamiya: XF02, Flat White
	~7875			Testors: 1168, White
	~7875			Vallejo Model Air: 001, White
	~7875			Xtracolor: X141, White
Aluminium			Overall Post-war	Aster: 201, Aluminium
	~7178			Compucolor: CIS12, Aluminium
				Halford Acrylic: Aluminium
				Halford Acrylic: Nissan Silver (Met)
				Humbrol Super Enamel: No.11, Silver
				Humbrol Super Enamel: No.191, Chrome Silver
	~7178			Lifecolor: LC24, Natural Metal
	~7178			ModelMaster: 1790, Chrome Silver
				ModelMaster Metalizer: 1401 Aluminium Plate
	~7178			Polly-S: IJ-17
	~7178			Tamiya: XF16, Flat Aluminium
	~7178			Testors: 1146, Aluminium
		RAL9006		Vallejo Model Air: 062, Aluminium
	~7178			Xtracolor: X142, Aluminium
Identification			Markings, Wing	AeroMaster Warbird Enamel: 9003, Yellow
Yellow	~3538		Leading Edges,	Gunze Sangyo Acrylic: H024, Orange Yellow
	~3538		Target Tug undersides	Gunze Sangyo Acrylic: H329, Yellow
			with Night & Trainer bands	Humbrol Super Enamel: No.24, Trainer Yellow
				Humbrol Super Enamel: No.154, Insignia Yellow
	~3538			Lifecolor: UA140, RLM 04 Yellow
	~3538			ModelMaster: 1707, Chrome Yellow
	~3538			ModelMaster: 1708, Insignia Yellow
	~3538			Pactra Acrylics: A27, Flat Yellow
	~3538			Polly-S: F-3, Yellow
	~3538			Polly-S: PF-40, Yellow
	~3538			Testors: 1169, Yellow
	~3538			Vallejo Model Air: 002, Yellow
				Xtracolor: X11, Trainer Yellow
	~3538			Xtracolor: X106, Insignia Yellow
PR Blue			Undersurfaces on PR aircraft	AeroMaster Warbird Acrylic: 1117, PR Blue
				Model Master Enamel: 2061, RAF PRU Blue
				Polly-S (Acrylic): 505268 RAF PRU Blue
		636		Xtracolor: X8, PR Blue
Dayglo Orange			Hi-Vis Markings	Gunze Sangyo Aqueous: H98, Fluorescent Orange
	~8903			Lifecolor: LC23, Fluorescent Orange
	~8913			ModelMaster: 2041, Fluorescent Red-Orange

ARGENTINA - Fuerza Aérea Argentina (Argentine Air Force)

COLOUR	FS 595A	BS or RAL	USE	AVAILABLE PAINTS
Aluminium	~7178		Overall	See entry under 'Royal Air Force' section
Dark Green	~4079		Uppersurface camouflage over Ocean Grey	See entry under 'Royal Air Force' section
Ocean Grey			Upper surface camouflage with Dark Green	See entry under 'Royal Air Force' section
Middle Blue			Undersurfaces & Roundels	Humbrol: 89, Middle Blue
White	~7875		Roundels & Codes	See entry under 'Royal Air Force' section

AUSTRALIA - Royal Australian Air Force (RAAF)

COLOUR	FS 595A	BS or RAL	USE	AVAILABLE PAINTS
Aluminium	~7178		Overall	See entry under 'Royal Air Force' section
White	~7875		Roundels & Codes	See entry under 'Royal Air Force' section
Dayglo Orange			Hi-Vis Markings & Drones	See entry under 'Royal Air Force' section

BELGIUM - Force Aérienne Belge (Belgian Air Force)

Meteors were delivered to this country in standard RAF schemes. Therefore see the entries for Ocean Grey, Dark Green, Medium Sea Grey and Aluminium in the 'Royal Air Force' section.

COLOUR	FS 595A	BS or RAL	USE	AVAILABLE PAINTS
Red	~1105		Roundels	Gunze Sangyo Acrylic: H003, Red
	~1105			Gunze Sangyo Acrylic: H013, Flat Red
	~1105			Humbrol Authentic: HM09, Scarlet
				Humbrol Super Enamel: No.19, Bright Red
		RAL 3000		Revell: 31, Fiery Red
	~1105			Tamiya: X07, Red
				Testors: 1503, Red
Identification Yellow	~3538		Wing & Fuselage Bands	See entry under 'Royal Air Force' section
Yellow			Roundels	Gunze Sangyo Acrylic: H004, Yellow
	~3655			Humbrol Authentic: HT06, Insignia Yellow
				Humbrol Super Enamel: No.69, Lemon Yellow
		RAL 1026		Revell: Luminous Yellow
	~3655			Tamiya: XF00, Lemon Yellow
	~3655			Tamiya: XF03, Flat Yellow
				Testors: 1514, Yellow
	~3655			Xtracolor: X108, Blue Angels Yellow FS13655
Black	~7038		Codes	See entry under 'Royal Air Force' section

BRAZIL - Força Aérea Brasileira (Brazilian Air Force)

COLOUR	FS 595A	BS or RAL	USE	AVAILABLE PAINTS
Tan	~0219		Uppersurface camouflage with Medium & Dark Green	AeroMaster Warbird Acrylics: 1059, Dark Tan
	~0219			Floquil Classic Enamel: 303345, Dark Tan
	~0219			Gunze Sangyo Aqueous: H310, Brown FS30219
				Humbrol: 119, Matt Light Earth
	~0219			Model Master Acrylic: 50142, Dark Tan
	~0219			Model Master Enamel: 1742, Dark Tan
	~0219			Polly Scale: 505392, Dark Tan
	~0219			Polly-S: 500816, Dark Tan
	~0219			Tamiya: XF52, Flat Earth
	~0219			Vallejo Model Air: 026, US Flat Brown
Medium Green	~4187		Uppersurface camouflage with Tan & Dark Green	ModelMaster Enamel: 2028, Willow Green
				Xtracolor: X151, Willow Green (ANA503)
Dark Green	~4079		Uppersurface camouflage with Tan & Medium Green	See entry under 'Royal Air Force' section

CANADA - Royal Canadian Air Force

Meteors were delivered to this country in standard RAF schemes. Therefore see the entries for Dark Green, Ocean Grey, Medium Sea Grey and Dark Sea Grey in the 'Royal Air Force' section.

DENMARK - Royal Danish Air Force

COLOUR	FS 595A	BS or RAL	USE	AVAILABLE PAINTS
Dark Green	~4079		Uppersurface camouflage over Medium Sea Grey	See entry under 'Royal Air Force' section
Medium Sea Grey	~6270		Overall or on Undersurfaces	See entry under 'Royal Air Force' section
Dark Sea Grey			Upper surface camouflage with Dark Green	See entry under 'Royal Air Force' section

ECUADOR - Fuerza Aérea Ecuatoriana (Ecuadorian Air Force)

COLOUR	FS 595A	BS or RAL	USE	AVAILABLE PAINTS
Aluminium	~7178		Overall colour	See entry under 'Royal Air Force' section

EGYPT - (Royal) Egyptian Air Force

COLOUR	FS 595A	BS or RAL	USE	AVAILABLE PAINTS
Aluminium	~7178		Overall colour	See entry under 'Royal Air Force' section

FRANCE - Armée de l'Air

COLOUR	FS 595A	BS or RAL	USE	AVAILABLE PAINTS
Dark Green	~4079		Uppersurface camouflage with Medium Sea Grey	See entry under 'Royal Air Force' section
Medium Sea Grey	~6270		Uppersurface camouflage with Dark Green	See entry under 'Royal Air Force' section
Gloss Olive	~4128		Nacelles of CEV NF.11s	Lifecolor: UA146, French Green
Green	~4128			Tamiya: XF26, Deep Green
Dayglo Orange			Hi-Vis Markings	See entry under 'Royal Air Force' section

ISRAEL - Israeli Defence Force (Air Force)

Meteors were delivered to this country in standard RAF schemes. Therefore see the entries for Dark Green, Ocean Grey, Medium Sea Grey and Dark Sea Grey in the 'Royal Air Force' section.

COLOUR	FS 595A	BS or RAL	USE	AVAILABLE PAINTS
Brown	~0219		Uppersurface camouflage with Dark Blue	AeroMaster Warbird Acrylics: 1059, Dark Tan
	~0219			Floquil Classic Enamel: 303345, Dark Tan
	~0219			Gunze Sanyo Aqueous: H310, Brown FS30219
				Humbrol: 119, Matt Light Earth
	~0219			ModelMaster Acrylic: 50142, Dark Tan
	~0219			ModelMaster Enamel: 1742, Dark Tan
	~0219			Polly Scale: 505392, Dark Tan
	~0219			Polly-S: 500816, Dark Tan
	~0219			Tamiya: XF52, Flat Earth
	~0219			Vallejo Model Air: 026, US Flat Brown
Dark Blue		RAL 5008	Upper surface camouflage with Brown	N/A
Oxford Blue	~5044		Uppersurface camouflage with Dark Earth on NF.13s	Gunze Sangyo Aqueous: H326, Blue FS15044
				Humbrol: 189, Oxford Blue
	~5044			ModelMaster Enamel: 1719, Insignia Blue
	~5044			Polly Scale Acrylic: 505023, Insignia Blue
	~5044			Polly-S Acrylic: 500878, Insignia Blue
	~5044			Tamiya: XF17, Sea Blue
	~5044			Xtracolor: X122, Insignia Blue
Light Grey	~6492		Undersurfaces	Compucolour: CAC29, Light Grey
				Humbrol Authentic: HJ02, Grey A/N2
Dark Grey	~6081		Undersurfaces	Compucolor: CAC14, Dark Grey
	~6081			Floquil Classic Enamel: 303384, Euro 1 Grey
	~6081			Gunze Sangyo Aqueous: H339, Engine Grey FS16081
	~6081			Gunze Sangyo Aqueous: H068, RLM 74
	~6081			Gunze Sangyo Aqueous: H301, Grey FS36081
	~6081			Humbrol Authentics: HG04, RLM 74
	~6081			Humbrol: 32, Matt Dark Grey
	~6081			ModelMasterAcrylic: 50188, Dark Grey FS36081
	~6081			ModelMaster Enamel: 1788, Dark Grey FS36081
	~6081			Mr Color: 339, Engine Grey FS16081
	~6081			Mr Color: 301, Grey FS36081
	~6081			Polly-S: 500822, Dark Grey FS36081
	~6081			Polly Scale: 505204, Dark Grey FS36081
	~6081			Tamiya: XF63, German Grey
	~6081			Vallejo Model Air: 055, RLM 66/FS36081
	~6081			Xtracolor: X129, Dark Grey FS16081
Extra Dark Sea Grey	~6118		Undersurfaces (NF.13s)	AeroMaster Warbird Acrylic: 1057, Neutral Grey
	~6118			AeroMaster Warbird Enamels: 9050, Gunship Grey
	~6118			Compucolor: CAC10, Gunship Grey
	~6118			Floquil Classic Enamel: 303333, Gunship Grey
	~6118			Gunze Sangyo Aqueous: H032, Field Grey
	~6118			Gunze Sangyo Aqueous: H075, Dark Sea Grey
	~6118			Gunze Sangyo Aqueous: H305, Grey FS36118
		BS638		Gunze Sangyo Aqueous: H331, Dark Sea Grey
	~6118			Humbrol Authentic: HF05, Gris-Bleu Fonce
	~6118			Humbrol Authentic: HM04, German Panzer Grey
	~6118			Humbrol Authentic: HU03, Neutral Grey 43
	~6118			Humbrol Authentic: HU22, Blue Grey ANA603
	~6118			Humbrol Authentic: USN1, Dark Grey 36118
	~6118			Humbrol: 125, US Dark Grey
	~6118			ModelMaster Acrylic: 50123, Gunship Grey
	~6118			ModelMaster Enamel: 1723, Gunship Grey
	~6118			Monogram ProModeler: 88-00037, Neutral Grey
	~6118			Mr Color: 822, Grey FS36118
	~6118			Polly-S: 500822, Sea Grey
	~6118			Polly Scale: 505382, Gunship Grey
	~6118			Tamiya: XF53, Neutral Grey
		BS640		Xtracolor: X005, Extra Dark Sea Grey BS640
	~6118			Xtracolor: X130, Gunship Grey FS16118
Aluminium	~7178		Overall	See entry under 'Royal Air Force' section
White	~7875		Roundels & Codes	See entry under 'Royal Air Force' section
Dayglo Orange			Hi-Vis Markings	See entry under 'Royal Air Force' section

THE NETHERLANDS - Royal Netherlands Air Force and Royal Netherlands Navy

COLOUR	FS 595A	BS or RAL	USE	AVAILABLE PAINTS
Dark Green	~4079		Uppersurface camouflage with Dark Sea Grey	See entry under 'Royal Air Force' section
Dark Sea Grey			Uppersurface camouflage with Dark Green	See entry under 'Royal Air Force' section
Aluminium	~7178		Overall	See entry under 'Royal Air Force' section
Identification Yellow	~3538		Band on Trainer A/C	See entry under 'Royal Air Force' section
Light Blue			Squadron Colour	Roundel Blue(*) with 50% white * See entry under 'Royal Air Force' section
White	~7875		Roundels & Codes	See entry under 'Royal Air Force' section

NEW ZEALAND - Royal New Zealand Air Force (RNZAF)

Meteors were delivered to this country in standard RAF schemes. Therefore see the entries for Dark Green, Ocean Grey, Medium Sea Grey and Dark Sea Grey in the 'Royal Air Force' section.

SWEDEN - Flygvapnet

Meteors were delivered to this country in standard RAF schemes. Therefore see the entries for Dark Green, Ocean Grey, Medium Sea Grey and Dark Sea Grey in the 'Royal Air Force' section.

COLOUR	FS 595A	BS or RAL	USE	AVAILABLE PAINTS
Identification White	~7875		Codes	See entry under 'Royal Air Force' section
Identification Yellow	~3538		Codes	See entry under 'Royal Air Force' section
Yellow	~3655		Overall	Humbrol Authentic: HT06, Insignia Yellow
	~3655			Tamiya: X08, Lemon Yellow
	~3655			Tamiya: XF03, Flat Yellow
	~3655			Xtracolor: X108, Blue Angels Yellow FS13655
Black	~7038		Codes (on Yellow)	See entry under 'Royal Air Force' section

SYRIA - Syrian Air Force

COLOUR	FS 595A	BS or RAL	USE	AVAILABLE PAINTS
Dark Green	~4079		Uppersurface camouflage with Light Earth	See entry under 'Royal Air Force' section
Light Earth	~0257		Uppersurface camouflage with Dark Green	N/A
Sky Blue	~5622		Undersurfaces	Compucolor: CAC21, Pale Blue
	~5622			Floquil: M203, Pale Blue
	~5622			Gunze Sangyo Acrylic: H314, Blue
	~5622			Humbrol Authentic: IAF4, Pale Blue
	~5622			ModelMaster: 1722, Duck Egg Blue
	~5622			Mr Color: 314, Blue
	~5622			Pactra: M4, Artillery Olive
	~5622			Polly-S: 877, Blue
Aluminium	~7178		Overall colour	See entry under 'Royal Air Force' section
White	~7875		Roundels	See entry under 'Royal Air Force' section

NOTE

The above listed references to Federal Standard (FS 595A) numbers do not include the prefix number. This just denotes the sheen of the colour e.g. 1=Gloss, 2=Semi-gloss and 3=Matt.

The above list has been compiled using manufacturers' paint lists and in conjunction with the Testors Modelers' Technical Guide and the IPMS Color Cross-Reference Guide by David Klaus. Although every care has been taken to offer modellers the broadest spectrum of appropriate colours, further research for each scheme is advisable.

Although the correct term for many American shades would be 'Gray' we have used 'Grey' throughout for consistency.

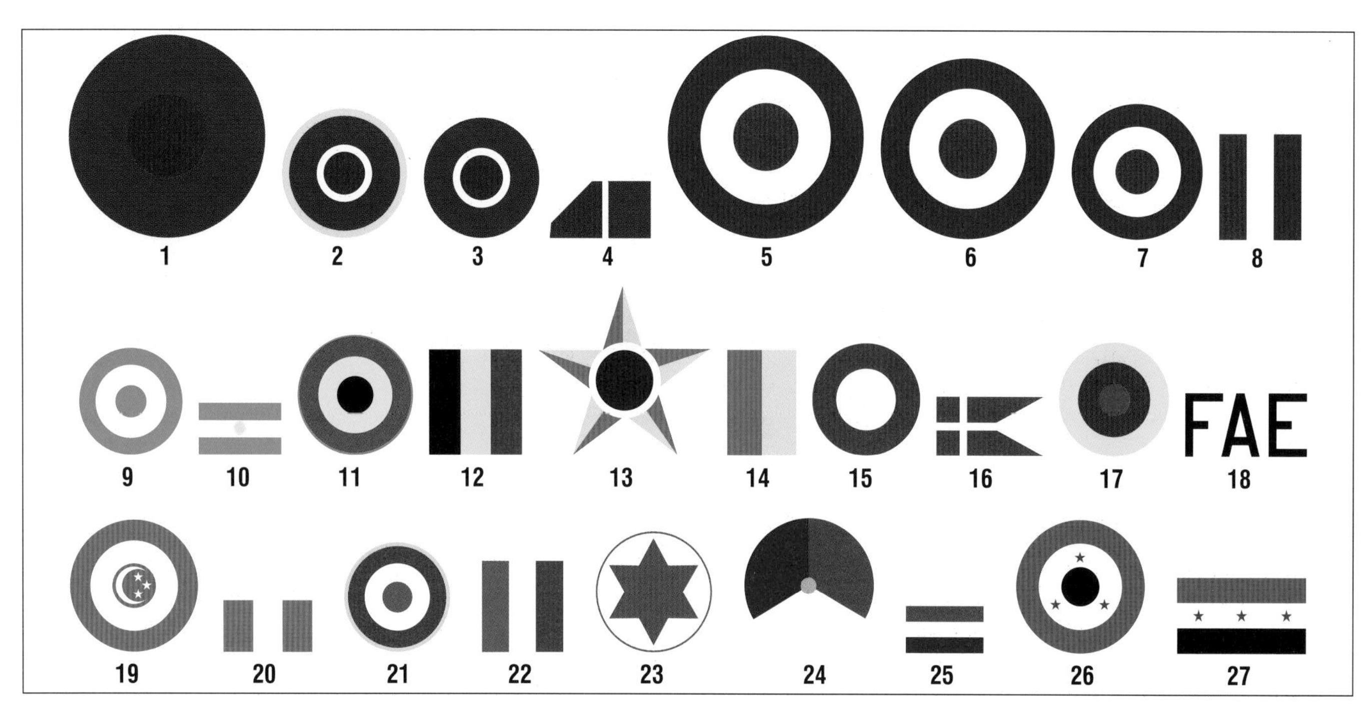

RAF/RN Markings
1 54" Overwing B Type Roundel (Dull Colours)
2 36" Fuselage C1 Type Roundel (Dull Colours)
3 32" C Type Underwing Roundel (Dull Colours); 48" Overwing when replacing B Type
4 11"x2"x11" Fin Flash (Dull Colours)
5 54" Overwing Post-War Roundel (Bright Colours)
6 48" Overwing Post-War Roundel - two-seat versions except T.7 (Bright Colours)
7 36" Fuselage & Underwing Post-War Roundel (Bright Colours)
8 8"x8"x8"x24" Post-War Fin Flash (Bright Colours)

Other Operators
9 Argentinian Air Force Roundel (six positions)
10 Argentinian Air Force Fin Flash
11 Royal Belgian Air Force Roundel (outer mid-blue on fuselage and above wing only)
12 Royal Belgian Air Force Fin Flash
13 Brazilian Air Force Wing Insignia
14 Brazilian Air Force Fin Flash
15 Royal Danish Air Force Roundel
16 Royal Danish Air Force Fin Flash
17 Ecuadorian Air Force Roundel (top of port wing)
18 Ecuadorian Air Force Insignia (above starboard wing)
19 Royal Egyptian Air Force Roundel
20 Royal Egyptian Air Force Fin Flash
21 French Air Force Roundel
22 French Air Force Fin Flash
23 Israeli Air Force Roundel (blue outline on Aluminium finish only)
24 Royal Netherlands Air Force Roundel
25 Royal Netherlands Air Force Fin Flash
26 Syrian Air Force Roundel
27 Syrian Air Force Fin Flash

probably the aircraft that carried the widest variety, and an extensive selection of these markings is reproduced on two full pages in this section.

Night fighter versions of the Gloster Meteor were finished in a similar camouflage scheme to that carried by the F Mk 8s, in Gloss Dark Green (BS381C: 641) and Gloss Dark Sea Grey (BS381C: 638) for the upper surfaces. However, undersides were always finished in Medium Sea Grey. Eventually, most Meteors NF Mk 11, 12 and 13 did not have the Dark Sea Grey of the upper surfaces applied; it would appear from photographic evidence that the NF Mk 14s retained both top colours throughout their service life. Underwing serials were carried as standard, however, no underwing roundels were ever carried by NF Meteors.

Meteors used for training purposes wore a variety of finishes, changing through the long period that these remained in service. Originally they were finished in Aluminium overall and had 36in (91.4cm) wide bands in Yellow applied to the outer wing panels, just outboard of the engine nacelles. These, however, did not overlap onto the ailerons, and a rectangular 'cut-out' was produced around the underside serial numbers. Dayglo Orange was, at times, generously applied as from the mid-1950s and although flying schools and training establishments carried fairly standard markings, those T Mk 7s assigned to operational squadrons carried a variety of finishes and markings, including their squadron's colours flanking the fuselage roundel. Most Meteors still operational after 1968 had their Aluminium finish replaced by Light Grey.

NF Mk 11, EN-11, KT•T seen at Ostend airfield in 1958. By this time this machine had been sold, and as you can see civil registration (OO-ARX) had been applied *(©via Rudy Binnemans)*

Towards the end of their front-line service, a number of Meteors were converted to target-towing duties, invariably finished Aluminium overall. Target tug Yellow/Night stripes were applied to the undersides while the fixed part of the elevators was painted Night, their movable surfaces in Yellow. Trainer-style bands in Yellow were also applied to the top of the outer wing panels. Dayglo Orange appeared around 1962, this being applied to the nose, wingtips and rear fuselage. This weathered very quickly to a yellowish tint and as a replacement, strips of self-adhesive dayglo film were applied instead.

Exported Meteors in many cases retained their original colours, although the respective air arms at times touched up or even repainted them altogether. Such changes are described in the captions of the individual colour profiles (see opposite).

A wheels-up landing for F Mk 4, EF-3 at Koksyde in 1955. This is one of two F MK 4s (the other being EF-24) that received NATO camouflage and markings *(©via Rudy Binnemans)*

This FR Mk 9 was operated by No.2 Squadron and although the codes are not visible here, this machine is WB116 with the code letter 'G' on the tail. It had previously carried the code B-G and it eventually ended up at No.10 SoTT as Inst. Airframe 7384M
(© R.J. Caruana)

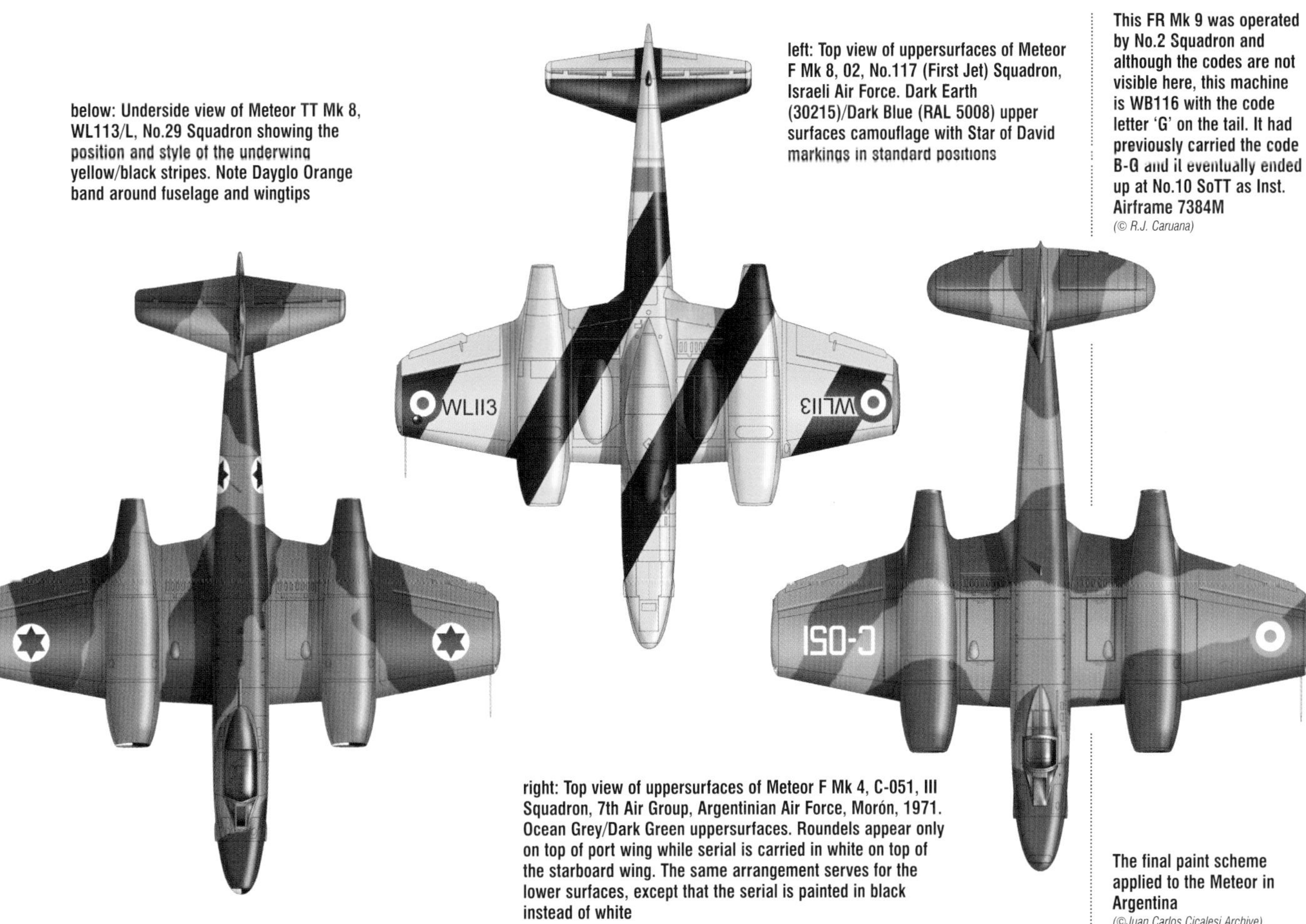

below: Underside view of Meteor TT Mk 8, WL113/L, No.29 Squadron showing the position and style of the underwing yellow/black stripes. Note Dayglo Orange band around fuselage and wingtips

left: Top view of uppersurfaces of Meteor F Mk 8, 02, No.117 (First Jet) Squadron, Israeli Air Force. Dark Earth (30215)/Dark Blue (RAL 5008) upper surfaces camouflage with Star of David markings in standard positions

right: Top view of uppersurfaces of Meteor F Mk 4, C-051, III Squadron, 7th Air Group, Argentinian Air Force, Morón, 1971. Ocean Grey/Dark Green uppersurfaces. Roundels appear only on top of port wing while serial is carried in white on top of the starboard wing. The same arrangement serves for the lower surfaces, except that the serial is painted in black instead of white

The final paint scheme applied to the Meteor in Argentina
(©Juan Carlos Cicalesi Archive)

Kit Listing

MANUFACTURER	SCALE	TYPE	SUBJECT	RELEASED	NOTES
Aeroclub	1/48th	VF/IM/WM	Gloster Meteor F Mk 4		
Aeroclub	1/72nd	IM/VF/WM	Gloster Meteor F Mk 8		
Aeroclub	1/48th	VF/IM/WM	Gloster Meteor F Mk 8		
Aeroclub	1/72nd	IM/VF/WM	Gloster Meteor T Mk 7		
Aeroclub	1/48th	VF/IM/WM	Gloster Meteor T Mk 7		
Aeroclub	1/48th	VF/IM/WM	A.W. Meteor NF Mk 11		
Aeroclub	1/48th	VF/IM/WM	A.W. Meteor NF Mk 14		
Aeroclub	1/48th	VF/IM/WM	A W Meteor NF Mk 12		
Airfix	**1/72nd**	**IM**	**Gloster Meteor Mk III**	**1970**	
Air Lines	1/72nd	IM	Gloster Meteor F Mk 8	1964–66	Ex-Frog
Airmodel	1/72nd	VF	Gloster Meteor T Mk 7	1969–80	Reissued by Frank Modellbau
AMT	1/48th	IM	Gloster Meteor F Mk I	1975–77	c/w Fieseler Fi 103 (V-1)
By-Planes	1/48th	VF	Gloster Meteor F Mk 8	1976–78	See Pamela Veal & Slipstream
Classic Airframes	**1/48th**	**IM/R/EB**	**Gloster Meteor F Mk 4**	**2003**	
Classic Airframes	**1/48th**	**IM/R/EB**	**Gloster Meteor F Mk 8**	**2003**	
Classic Airframes	**1/48th**	**IM/R/EB**	**Gloster Meteor F Mk 8**	**2004**	**Early Version**
Classic Airframes	**1/48th**	**IM/R/EB**	**Gloster Meteor FR Mk 9**	**2004**	
Classic Airframes	**1/48th**	**IM/R/EB**	**Gloster Meteor T Mk 7**	**2004**	
Classic Airframes	1/48th	IM/R/EB	A.W. Meteor NF Mk 11/13	Due 2004	
Classic Airframes	1/48th	IM/R/EB	A.W. Meteor NF Mk 12/14	Due 2004	
CzechMaster Resin	**1/72nd**	**R/VF**	**Gloster Meteor F Mk 8/FR Mk 9**		
Epoxy	1/72nd	R/VF	A.W. Meteor NF Mk 11	Mid-1980s	
Frank Modellbau	1/72nd	VF	Gloster Meteor T Mk 7	1969–80	Ex-Airmodel
Frog	1/72nd	IM	Gloster Meteor F Mk 4	1970	See Footnote
Frog	1/72nd	IM	Gloster Meteor F Mk 8	1955	
Frog Penguin	1/72nd	IM	Gloster Meteor F Mk 4	1947	
Gunze Sangyo	1/72nd	IM	Gloster Meteor Mk III	1980s	Ex-Airfix
Hasegawa	1/72nd	IM	Gloster Meteor F Mk 4	1960s–70s	Ex-Frog
Hawk	1/48th	IM	Gloster Meteor	1966	
ID Models	1/32nd	VF	Gloster Meteor F Mk 8		
Matchbox	1/72nd	IM	A.W. Meteor NF Mk 11/12/14	1977	
Merlin Models	1/72nd	IM/WM/VF	Gloster Meteor F Mk 8	1984–90s	
MPM	1/72nd	IM	Gloster Meteor F Mk 8	Due 2004	
Novo	1/72nd	IM	Gloster Meteor F Mk 4	1977	Never released. Ex-Frog
Novo-Export	1/72nd	IM	Gloster Meteor F Mk 4	1982	Never released. Ex-Frog
Pamela Veal	1/48th	VF	Gloster Meteor F Mk 8	Ex-Slipstream	
Panther	1/32nd	R/VF	Gloster Meteor F Mk 8	Due 2004	
PJ Productions	**1/72nd**	**R/VF**	**Gloster Meteor F Mk 4**	**'RAF'**	
PJ Productions	**1/72nd**	**R/VF**	**Gloster Meteor F Mk 4**	**'Belgian AF'**	
PJ Productions	**1/72nd**	**R/VF**	**Gloster Meteor F Mk 8**	**'RAF'**	
PJ Productions	**1/72nd**	**R/VF**	**Gloster Meteor F Mk 8**	**'Belgian AF'**	
PJ Productions	**1/72nd**	**R/VF**	**Gloster Meteor T Mk 7**	**'RAF'**	
PJ Productions	**1/72nd**	**R/VF**	**A.W. Meteor NF Mk 11**	**'RAF'**	
PJ Productions	1/72nd	R/VF	A.W. Meteor NF Mk 11	'Belgian AF'	
PJ Productions	1/72nd	R/VF	A.W. Meteor NF Mk 11	'French AF'	
Rareplanes	1/72nd	VF	Gloster Meteor F Mk 8		
Rareplanes	1/72nd	VF	A.W. Meteor NF Mk 11/12/13/14		
Revell	1/72nd	IM	A.W. Meteor NF Mk 11/12/14	1998	Ex-Matchbox
Slipstream	1/48th	VF	Gloster Meteor F Mk 8		See also By-Planes
Tamiya	1/48th	IM	Gloster Meteor F Mk I	1998	
Tamiya	**1/48th**	**IM**	**Gloster Meteor F Mk I**	**1999**	**Revised Tooling**
Tamiya	**1/48th**	**IM**	**Gloster Meteor F Mk I**	**2000**	**Includes Fi 103 V-1**
Tamiya	**1/48th**	**IM**	**Gloster Meteor F Mk III**	**2002**	**Updated (Revised) F.I kit**
Tri-ang/Frog	1/72nd	IM	Gloster Meteor F Mk 8	1960s–71	Ex-Frog [NZ Dist of Frog]
USAirfix	1/72nd	IM	Gloster Meteor Mk III	1980–81	Ex-Airfix
Ventura	1/72nd	IM/WM/VF	Gloster Meteor F Mk 8		
Ventura	1/72nd	IM/WM/VF	Gloster Meteor T Mk 7		No confirmation of production
Welsh Models	**1/144th**	**IM/VF**	**Gloster Meteor F Mk 8**	**1984**	
Welsh Models	**1/144th**	**IM/VF**	**Gloster Meteor T Mk 7**	**1984**	
WK Model	1/72nd	R/VF	Gloster Meteor F Mk 4	1988–90s	

Note: The Frog Meteor F.4 kit has been released by a number of Russian manufacturers since the late 1970s, none of which are listed above due to the limited nature of the release and the difficulty in identifying the manufacturer's name.

KEY

IM = Injection-Moulded Plastic (Inc Limited-Run Injection-Moulded Plastic)
R = Resin
VF = Vac-formed Plastic
WM = White Metal (Inc Pewter)

Note: This list contains all known Meteor kits, along with their original release date (if known). Subsequent reissue details are not included, nor are there any listings for these kits if they were released in 'sets' or used for special promotions.

All items emboldened were still readily available in the UK at the time of writing (May 2004), although during the printing of this title some may go out of production as they may also do subsequently.

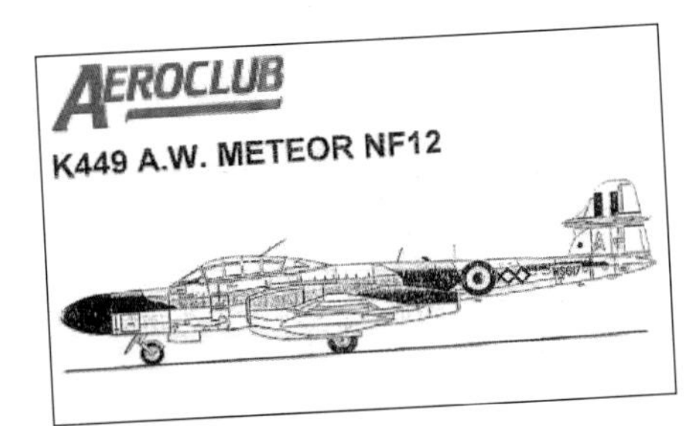

Aeroclub 1/48th NF Mk 12 (#K449)

PJ Productions F Mk 4 'RAF' (#721003)

PJ Productions F Mk 8 'RAF' (#721005)

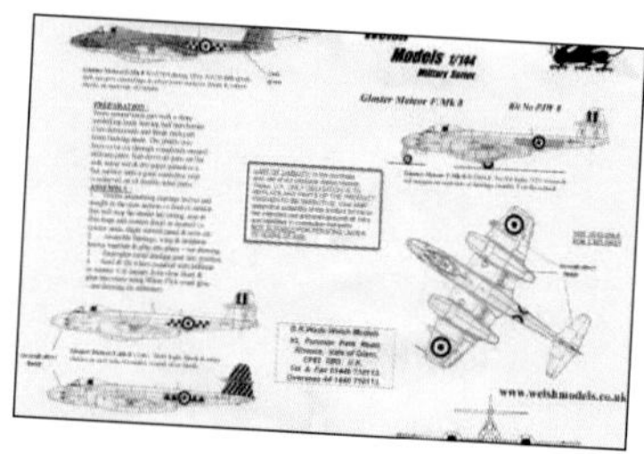

Welsh Models 1/144th Meteor F Mk 8 (#PJW8)

PJ Productions T Mk 7 'RAF' (#721009)

PJ Productions F Mk 8 'Belgian AF' (#721006)

PJ Productions NF Mk 11 'RAF' (#721011)

PJ Productions NF Mk 11 'Belgian AF' (#721012)

PJ Productions NF Mk 11 'Armée de l'Air' (#721013)

Accessories & Conversions

Appendix II

MANUFACTURER	SCALE	TYPE	PRODUCT NO	ITEM	DESIGNED FOR/NOTES
Aeroclub	1/72nd	IM/VF		Meteor T Mk 7 Conversion	Matchbox
Aeroclub	1/72nd	IM/VF/WM		Meteor F Mk 8 Conversion	Matchbox
Aeroclub	1/72nd	IM/VF/WM		Meteor F Mk 8 Conversion	Matchbox
Aeroclub	1/72nd	IM/VF/WM		Meteor FR Mk 9 Conversion	Matchbox
Aeroclub	**1/72nd**	**VF**	**C017**	**Meteor Mk I, III & IV Canopy**	
Aeroclub	**1/72nd**	**VF**	**C018**	**Meteor T Mk 7 Canopy**	
Aeroclub	**1/72nd**	**VF**	**C019**	**Meteor NF Mk 14 Canopy**	
Aeroclub	**1/72nd**	**VF**	**C020**	**Meteor F Mk 8 Canopy**	**Early & Late Types**
Aeroclub	**1/48th**	**VF**	**C070**	**Meteor F Mk I Canopy**	
Aeroclub	**1/48th**	**VF**	**C071**	**Meteor Mk III & IV Canopy**	
Aeroclub	**1/48th**	**VF**	**C088**	**Meteor F Mk 8 (Late) Canopy**	**Classic Airframes**
Aeroclub	**1/48th**	**VF**	**C089**	**Meteor T Mk 7 Canopy**	**Classic Airframes**
Aeroclub	**1/72nd**	**WM**	**EJ001**		**M-B Mk 2 Ejection Seat**
Aeroclub	**1/72nd**	**WM**	**EJ008**		**M-B Mk 3 Ejection Seat**
Aeroclub	**1/48th**	**WM**	**EJ401**		**M-B Mk 2 Ejection Seat**
Aeroclub	**1/48th**	**WM**	**EJ402**		**M-B Mk 3 Ejection Seat**
Aeroclub	**1/48th**	**R**	**EJ423**		**M-B Mk 2 Ejection Seat**
Aeroclub	**1/72nd**	**WM**	**V037**		**Gloster Meteor Undercarriage**
Aeroclub	**1/72nd**	**IM**	**V079**		**ML Type Target Tug Winch**
Aeroclub	**1/48th**	**R**	**V217**	**Meteor F Mk 8 Mainwheels**	**Classic Airframes**
Aeroclub	**1/48th**	**WM**	**V218**	**Meteor F Mk 8 Mainwheels**	**Classic Airframes**
Airmodel	1/72nd	VF	AM-144	Meteor PR Mk 10 Conversion	Airfix or Frog
Airwaves	1/72nd	EB	AC72097	Meteor NF Mk 14 Detail Set	Matchbox
Cutting Edge	**1/48th**	**Ma**	**BM48133**	**Meteor F Mk I Canopy and Wheel Masks**	**Tamiya**
Eduard	**1/48th**	**EB**	**48-211**	**Meteor F Mk I Detail Set**	**Tamiya**
Eduard	**1/48th**	**EB**	**48-213**	**Meteor F Mk III Detail Set**	**Tamiya**
Eduard	**1/48th**	**EB**	**FE116**	**Meteor F Mk I Detail Set**	**Tamiya**
Eduard	**1/48th**	**Ma**	**XF182**	**Meteor F Mk I Canopy and Wheel Masks**	**Tamiya**
E-Z Mask	**1/48th**	**Ma**	**038**	**Meteor F Mk I Canopy Mask**	**Tamiya**
Final Touch	1/72nd	R/VF		Prone Pilot Meteor Conversion	Matchbox
Intermodel	1/72nd	VF	IM-19	Meteor F Mk 8 Conversion	Frog
Neomega	**1/48th**	**R**		**M-B Mk 2 Ejection Seat**	
Squadron	**1/48th**	**VF**	**9624**	**Meteor Mk I/IV Canopy**	
Tasman	**1/72nd**	**VF**	**202**	**Meteor F Mk 8 Canopy**	
True Details	**1/48th**	**Ma**	**41045**	**Meteor F Mk I Canopy Frames**	**Tamiya**
True Details	**1/48th**	**R**	**48107**	**Meteor F Mk 1 Wheels**	**Tamiya**

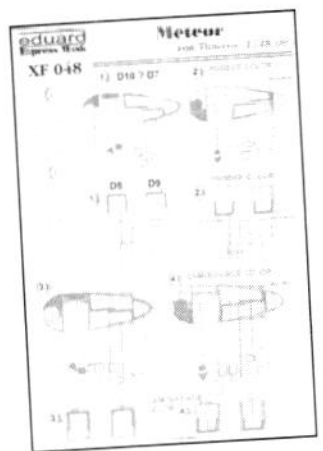
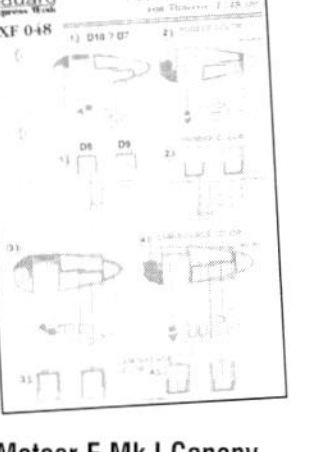

Meteor F Mk I Canopy and Wheel Masks (Eduard XF048)

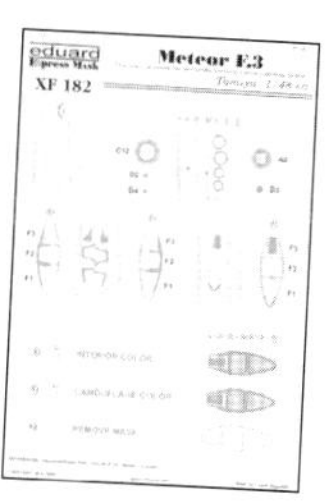
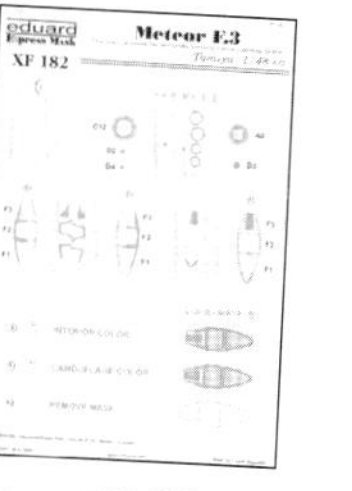

Meteor F Mk III Canopy and Wheel Masks (Eduard XF182)

KEY

A – Acetate
AC = Acetate Film
EB = Etched Brass
IM = Injection Moulded Plastic
M = Metal/Pewter
Ma = Mask (Die-Cut)
P = Paper
R = Resin
Rb = Rubber
Vi = Vinyl
VF = Vac-form Plastic

Note: All of the above emboldened items were still readily available in the UK at the time of writing (May 2004). These may, however, go out of production subsequently, so check with your local model shop for availability.

Meteor F Mk I, III & IV Canopy (Aeroclub C017)

Meteor T Mk 7 Canopy (Aeroclub C018)

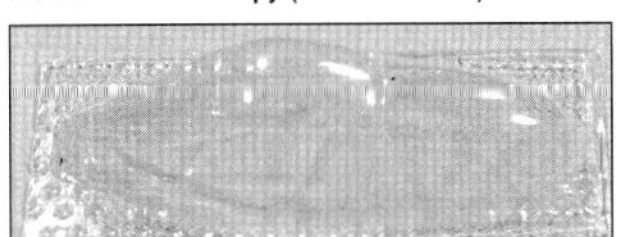

Meteor F Mk III & IV Canopy (Aeroclub C071)

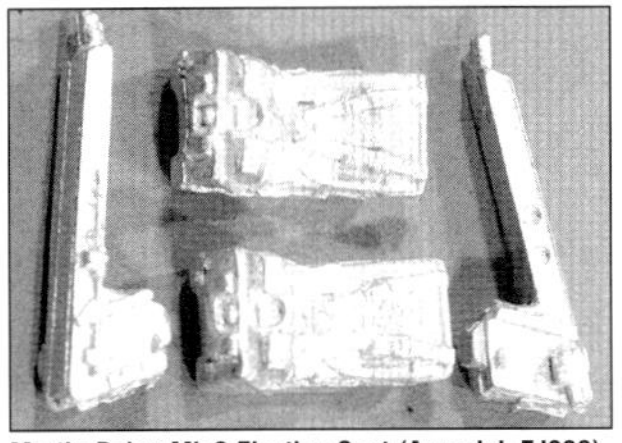

Martin-Baker Mk 3 Ejection Seat (Aeroclub EJ008)

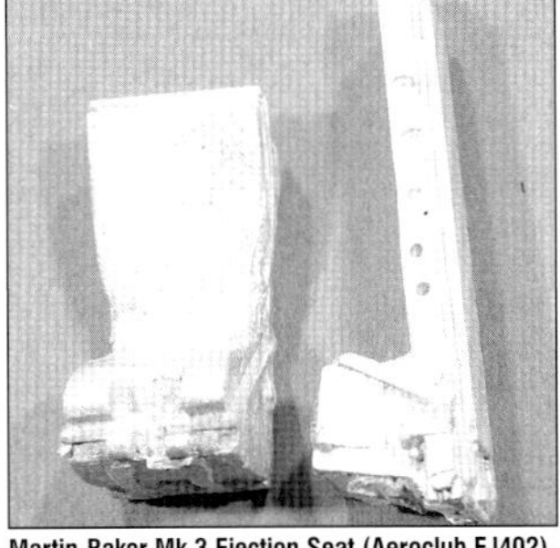

Martin-Baker Mk 3 Ejection Seat (Aeroclub EJ402)

Meteor F Mk I Detail Set (Eduard 48-211)

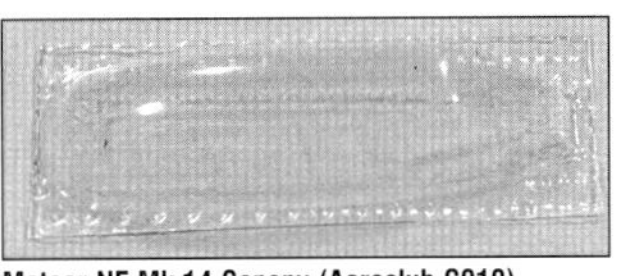

Meteor NF Mk 14 Canopy (Aeroclub C019)

Meteor F Mk 8 Late Canopy (Aeroclub C088)

Martin-Baker Mk 2 Ejection Seat (Aeroclub EJ401)

ML Type Target Tug Winch (Aeroclub V079)

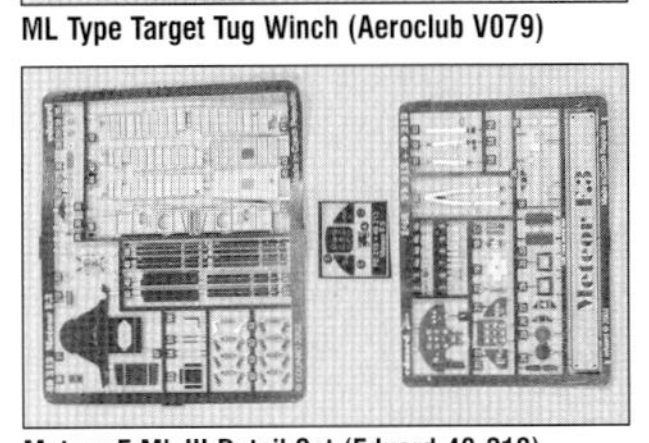

Meteor F Mk III Detail Set (Eduard 48-213)

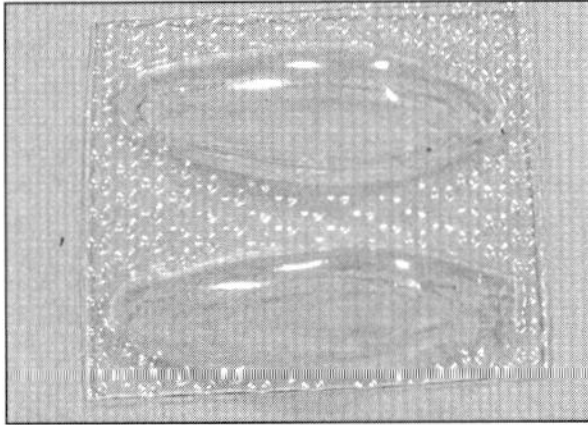

Meteor F Mk 8 Canopy 'Early & Late' (Aeroclub C020)

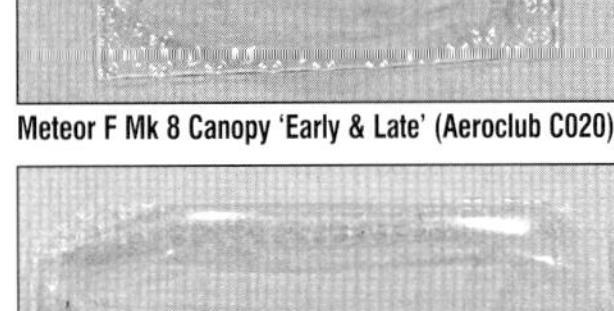

Meteor T Mk 7 Canopy (Aeroclub C089)

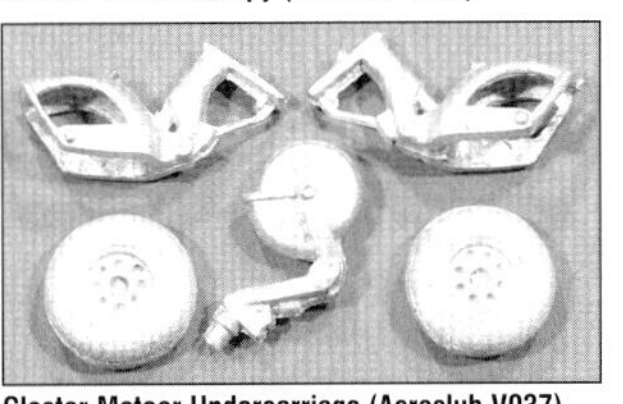

Gloster Meteor Undercarriage (Aeroclub V037)

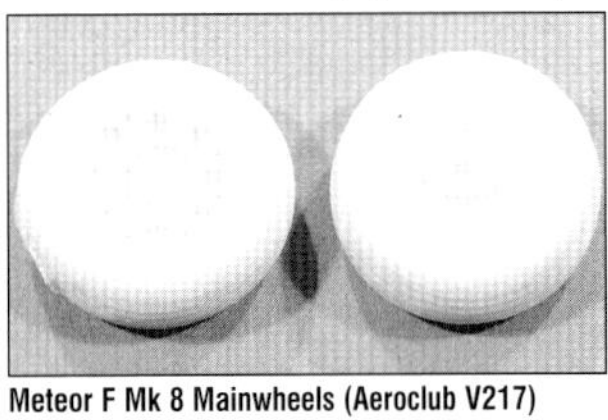

Meteor F Mk 8 Mainwheels (Aeroclub V217)

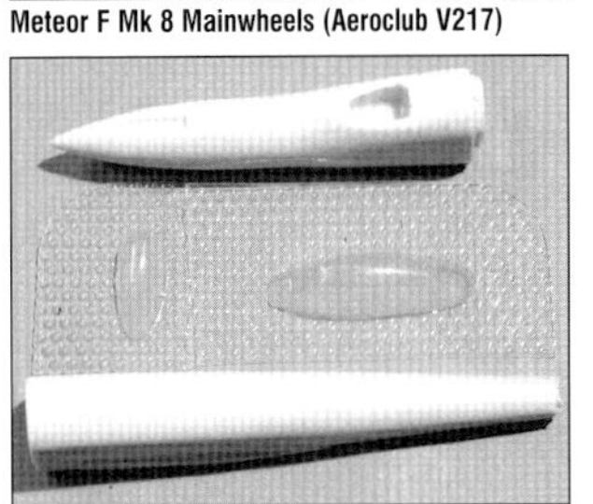

Prone Pilot Meteor Conversion (Final Touch)

Meteor F Mk I Canopy (Aeroclub C070)

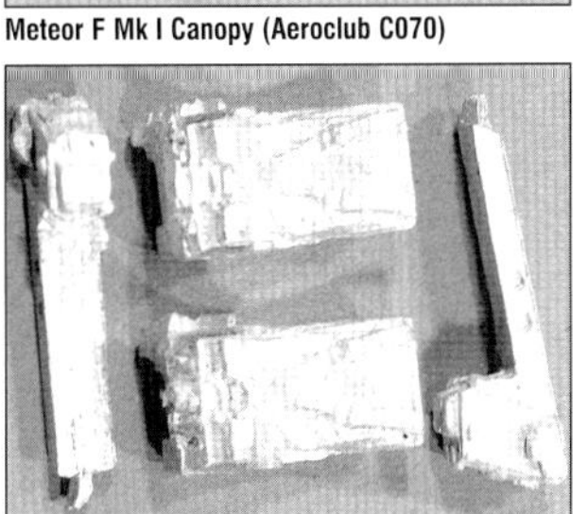

Martin-Baker Mk 2 Ejection Seat (Aeroclub EJ001)

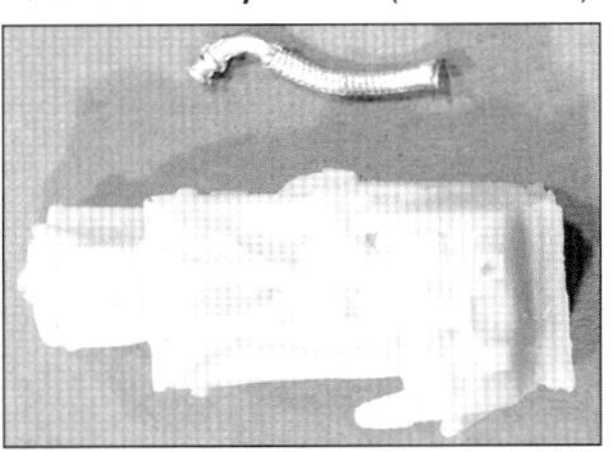

Martin-Baker Mk 2 Ejection Seat (Aeroclub EJ423)

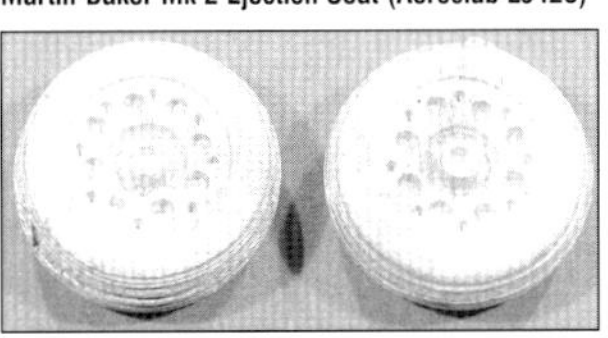

Meteor F Mk 8 Mainwheels (Aeroclub V218)

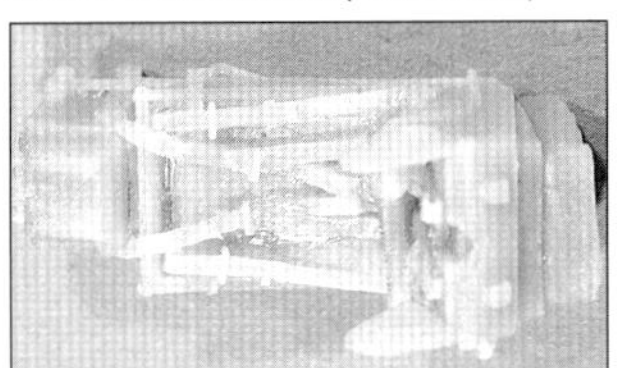

Martin-Baker Mk 2 Ejection Seat (Neomega)

Decals

MANUFACTURER	SCALE	SHEET NO.	TITLE
Aerocalcas	1/72nd	72004	
Inc. F Mk 4, C-090, Escuadrille Acrobática 46. Airport of Carrasco, R.O. del Uruguay, circa 1964			
Aerocalcas	1/72nd	72009	
F Mk 4, C-084 or C-086 [I-084 or I-086], used for aerobatics during 1958			
Aeroclub	1/72nd	AD013	Meteor Mk I/III
F Mk 1, EE227, YQ•Y, No.616 Squadron, 1944			
F Mk 3, EE354, XL•H, No.135 Conversion Unit			
The sheet also includes serial for EE214/G, DG202/G, EE317, EE219 & EE240			
Dutch Decal	1/72nd	72041	LSK, KLu & RNethNa
F Mk 4, Y9 2, NethAF, No.323 Sqn. VLB Leeuwarden 1952–53			
F Mk 4, 7E 2, NethAF, No.327 Sqn. VLB Volkel 1950–51			
F Mk 4, I 60, RNethAF, JVO (Fighter Training School) VLB Woensdrecht			
F Mk 4, I 62, RNethAF, JVO (Fighter Training School) VLB Woensdrecht			
F Mk 4, I 53, NethAF, No.327 Sqn. VLB Soesterberg 1952			
F Mk 4, 9I 4, NethAF, No.326 Sqn. VLB Leeuwarden 1950–51			
F Mk 4, 4R 10, NethAF, No.325 Sqn. VLB Leeuwarden 1949–51			
F Mk 8, 3W 31, RNethAF, No.322 Sqn. VLB Soesterberg 1953–57			
F Mk 8, 3W 55, RNethAF, No.322 Sqn. VLB Soesterberg 1953–57			
F Mk 8, 3P 13, RNethAF, No.324 Sqn. VLB Leeuwarden 1953–57			
F Mk 8, 3P 10, RNethAF, No.324 Sqn. VLB Leeuwarden 1953–57			
F Mk 8, 4R 8, RNethAF, No.325 Sqn. VLB Leeuwarden 1951–56			
F Mk 8, 9I 17, RNethAF, No.326 Sqn. VLB Leeuwarden 1951–56			
F Mk 8, I-207, RNethAF, Target Tug No.323 Sqn. VLB Leeuwarden 1951–56			
F Mk 8, I-241, RNethAF, JVO VLB Woensdrecht 1956			
F Mk 8, S8 11, RNethAF, No.328 Sqn. VLB Soesterberg 1951–55			
F Mk 8, 7E 1, RNethAF, No.327 Sqn. VLB Soesterberg 1951 55			
F Mk 8, Y9 18/30, RNethAF, No.323 Sqn. VLB Leeuwarden 1954–58			
T.Mk.7, I-306, RNethAF, No.323 Sqn. VLB Leeuwarden 1956			
T.Mk.7, I-10, RNethAF, No.322 Sqn. VLB Soesterberg			
T.Mk.7, 135 RNethNavy, No.3 Sqn. VLB Valkenburg 1957–61			
T.Mk.7, I-19, RNethAF, No.500 Sqn. VLB Soesterberg 1956			
Dutch Decal	1/48th	RAF/1	
Sqn markings for Nos. 19, 64, 65, 85, 89, 151, 245, 253, 500, 610, 615 & 616 Squadron, RAF			
All above for Meteor T Mk 7 and F Mk 8			
Dutch Decal	1/48th	RAF/2	
Sqn markings for Nos. 29, 46, 60, 72, 141, 219, 263, 601 Squadron, RAF Sqn markings for No.2 Air Navigation School			
All above for Meteor F Mk 8, NF Mk 11, 13 & 14			
Dutch Decal	1/48th	48025	Dutch Assortment
Inc. F Mk 8, Y9•18, No.323 Sqn, RNethAF			
Dutch Decal	1/48th	48027	
Inc. F Mk 4, I•62, RNethAF, JVO (Fighter Training Schol), VLB Woensdrecht			
T Mk 7, 135, RNethNavy, No.3 Sqn, MVLK Valkenburg, 1957–61			
Dutch Decal	1/48th	48040	Gloster Meteor
F Mk 4, I-62, Y9•8, No.323 Sqn, RNethAF, VLB Leeuwarden, 1952-53			
F Mk 8, 3W•55, No.322 Sqn, RNethAF, VLB Soestrberg 1953–57			
T Mk 7, I•306, No.323 Sqn, RNethAF, VLB Leeuwarden, 1956			
F Mk 8, 7E•14, No.327 Sqn, RNethAF, VLB Soesterberg 1951–57			
F Mk 8, I•241, RNeth AF, JachtVliegOpleiding, VLB Woensdrecht, 1956			
F Mk 8, I•207, RNeth AF, No.323 (Target-Tug) Sqn, VLB Leeuwarden, 1951–57			
FCM	1/72nd	72-12	
Inc. F Mk 8, S/No.4406, 'AI' of Esq. Jambock, 1º/1º G.A.C., Brazilian Air Force, 1956			
IsraDecal	1/72nd	IAF26	Gloster Meteor
T Mk 7, S/No.a13, First Jet Squadron, IAF, 1953			
T Mk 7, S/No.a14, First Jet Squadron, IAF, 1953			
T Mk 7, S/No.a15, First Jet Squadron, IAF, 1953			
T Mk 7, S/No.a13, First Jet Squadron, IAF, 1953			
FR Mk 9, S/No.36, First Jet Squadron, 1956			
F Mk 8, S/No.02, Knights of the North Sqn, 1960			
FR Mk 9, S/No.33, Knights of the North Sqn, 1958			
F Mk 8, S/No.04, Knights of the North Sqn, 1960			
F Mk 8, S/No.04, First Jet Sqn, 1956			
F Mk 8, S/No.09, Knights of the Orange Tail Sqn, 1963			
T Mk 7, S/No.15, Knights of the North Sqn, 1969			
T Mk 7, S/No.21, Knights of the North Sqn, 1969			
T Mk 7, S/No.17, Knights of the North Sqn, 1969			
NF Mk 13, S/No.52, Bat Sqn, 1956			
IsraDecal	1/48th	IAF25	Gloster Meteor
T Mk 7, S/No.a13, First Jet Squadron, IAF, 1953			
T Mk 7, S/No.a14, First Jet Squadron, IAF, 1953			
T Mk 7, S/No.a15, First Jet Squadron, IAF, 1953			
T Mk 7, S/No.a13, First Jet Squadron, IAF, 1953			
FR Mk 9, S/No.36, First Jet Squadron, 1956			
F Mk 8, S/No.02, Knights of the North Sqn, 1960			
FR Mk 9, S/No.33, Knights of the North Sqn, 1958			

MANUFACTURER	SCALE	SHEET NO.	TITLE
IsraDecal continued...			
F Mk 8, S/No.04, Knights of the North Sqn, 1960			
F Mk 8, S/No.04, First Jet Sqn, 1956			
F Mk 8, S/No.09, Knights of the Orange Tail Sqn, 1963			
T Mk 7, S/No.15, Knights of the North Sqn, 1969			
T Mk 7, S/No.21, Knights of the North Sqn, 1969			
T Mk 7, S/No.17, Knights of the North Sqn, 1969			
NF Mk 13, S/No.52, Bat Sqn, 1956			
Kits at War	1/72nd	K7/3	
Inc. Mk 4, EE455, RAF High-Speed Flight, 603.125 mph in 1945, flown by Eric Greenwood			
Kits at War	1/72nd	K7/10	Belgian Air Force
Inc. NF Mk 11, ND•D, EN16, 1e Wing, 10e Smaldeel, Bevekom, Belgium, 1956			
Kits at War	1/48th	K4/5	
Inc. Mk 4, EE455, RAF High Speed Flight, 603.125 mph in 1945, flown by Eric Greenwood			
LPS Hobby	1/72nd	72014	Meteor F Mk 8/T Mk 7
F Mk 8, S/No.4430, 'E3', 2º/1º Grupo de Caça, Santa Cruz AFB, Brazilian AF, 1954			
F Mk 8, S/No.4408, 'A1', 1º/1º Grupo de Caça, Santa Cruz AFB, Brazilian AF, 1957			
F Mk 8, S/No.4452, 1º/1º Grupo de Caça, Santa Cruz AFB, Brazilian AF, 1967			
F Mk 8, S/No.4412, 2º/1º Grupo de Caça, Santa Cruz AFB, Brazilian AF, 1960			
F Mk 8, S/No.4448, 1º/14º Grupo de Caça, Canoas AFB, Brazilian AF, 1959			
F Mk 8, S/No.4460, target-tug used by 1º/1º Grupo de Caça, Brazilian AF			
T Mk 7, S/No.4301, first Brazilian AF jet, first flown from Galeão AFB, May 1953			
T Mk 7, S/No.4308, 2º/1º Grupo de Caça, Santa Cruz AFB, Brazilian AF			
F Mk 8, S/No.4449, 1º/14º Grupo de Caça, Canoas AFB, Brazilian AF			
T Mk 7, S/No.4301, 2º/1º Grupo de Caça, Santa Cruz AFB, Brazilian AF			
Model Art	1/72nd	72-002	
TT Mk 20, WM159, 040, Airwork FRU, Royal Navy, Hurn, 1967			
TT Mk 20, WD592, HF, 864, No.728 NAS, Royal Navy, Hal Far (Malta), 1966			
TT Mk 20, '518', Royal Danish Air Force circa 1960			
NF Mk 11, NF11-24, Centre d'Essais en Vol, Bretigny, circa 1963			
NF Mk 11, NF11-1, C.E.V Bretigny circa 1975			
NF Mk 11, '501', No.723 Sqn, RDanish AF, Aalborg, 1955			
NF Mk 11, '518', No.723 Sqn, RDanish AF, Aalborg, 1955			
F Mk 4, EE455, RAF High-Speed Flight, Tangmere, 1945			
Model Art	1/72nd	72-003	
NF Mk 14, S/No. NF14-747, Centre d'Essais en Vol, Bretigny, 1984			
NF Mk 13, '57', Israeli Air Force, circa 1957			
NF Mk 13, No.474 (ex-RAF WM337), Syrian Air Force, Damascus, 1955			
NF Mk 13, No.1429, Royal Egyptian Air Force, 1956			
Model Art	1/72nd	72-020	
F Mk 8, WH261, 'Z', No. 600 Sqn, 1954			
F Mk 8, WK784, No.604 Sqn, 1953			
F Mk 8, WH503, 'F', No.611 Sqn, Woodvale, 1953			
F Mk 8, WK810, 'E', No.615 Sqn, Biggin Hill, 1955			
Modeldecal	1/72nd	088	RAF Meteors
F Mk 8, WA844, 'E', No.604 Sqn, RAuxAF, North Weald, February 1957			
F Mk 8, WH450, 'R', No.153 Sqn, West Malling, 1956			
F Mk 8, WF654, 'R', No.64 Sqn, Duxford, 1957			
NF Mk 11, WM293, 'B', No.68 Sqn, West Germany, 2nd TAF, circa 1958			
FR Mk 9, WX978, 'Z', No.8 Sqn, Khormaksar, Aden, 1959			
NF Mk 12, WS605, 'D', No.64 Sqn, Duxford, 1957			
NF Mk 11, No.68 Sqn			
NF Mk 14, WS729, 'A', No.153 Sqn, West Malling, 1957			
NF Mk 12, WS665, 'L', No.153 Sqn, West Malling 1957			
NF.14, WS811, 'O', No.64 Sqn, Duxford, 1958			
Modeldecal	1/72nd	092	RAF Meteor Night Fighters
NF Mk 11, WD663 'C', No.5 Sqn, RAF Laarbruch, Germany 1959			
NF Mk 11, WM238 'Y', No.11 Sqn, RAF Geilenkirchen, Germany 1959–60			
NF Mk 14, WS750 'W', No.25 Sqn, RAF West Malling 1956			
NF Mk 14, WS726 'H', No.25 Sqn, RAF West Malling 1955			
NF Mk 12, WS665 'L', No.25 Sqn, RAF Waterbeach 1958			
NF Mk 11, WM145 'A', No.29 Sqn, RAF Tangmere 1955			
NF Mk 13, WM315 'F', No.39 Sqn, RAF Nicosia, Cyprus, 1958			
NF Mk 11, WM311, No.39 Sqn, RAF Luqa, Malta, ca 1955. C.O.'s aircraft			
NF Mk 12, WS609 'B', No.46 Sqn, RAF Odiham, ca 1955			
NF Mk 14, WS830 'H', No.46 Sqn, RAF Odiham, ca. 1955, C.O.'s aircraft			
NF Mk 14, WS800, No.60 Sqn, RAF Tengah, Singapore, 1960. C.O.'s aircraft			
NF Mk 12, WS609 'B', No.72 Sqn, RAF Church Fenton, 1958.			
NF Mk 14, WS833 'MS', No.72 Sqn, RAF Church Fenton. 1955, Wg Cdr Maurice Shaw (CO)			
Modeldecal	1/72nd	093	RAF Meteor Night Fighters
NF Mk 14, WS844/NP, No.33 Sqn, RAF Leeming, early 1958, CO's aircraft (Wg Cdr N. Poole)			
NF Mk 14, WS790/H, No.33 Sqn, 'A' Flight commander's aircraft, 1958			
NF Mk 14, WS836/P, No.33 Sqn, 'B' Flight commander's aircraft, 1958			
NF Mk 11, WD673/F, No.87 Sqn, Wahn, W. Germany, circa 1956			
NF Mk 11, WM158/T, No.96 Sqn, 125 Wing, Ahlhorn, W. Germany, circa 1956			
NF Mk 11, WM260/H, No.125 Sqn, Stradishall, July 1955			

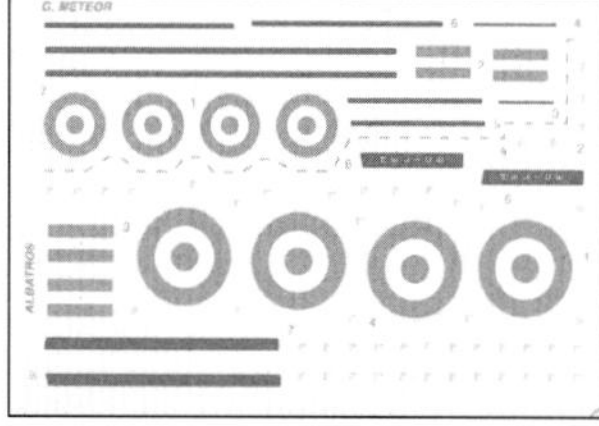

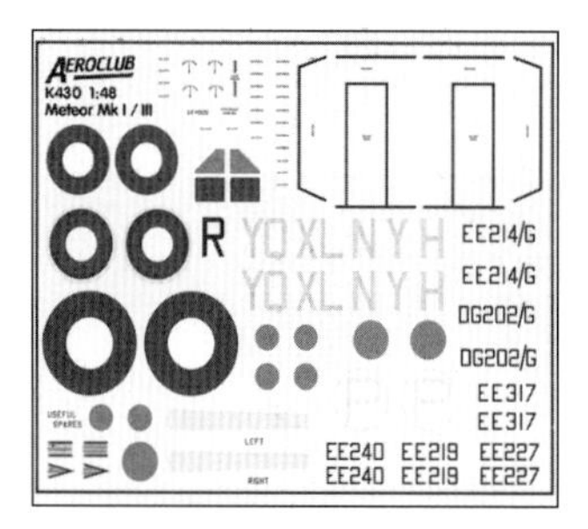

Aeroclub AD013

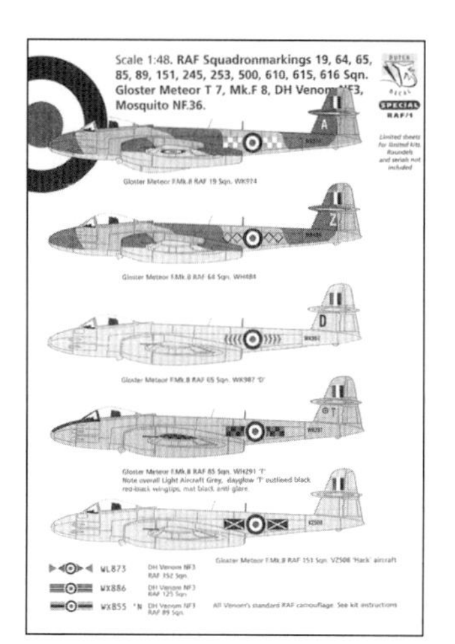

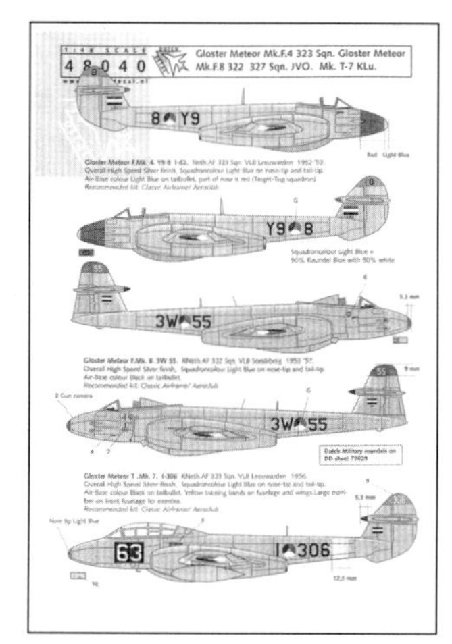

Dutch Decal 72041

Aerocalcas 72009

Dutch Decal RAF/1

Dutch Decal 48040

IsraDecal IAF26

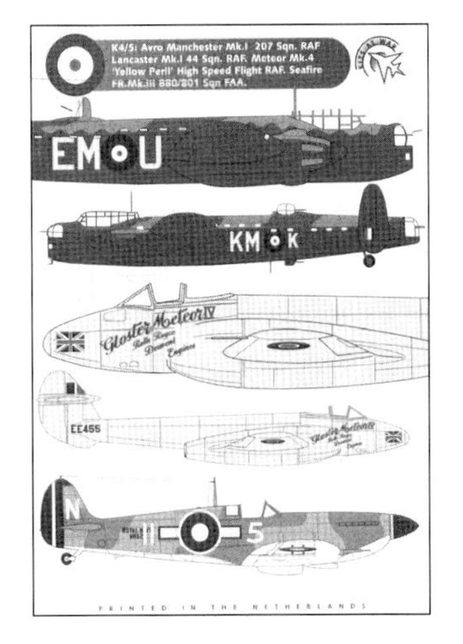

Kits at War K4/5

Kits at War K7/10

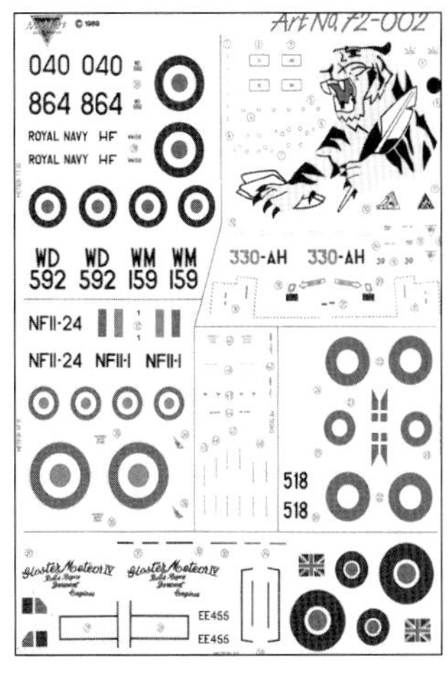

Model Art 72-002

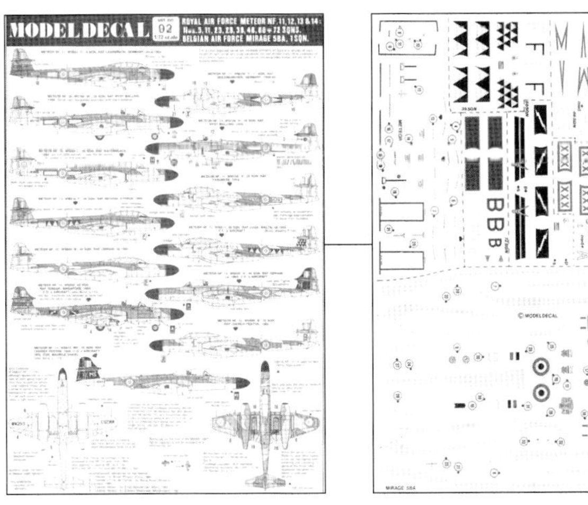

Modeldecal 092

Xtradecal X72-057

MANUFACTURER	SCALE	SHEET NO.	TITLE
Model Decal continued...			
NF Mk 11, WM151/C, 'A' Flight, No.125 Sqn			
NF Mk 11, WM237/R, 'B' Flight, No.125 Sqn			
NF Mk 11, WD770/S, No.141 Sqn, Coltishall, circa 1952			
NF Mk 11, WD643/L, No.151 Sqn, Leuchars, circa 1954			
NF Mk 12, WS674/V, No.152 Sqn, Stradishall, 1958			
NF Mk 12, WS633/J, No.151 Sqn. 1958			
NF Mk 11, WM223/U, No.151 Sqn			
NF Mk 11, WM238/R, No.256 Sqn			
NF Mk 11, WD642/A, No.256 Sqn, 125 Wing, Geilenkirchen, 1958			
NF Mk 14, WS783/T, No.152 Sqn, Stradishall, 1958			
NF Mk 13, WM321, No.219 Sqn, Kabrit, Egypt, 1954			
NF Mk 12, WS604/U, No.264 Sqn, Middleton St. George, August 1957			
NF Mk 11, WM143/X, No.264 Sqn, Linton-on-ouse, 1954			
NF Mk 14, WS827, No.264 Sqn, circa 1955			
NF Mk 14, WS841/HMT, No.264 Sqn, Linton-On-Ouse, 1955, Sqn Ldr H.M. Tudor			
NF Mk 14, WS774/D, No.2 Air Navigation School, Thorney Island, circa 1960			
NF Mk 14, WS844/JCF, No.264 Sqn. Middleton St. George, September 1957			
PD Decals	**1/72nd**	**72-017**	**Jet Killers (Part 1)**
Inc. F Mk 8, A77-15, Fg Off B. Gogerly, No. 77 Sqn, RAAF			
F Mk 8, A77-258, Plt Off J. Sturman, No.77 Sqn, RAAF			
PD Decals	**1/72nd**	**72-018**	**Jet Killers (Part 2)**
F Mk 8, A77-29, Fg Off Les Reading, No.77 Sqn, Korea, October 1951			
F Mk 8, A77-851, Sgt George Hale, No.77 Sqn, Korea, March 1953			
F Mk 8, A77-385, Plt Off Bill Simmonds, No.77 Sqn, Korea, May 1952			
PD Decals	**1/48th**	**48-017**	**Jet Killers (Part 1)**
Inc. F Mk 8, A77-15, Fg Off B. Gogerly, No.77 Sqn, RAAF			
F Mk 8, A77-258, Plt Off J. Sturman, No.77 Sqn, RAAF			
PD Decals	**1/48th**	**48-018**	**Jet Killers (Part 2)**
F Mk 8, A77-29, Fg Off Les Reading, No.77 Sqn, Korea, October 1951			
F Mk 8, A77-851, Sgt George Hale, No.77 Sqn, Korea, March 1953			
F Mk 8, A77-385, Plt Off Bill Simmonds, No.77 Sqn, Korea, May 1952			
RAFDEC	**1/72nd**	**RF7201**	**Gloster Meteor**
F Mk 4, VT229, '60', No.12 FTS, RAF Westonzoyland, 1954			
T Mk 7, VW440, FMK•H, No.203 AFS, RAF Driffield, 1949			
T Mk 7, WHI94, I9•S, RAF Full Sutton, 1953			
F Mk 8, WK947, 'W', No.245 Sqn, RAF Stradishall, May 1957, Exercise Vigilant			
FR Mk 9, VZ602, UU•A, No.226 OCU, RAF Stradishall, 1951			
PR Mk 10, VS975, A•N, No.541 Sqn, RAF Buckeburg, 1953			
RAFDEC	**1/72nd**	**RF7202**	**Gloster Meteor**
F Mk 4, RA482, HX•W, No.226 OCU, RAF Stradishall, June 1950			
T Mk 7, WH228, '46', No.209 AFS, RAF Weston Zoyland, 1953			
T Mk 7, WG946, 72•Y, No.206 AFS, RAF Oakington, 1953			
T Mk 7, WF88I, 55•X, No.203 AFS, RAF Driffield, October 1953			
T Mk 7, WA733, No.85 Sqn, RAF Church Fenton, August 1958			
F Mk 8, WH40I, L•M, Linton-on-Ouse Station Flight, 1953, flown by Wg Cdr L. G. Martin			
PR Mk 10, WBI56, A•B, No.541 Sqn, RAF Buckeburg, 1954			
Scale Decals	**1/72nd**	**SD5**	
NF Mk 11, WM165, Z, No.141 Squadron			
NF Mk 11, WM223, No.151 Squadron, 1956			
NF Mk 11, WD585, 'B', No.256 Squadron			
TT Mk 20, WM292, 'Q41', Airwork FRU, 1959			
NF Mk 13, '57', Israeli Air Force, 1957			
Xtradecal	**1/72nd**	**X72-057**	**RAF Gloster Meteors**
F Mk 8, WK681/H of No.65 Sqn, Aerobatic Team, RAF Duxford, Dec 1953			
F Mk 8, WE947/L of No.1 Sqn, RAF Tangmere in 1951			

MANUFACTURER	SCALE	SHEET NO	TITLE
Xtradecal continued...			
F Mk 8, WA826/F of No.245 Sqn, RAF Horsham St. Faith, undertaking trials with aerial refuelling in 1951			
F Mk 8, WL135 of the CO, No.245 Sqn, RAF Horsham St. Faith, 1955			
F Mk 8, WK672/X of No.247 Sqn, RAF Odiham, 1951–52			
F Mk 8, WA852/J of No.257 Sqn, RAF Horsham St. Faith, 1953			
F Mk 8, WA893/C of No.263 Sqn, RAF Wattisham, 1956			
F Mk 8, WK803/V of No.56 Sqn, RAF Waterbeach, 1953 This aircraft participated in the Coronation flypast			
F Mk 8, VZ531/K of No.609 Sqn, Royal Aux. AF. Finningley, 1957			
F Mk 8, WE876 of RAF Church Fenton Station Flight, carrying the markings of the resident Nos.19, 72 and 85 Squadrons			
F Mk 8, WA794/X of No.43 Sqn, RAF Leuchars in the early 1950s			
F Mk 8, WF654/R of No.64 Sqn, RAF Duxford, 1957			
F Mk 8, WH263/N of No.616 Sqn, RAuxAF, RAF Finningley in the mid-1960s			
F Mk 8, WH378/N of No.54 Sqn, RAF Odiham in the early 1950s			
F Mk 8, WH476/T, used as a 'hack' on the Venom NF.3 equipped No.89 Sqn, RAF Stradishall in 1956			
F Mk 8, VZ547/B of No.74 Sqn, RAF Horsham St. Faith, circa 1950-1			
F Mk 8, VZ547/B of No.74 Sqn, RAF Horsham St. Faith, circa 1952, as it may have appeared after the introduction of squadron markings			
Xtradecal	**1/48th**	**X48-043**	**RAF Gloster Meteors**
F Mk 8, WA826/F of No.245 Sqn, RAF Horsham St. Faith, undertaking trials with aerial refuelling in 1951			
F Mk 8, WL135 of the CO, No.245 Sqn, RAF Horsham St. Faith, 1955			
F Mk 8, WA852/J of No.257 Sqn, RAF Horsham St. Faith, 1953			
F Mk 8, WK672/X, No.247 Sqn, RAF Odiham, 1951–52			
F Mk 8, WA893/C of No.263 Sqn, RAF Wattisham, 1956			
F Mk 8, WF654/R of No.64 Sqn, RAF Duxford, 1957			
F Mk 8, WH263/N of No.616 Sqn, RAuxAF, RAF Finningley in the mid-1960s			
F Mk 8, VZ547/B of No.74 Sqn, RAF Horsham St. Faith, circa 1950–51			
F Mk 8, VZ547/B of No.74 Sqn, RAF Horsham St. Faith, circa 1952, as it may have appeared after the introduction of squadron markings			
Xtradecal	**1/48th**	**X48-046**	**RAF Gloster Meteors**
F Mk 4, RA444, A6•B, No.257 Sqn, RAF Horsham St.Faith, circa late 1940s			
F Mk 4, VW261, No.609 Sqn, RAuxAF, RAF Church Fenton, circa 1951			
F Mk 4, VT133, 4D•J, No.74 Sqn, RAF Horsham St.Faith, circa late 1940s			
F Mk 4, VZ417/A, No.63 Sqn. RAF Waterbeach, circa 1951			
T Mk 7, VW439/R, No.607 Sqn, RAuxAF, RAF Ouston, circa 1950s			
T Mk 7, WA718/X, No.611 Sqn, RAuxAF, RAF Woodvale, circa mid-1950s			
T Mk 7, WA725/Y, RAF Leuchars Station Flight, circa late 1950s			
T Mk 7, WA659/Y, No.33 Sqn, RAF Middleton St. George, circa 1958–59			
T Mk 7, WS116/936 of the Station Flight, RNAS Lossiemouth FAA, early 1960s			
T Mk 7, WH224/Z, No.500 Sqn, RAuxAF, RAF West Malling, circa mid-1950s			
T Mk 7, WL349/Z, No.229 OCU, RAF Chivenor, 1973			

Note: Blue Rider included a free decal sheet that included decals for the Martin-Baker T Mk 7 (WL419) in one of their editions of Insignia magazine in the 1990s. We have not included the details of this sheet above, as it was never available separately.

Some of the above-listed manufacturers are no longer in business and/or some of the sheets may no longer be in production.

Meteor Variants

Appendix IV

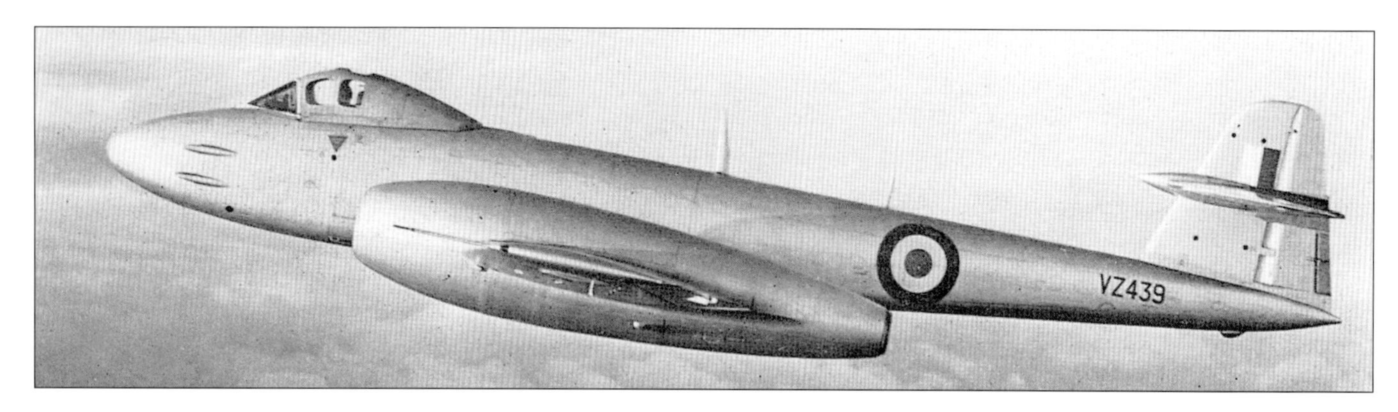

High-altitude and pressurisation trials were conducted with VZ439, which is seen here in flight with its specially modified canopy fitted

Note: The various special engine and system test aircraft built using the Meteor airframe are not included here. For more details of these machines see Chapter 8.

Designation:	**Prototype (F.9/40)**
Type:	Single-seat Fighter
Gloster Type No.:	G.41
Span:	43ft 0in (13.1m)
Length:	41ft 3in (12.5m)
Height:	13ft 0in (3.9m)
Engine:	(DG202/G) Two Rolls-Royce W.2B/23C Welland turbojets of 1,700lb (771kg) thrust each; (DG203/G) Two Power Jets W.2/500 turbojets of 1,400lb (636kg) thrust each [later fitted with W.2/700 engines of 1,760lb (800kg) thrust each]; (DG204/G) Two Metro-Vick F.2 turbojets of 1,900lb (863kg) thrust each; (DG205/G) Two Rolls-Royce W.2B/23 Welland turbojets of 1,600lb (727kg) thrust each; (DG206/G & DG207/G) Two Halford H.1 (later de Havilland Goblin) turbojets of 2,300lb (1,045kg) thrust each; (DG208/G) Two Rolls-Royce W.2B/23 turbojets of 1,600lb (727kg) thrust each; (DG209/G) Two Rolls-Royce W.2B/37 Welland turbojets of 2,000lb (909kg) thrust each
Weight*:	Empty 8,140lb (3,737kg); Loaded 13,795lb (6,258kg)
Max Speed*:	415mph (674km/h) @ 10,000ft (3,048m)
Service Ceiling*:	40,000ft (12,192m)
Armament:	Four 20mm Hispano cannon with a total of 780 rounds
Production:	8

Note: * These figures only relate to one prototype (probably DG202/G) and obviously differ depending on the engine installed. They are only included here as a representation of the type's likely performance etc.

Designation:	**F Mk I**
Type:	Single-seat Fighter
Gloster Type No.:	G.41A
Span:	43ft 0in (13.1m)
Length:	41ft 3in (12.5m)
Height:	13ft 0in (3.9m)
Engine:	Two Rolls-Royce W.2B/23C Welland I turbojets of 1,700lb (771kg) thrust each
Fuel Capacity:	300 Imp. Gal. (1,363lt)
Weight:	Empty 8,140lb (3,737kg); Loaded 13,795lb (6,258kg)
Max Speed:	415mph (674km/h) @ 10,000ft (3,048m)
Service Ceiling:	40,000ft (12,192m)
Armament:	Four 20mm Hispano cannon with a total of 780 rounds
Production:	20

Designation:	**F Mk II**
Type:	Single-seat Fighter
Gloster Type No.:	G.41B
First Flight:	24th July 1945
Span:	44ft 4in (13.5m)
Length:	41ft 5in (12.6m)
Height:	13ft 0in (3.9m)
Engine:	Two Halford H.1b (later de Havilland Goblin) turbojets of 2,700lb (1,227kg) thrust each
Fuel Capacity:	325 Imp. Gal. (1,477lt)
Weight:	Empty 10,519lb (4,771kg)
Service Ceiling:	ft (m)
Armament:	Four 20mm Hispano cannon with a total of 720 rounds
Production:	1 (DG207/G)

Designation:	**F Mk III (Early Production)**
Type:	Single-seat Fighter
Gloster Type No.:	G.41C
Span:	43ft 0in (13.1m)
Length:	41ft 3in (12.5m)
Height:	13ft 0in (3.9m)
Engine:	Two Rolls-Royce W.2B/23C Welland I turbojets of 1,700lb (771kg) thrust each
Fuel Capacity:	500 Imp. Gal. (2,275lt)
Weight:	Empty 8,140lb (3,737kg); Loaded 13,795lb (6,258kg)
Max Speed:	415mph (674km/h) @ 10,000ft (3,048m)
Service Ceiling:	40,000ft (12,192m)
Armament:	Four 20mm Hispano cannon with a total of 780 rounds
Production:	15 (EE230 to EE244)

Designation:	**F Mk III (Late Production)**
Type:	Single-seat Fighter
Gloster Type No.:	G.41D
Span:	43ft 0in (13.1m)
Length:	41ft 3in (12.5m)
Height:	13ft 0in (3.9m)
Engine:	Two Rolls-Royce W.2B/37 Derwent 1 turbojets of 2,000lb (907kg) thrust each
Fuel Capacity:	500 Imp. Gal. (2,275lt) plus provision for 100 Imp. Gal. (455lt) ventral drop tank. Note some later versions could carry a 180 Imp. Gal. (818lt) drop tank
Weight:	Empty 8,140lb (3,737kg); Loaded 13,795lb (6,258kg)
Max Speed:	415mph (674km/h) @ 10,000ft (3,048m)
Service Ceiling:	40,000ft (12,192m)
Armament:	Four 20mm Hispano cannon with a total of 780 rounds
Production:	180

Designation:	**F Mk III (Long-Chord Nacelles)**
Type:	Single-seat Fighter
Gloster Type No.:	G.41E
Span:	43ft 0in (13.1m)
Length:	41ft 3in (12.5m)
Height:	13ft 0in (3.9m)
Engine:	Two Rolls-Royce Derwent 5 turbojets of 3,500lb (1,587kg) thrust each
Fuel Capacity:	500 Imp. Gal. (2,275lt) plus provision for 100 Imp. Gal. (455lt) or 180 Imp. Gal. (818lt) ventral drop tank
Weight:	Empty 8,140lb (3,737kg); Loaded 13,795lb (6,258kg)
Max Speed:	415mph (674km/h) @ 10,000ft (3,048m)
Service Ceiling:	40,000ft (12,192m)
Armament:	Four 20mm Hispano cannon with a total of 780 rounds
Production:	15 (EE479-493, Last Mk IIIs built)

Designation:	**F Mk 4 (Early Production)**
Type:	Single-seat Fighter
Gloster Type No.:	G.41F
Span:	43ft 0in (13.1m)
Length:	41ft 0in (12.49m)
Height:	13ft 0in (3.9m)
Engine:	Two Rolls-Royce Derwent 5 turbojets of 3,500lb (1,587kg) thrust each
Fuel Capacity:	500 Imp. Gal. (2,275lt)
Weight:	Empty 10,519lb (4,771kg)
Max Speed:	575mph (925km/h) @ 10,000ft (3,048m)
Service Ceiling:	52,500ft (15,849m)
Armament:	Four 20mm Hispano cannon
Production:	443 (Total F Mk 4 production)

Designation:	**F Mk 4**
Type:	Single-seat Fighter
Gloster Type No.:	G.41G
Span:	37ft 2in (11.3m)
Length:	41ft 0in (12.49m)
Height:	13ft 0in (3.9m)
Engine:	Two Rolls-Royce Derwent 5 turbojets of 3,500lb (1,587kg) thrust each
Fuel Capacity:	500 Imp. Gal. (2,275lt)
Weight:	Empty 11,217lb (5,088kg); Loaded 14,545lb (6,597kg)
Max Speed:	580mph (933km/h) @ 10,000ft (3,048m)
Service Ceiling:	45,000ft (13,716m)
Armament:	Four 20mm Hispano cannon
Production:	443 (Total F Mk 4 production)

Designation:	**PR Mk 5**
Type:	Single-seat Photo-Reconnaissance
Gloster Type No.:	G.41H
First Flight:	13th July 1949 (Fatal Crash)
Span:	37ft 2in (11.3m)
Length:	41ft 0in (12.49m)
Height:	13ft 0in (3.9m)
Engine:	Two Rolls-Royce Derwent 8 turbojets of 3,500lb (1,587kg) thrust each
Fuel Capacity:	500 Imp. Gal. (2,275lt)
Weight:	Empty 11,217lb (5,088kg); Loaded 14,545lb (6,597kg)
Max Speed:	580mph (933km/h) @ 10,000ft (3,048m)
Service Ceiling:	45,000ft (13,716m)
Armament:	None
Cameras:	One oblique (nose-mounted) F.24 and two ventral (rear fuselage-mounted) F.36s
Production:	One prototype, converted F Mk 4 VT347 (disintegrated in flight, design not proceeded with)

Designation:	**F Mk 6**
Type:	Single-seat Fighter
Gloster Type No.:	G.41J
Span:	37ft 2in (11.3m)
Length:	44ft 7in (13.5m)
Height:	13ft 0in (3.9m)
Engine:	Two Rolls-Royce Derwent 7 turbojets

One of the most drastic conversions was undertaken with RA490, as can be seen here with the huge nacelles housing the Rolls-Royce Nenes fitted to it

Fuel Capacity: N/K
Weight: Empty N/K
Max Speed: Projected at Mach 0.88
Service Ceiling: 54,000ft (16,460m)
Production: None, project only

Designation: T Mk 7
Type: Two-seat Operational Trainer
Specification: T.1/47
Gloster Type No.: G.43
Span: 37ft 2in (11.3m)
Length: 43ft 6in (13.2m)
Height: 13ft 0in (3.9m)
Engine: Two Rolls-Royce Derwent 5 or 8 turbojets of 3,500lb (1,587kg) thrust each
Fuel Capacity: 500 Imp. Gal. (2,275lt)
Range: 580 miles (933km)
Weight: Empty 10,645lb (4,829kg); Loaded 14,230lb (6,454kg)
Max Speed: 590mph (949km/h) @ 10,000ft (3,048m)
Service Ceiling: 45,000ft (13,716m)
Armament: None
Production: 640

Designation: F Mk 8
Type: Single-seat Fighter
Gloster Type No.: G.41K
Span: 37ft 2in (11.3m)
Length: 44ft 7in (13.5m)
Height: 13ft 0in (3.9m)
Engine: Two Rolls-Royce Derwent 8 turbojets of 3,500lb (1,587kg) thrust each
Fuel Capacity: 795 Imp. Gal. (3,617lt)
Weight: Empty 10,684lb (4,846kg); Loaded 15,700lb (7,122kg)
Max Speed: 590mph (962.3km/h) @ 10,000ft (3,048m)
Service Ceiling: 43,000ft (13,106m)
Armament: Four 20mm Hispano Mk 5 cannon with 190 rounds per gun
Production: 1,079

Designation: FR Mk 9
Type: Single-seat Fighter-Reconnaissance
Gloster Type No.: G.41L
Span: 37ft 2in (11.3m)
Length: 44ft 7in (13.5m)
Height: 13ft 0in (3.9m)
Engine: Two Rolls-Royce Derwent 8 turbojets of 3,500lb (1,587kg) thrust each
Fuel Capacity: 795 Imp. Gal. (3,617lt) plus provision to carry a 178 Imp. Gal (796lt) ventral drop tank
Weight: Empty 10,790lb (4,894kg); Loaded 15,770lb (7,153kg)
Max Speed: 598mph (962.3km/h) @ Sea Level, 550mph (885.1km/h) @ 30,000ft (9,144m)
Service Ceiling: 41,000ft (12,497m)
Armament: Four 20mm Hispano Mk 3 cannon
Cameras: One F.24 in nose. Later replaced with three F.95s
Production: 79

Designation: PR Mk 10
Type: Single-seat High-altitude Photographic Reconnaissance
Gloster Type No.: G.41M
Span: 43ft 0in (13.1m)
Length: 44ft 3in (13.4m)
Height: 13ft 0in (3.9m)
Engine: Two Rolls-Royce Derwent 8 turbojets of 3,500lb (1,587kg) thrust each
Fuel Capacity: 795 Imp. Gal. (3,617lt)
Weight: Empty 10,993lb (4,986kg); Loaded 15,400lb (6,985kg)
Max Speed: 501mph (806km/h) @ Sea Level, 541mph (870.6km/h) @ 41,000ft (9,144m)
Service Ceiling: Clean 47,000ft (14,326m) or 44,000ft (13,411m) with drop tanks
Range: 1,085 miles (1,746km)
Armament: None
Cameras: One F.24 in nose and two (vertical or split-vertical) F.52s in rear fuselage
Production: 59

Designation: NF Mk 11
Type: Two-seat Night Fighter
Gloster Type No.: G.47
Specification: F.24/48
Span: 43ft 0in (13.1m)
Length: 48ft 6in (14.7m)
Height: 13ft 11in (4.2m)
Engine: Two Rolls-Royce Derwent 8 turbojets of 3,700lb (1,678kg) thrust each
Fuel Capacity: 600 Imp. Gal. (2,370lt)
Weight: Empty 12,019lb (5,541kg); Loaded 20,035lb (9,058kg)
Max Speed: 580mph (933km/h) @ 10,000ft (3,048m)
Service Ceiling: 40,000ft (12,192m)
Armament: Four wing-mounted 20mm Hispano Mk 5 cannon with 160 rounds per gun
Radar: SCR-720 (A.I. Mk 10)
Production: 307

Designation: NF Mk 12
Type: Two-seat Night Fighter
Gloster Type No.: G.47
Span: 43ft 0in (13.1m)
Length: 49ft 11in (15.2m)
Height: 13ft 11in (4.2m)
Engine: Two Rolls-Royce Derwent 9 turbojets of 3,800lb (1,723kg) thrust each
Fuel Capacity: 600 Imp. Gal. (2,370lt)
Weight: Empty 12,292lb (5,575kg); Loaded 17,223lb (7,012kg)
Max Speed: 580mph (933km/h) @ 10,000ft (3,048m)
Service Ceiling: 40,000ft (12,192m)
Armament: Four wing-mounted 20mm Hispano Mk 5 cannon with 160 rounds per gun
Radar: A.I. Mk 21 (AN/APS-21)
Production: 97

Designation: NF Mk 13
Type: Two-seat Tropicalised Night Fighter
Gloster Type No.: G.47
Span: 43ft 0in (13.1m)
Length: 48ft 6in (14.7m)
Height: 13ft 11in (4.2m)
Engine: Two Rolls-Royce Derwent 8 turbojets of 3,700lb (1,678kg) thrust each
Fuel Capacity: 600 Imp. Gal. (2,370lt)
Weight: Empty 12,347lb (5,600kg); Loaded 20,485lb (9,291kg)
Max Speed: 585mph (940km/h) @ 10,000ft (3,048m)
Service Ceiling: 36,000ft (10,972m)
Armament: Four wing-mounted 20mm Hispano Mk 5 cannon with 160 rounds per gun
Radar: SCR-720 (A.I. Mk 10)
Production: 40

Designation: NF Mk 14
Type: Two-seat Night Fighter
Gloster Type No.: G.47
Span: 43ft 0in (13.1m)
Length: 51ft 4in (15.63m)
Height: 13ft 11in (4.2m)
Engine: Two Rolls-Royce Derwent 9 turbojets of 3,800lb (1,723kg) thrust each
Fuel Capacity: 600 Imp. Gal. (2,370lt)
Weight: Empty 12,620lb (5,724kg); Loaded 21,200lb (9,626kg)
Max Speed: 585mph (940km/h) @ 10,000ft (3,048m)
Service Ceiling: 43,000ft (13,106m)
Armament: Four wing-mounted 20mm Hispano Mk 5 cannon with 160 rounds per gun
Radar: A.I. Mk 21 (AN/APS-21)
Production: 100

Designation: U Mk 15
Type: Radio-controlled, Unmanned Check and Target
Span: 37ft 2in (11.3m)
Length: 41ft 0in (12.49m)
Height: 13ft 0in (3.9m)
Engine: Two Rolls-Royce Derwent 5 turbojets of 3,500lb (1,587kg) thrust each
Fuel Capacity: 500 Imp. Gal. (2,275lt)

A77-157 'Cock of the North' (formerly WE889). It also carried the name 'Inda Grippa da Grog' at one time. This Meteor was subsequently converted to U Mk 21A target aircraft and in this role it was shot down in September 1969
(© Courtesy of the Aviation Heritage Museum of WA)

Weight: This depended on the equipment fitted for each sortie/task undertaken, so no specifics are available
Service Ceiling: This was dependant on the range of the guidance system installed, so no specifics are available
Camera Equip: wing tip-mounted camera pods containing two WRETAR cameras, one looking above, the other below the wing with 180° field of view. These pods were jettisonable, had recovery parachutes, buoyancy aids and location beacons installed so they could be recovered if the drone was destroyed
Production: 91 (although some sources quote 94, only 91 serial numbers exist in the records)

Designation: U Mk 16 (or D Mk 16)
Type: Radio-controlled, Unmanned Check and Target
First Flight: 22nd October 1966 (WA775)
Span: 37ft 2in (11.3m)
Length: 48ft 6in (14.7m)
Height: 13ft 0in (3.9m)
Engine: Two Rolls-Royce Derwent 8 turbojets of 3,500lb (1,587kg) thrust each
Fuel Capacity: 500 Imp. Gal. (2,275lt)
Weight: This depended on the equipment fitted for each sortie/task undertaken, so no specifics are available
Max Speed: This varied depending on the equipment carried for each sortie/task undertaken, so no specifics are available
Service Ceiling: This was dependant on the range of the guidance system installed, so no specifics are available
Production: 91 (All converted F Mk 8s)

Designation: TT Mk 20
Type: Two-seat Target Tug
Length: 48ft 6in (14.7m)
Height: 13ft 0in (3.9m)
Engine: Two Rolls-Royce Derwent 8 turbojets of 3,500lb (1,587kg) thrust each
Fuel Capacity: 600 Imp. Gal. (2,370lt)
Weight: This depended on the equipment fitted for each sortie undertaken, so no specifics are available
Max Speed: 560mph (910km/h) @ 10,000ft (3,048m)
Service Ceiling: 40,000ft (12,192m)
Armament: None (although wing-mounted cannon fairings retained)
Radar: None (replaced with lead ballast)
Winch: ML Aviation Type G Wind-driven. Later machines used the Del-Mar winch with a single Rushton target on a drop-down loader
Production: 43 (All conversions)

Designation: U Mk 21
Type: Radio-controlled, Unmanned Check and Target
Span: 37ft 2in (11.3m)
Height: 13ft 0in (3.9m)
Engine: Two Rolls-Royce Derwent 8 turbojets of 3,500lb (1,587kg) thrust each
Weight: This depended on the equipment fitted for each sortie/task undertaken, so no specifics are available
Max Speed: This varied depending on the equipment carried for each sortie/task undertaken, so no specifics are available
Service Ceiling: This was dependant on the range of the guidance system installed, so no specifics are available
Production: 8 (All converted by Flight Refuelling Ltd for the RAAF)

Designation: U Mk 21A
Type: Radio-controlled, Unmanned Check and Target
Span: 37ft 2in (11.3m)
Height: 13ft 0in (3.9m)
Engine: Two Rolls-Royce Derwent 8 turbojets of 3,500lb (1,587kg) thrust each
Weight: This depended on the equipment fitted for each sortie/task undertaken, so no specifics are available
Max Speed: This varied depending on the equipment carried for each sortie/task undertaken, so no specifics are available
Service Ceiling: This was dependant on the range of the guidance system installed, so no specifics are available
Production: 15 (All ex-RAAF F Mk 8s converted by Fairey Aviation at Bankstown)

NF(T) Mk 14, WS739 'F' of No.1 Air Navigation School. This machine later became Inst. Airframe 7961M, was later sold to a Mr L. Jackson and ended up at the Nostell Aviation Museum
(© R.J. Caruana)

Meteor Genealogy

Appendix V

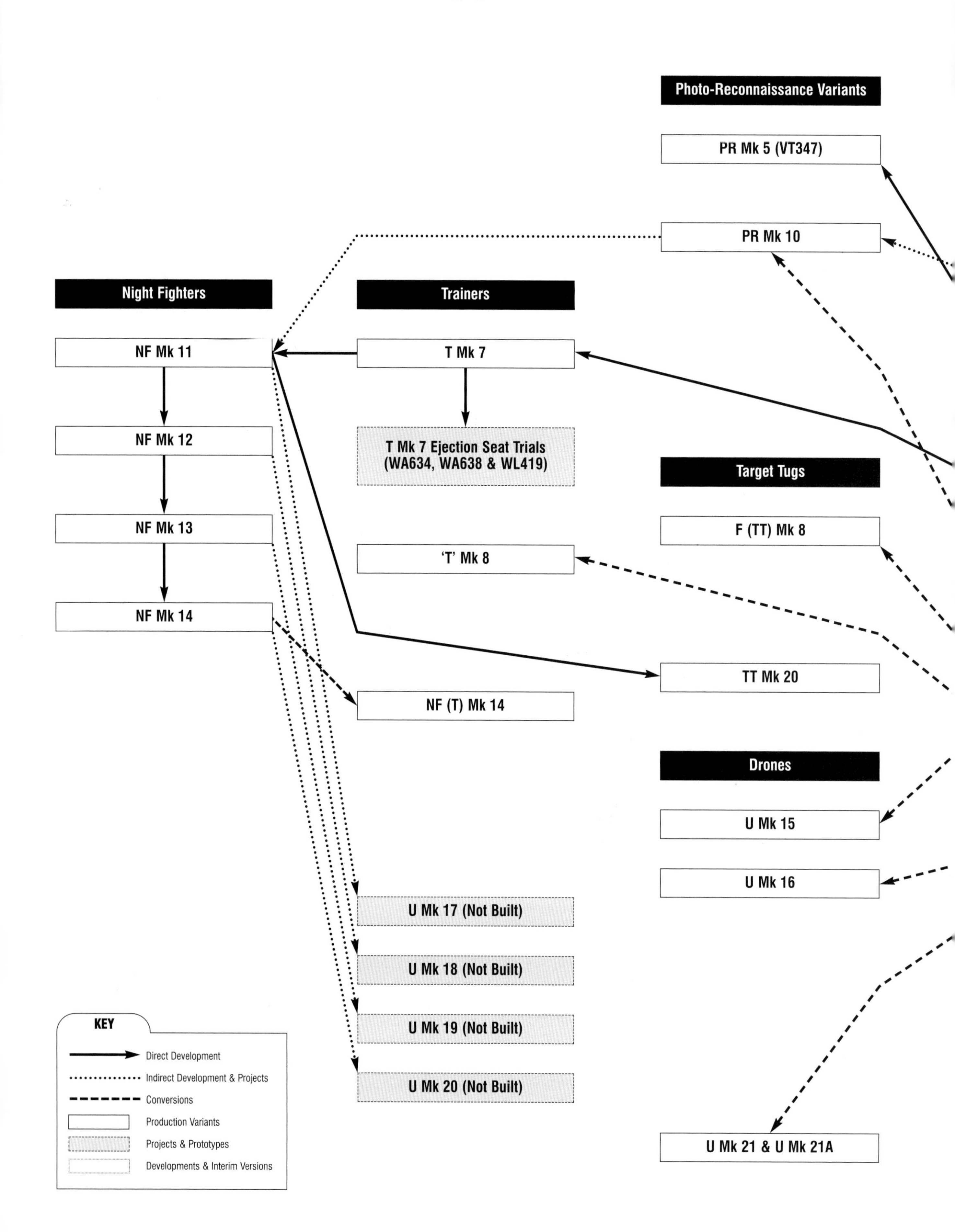

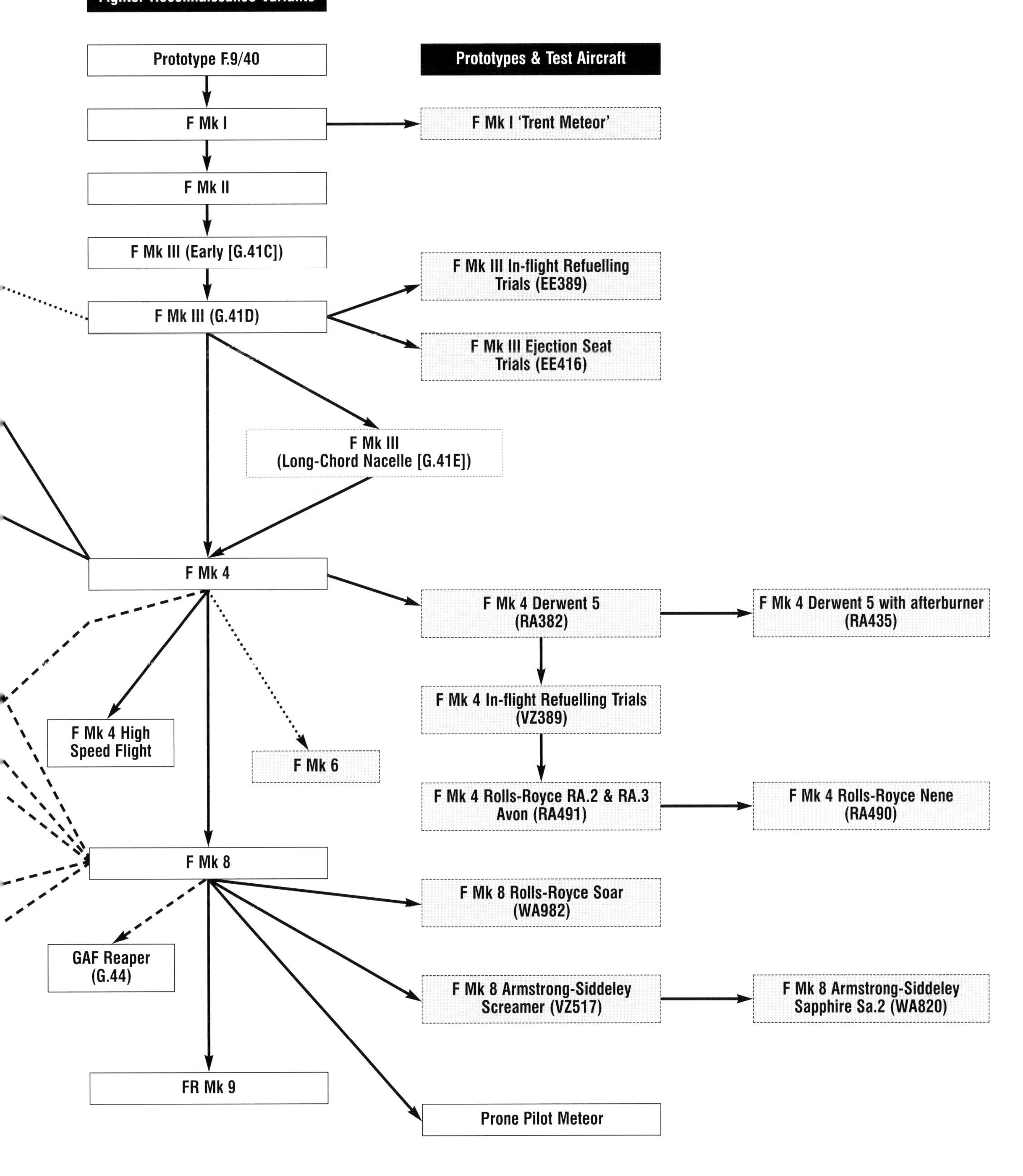

Fighter, Fighter-Bomber & Fighter-Reconnaissance Variants
Prototype F.9/40
Prototypes & Test Aircraft
F Mk I
F Mk I 'Trent Meteor'
F Mk II
F Mk III (Early [G.41C])
F Mk III In-flight Refuelling Trials (EE389)
F Mk III (G.41D)
F Mk III Ejection Seat Trials (EE416)
F Mk III (Long-Chord Nacelle [G.41E])
F Mk 4
F Mk 4 Derwent 5 (RA382)
F Mk 4 Derwent 5 with afterburner (RA435)
F Mk 4 In-flight Refuelling Trials (VZ389)
F Mk 4 High Speed Flight
F Mk 6
F Mk 4 Rolls-Royce RA.2 & RA.3 Avon (RA491)
F Mk 4 Rolls-Royce Nene (RA490)
F Mk 8
F Mk 8 Rolls-Royce Soar (WA982)
GAF Reaper (G.44)
F Mk 8 Armstrong-Siddeley Screamer (VZ517)
F Mk 8 Armstrong-Siddeley Sapphire Sa.2 (WA820)
FR Mk 9
Prone Pilot Meteor

Foreign Operators

Appendix VI

A77-1 (formerly EE427). The first Meteor, a F Mk 3, delivered to the RAAF, seen after a crash landing at Darwin in February 1947

(© Courtesy of the Aviation Heritage Museum of WA)

What follows is a brief run-down of the countries that operated the Meteor and their aircraft.

Argentina

Fuerza Aérea Argentina (Argentine Air Force)

Serial Numbers

Meteor F Mk 4

FAA serial:	*Ex-RAF serial:*
I-101	RA384
I-102	RA386
I-103	RA388
I-104	RA389
I-105	RA390
I-106	RA391
I-107	RA370
I-108	RA385
I-109	RA392
I-110	RA393
I-111	RA395
I-112	RA396
I-113	EE570
I-114	EE575
I-115	EE551
I-116	EE569
I-117	EE554
I-118	EE571
I-119	EE553
I-120	EE546
I-121	EE544
I-122	EE552
I-123	EE576
I-124	EE548
I-125	EE532
I-126	EE572
I-127	EE527
I-128	EE535
I-129	EE537
I-130	EE542
I-131	EE588
I-132	EE581
I-133	EE582
I-134	EE574
I-135	EE580
I-136	EE577
I-137	EE583
I-138	EE587
I-139	EE585
I-140	EE589
I-141	EE586
I-142	EE526
I-143	EE540
I-144	EE534
I-145	EE547
I-146	EE543
I-147	EE533
I-148	EE539
I-149	EE536
I-150	EE541

I-051 to I-100 were all new build aircraft with no previous identity. The 'I' prefix (Interceptor) was changed to 'C'(Caza-Bombardero/ fighter-bomber) in 1950

Australia

Royal Australian Air Force

Serial Numbers

Meteor F Mk 3

RAAF serial:	*Ex-RAF serial:*
A77-1	EE427

Meteor F Mk 8

RAAF serial	*Ex-RAF serial:*
A77-11	WH259
A77-15	WE911
A77-17 *	WA964
A77-29	WE938
A77-31 *	WE903
A77-46	WF746
A77-65	WH475
A77-120	WE880
A77-128	WE908
A77-134	WE898
A77-139	WA949
A77-157 +	WE889
A77-163	WA941
A77-189	WA961
A77-193 +	WE969
A77-207 +	WE905
A77-231	WA944
A77-251	WE906
A77-258 *	WH254
A77-300	WA935
A77-316	WE945
A77-343	WH274
A77-354	WA934
A77-368 *	WA952
A77-373	WA936
A77-385	WE918
A77-393	WE877
A77-397 *	WE896
A77-415	WE900
A77-422 +	WF750
A77-436	WE971
A77-446 *	WA783
A77-464	WA958
A77-510 +	WH251
A77-559	WE910
A77-570	WE890
A77-587	WA939
A77-616	WA956
A77-627	WE928
A77-643	WE886
A77-645	WE886
A77-721	WA954
A77-726	WA957
A77-728	WA951
A77-730	WA782
A77-734 *	WE907
A77-735	WA942
A77-740	WA948
A77-741	WA947
A77-744 *	WA786
A77-793 *	WH252
A77-802 *+	WA998
A77-811	WA937
A77-851 *+	WK683
A77-852	WH479
A77-853	WK715
A77-854 *	WK650
A77-855 *	WK728
A77-856	WK686
A77-857	WK684
A77-858	WK682
A77-859	WK688
A77-860	WK670
A77-861 *	WH481
A77-862	WH417
A77-863 +	WK730
A77-864	WK735
A77-865	WH405
A77-866	WH414
A77-867 *	WK685
A77-868 *	WK674
A77-869 *	WK727
A77-870 *	WK748
A77-871 *	WK791
A77-872 *+	WK792
A77-873 *+	WK796
A77-874 *	WK909
A77-875 *	WK798
A77-876 *+	WK800
A77-877 *	WK913
A77-878 *	WK907
A77-879 *	WK821
A77-880 *	WK910
A77-881 *	WK944
A77-882 *+	WK937
A77-883 *	WK912
A77-884 *+	WK931
A77-885 *+	WK973
A77-886 *	WK938
A77-911	WA946
A77-920	WF653
A77-949	WA960
A77-953	WE874
A77-959	WE909
A77-982	WA950

+ Converted to U Mk 21 in Australia by Fairey Aviation Australasia Pty Ltd

* Airframes returned to Australia after the end of the Korean war

Meteor NF Mk 11

RAAF serial:	*Ex-RAF serial:*
A77-3	VW410

Meteor T Mk 7

RAAF serial	*Ex-RAF serial:*
A77-2	WM262
A77-4	WN321
A77-229	WA731
A77-305	WA732
A77-380	WG974
A77-577	WG977
A77-701	WA731
A77-702	WA732
A77-703	WG974
A77-704	WG977
A77-705	WA680
A77-706	WF843
A77-707	WH118
WH220	WH220
WH238	WH238
WH482	WH482

Meteor U Mk 16

Ex-RAF serial:
VT106
VT112
VT113
VT130
VT139
VT142
VT177
VT179
VT184
VT191
VT192
VT197
VT219
VT222
VT270
VT286
VT294
VT316
VT319
VT329
VT386
VT401
VT403
VT414
RA367
RA371
RA398
RA421
RA433
RA454
VW266
VW303
VW791

Belgium

Force Aérienne Belge (Belgian Air Force)

Serial Numbers

Meteor F Mk 4
EF-1 to EF-48

Meteor T Mk 7
ED-1 to ED-3 New build
ED-4 to ED-42
Of which the following came from ex-RAF stocks:
WA684, WA688, WF814, WF817, WF818, WF827, WG970, WH114, WH117, WH171, WH174, WL399, WL415, WL427, WL428, WL486, WN320, WS140, WS141
The balance (20) converted from surplus F Mk 4s by Avions Fairey, using kits supplied by Gloster.

Meteor F Mk 8
EG-201 to EG-223
Ex-RAF serials:
VZ450, VZ457, VZ459, VZ499, VZ553, VZ562, VZ566, WA755, WA870, WA876, WA878, WA881, WA883, WA884, WA887, WA888, WA889, WA892, WA895, WA898, WA900, WA901, WA902
New build by Avions Fairey:
EG-1 to EG-150

Meteor NF Mk 11
EN-1 to EN-24
Ex-RAF serials:
WD590, WD594, WD596, WD602, WD622, WD661, WD724 WD726 to WD733, WD735, WD736, WD741, WD743, WD744, WD760, WD763, WD775, WD777

Brazil

Força Aérea Brasileira (Brazilian Air Force)

Serial Numbers

Meteor F Mk 8
New-build Meteors:
FAB 4400 to FAB 4460
of which the following were ex-Royal Egyptian Air Force (REAF) [ex-RAF]

FAB Serial	*Ex-REAF:*	*Ex-RAF:*
FAB 4455	EAF 1415	WK877
FAB 4456	EAF 1419	WK887
FAB 4457	EAF 1420	WK888
FAB 4458	EAF 1421	WK889

Meteor TF Mk 7

FAB Serial	*Ex-RAF Serial:*
FAB 4300	WS142
FAB 4301	WS143
FAB 4302	WS144
FAB 4303	WS145
FAB 4304	WS146
FAB 4305	WS147
FAB 4306	WS148
FAB 4307	WS149
FAB 4308	WS150
FAB 4309	WS151

Canada

Royal Canadian Air Force

Serial Numbers

F Mk 3
EE311
For cold weather trials only

F Mk 4
RA421
Replaced EE311 for trials
VT196
Avro Orenda 10 engine trials

T Mk 7
WA740
No.421 Squadron, No.2 Wing, Odiham (*)
WA742
No.421 Squadron, No.2 Wing, Odiham (*)
*These were loaned from the RAF for a period of training with the RAF Vampire Wing between January and November 1951.

Denmark

Royal Danish Air Force

Serial Numbers

Meteor F Mk 4
461 to 480

Meteor F Mk 8
481 to 500

Meteor NF Mk 11
501 to 520*
Ex-RAF serials:
WM384 to WM403

Meteor T Mk 7
261 to 269
Apart from NF Mk 11s, all were new-build aircraft
*Of these, 504, 508, 512, 517, 518 and 519 were returned to Armstrong-Whitworth for reconditioning and conversion to TT Mk 20 standard

One of the ten T Mk 7s operated by the Fôrça Aérea Brasileira. This is probably FAB 4301, the second T Mk 7 supplied to Brazil and it is seen flying over England prior to delivery in February 1953

(FAB via Juan Carlos Cicalesi)

Ecuador

Fuerza Aérea Ecuatoriana (Ecuadorian Air Force)

Serial Numbers

Meteor FR Mk 9

FAE serials:	*Ex-RAF serials:*
701	VZ597
702	WH547
703	VW336
704	WB136
705	VZ610
706	WH540
707	WH543
708	WH549
709	WH550
710	WH553
711	WH554
712	WH555

Later renumbered in the FF-11? to FF-12? range, full numbers not known.

Egypt

(Royal) Egyptian Air Force

Serial Numbers

Meteor T Mk 7
New build:
1400, 1413, 1414
From ex-RAF Stocks:

Egyptian AF:	*Ex-RAF serials:*
1439	VW435
1440	WA730
1441	WG994

Meteor F Mk 8

Egyptian AF:	*Ex-RAF serials:*
1415	WH350
1419	WL188
1420	WH371
1421	WL186
1423	WL183
1424	WL185
1425	WL187
1426	WL191

Meteor NF Mk 13

Egyptian AF:	*Ex-RAF serials:*
1427	WM325
1428	WM326
1429	WM328
1430	WM338
1431	WM340
1432	WM362

France

Armée de l'Air

Serial Numbers

Meteor F Mk 4

EE523 (F-BEPQ & F-WEBQ)
RA491

Meteor T Mk 7

WA607 (F-BEAR) used by CEV/SNCASO for ejection seat trials from April 1955.

New build:	*Reg:*	*Source/ Ex-RAF serial:*
F-1	F-ZJOT F-ZABB	Ex-Syria ('91')
F-2	F-ZLAJ F-ZJNM F-ZABJ	Ex-RAF/Syria (WH136/'92')
F-3	F-BEAR?	
F-4		WL476
F-5	30-OY 30-MU 346-QV F-ZABC (CEV)	WL425
F-6	30-MV 30-FY 346-QW 346-QV F-ZADB (EPNER)	WL471
F-7	30-OZ 30-MW 346-QX F-ZACM	WF776
F-8		WH168
F-9	30-MY 346-QY F-ZADC (EPNER)	WH832
F-10	30-MZ	WN312
F-11	T7-51 30-FZ	WL485
228	MK7-228 T7-228 (EPNER)	WH228
997	F-ZLAI T7-F1(?)	WG997
F-BEAR	WA607 (*see above)	

Meteor NF Mk 11

New build: serial:	*Reg:*	*Source/ Ex-RAF*
NF11-1	F-ZABH(*)	WM296
NF11-2	F-ZABO(*)	WM297
NF11-3	F-ZWSC(*)	WM298
NF11-4	F-ZABE(*)	WM299
NF11-5	F-ZABC(*)	WM300
NF11-6 (•)	F-ZJOQ(*)	WM301
NF11-7	F-ZABP(*)	WM302
NF11-8	F-ZABG(*)	WM303
NF11-9	F-ZABF(*)	WM304
NF11-10	30-MA (^)	
NF11-11	F-ZABG(*) MM(+) 30-MB (^)	
NF11-12	30-MC (^)	
NF11-13	MN (+) 30-MD (^)	
NF11-14	F-ZABV(*) 30-ME (^)	
NF11-15	30-MF (^)	
NF11-16	30-MG (^) 346-QA (±)	
NF11-17	30-MH (^) 346-QB (±)	
NF11-18	30-FA (@)	
NF11-19	30-FB (@) 346-QC (±)	
NF11-20	F-ZACS(*) 30-FC (@)	
NF11-21	30-FD (@)	
NF11-22	F-ZACB(*) 30-FE (@)	
NF11-23	30-FF (@)	
NF11-24	F-ZAGM(*) 30-FG (@)	
NF11-25	30-FH (@)	
NF11-26	346-QD (±)	
NF11-27	30-OA (~)	
NF11-28	30-OB (~)	
NF11-29	30-OC (~) 346-QE (±)	
NF11-30	30-OD (~)	
NF11-31	30-OE (~) 346-QF (±)	
NF11-32	30-OF (~)	
NF11-33	30-OG (~) 346-QG (±)	
NF11-34	30-OH (~) 346-QH (±)	
NF11-35	30-OI (~)	
NF11-36	30-OJ (~) 346-QI (±)	
NF11-37	30-OK (~) 346-QJ (±)	
NF11-38	30-OL (~) 346-QK (±)	
NF11-39	30-OM (~) 346-QL (±)	
NF11-40	30-ON (~) 346-QM (±)	
NF11-41	30-OO (~) 346-QN (±)	

* - CEV registration
\+ - CTB registration
~ - 1/30 Loire
^ - 2/30 Camargue
@ - 3/30 Lorraine
± - CITT 346
• Note: NF11-6 acted as chase plane to Concorde 001 during her initial flights.

Meteor NF Mk 13

French:	*Ex-RAF:*	*Civil:*
NF13-364	WM364	F-AZCG
NF13-365	WM365	F-ZACH

Meteor NF Mk 14

French:	*Ex-RAF:*	*Civil:*
NF-14-747	WS747	F-ZABM
NF-14-796	WS796	F-ZABW

Israel

Heyl Ha'Avir (Israeli Air Force)

Serial Numbers

Meteor T Mk 7

2162 to 2165
111 and 112 fitted with E.1/44 tail by Avions Fairey

Meteor F Mk 8

2166 to 2169
2172 to 2178

Meteor FR Mk 9

Israeli serials:	*Ex-RAF serials:*
211	WX967
212	WL259
213	WB129
214	WB140
215	WX975
216	WX963
217	WX980

Meteor NF Mk 13

Israeli serials:	*Ex-RAF serials:*
4X-FNA	WM366
4X-FNB	WM334
4X-FNC	WM362
4X-FND	WM309
4X-FNE	WM320
4X-FNF	WM335

Netherlands

Koninklijke Luchtmacht (Royal Netherlands Air Force)

Serial Numbers

Meteor F Mk 4

New-build Meteors:
I-21 to I-64

RNAF serials:	*Ex-RAF serials:*
I-55	VZ391
I-56	VZ393
I-57	VZ395
I-58	VZ396
I-59	VZ397
I-60	VZ387
I-61	VZ400
I-62	VZ388
I-63	VZ390
I-64	VZ399
I-65	VW309
I-66	VW286
I-67	VZ398
I-68	VZ402
I-69	VZ409
I-70	VZ408
I-71	VW288
I-72	VW264
I-73	VW291
I-74	VW310
I-75	VW313
I-76	VT333
I-77	VW263
I-78	VZ394
I-79	VW295
I-80	VW296
I-81	VW315

Photographs of Meteors operated by Ecuador are few and far between; this shot shows one of the FR Mk 9s prior to delivery

Meteor F Mk 8

Direct from Glosters (undelivered ex-RAF):

I-90	WF697
I-91	WF698
I-92	WF699
I-93	WF693
I-94	WF696

License-built by Fokker:
I-101 to I-255

Meteor T Mk 7

New-build Meteors:
I-1 to I-7, I-310 to I-312, I-315, I-317, I-312

RNAF serials:	*Ex-RAF serials/regs:*
I-1	G-AKPK
I-8	WA623
I-9	WA626
I-10	WA633
I-11	WH165
I-12	WH203
I-13	WH193
I-14	WH196
I-15	WH199
I-16	WH179
I-17	WH202
I-18	WH469
I-19	WH203
I-20	WH482
I-301	WH207
I-302	WH222
I-303	WH487
I-304	WG998
I-305	WH125
I-306	WL426
I-307	WN315
I-308	WN237
I-309	WL477
I-313	XF279
I-314	XF278
I-316	WH135
I-318	WL412
I-319	WA674
I-320	VW417
I-322	WA592
I-323	WF856
I-324	WH247
I-325	WH177

New Zealand

Royal New Zealand Air Force (RNZAF)

Serial Numbers

Meteor F Mk 3

RNZAF Serial:	*Ex-RAF serial:*
NZ6001	EE395

South Africa

South African Air Force (SAAF)

Serial Numbers

Meteor F Mk 3

EE429
Loaned to SAAF, March 1946 to June 1949

Sweden

Svenska Flygtjänst AB (Swedair Ltd)

Serial Numbers

Meteor T Mk 7

Civil registration:	*Ex-RAF serial:*
SE-CAS	WF833
SE-CAT	WH128
SE-DCC	
SE-DCF	
SE-DCG	
SE-DCH	
SE-DCI	

Syria

Al Quwwat al-Jawwiya al Arabia as-Suriya (Syrian Air Force)

Serial Numbers

Meteor T Mk 7

From ex-RAF stocks:

91	WL471
92	WL472

Meteor F Mk 8

New-build:
101 to 112

From ex-RAF stocks:

414	WL174
415	WK868
416	WK984
417	WH503
418	WE965
419	WH260

Meteor FR Mk 9

From ex-RAF stocks:

480	WB133
481	WX972

Meteor NF Mk 13

From ex-RAF stocks:

471	WM332
472	WM336
473	WM330
474	WM337
475	WM341
476	WM333

United States of America

United States Army Air Force (USAAF)

Serial Numbers

F Mk I

DG210/G
Loaned for evaluation in 1944

An F Mk 8 of the Syrian Air Force prior to delivery

An impressive line-up of Fôrça Aérea Brasileira F Mk 8s, all of which were operated by the two squadrons of 1° GavCa based at Santa Cruz [in this case 1°/14°]

(FAB via César Del Gaizo)

Meteor Production

Appendix VII

One of the Meteor T Mk 7s shortly after arrival in Israel. The intake and the nose are not yet painted white and black
(© R. Weiss)

Contract Number: SB21179/C.23(2)
Air Ministry Specification: F.9/40
Gloster Type No.: Gloster Whittle F.9/40 Prototype
Quantity: 8
Built by: Gloster Aircraft, Hucclecote
DG202/G to DG209/G

Contract Number: A/C1490/41
Meteor Mk: F Mk I
Gloster Type No.: Gloster G.41A
Quantity: 20
Built by: Gloster Aircraft, Hucclecote
EE210 to EE229

Contract Number: SB21179/C.23(2)
Meteor Mk: F Mk II
Gloster Type No.: Gloster G.41B
Quantity: 1
Built by: Gloster Aircraft, Hucclecote
See Whittle F.9/40 prototype – DG207/G was prototype for proposed F Mk I version with DH-Halford Goblin engines; not proceeded with

Contract Number: 6/ACFT/1490 C.B. 7(b)
Meteor Mk: F Mk III
Gloster Type No.: Gloster G.41C
Quantity: 15
Built by: Gloster Aircraft, Hucclecote
EE230 to EE244 - Welland engines

Contract Number: 6/ACFT/1490 C.B. 7(b)
Meteor Mk: F Mk III
Gloster Type No.: Gloster G.41D
Quantity: 180
Built by: Gloster Aircraft, Hucclecote
EE245 to EE254 – Derwent engines
EE269 to EE319 – Derwent engines
EE331 to EE369 – Derwent engines
EE384 to EE429 – Derwent engines
EE444 to EE446 – Derwent engines

Contract Number: 6/ACFT/1490 C.B. 7(b)
Meteor Mk: F Mk III
Gloster Type No.: Gloster G.41E
Quantity: 15
Built by: Gloster Aircraft, Hucclecote
EE479 to EE493 – Long-chord engine cowlings
Allocated but cancelled:
TX386 to TX428
TX531 to TX567
TX572 to TX614
TX618 to TX645
TX649 to TX688
TX693 to TX737
TX739 to TX776
TX779 to TX804

Contract Number: 6/ACFT/1490 C.B. 7(b)
Meteor Mk: F Mk 4
Gloster Type No.: Gloster G.41F
Quantity: 170
Built by: Gloster Aircraft, Hucclecote
EE517 to EE554
EE568 to EE599
RA365 to RA398
RA413 to RA457
RA473 to RA493

Contract Number: 6/ACFT/658 C.B. 7(b)
Meteor Mk: F Mk 4
Gloster Type No.: Gloster G.41G
Quantity: 200
Built by: Gloster Aircraft, Hucclecote
VT102 to VT150
VT168 to VT199
VT213 to VT247
VT256 to VT294
VT303 to VT347
VW255 to VW315
VW780 to VW791

Contract Number: 6/ACFT/1389 C.B. 7(b)
Meteor Mk: F Mk 4
Gloster Type No.: Gloster G.41G
Quantity: 73
Built by: Armstrong-Whitworth Aircraft, Baginton
VZ386 to VZ419
VZ427 to VZ429
VZ436 & VZ437

Contract Number: Part of 6/ACFT/658 C.B. 7(b)
Meteor Mk: PR Mk 5
Gloster Type No.: Gloster G.41H
Quantity: 1
Built by: Gloster Aircraft, Hucclecote
VT347 – Crashed first flight; not proceeded with

Contract Number: 6/ACFT/1389 C.B. 7(b)
Meteor Mk: T Mk 7
Gloster Type No.: Gloster G.43
Quantity: 91
Built by: Gloster Aircraft, Hucclecote
VW410 to VW459
VW470 to VW489
VZ629 to VZ649

Contract Number: 6/ACFT/2982 C.B. 7(b)
Meteor Mk: T Mk 7
Gloster Type No.: Gloster G.43
Quantity: 137
Built by: Gloster Aircraft, Hucclecote
WA590 to WA639
WA649 to WA698
WA707 to WA743

Contract Number: 6/ACFT/5044 C.B. 7(b)
Meteor Mk: T Mk 7
Gloster Type No.: Gloster G.43
Quantity: 89
Built by: Gloster Aircraft, Hucclecote
WF766 to WF795
WF813 to WF862
WF875 to WF883

Contract Number: 6/ACFT/5621 C.B. 7(b)
Meteor Mk: T Mk 7
Gloster Type No.: Gloster G.43
Quantity: 160
Built by: Gloster Aircraft, Hucclecote
WG935 to WG950
WG961 to WG999
WH112 to WH136
WH164 to WH209
WH215 to WH248

Contract Number: 6/ACFT/6066 C.B. 7(b)
Meteor Mk: T Mk 7
Gloster Type No.: Gloster G.43
Quantity: 139
Built by: Gloster Aircraft, Hucclecote
WL332 to WL381
WL397 to WL436
WL453 to WL488
WN309 to WN321

Contract Number: 6/ACFT/6410 C.B. 7(b)
Meteor Mk: T Mk 7
Gloster Type No.: Gloster G.43
Quantity: 24
Built by: Gloster Aircraft, Hucclecote
WS103 to WS117
WS140 to WS151
XF273 to XF279
Allocated but cancelled:
WZ154 to WZ203
WZ227 to WZ267

Contract Number: 6/ACFT/2430 C.B. 7(b)
Meteor Mk: F Mk 8
Gloster Type No.: Gloster G.41K
Quantity: 73
Built by: Gloster Aircraft, Hucclecote
VZ438 to VZ485
VZ493 to VZ517
Quantity: 45
Built by: Armstrong-Whitworth Aircraft, Baginton
VZ518 to VZ532

VZ540 to VZ569
Quantity: 209
Built by: Gloster Aircraft, Hucclecote
WA755 to WA794
WA808 to WA857
WA867 to WA909
WA920 to WA969
WA981 to WA999
WB105 to WB112

Contract Number: 6/ACFT/4040 C.B. 7(b)

Meteor Mk: F Mk 8
Gloster Type No.: Gloster G.41K
Quantity: 48
Built by: Armstrong-Whitworth Aircraft, Baginton
WE852 to WE891
WE895 to WE902
Quantity: 72
Built by: Gloster Aircraft, Hucclecote
WE903 to WE939
WE942 to WE976

Contract Number: 6/ACFT/5043 C.B. 7(b)

Meteor Mk: F Mk 8
Gloster Type No.: Gloster G.41K
Quantity: 36
Built by: Armstrong-Whitworth Aircraft, Baginton
WF639 to WF662
WF677 to WF688
Quantity: 53
Built by: Gloster Aircraft, Hucclecote
WF639 to WF716
WF736 to WF760

Contract Number: 6/ACFT/5621 C.B. 7(b)

Meteor Mk: F Mk 8
Gloster Type No.: Gloster G.41K
Quantity: 200
Built by: Armstrong-Whitworth Aircraft, Baginton
WH249 to WH263
WH272 to WH300
WH342 to WH386
WH396 to WH426
WH442 to WH484
WH498 to WH513

Contract Number: 6/ACFT/6066 C.B. 7(b)

Meteor Mk: F Mk 8
Gloster Type No.: Gloster G.41K
Quantity: 50
Built by: Gloster Aircraft, Hucclecote
WK647 to WK699
Quantity: 50
Built by: Armstrong-Whitworth Aircraft, Baginton
WK710 to WK756
Quantity: 90
Built by: Gloster Aircraft, Hucclecote
WK783 to WK827
WK849 to WK893
Quantity: 29
Built by: Armstrong-Whitworth Aircraft, Baginton
WK906 to WK935
Quantity: 124
Built by: Gloster Aircraft, Hucclecote
WK936 to WK955
WK966 to WK994
WL104 to WL143
WL158 to WL191
Allocated but cancelled:
WL192 to WL207
WL221 to WL234
WS230 to WS558

Contract Number: 6/ACFT/2983 C.B. 7(b)

Meteor Mk: FR Mk 9
Gloster Type No.: Gloster G.41L
Quantity: 23
Built by: Gloster Aircraft, Hucclecote
VW360 to VW371
VZ577 to VZ611
WB113 to WB125
WB138 to WB143

Contract Number: 6/ACFT/5621 C.B. 7(b)

Meteor Mk: FR Mk 9
Gloster Type No.: Gloster G.41L
Quantity: 25
Built by: Gloster Aircraft, Hucclecote
WH533 to WH557

Contract Number: 6/ACFT/6066 C.B. 7(b)

Meteor Mk: FR Mk 9
Gloster Type No.: Gloster G.41L
Quantity: 11
Built by: Gloster Aircraft, Hucclecote
WL255 to WL265

Contract Number: 6/ACFT/7252 C.B. 7(b)

Meteor Mk: FR Mk 9
Gloster Type No.: Gloster G.41L
Quantity: 20
Built by: Gloster Aircraft, Hucclecote
WX962 to WX981
Allocated but cancelled:
WX982 to WX994
WZ103 to WZ151

Contract Number: 6/ACFT/658 C.B. 7(b)

Meteor Mk: PR Mk 10
Gloster Type No.: Gloster G.41M
Quantity: 20
Built by: Gloster Aircraft, Hucclecote
VS968 to VS987

Contract Number: 6/ACFT/1389 C.B. 7(b)

Meteor Mk: PR Mk 10
Gloster Type No.: Gloster G.41M
Quantity: 4
Built by: Gloster Aircraft, Hucclecote
VW376 to VW379

Contract Number: 6/ACFT/2430 C.B. 7(b)

Meteor Mk: PR Mk 10
Gloster Type No.: Gloster G.41M
Quantity: 1
Built by: Gloster Aircraft, Hucclecote
VZ620

Contract Number: 6/ACFT/2983 C.B. 7(b)

Meteor Mk: PR Mk 10
Gloster Type No.: Gloster G.41M
Quantity: 29
Built by: Gloster Aircraft, Hucclecote
WB153 to WB181

Contract Number: 6/ACFT/3433 C.B. 7(b)

Meteor Mk: PR Mk 10
Gloster Type No.: Gloster G.41M
Quantity: 5
Built by: Gloster Aircraft, Hucclecote
WH569 to WH573
Allocated but cancelled:
WL286 to WL305

Contract Number: 6/ACFT/3433 C.B. 7(b)

Meteor Mk: NF Mk 11
Gloster Type No.: Gloster G.47
Quantity: 200
Built by: Armstrong-Whitworth Aircraft, Baginton
WA546 & WA547 (Prototypes)
WD585 to WD634
WD640 to WD689
WD696 to WD745
WD751 to WD800

Contract Number: 6/ACFT/6141 C.B. 7(b)

Meteor Mk: NF Mk 11
Gloster Type No.: Gloster G.47
Quantity: 107
Built by: Armstrong-Whitworth Aircraft, Baginton
WM143 to WM192
WM221 to WM270
WM292 to WM302
WM372 to WM375 – Special batch on an MofS order, sent to Fairey Aviation for Firestreak missile tests. Subsequently, WM372 & WM373 undertook these trials in Australia
WM384 to WM403 – 20 aircraft delivered to Danish Air Force
WM368 to WM403 – WM372, WM373 to Australia for Fireflash trials

Contract Number: 6/ACFT/6412 C.B. 7(b)

Meteor Mk: NF Mk 12
Gloster Type No.: Gloster G.47
Quantity: 97
Built by: Armstrong-Whitworth Aircraft, Baginton
WS590 to WS639
WS658 to WS700
WS715 to WS721

Contract Number: 6/ACFT/6141 C.B. 7(b)

Meteor Mk: NF Mk 13
Gloster Type No.: Gloster G.47
Quantity: 40
Built by: Armstrong-Whitworth Aircraft, Baginton
WM308 to WM341
WM362 to WM367

Contract Number: 6/ACFT/6412 C.B. 7(b)

Meteor Mk: NF Mk 14
Gloster Type No.: Gloster G.47
Quantity: 100
Built by: Armstrong-Whitworth Aircraft, Baginton
WS722 to WS760
WS774 to WS812
WS827 to WS848

Meteor Mk: TT Mk 20

Conversions: 43
WD585, WD591, WD592, WD606, WD610, WD612, WD623, WD629, WD630, WD643, WD645, WD646, WD647, WD649, WD652, WD657, WD678, WD679, WD702, WD706, WD711, WD767, WD780, WD785 WM147, WM148, WM151, WM159, WM160, WM167, WM181, WM223, WM224, WM230, WM234, WM242, WM245, WM246, WM255, WM260, WM270, WM292, WM293
These conversions took place at Gloster and Armstrong-Whitworth's factories at Baginton, Bitteswell and Moreton Valence, as well as RNAY Sydenham. WD677, WM163 and WM172 were sent to Lossiemouth for potential conversion, but their condition was such that they were returned to the RAF for scrapping

Meteor Mk: U Mk 15

Conversions: 91
EE521, EE524
RA367, RA371, RA373, RA375, RA387; RA397, RA398, RA415, RA417, RA420, RA421, RA430, RA432, RA433, RA438, RA439, RA441, RA442, RA454, RA457, RA473, RA479
VT104, VT105, VT106, VT107, VT110, VT112, VT113, VT118, VT130, VT135, VT139, VT142, VT168, VT175, VT177, VT179, VT184, VT187, VT191, VT192, VT196, VT197, VT219, VT220, VT222, VT226, VT230, VT243, VT256, VT259, VT262, VT268, VT270, VT282, VT286, VT289, VT291, VT294, VT310, VT316, VT319, VT329, VT330, VT332, VT334, VT338
VW258, VW266, VW273, VW275, VW276, VW280, VW285, VW293, VW299, VW303, VW308, VW781, VW791
VZ386, VZ389, VZ401, VZ403, VZ407, VZ414, VZ415, VZ417

Meteor Mk: U Mk 16

Conversions: 91
VZ445, VZ485, VZ506, VZ508, VZ514, VZ551
WA756, WA775, WA842, WA982, WA991
WE867, WE872, WE815, WE932, WE934, WE960, WE962
WF706, WF707, WF711, WF716, WF741, WF743, WF751, WF755, WF756
WH258, WH284, WH286, WH309, WH320, WH344, WH349, WH359, WH365, WH369, WH372, WH373, WH376, WH381, WH420, WH453, WH499, WH500, WH505, WH506, WH509
WK648, WK693, WK709, WK717, WK729, WK738, WK743, WK783, WK784, WK789, WK790, WK793, WK795, WK797, WK799, WK800 (redesignated ex-RAAF U Mk 21A), WK807, WK812, WK852, WK855, WK859, WK870, WK877, WK883, WK885, WK911, WK925, WK926, WK932, WK941, WK942, WK949, WK971, WK980, WK989, WK993, WK994 WL110, WL124, WL127, WL160, WL162, WL163
The following aircraft were delivered to Flight Refuelling Ltd as spares ships, and so were never actually converted to U Mk 16 configuration
VZ439, VZ448, VZ458, VZ462, VZ513, VZ520, VZ530, VZ554, WA781, WA850, WA984, WE881, WE919, WE924, WE925, WE946, WF646, WF681, WF685, WF741, WH281, WH469(*), WK660, WK675, WK716, WK721, WK731, WK737, WK744, WL111 and WL134
This latter airframe may well have subsequently been converted. On top of this WK745, WK746 and WK747 were all designated to become U Mk 16 but records do not confirm their actual conversion
*Serial number suspect

Meteor Mk: U Mk 21

Conversions: 8 (+ 2 redesignated ex-U Mk 16s)
VZ455, VZ503
WE902, WE920(*)
WF659
WH460
WK710, WK797(*), WK879
WL136
* These two machines were U Mk 16s already in Australia, so they were subsequently redesignated U Mk 21s

Meteor Mk: U Mk 21A

Conversions: 15 (all Ex-RAAF)
A77-157, A77-193, A77-207, A77-422, A77-510, A77-802, A77-851, A77-855, A77-863, A77-872, A77-873, A77-876(*), A77-882, A77-884, A77-885
* A77-876 returned to the UK in 1971 where it reverted to its ex-RAF serial of WK800 and was redesignated as a U Mk 16

F Mk III EE419, coded MR•V of No.245 Squadron. It is seen here at RAF Coltishall (where it had been received, but was marked as Inst Airframe 7247M). It was finally burnt in 1969
(© R.J. Caruana)

Meteor Squadrons

Appendix VIII

No. 1 Squadron

Code: JX (Not used after 1950)
Started Meteor Operations: Tangmere (Oct 1946)
UK-Based: Tangmere (10/46-9/55)
Foreign-Based: N/A
Reformed: N/A
Disbanded: N/A
Re-equipped: Hunter F Mk 4
Variants Operated: F Mk 3, F Mk 4 & F Mk 8

No. 2 Squadron

Code: None
Started Meteor Operations: Bückeburg, Germany (December 1950)
UK-Based: N/A
Foreign-Based: Bückeburg (12/50-5/52), Wahn (5/52-10/55), Geilenkirchen (10/55-3/56)
Reformed: N/A
Disbanded: N/A
Re-equipped: March 1956 (Supermarine Swift FR Mk 5)
Variants Operated: FR Mk 9, PR Mk 10

No. 5 Squadron

Code: None
Started Meteor Operations: Laarbruch, Germany (by reforming No. 68 Sqn, 12/01/59)
UK-Based: N/A
Foreign-Based: Laarbruch (1/59-6/60)
Reformed: N/A
Disbanded: N/A
Re-equipped: June 1960 (Gloster Javelin FAW Mk 5)
Variants Operated: NF Mk 11

No. 8 Squadron

Code: None
Started Meteor Operations: Khormaksar (January 1958*)
UK-Based: N/A
Foreign-Based: Khormaksar
Reformed: August 1960 (a/c returned by Arabian Peninsula Reconnaissance Flight)
Disbanded: August 1958 (became the Arabian Peninsula Reconnaissance Flight)
Re-equipped: Retired Meteor from Sqn in April 1963
Variants Operated: Mk FR Mk 9
* - Took over the FR.9s of No. 208 squadron and operated them as C Flight alongside the unit's main force of Venom FB Mk 4s

No. 11 Squadron

Code: None
Started Meteor Operations: Geilenkirchen by renumbering No. 256 Sqn (January 1959)
UK-Based: N/A
Foreign-Based: Geilenkirchen (1/59-1960)
Reformed: N/A
Disbanded: N/A
Re-equipped: 1960 (Gloster Javelin FAW Mk 4)
Variants Operated: NF Mk 11

No. 13 Squadron

Code: None
Started Meteor Operations: Ein Shemer by renumbering No. 680 Sqn (1st September 1946)
UK-Based: N/A
Foreign-Based: Ein Shemer (1/9/46-12/46), Kabrit (12/46-2/47), Fayid (2/47-1/55), Abu Sueir (1/55-2/56), Akrotiri (2/56-5/56)
Reformed: N/A
Disbanded: N/A
Re-equipped: May 1956 (E.E. Canberra PR Mk 7)
Variants Operated: PR Mk 10

No. 19 Squadron

Code: None
Started Meteor Operations: Church Fenton (January 1951)
UK-Based: Church Fenton (1/51-1/57)
Foreign-Based: N/A
Reformed: N/A
Disbanded: N/A
Re-equipped: January 1957 (Hawker Hunter F Mk 6)
Variants Operated: F Mk 4 & F Mk 8

No. 25 Squadron

Code: None
Started Meteor Operations: West Malling (January 1954)
UK-Based: West Malling (1/54-9/57), Tangmere (9/57-7/58), Waterbeach (7/58-4/59)
Foreign-Based: N/A
Reformed: Waterbeach 1st July 1958 (by renumbering No. 153 Squadron)
Disbanded: Tangmere 1st July 1958
Re-equipped: April 1959 (Gloster Javelin FAW Mk 7)
Variants Operated: NF Mk 12 & NF Mk 14

No. 29 Squadron

Code: None
Started Meteor Operations: Tangmere (January 1957)
UK-Based: Tangmere (1/57), Acklington (1/57-12/57)
Foreign-Based: N/A
Reformed: N/A
Disbanded: N/A
Re-equipped: December 1957 (Gloster Javelin FAW Mk 6)
Variants Operated: NF Mk 11

No. 33 Squadron

Code: None
Started Meteor Operations: Leeming, by renumbering No. 264 Squadron (1st October 1957)
UK-Based: Leeming (10/57-7/58), Middleton St. George (7/58-8/58)
Foreign-Based: N/A
Reformed: N/A
Disbanded: N/A
Re-equipped: August 1958 (Gloster Javelin FAW Mk 7)
Variants Operated: NF Mk 12 & NF Mk 14

No. 34 Squadron

Code: None
Started Meteor Operations: Tangmere (July 1954)
UK-Based: Tangmere (7/54-2/56)
Foreign-Based: N/A
Reformed: N/A
Disbanded: N/A
Re-equipped: February 1956 (Hawker Hunter F Mk 5)
Variants Operated: F Mk 8

No. 39 Squadron

Code: None
Started Meteor Operations: Kabrit (November 1952)
UK-Based: N/A
Foreign-Based: Kabrit (11/52-1/55), Luqa (1/55-8/56), Nicosia (8/56-6/58)
Reformed: N/A
Disbanded: Nicosia 30th June 1958
Re-equipped: N/A
Variants Operated: NF Mk 13

No. 41 Squadron

Code: None
Started Meteor Operations: Church Fenton (January 1951)
UK-Based: Church Fenton (1/51-3/51), Biggin Hill (3/51-7/55)
Foreign-Based: N/A
Reformed: N/A
Disbanded: N/A
Re-equipped: July 1955 (Hawker Hunter F Mk 5)
Variants Operated: F Mk 4 & F Mk 8

No. 43 Squadron

Code: SW
Started Meteor Operations: Tangmere, by renumbering No. 266 Squadron (11th February 1949)
UK-Based: Tangmere (2/49-11/50), Leuchars (11/50-7/54)
Foreign-Based: N/A
Reformed: N/A
Disbanded: N/A
Re-equipped: July 1954 (Hawker Hunter F Mk 1)
Variants Operated: F Mk 4 & F Mk 8

No. 46 Squadron

Code: None
Started Meteor Operations: Odiham (August 1954)
UK-Based: Odiham (8/54-2/56)
Foreign-Based: N/A
Reformed: N/A
Disbanded: N/A
Re-equipped: February 1956 (Gloster Javelin FAW Mk 1)
Variants Operated: NF Mk 12 & NF Mk 14

No. 54 Squadron

Code: None
Started Meteor Operations: Odiham (April 1952)
UK-Based: Odiham (4/52-3/55)
Foreign-Based: N/A
Reformed: N/A
Disbanded: N/A
Re-equipped: March 1955 (Hawker Hunter F Mk 1)
Variants Operated: F Mk 8

No. 56 Squadron

Code: None
Started Meteor Operations: Bentwaters, by renumbering No. 124 Squadron (1st April 1946)
UK-Based: Bentwaters (4/46-9/46), Boxted (9/46-11/46), Wattisham (11/46-4/47), Duxford (4/47-3/48), Thorney Island (3/48-5/50), Waterbeach (5/50-2/54)
Foreign-Based: N/A
Reformed: N/A
Disbanded: N/A
Re-equipped: February 1954 (Supermarine Swift F Mk 1)
Variants Operated: F Mk 3, F Mk 4 & F Mk 8

No. 60 Squadron

Code: None
Started Meteor Operations: Tengah (October 1959)
UK-Based: N/A
Foreign-Based: Tengah (10/59-8/61)
Reformed: N/A
Disbanded: N/A
Re-equipped: August 1961 (Gloster Javelin FAW Mk 9)
Variants Operated: NF Mk 12 & NF Mk 14

No. 63 Squadron

Code: UB (only on F Mk 3s)
Started Meteor Operations: Thorney Island (April 1948)
UK-Based: Thorney Island (4/48-5/50), Waterbeach (5/50-11/56)
Foreign-Based: N/A
Reformed: N/A
Disbanded: N/A
Re-equipped: November 1956 (Hawker Hunter F Mk 6)
Variants Operated: F Mk 3 & F Mk 4

No. 64 Squadron

Code: None
Started Meteor Operations: Linton-on-Ouse (April 1951)
UK-Based: Linton-on-Ouse (4/51-8/51), Duxford (8/51-9/58)
Foreign-Based: N/A
Reformed: N/A
Disbanded: N/A
Re-equipped: September 1958 (Gloster Javelin FAW Mk 7)
Variants Operated: F Mk 8, NF Mk 12 & NF Mk 14

No. 65 Squadron

Code: None
Started Meteor Operations: Linton-on-Ouse (April 1951)
UK-Based: Linton-on-Ouse (4/51-8/51), Duxford (8/51-3/57)
Foreign-Based: N/A
Reformed: N/A
Disbanded: N/A
Re-equipped: March 1957 (Hawker Hunter F Mk 6)
Variants Operated: F Mk 8

No. 66 Squadron

Code: HI & LZ (only on F Mk 3 & 4s)
Started Meteor Operations: Duxford (March 1947)
UK-Based: Duxford (3/47-10/49), Linton-on-Ouse (10/49-12/53)
Foreign-Based: N/A
Reformed: N/A
Disbanded: N/A

Meteor F Mk IIIs of No.222 Squadron seen in flight. EE450, ZD•K is nearest the camera

Re-equipped: December 1953 (Canadair Sabre F Mk 4)
Variants Operated: F Mk 3, F Mk 4 & F Mk 8

No. 68 Squadron

Code: None
Started Meteor Operations: Wahn (1st January 1952)
UK-Based: N/A
Foreign-Based: Wahn (1/52-7/57), Laarbruch (7/57-1/59)
Reformed: N/A
Disbanded: 20th January 1959
Re-equipped: N/A
Variants Operated: NF Mk 11

No. 72 Squadron

Code: None
Started Meteor Operations: North Weald (July 1952)
UK-Based: North Weald (7/52-7/53), Church Fenton (7/53-6/59)
Foreign-Based: N/A
Reformed: N/A
Disbanded: N/A
Re-equipped: June 1959 (Gloster Javelin FAW Mk 4)
Variants Operated: F Mk 8, NF Mk 12 & NF Mk 14
Note: Last unit to fly Meteors in Fighter Command

No. 74 Squadron

Code: 4D
Started Meteor Operations: Colerne (May 1945)
UK-Based: Colerne (5/45-9/46), Bentwaters (9/46-10/46), Horsham St. Faith (10/46-3/57)
Foreign-Based: N/A
Reformed: N/A
Disbanded: N/A
Re-equipped: March 1957 (Hawker Hunter F Mk 4)
Variants Operated: F Mk 8

No. 79 Squadron

Code: T
Started Meteor Operations: Bückeburg (15th November 1951)
UK-Based: N/A
Foreign-Based: Bückeburg (11/51), Gütersloh (11/51-6/56)
Reformed: N/A
Disbanded: N/A
Re-equipped: June 1956 (Supermarine Swift FR Mk 5)
Variants Operated: FR Mk 9

No. 81 Squadron

Code: None
Started Meteor Operations: Butterworth (December 1953)
UK-Based: N/A
Foreign-Based: Seletar with detachments to Butterworth, Kai Tak & Labuan (12/53-4/58), Tengah with detachment to Labuan (4/58-7/61)
Reformed: N/A
Disbanded: N/A
Re-equipped: July 1961 (E.E. Canberra PR Mk 7)
Variants Operated: PR Mk 10

No. 85 Squadron

Code: None
Started Meteor Operations: West Malling (October 1951)
UK-Based: West Malling (10/51-9/57), Church Fenton (9/57-11/58)
Foreign-Based: N/A
Reformed: N/A
Disbanded: Church Fenton, 30th November 1958
Re-equipped: N/A
Variants Operated: NF Mk 11, NF Mk 12 & NF Mk 14

No. 87 Squadron

Code: None
Started Meteor Operations: Wahn (1st January 1952)
UK-Based: N/A
Foreign-Based: Wahn (1/52-8/57)
Reformed: N/A
Disbanded: N/A
Re-equipped: August 1957 (Gloster Javelin FAW Mk 1)
Variants Operated: NF Mk 11

No. 91 Squadron

Code: DL
Started Meteor Operations: Duxford (October 1946)
UK-Based: Duxford (10/46-11/46), Debden (11/46-1/47), Acklington (1/47)
Foreign-Based: N/A
Reformed: N/A
Disbanded: 31st January 1947 (renumbered as No. 92 Squadron)
Re-equipped: N/A
Variants Operated: F Mk 3

No. 92 Squadron

Code: DL & 8L
Started Meteor Operations: Acklington (31st January 1947)
UK-Based: Acklington (1/47-2/47), Duxford (2/47-10/49), Linton-on-Ouse (10/49-2/54)
Foreign-Based: N/A
Reformed: N/A
Disbanded: N/A
Re-equipped: February 1954 (Canadair Sabre F Mk 4)
Variants Operated: F Mk 3, F Mk 4 & F Mk 8

No. 96 Squadron

Code: None
Started Meteor Operations: Ahlhorn (1st October 1952)
UK-Based: N/A
Foreign-Based: Ahlhorn, Germany (10/52-1/59)
Reformed: N/A
Disbanded: Ahlhorn (21st January 1959), renumbered as No. 3 Squadron
Re-equipped: N/A
Variants Operated: NF Mk 11

No. 111 Squadron

Code: None
Started Meteor Operations: North Weald (2nd December 1953)
UK-Based: North Weald (12/53-6/55)
Foreign-Based: N/A
Reformed: N/A
Disbanded: N/A
Re-equipped: June 1955 (Hawker Hunter F Mk 4)
Variants Operated: F Mk 8

No. 124 Squadron

Code: None
Started Meteor Operations: Hutton Cranwick (August 1945)
UK-Based: Huton Cranwick (8/45), Molesworth (8/45-10/45), Bentwaters (10/45-4/46)
Foreign-Based: N/A
Reformed: N/A
Disbanded: 1st April 1946 (Bentwaters), renumbered as No. 56 Squadron
Re-equipped: N/A
Variants Operated: F Mk 3

No. 125 Squadron

Code: None
Started Meteor Operations: Stradishall (March 1955)
UK-Based: Stradishall (3/55-1/56)
Foreign-Based: N/A
Reformed: N/A
Disbanded: N/A
Re-equipped: January 1956 (D.H. Venom NF Mk 3)
Variants Operated: NF Mk 11

No. 141 Squadron

Code: None
Started Meteor Operations: Coltishall (September 1951)
UK-Based: Coltishall (9/51-6/55)
Foreign-Based: N/A
Reformed: N/A
Disbanded: N/A
Re-equipped: June 1955 (D.H. Venom NF Mk 3)
Variants Operated: NF Mk 11

No. 151 Squadron

Code: None
Started Meteor Operations: Leuchars (March 1953)
UK-Based: Leuchars (3/53-10/55)
Foreign-Based: N/A
Reformed: N/A
Disbanded: N/A
Re-equipped: October 1955 (D.H. Venom NF Mk 3)
Variants Operated: NF Mk 11 (also had an F Mk 8 as the squadron hack)

No. 152 Squadron

Code: None
Started Meteor Operations: Wattisham (June 1954)
UK-Based: Wattisham (6/54-6/56), Stradishall (6/56-7/58)
Foreign-Based: N/A

Reformed: N/A
Disbanded: Stradishall, 11th July 1958
Re-equipped: N/A
Variants Operated: NF Mk 12 & NF Mk 14

No. 153 Squadron

Code: None
Started Meteor Operations: West Malling (28th February 1955)
UK-Based: West Malling (2/55-9/57), Waterbeach (9/57-6/58)
Foreign-Based: N/A
Reformed: N/A
Disbanded: Waterbeach, 23rd June 1958, renumbered as No. 25 Squadron
Re-equipped: N/A
Variants Operated: NF Mk 12 & NF Mk 14

No. 208 Squadron

Code: None
Started Meteor Operations: Fayid (January 1951)
UK-Based: N/A
Foreign-Based: Fayid (1/51-10/51), Abu Sueir (10/51-1/56), Hal Far (1/56-3/56), Akrotiri (3/56-8/56), Ta'Qali with detachment to Khormaksar (8/56-3/58), Nicosia with detachment to Khormaksar (3/58-12/58)
Reformed: N/A
Disbanded: Nicosia, December 1958
Re-equipped: N/A
Variants Operated: FR Mk 9

No. 219 Squadron

Code: None
Started Meteor Operations: Kabrit (March 1951)
UK-Based: N/A
Foreign-Based: Kabrit (3/51-9/54)
Reformed: N/A
Disbanded: Wittering, 1st September 1954
Re-equipped: N/A
Variants Operated: NF Mk 13

No. 222 Squadron

Code: ZD
Started Meteor Operations: Westonzoyland (October 1945)
UK-Based: Westonzoyland (10/45), Fairwood Common, Molesworth, Spilsby (10/45-6/46), Exeter (6/46-7/46), Westonzoyland (7/46-10/46), Tangmere (10/46-5/47), Tangmere (6/47-6/48), Thorney Island (7/48-3/50), Waterbeach (3/50-5/50), Leuchars (5/50-12/54)
Foreign-Based: Gilze-Rijen [B.77] (2/45-4/45), Nijmegen (4/45), Quackenbrück (4/45-6/45), Lübeck (5/47-6/47), Lübeck (6/48-7/48)
Reformed: N/A
Disbanded: N/A
Re-equipped: December 1954 (Hawker Hunter F Mk 1)
Variants Operated: F Mk 3, F Mk 4 & F Mk 8

No. 234 Squadron

Code: FX
Started Meteor Operations: Molesworth (February 1946)
UK-Based: Molesworth (2/46-3.46), Boxted (3/46-9/46)
Foreign-Based: N/A
Reformed: N/A
Disbanded: Boxted, 1st September 1946, renumbered as No. 266 Squadron
Re-equipped: N/A
Variants Operated: F Mk 3

No. 245 Squadron

Code: MR
Started Meteor Operations: Colerne (August 1945)
UK-Based: Colerne (8/45-6/46), Bentwaters (6/46-10/46), Horsham St. Faith (10/46-6/55), Stradishall (6/55-4/57)
Foreign-Based: N/A
Reformed: N/A
Disbanded: N/A
Re-equipped: April 1957 (Hawker Hunter F Mk 4)
Variants Operated: F Mk 3, F Mk 4 & F Mk 8

No. 247 Squadron

Code: None
Started Meteor Operations: Odiham (April 1952)
UK-Based: Odiham (4/52-6/55)
Foreign-Based: N/A
Reformed: N/A
Disbanded: N/A
Re-equipped: June 1955 (Hawker Hunter F Mk 1)
Variants Operated: F Mk 8

No. 256 Squadron

Code: None
Started Meteor Operations: Ahlhorn (November 1952)
UK-Based: N/A
Foreign-Based: Ahlhorn (11/52-2/58), Geilenkirchen (2/58-1/59)
Reformed: N/A
Disbanded: Geilenkirchen, 21st January 1959, renumbered No. 11 Squadron.
Re-equipped: N/A
Variants Operated: NF Mk 11

No. 257 (Burma) Squadron

Code: A6
Started Meteor Operations: Church Fenton (September 1946)
UK-Based: Church Fenton (9/46-9/47), Horsham St. Faith (9/47-10/50), Wattisham (10/50-11/54)
Foreign-Based: N/A
Reformed: N/A
Disbanded: N/A
Re-equipped: November 1954 (Hawker Hunter F Mk 2)
Variants Operated: F Mk 3 and F Mk 4

No. 263 Squadron

Code: HE
Started Meteor Operations: Acklington (September 1945)
UK-Based: Acklington (9/45), Church Fenton (9/45-6/46), Boxted with detachment to Lübeck (6/46-9/46), Horsham St. Faith with detachment to Lübeck (9/46-10/50), Wattisham (10/50-2/55)
Foreign-Based: See above
Reformed: N/A
Disbanded: N/A
Re-equipped: February 1955 (Hawker Hunter F Mk 2)
Variants Operated: F Mk 3, F Mk 4 & F Mk 8

No. 264 Squadron

Code: None
Started Meteor Operations: Linton-on-Ouse (December 1951)
UK-Based: Linton-on-Ouse (12/51-2/52), Leuchars (2/52-8/52), Unrecorded (8/52-3/57), Middleton St. George (3/57-9/57), Leeming (9/57-10/57)
Foreign-Based: N/A
Reformed: N/A
Disbanded: Leeming, October 1957, renumbered No. 33 Squadron.

Re-equipped: N/A
Variants Operated: NF Mk 11, NF Mk 12 & NF Mk 14

No. 266 Squadron

Code: FX
Started Meteor Operations: Boxted (1st September 1946)
UK-Based: Boxted (9/46), Acklington (9/46-11/46), Wattisham (11/46-4/47), Tangmere (4/47), Tangmere (6/47-2/49)
Foreign-Based: Lübeck (4/47-6/47)
Reformed: N/A
Disbanded: Tangmere, 11th February 1949, renumbered No. 43 Squadron.
Re-equipped: N/A
Variants Operated: F Mk 3 & F Mk 4

No. 500 Squadron

Code: RAA
Started Meteor Operations: (July 1948)
UK-Based: West Malling with detachments to Horsham St. Faith, Thorney Island, Leuchars, Ta'Qali & Celle [Summer Camps] (7/48-3/57)
Foreign-Based: See above
Reformed: N/A
Disbanded: 10th March 1957 (West Malling)
Re-equipped: N/A
Variants Operated: F Mk 3, F Mk 4 & F Mk 8

No. 504 Squadron

Code: RAD
Started Meteor Operations: Colerne (28th March 1945)
UK-Based: Colerne with detachment to Lübeck (3/45-8/45), Wymeswold with detachments to Manston, Horsham St. Faith, Celle and Ta'Qali [Summer Camp] (3/50-2/57)
Foreign-Based: See above
Reformed: Wymeswold, 10th May 1946
Disbanded: Colerne, 10th August 1945 and Wymeswold, 12th February 1957
Re-equipped: N/A
Variants Operated: F Mk 3, F Mk 4 & F Mk 8

No. 541 Squadron

Code: None
Started Meteor Operations: Benson (July 1945)
UK-Based: Benson (7/45-4/46), Benson (12/50-6/51)
Foreign-Based: Bückeburg (6/51-6/55), Laarbruch (6/55-9/57)
Reformed: N/A
Disbanded: Laarbruch, 6th September 1957
Re-equipped: N/A
Variants Operated: F Mk 3 & PR Mk 10
Note: The three F Mk 3s (EE409, EE410 & EE411) were only received for evaluation

No. 600 (City of London) Squadron

Code: LJ
Started Meteor Operations: Biggin Hill (March 1950)
UK-Based: Biggin Hill with detachments to Tangmere, Thorney Island, Celle, Oldenburg & Ta'Qali [Summer Camp] (3/50-3/57)
Foreign-Based: See above
Reformed: N/A
Disbanded: Biggin Hill, 10th March 1957
Re-equipped: N/A
Variants Operated: F Mk 4 & F Mk 8

No. 601 (County of London) Squadron

Code: None
Started Meteor Operations: North Weald (August 1952)
UK-Based: North Weald with detachments to Horsham St. Faith, Sylt and Ta'Qali [Summer Camp] (8/52-3/57)
Foreign-Based: See above
Reformed: N/A
Disbanded: North Weald, 10th March 1957
Re-equipped: N/A
Variants Operated: F Mk 8

No. 604 (County of Middlesex) Squadron

Code: None
Started Meteor Operations: North Weald (August 1952)
UK-Based: North Weald with detachments to Thorney Island and Ta'Qali [Summer Camps] (8/52-3/57)
Foreign-Based: See above
Reformed: N/A
Disbanded: North Weald, 10th March 1957
Re-equipped: N/A
Variants Operated: F Mk 8

No. 609 Squadron

Code: None
Started Meteor Operations: Church Fenton (January 1951)
UK-Based: Church Fenton with detachments to Tangmere, Manston, Thorney Island, Chivenor, Sylt & Celle [Summer Camps] (4/51-3/57)
Foreign-Based: See above
Reformed: N/A
Disbanded: Church Fenton, 10th March 1957
Re-equipped: N/A
Variants Operated: F Mk 4 & F Mk 8

No. 610 (County of Chester) Squadron

Code: None
Started Meteor Operations: Hooton Park (April 1951)
UK-Based: Hooton Park (4/51-3/57)
Foreign-Based: N/A
Reformed: N/A
Disbanded: Hooton Park, 10th March 1957
Re-equipped: N/A
Variants Operated: F Mk 4 & F Mk 8

No. 611 (West Lancashire) Squadron

Code: None
Started Meteor Operations: Hooton Park (May 1951)
UK-Based: Hooton Park (5/51-3/57)
Foreign-Based: N/A
Reformed: N/A
Disbanded: Hooton Park, 10th March 1957
Re-equipped: N/A
Variants Operated: F Mk 4 & F Mk 8

No. 615 (County of Surrey) Squadron

Code: V6
Started Meteor Operations: Biggin Hill (September 1950)
UK-Based: Biggin Hill with detachments to Horsham St. Faith, Sylt and Celle [Summer Camp] (9/50-3/57)
Foreign-Based: N/A
Reformed: N/A
Disbanded: Hooton Park, 10th March 1957
Re-equipped: N/A
Variants Operated: F Mk 4, T Mk 7 & F Mk 8

No. 616 Squadron

Code: YQ
Started Meteor Operations: Culmhead (12th July 1944)

A formation of F Mk 4s from No.43 Squadron. Nearest is VT104 (SW•W), then VT243 (SW•Y) and RA489 (SW•N), while SW•P has its serial obscured
(©Glenn Sands)

UK-Based: Culmhead (7/44), Manston with detachment to Debden (7/44-1/45), Colerne with detachment to Melsbroek [B.58] (1/45-2/45), Andrews Field with detachment to Melsbroek [B.58] (2/45-3/45), Finningley with detachments to Tangmere, Colerne, Horsham St. Faith, Celle & Thorney Island [Summer Camp] (12/48-2/57)
Foreign-Based: Gilze-Rijen [B.77] (3/45-4/45), Nijmegen (4/45), B.109 (4/45-5/45), Lüneberg (5/45), Lübeck (5/45-8/45)
Reformed: 31st July 1946 (Finningley)
Disbanded: Lübeck, 29th August 1945, Finningley, 15th February 1957
Re-equipped: N/A
Variants Operated: F Mk I, F Mk 3, F Mk 4 & F Mk 8
Note: First operational RAF Meteor squadron

Secondary RAF Squadrons & Government Establishments

No. 1 Air Navigation Flight
No. 1 Air Navigation School
No. 1 Group Communications Flight
No. 1 Overseas Ferry Unit
No. 1 Tactical Weapons Unit
No. 2 Air Navigation Flight
No. 2 Air Navigation School
No. 2 Armament Practice Station, Acklington
No. 2 Ferry Pool
No. 2 Ferry Unit
No. 2 Group Communications Flight
No. 2 Tactical Air Force Communications Squadron
No. 3 Civilian Anti-Aircraft Co-operation Unit
No. 3 Flying Training School
No. 3 Group Communications Flight
No. 4 Civilian Anti-Aircraft Co-operation Unit
No. 4 Flying Training School
No. 5 Civilian Anti-Aircraft Co-operation Unit
No. 5 Flying Training School
No. 6 Joint Services Trials Unit (WRE)
No. 8 Flying Training School
No. 9 Flying Training School
No. 10 Flying Training School
No. 11 Group Communications Flight
No. 12 Group Communications Flight
No. 12 Flying Training School
No. 13 Group Communications Flight
No. 14 Group Communications Flight
No. 25 Group Communications Flight
No. 29 Air Fighting Development Squadron (CFE)
No. 32 Operational Training Unit
No. 41 Group Test Pilots Pool
No. 61 Operational Training Unit
No. 64 Group Communications Flight
No. 81 Group Communications Flight
No. 83 Group Communications Flight
No. 85 Air Fighting Development Squadron (CFE)
No. 101 Flying Refresher School
No. 102 Flying Refresher School
No. 103 Flying Refresher School
No. 105 Flying Refresher School
No. 110 Flying Refresher School
No. 141 Air Fighting Development Squadron (CFE)
No. 202 Advanced Flying School
No. 203 Advanced Flying School
No. 205 Advanced Flying School
No. 205 Group Communications Flight
No. 206 Advanced Flying School
No. 207 Advanced Flying School
No. 208 Advanced Flying School
No. 209 Advanced Flying School
No. 210 Advanced Flying School
No. 211 Advanced Flying School
No. 211 Flying Training School
No. 215 Advanced Flying School
No. 226 Operational Conversion Unit
No. 228 Operational Conversion Unit
No. 229 Operational Conversion Unit
No. 231 Operational Conversion Unit
No. 233 Operational Conversion Unit
No. 237 Operational Conversion Unit
No. 238 Operational Conversion Unit
No. 226 Operational Training Unit
No. 264 Air Fighting Development Squadron (CFE)
No. 1335 Conversion Unit
No. 1574 Target Facilities Flight, Changi
No. 1689 Ferry Pool Training Flight
Air Attaché, Paris
Air Fighting Development Squadron (CFE)
Airborne Forces Experimental Establishment
Air Observer School
Air Ministry Servicing Development Unit
All Weather Operational Conversion Unit
All Weather Development Squadron (CFE)
Armament and Instrument Experimental Unit
Armament Practice Station, Acklington
Armament Practice Station, Sylt
Bomber Command Communications Flight
Bomber Command Communications Squadron
Blind Landing Experimental Unit
College of Air Warfare
Central Bombing Establishment
Coastal Command Communications Flight
Central Flying Establishment
Central Flying School
Central Gunnery School
Central Photographic Establishment
Central Signals Establishment
Central Servicing Development Establishment
Controller of Research & Development
Day Fighter Leader School (CFE)
Empire Air Armament School
Empire Central Flying School
Empire Flying School
Empire Test Pilots School
Fighter Command Communications Squadron
Far East Communications Squadron
Far East Training Squadron
Fighter Interceptor Unit
Flying Refresher Flight, Aden
Ferry Training Unit
Fighter Weapons School
Guided Weapons Development Squadron
Institute of Aviation Medicine
Instrument Training Flight, Nicosia
Instrument Training Flight, Shallufa
Instrument Training Flight, Tangmere
Instrument Training Flight, West Raynham
Jet Conversion Flight
Jet Conversion Unit
Levant Communications Flight
Middle East Communications Squadron
Night and All Weather Conversion Unit
National Gas Turbine Establishment
Night Fighter Leader School
Overseas Ferry Unit
Protectorate Command Communications Squadron, Aden
Royal Aircraft Establishment
RAF College
RAF Flying College
Radar Research Establishment
Special Conversion Unit
Station Flight, Biggin Hill
Station Flight, Church Fenton
Station Flight, Coltishall
Station Flight, Duxford
Station Flight, Geilenkirchen
Station Flight, Horsham St. Faith
Station Flight, Leuchars
Station Flight, Linton-on-Ouse
Station Flight, North Weald
Station Flight, Odiham
Station Flight, Ouston
Station Flight, Stradishall
Station Flight, Tangmere
Station Flight, Waterbeach
Station Flight, Wattisham
Station Flight, West Malling
Station Flight, Wymeswold
Tactical Air Force Communications Squadron
Tactical Weapons Unit
Target Towing Flight, Gibraltar
Target Towing Flight, Kai Tak
Target Towing Flight, Nicosia
Target Towing Flight, Seletar
Target Towing Squadron, Malta
Telecommunications Flying Unit
Telecommunications Research Establishment
Temperature and Humidity (THUM) Flight
Winterisation Experimental Establishment

Fleet Air Arm Units

No. 700 NAS (TT Mk 20)
No. 700Z NAS (T Mk 7, Code: LM)
No. 702 NAS (T Mk 7, Code: CW)
No. 703 NAS (F Mk 3, Code: FD)
No. 703 NAS (T Mk 7, Code: FD)
No. 703 NAS (F Mk 8)
No. 728 NAS (T Mk 7, Code: HF & LM)
No. 728 NAS (TT Mk 20, Code: HF)
No. 728B NAS (U Mk 15)
No. 728B NAS (U Mk 16)
No. 736 NAS (T Mk 7, Code: LM)
No. 759 NAS (T Mk 7, Code: CW, HF & LM)
No. 767 NAS (T Mk 7)
No. 771 NAS (T Mk 7, Code: FD)
No. 776 FRU (T Mk 7)
No. 776 FRU (TT Mk 20)
No. 781 NAS (T Mk 7)
No. 806 NAS (T Mk 7)
No. 813 NAS (T Mk 7)
Station Flight, RNAS Brawdy
Station Flight, RNAS Sydenham
Station Flight, RNAS Yeovilton

Meteor Bibliography

Appendix 

Gloster Meteor - Postwar Military Aircraft 2
by Chaz Bowyer
Ian Allan ©1985
ISBN 0-7110-1477-9

Gloster Meteor - Super Profile
by M.J.Hardy
Winchmore Publishing Services Ltd ©1985
ISBN 0-85429-451-1

Gloster Meteor
by Barry Jones
The Crowood Press ©1998
ISBN 1-86126-162-4

Gloster Meteor & E.28/39 'Pioneer'
by Mike Chilestone
Mushroom Model Publications

The Gloster Meteor
by E. Shacklady
MacDonald ©1962

The Gloster Meteor - Close-up Classic 1
by Richard J. Caruana
Modelaid International Publications ©1990
ISBN 1-871767-02-4

Meteor
by Bryan Philpott
Patrick Stephens Ltd ©1986
ISBN 0-85059-734-X

Meteor - Gloster's First Jet Fighter
by Stephen J. Bond
Midland Counties Publications ©1985
ISBN 0-904597-55-5

Meteor In Action
by Glen Ashley
Squadron/Signal Publications ©1995
ISBN 0-89747-332-9

Meteor F Mk 8, Aircraft in Profile No.12
Profile Publications Ltd ©1966

Meteor, Sabre & Mirage in Australian Service
by Stewart Wilson
Aerospace Publications ©1989

Official Publications

Air Publication

Air Publication AP2210A F Mk I

Air Publication AP2210C F Mk III

Air Publication AP2210D F Mk 4

Air Publication AP2210G T Mk 7

Air Publication AP2210H F Mk 8

Air Publication AP2210J FR Mk 9

Air Publication AP2210K PR Mk 10

Air Publication AP2210L NF Mk 11

Air Publication AP2210M NF Mk 12

Air Publication AP2210N NF Mk 13

Air Publication AP2210P NF Mk 14

Air Publication AP2210Q U Mk 15

Air Publication AP2210R U Mk 16

Air Publication AP2210V TT Mk 20

General Titles

Aircam - Aerobatic Teams 1950-71 Vol.1 & 2
by Richard Ward
Osprey

Aircraft Camouflage & Markings 1907-1954
by Bruce Robertson
Harleyford ©1965

Aircraft Markings of the World 1912-1967
by Bruce Robertson
Harleyford ©1967

Aircraft of the RAF - A Pictorial Record 1918-1978
by J.W.R. Taylor
MacDonald & Janes ©1978

Aircraft of the Royal Air Force since 1918
by Owen Thetford
Putnam Publishing Ltd. © 1957, 58, 62, 68, 71, 76, 79 & 1988
ISBN 0-85177-810-0

The Airfields of Lincolnshire since 1912
by R. Blake, M. Hodgson & B. Taylor
Midland Counties Publications ©1984

Armament of British Aircraft 1909-1939
by H.F. King
Putnam Publishing Ltd © 1971

Aviation Photo Album Vols. 1 & 2
by Michael J.F. Bowyer
Patrick Stephens Ltd © 1978

Belgian Military Aviation 1945-1977
by Paul Jackson
Midland Counties Publications ©1977

British Aircraft of World War II
by David Monday
Hamlyn ©1982

British Civil Aircraft since 1919 - Volume 2
by A.J. Jackson
Putnam Publishing Ltd © 1973

The British Fighter since 1912
by P. Lewis
Putnam Publishing Ltd © 1965

British Military Aircraft Serials 1911-1979
by Bruce Robertson
Patrick Stephens Ltd ©1979

British Naval Aircraft since 1912
by Owen G. Thetford
Putnams ©1982

Camouflage and Markings, RAF Fighter Command 1936-1945
by James and Robert Jones
Ducimus Books ©1971

Camouflage & Markings: RAF 1939-45
by M. Reynolds
Argus Books ©1992

Coastal, Support and Special Squadrons of the RAF
by John D. R. Rawlings
Janes ©1982

Combat Aircraft of the World
edited by J.M.R. Taylor
Edbury Press & Michael Joseph ©1969

Dutch Military Aviation 1945-1978
by Paul Jackson
Midland Counties Publications ©1978

Famous Fighter Squadrons of the RAF Vol.1
by James J. Halley
Hylton Lacy ©1971

Fighters of the Fifties
by Bill Gunston
Patrick Stephens Ltd ©1981

Fighter Squadrons of the RAF and their Aircraft
by J.D.R. Rawlings
MacDonald & Jane's ©1969

Fighting Colours - RAF Fighter Camouflage and Markings 1937-1975
by M.J.F. Bowyer
Patrick Stephens Ltd © 1969, 1970, 1975
ISBN 0-85059-191-0

Flying Colours
by W. Green & G. Swanborough
Salamander ©1981

The Flying Navy
by Richard E. Gardner
Almarks Publications, 1971

French Military Aviation
by Paul Jackson
Midland Counties Publications ©1979

Gloster Aircraft since 1917
by D.N. James
Putnam ©1971

History of No.208 Squadron
by D.S.B. Marr
Official Squadron Publications ©1966

History of the RAF
by C. Bowyer
Hamlyn ©1977

Latin American Military Aviation
by J.M. Andrade
Midland Counties Publications ©1982

Jet Pioneers
by Tim Kershaw
Sutton Publishing ©2004
ISBN 0-7509-3212-0

Les Avions Britanniques aux couleurs Françaises
by Jean-Jacques Petit
Avia Editions ©2003
ISBN 2-915030-04-9

Lion over Korea - 77 Fighter Squadron RAAF 1950-55
by David Wilson
Banner Books, ©1994

MiG Alley - Air to air combat over Korea
by Larry Davis
Squadron/Signal Publications, ©1978

Pictorial History of the RAF Vol.3
by J.W.R. Taylor and P.J.R. Moyes
Ian Allan ©1970

RAF, A Pictorial History
by Bruce Robertson
Robert Hale Ltd ©1978

RAF Flying Training & Support Units
by R. Sturtivant, J. Hamlin & J.J. Halley
Air Britain ©1995

Royal Air Force - The Aircraft in Service since 1918
by C. Bowyer & M. Turner
Hamlyn © 1981

Royal Air Force - Unit Histories
by J.J. Halley
Air Britain ©1969 & 1973

Squadron Codes 1937-56
by Michael J.F. Bowyer & J.D.R. Rawlings
Patrick Stephens ©1979

Squadron Histories, RFC, RNAS and RAF since 1912
by Peter Lewis
Putnam ©1968

The Squadrons of the Fleet Air Arm
by R. Sturtivant & T. Ballance
Air Britain ©1994

Squadrons of the Royal Air Force
by J.J. Halley
Air Britain ©1980

Warplanes of the Second World War
by William Green
MacDonald & Jane's

Wings of the Navy
by Capt. Eric 'Winkle' Brown
Pilot Press © 1980

Yesterday's RAF Fighters
by P.J.R. Moyes
Vintage Aviation Publications ©1976

Periodicals & Journals

Aeromilitaria: 3/80, 3/87

Aeronautics: May 1946, December 1947, December 1948

Aeroplane Monthly: July 1975, November 1975, July 1977, August 1979, July 1982, August 1982, October 1983, May 1985, April 1990, November 1993, March 1994, December 1994, March to July 1995, January 1996, April 2003

Air: Vol.29 No.5

Air Britain Digest: Vol.39 No.5, Aug/Sept 1988

Air Classics Quarterly Review: Summer 1974

Air Clues: Vol.39 No.6

Aircraft Illustrated: November 1970, June 1972, April 1993, March 1999

Aircraft Illustrated Annual: 1987

Aircraft Modelworld: July & August 1986, March 1987

Air Enthusiast: No.25, No.50, No.55, No.77, No.106

Air Extra: No.20

Airfix Magazine: Vol.1 No.2, October 1992

Air Forces International: February 1988

Air Forces Monthly: November 1991

Air International: May 1982, October 1987

Air Mail: January-March 2000

Air Pictorial: January 1963, May 1965, July 1980, March 1993, February 1994, July 1994

Airplane: Vol.18 No.210

Air Review: Vol.7 No.4

Air World: December 1995

Aviation News: 11-24 September 1981, Vol.6 No.18, Vol.13 No.22, Vol.16 No.16, Vol. 16 No.26, Vol.18 No.3, Vol.19 No.9, Vol 20 No.16, Vol.21 No.2

Dateline: No.224 (5th June 1976)

Digby Digest: April 1989

Exclusively Aircraft: Issue No.4

Flight: 30th March 1956

Flypast: March 1989, February 1992, March 1993, July 1995, August 1995, May 2000

IAEE Journal: Jan/Feb 1964

IPMS(UK): 4/88

Le Fana de l'Aviation: No.244 (Nov 1989), No.274 (Sept 1992), No.275 (October 1992), No.276 (November 1992)

Military Aviation Review: August 1976, September 1976, October 1976, December 1979, June/July 1981

Modelaid Quarterly International: No.1 (December 1987)

Modelbouw in Plastic: 3/85

Mushroom Monthly: 4/7, 9/1, 9/4 & 9/5

Mushroom Model Magazine: Vol.1 No.3

PAM News: Vol.5 Iss 1 & 2, No.18

Plastic Kit Revue: No.12 & 13 (1993)

RAE News: Vol.42 No.5

RAF News: No.662 (1986), No.683 (1987)

RAF Yearbook: 1984, 2002

Roundel: February 1977, March 1977, July 1977, August 1977, October 1977, December 1977, May to November 1978, January 1979, March 1980

Scale Aircraft Modelling: Vol.1 No.6, Vol.2 No.9, Vol.3 No.5, Vol.5 No.2, Vol.7 No.1, Vol.9 No.2, Vol.9 No.3 and Vol.12 No.10

Target: No.7

The Aeroplane: 14th September 1945, 16th November 1945, 15th February 1946

The Air Cadet: June 1991

Wingspan: Sept/Oct 1986, November 1992, No.97 (March 1993), No.104 (October 1993), Jan/Feb 2001

World Air Power Journal: Spring 1991

Note:
The above periodical and journals listing is not, and cannot be, complete. The list above gives a broad overview of the subject and is offered as a reference guide for all those wishing to build the type. Further research into suitable source material is, however, still recommended

Index

Please note: this index does not reference the appendices.

A line-up of four Meteors, including A77-134 (formerly WE898). Whilst serving in Korea it was named 'Snookes' and at another time 'Marara I' *(© Courtesy of the Aviation Heritage Museum of WA)*

VZ608 was fitted with an RB108 lift engine in the mid-fuselage section for trials relating to the Short SC.1

Still going strong and long may it continue! Martin-Baker's modified T Mk 7 WL419 is seen making a low pass over their airfield
(© Martin-Baker Plc)

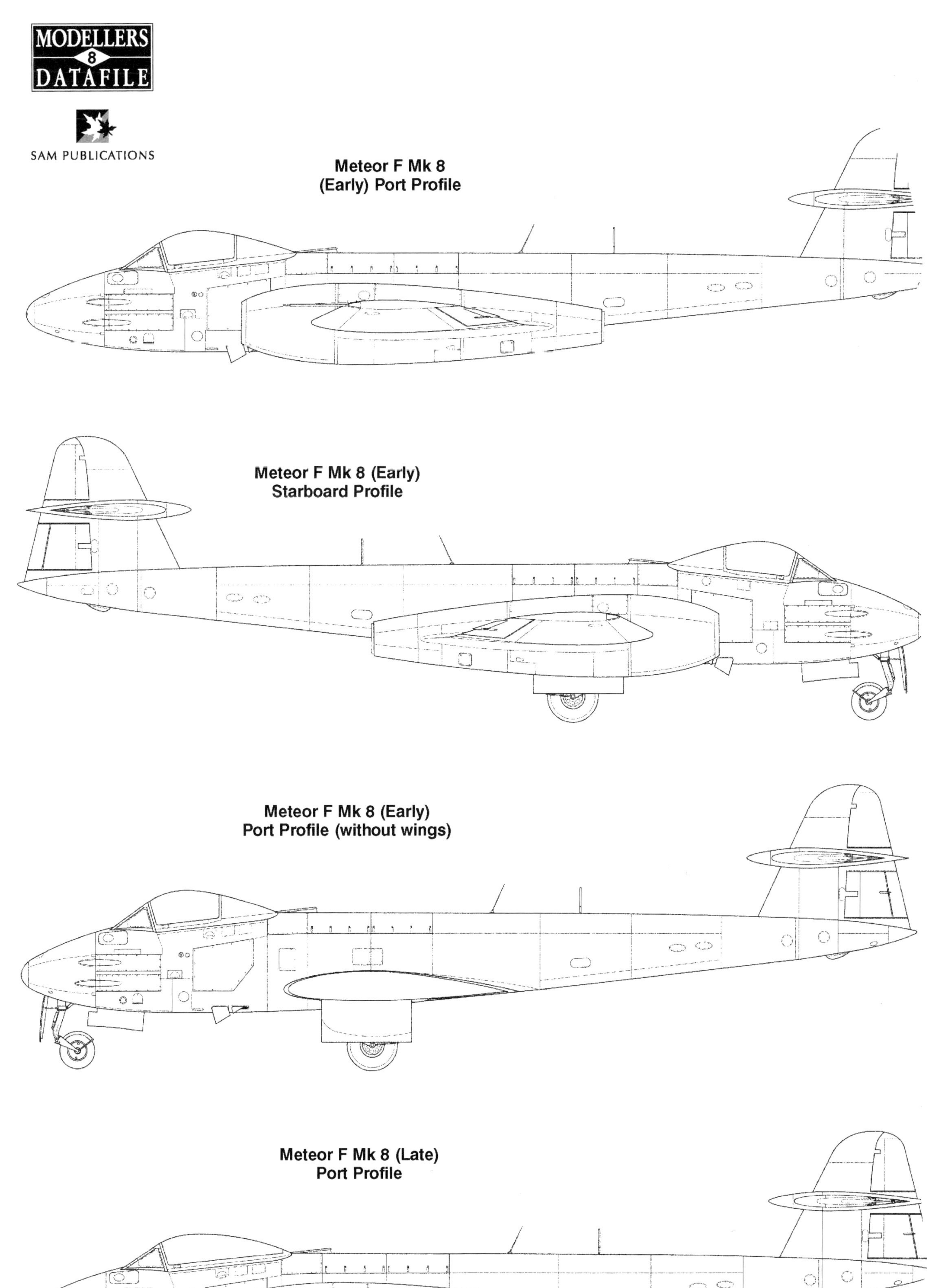
MODELLERS
8
DATAFILE
SAM PUBLICATIONS
Meteor F Mk 8
(Early) Port Profile
Meteor F Mk 8 (Early)
Starboard Profile
Meteor F Mk 8 (Early)
Port Profile (without wings)
Meteor F Mk 8 (Late)
Port Profile

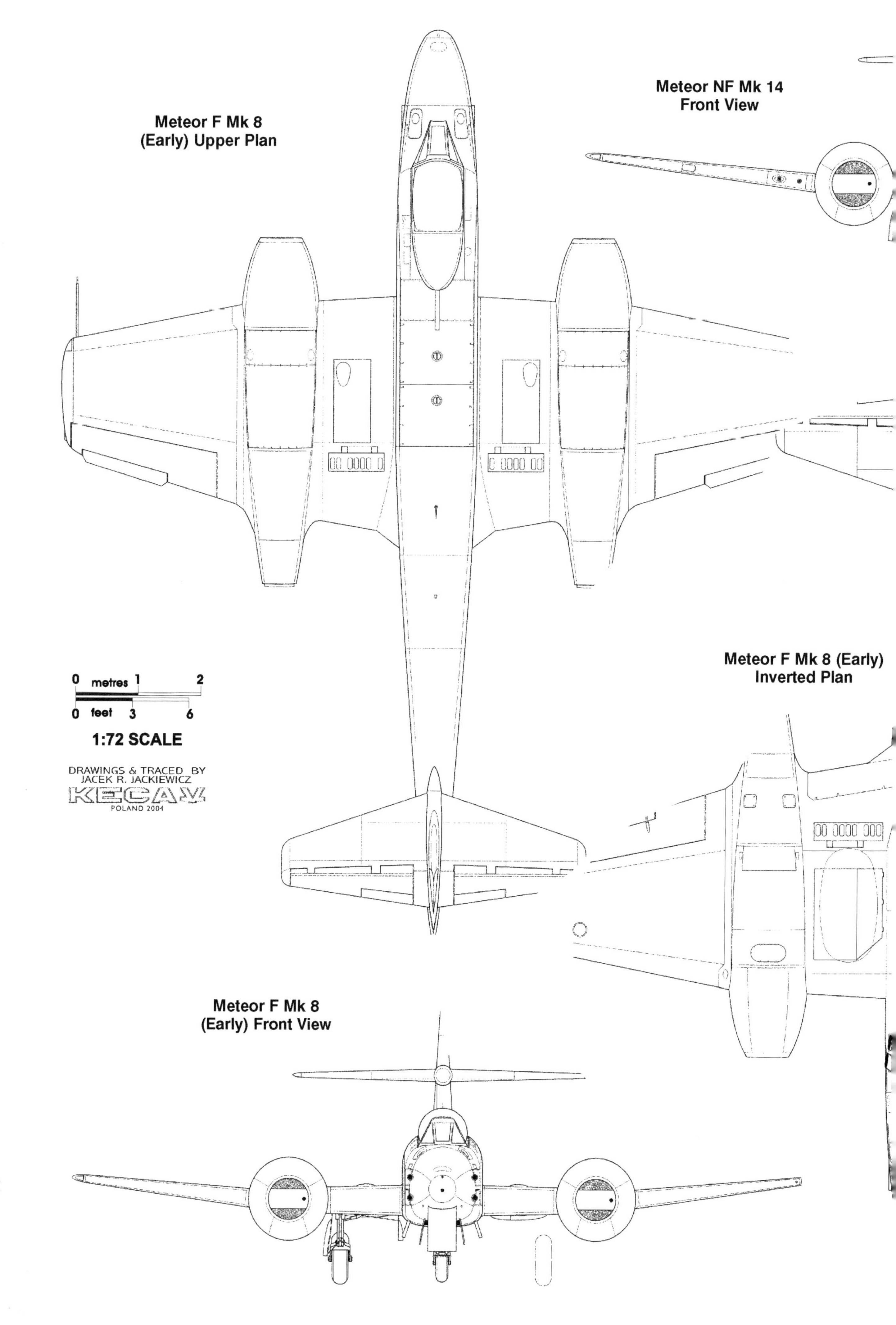
Meteor F Mk 8
(Early) Upper Plan
Meteor NF Mk 14
Front View
0 metres 1 2
0 feet 3 6
1:72 SCALE
DRAWINGS & TRACED BY
JACEK R. JACKIEWICZ
KECAY
POLAND 2004
Meteor F Mk 8 (Early)
Inverted Plan
Meteor F Mk 8
(Early) Front View

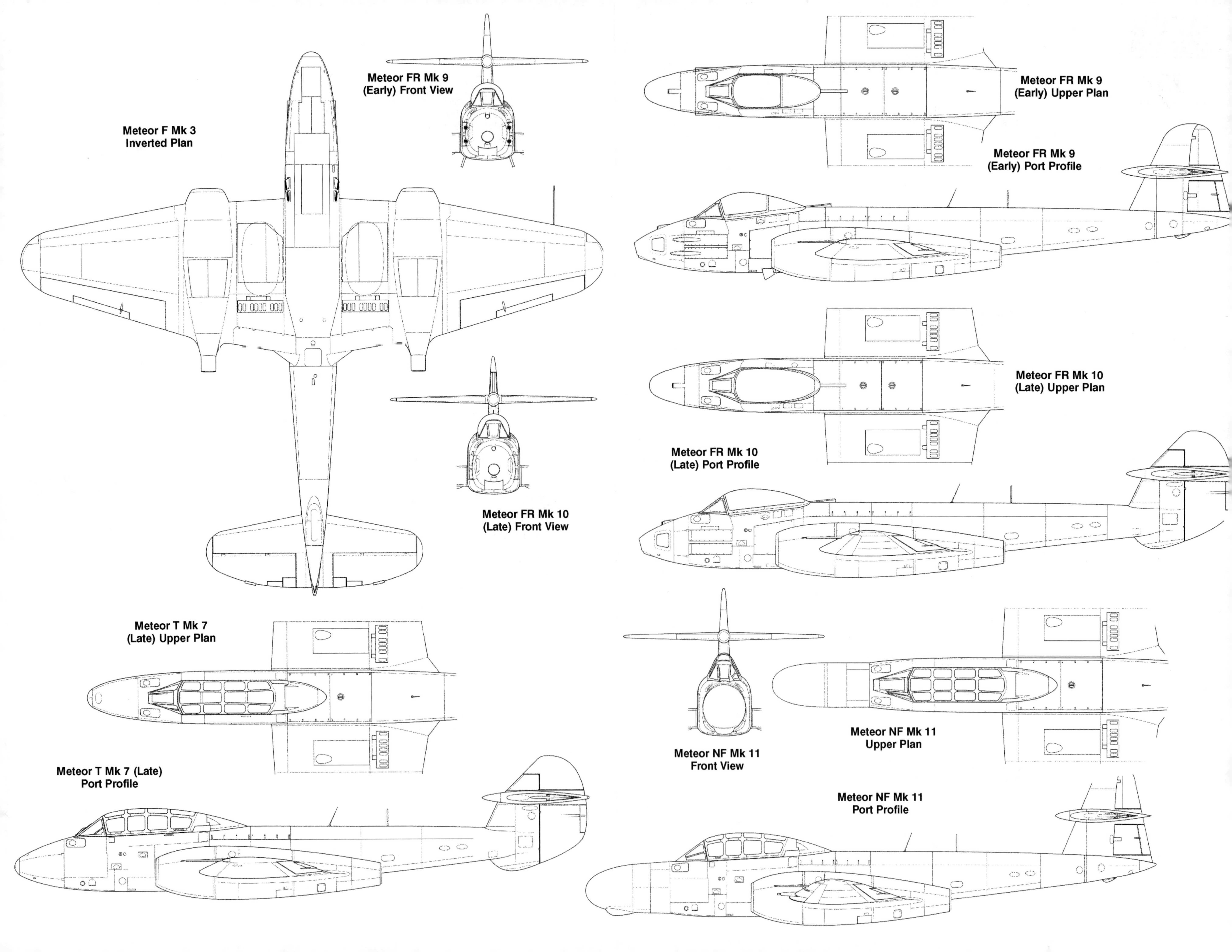
Meteor F Mk 3
Inverted Plan
Meteor FR Mk 9
(Early) Front View
Meteor FR Mk 9
(Early) Upper Plan
Meteor FR Mk 9
(Early) Port Profile
Meteor FR Mk 10
(Late) Upper Plan
Meteor FR Mk 10
(Late) Port Profile
Meteor FR Mk 10
(Late) Front View
Meteor T Mk 7
(Late) Upper Plan
Meteor T Mk 7 (Late)
Port Profile
Meteor NF Mk 11
Front View
Meteor NF Mk 11
Upper Plan
Meteor NF Mk 11
Port Profile

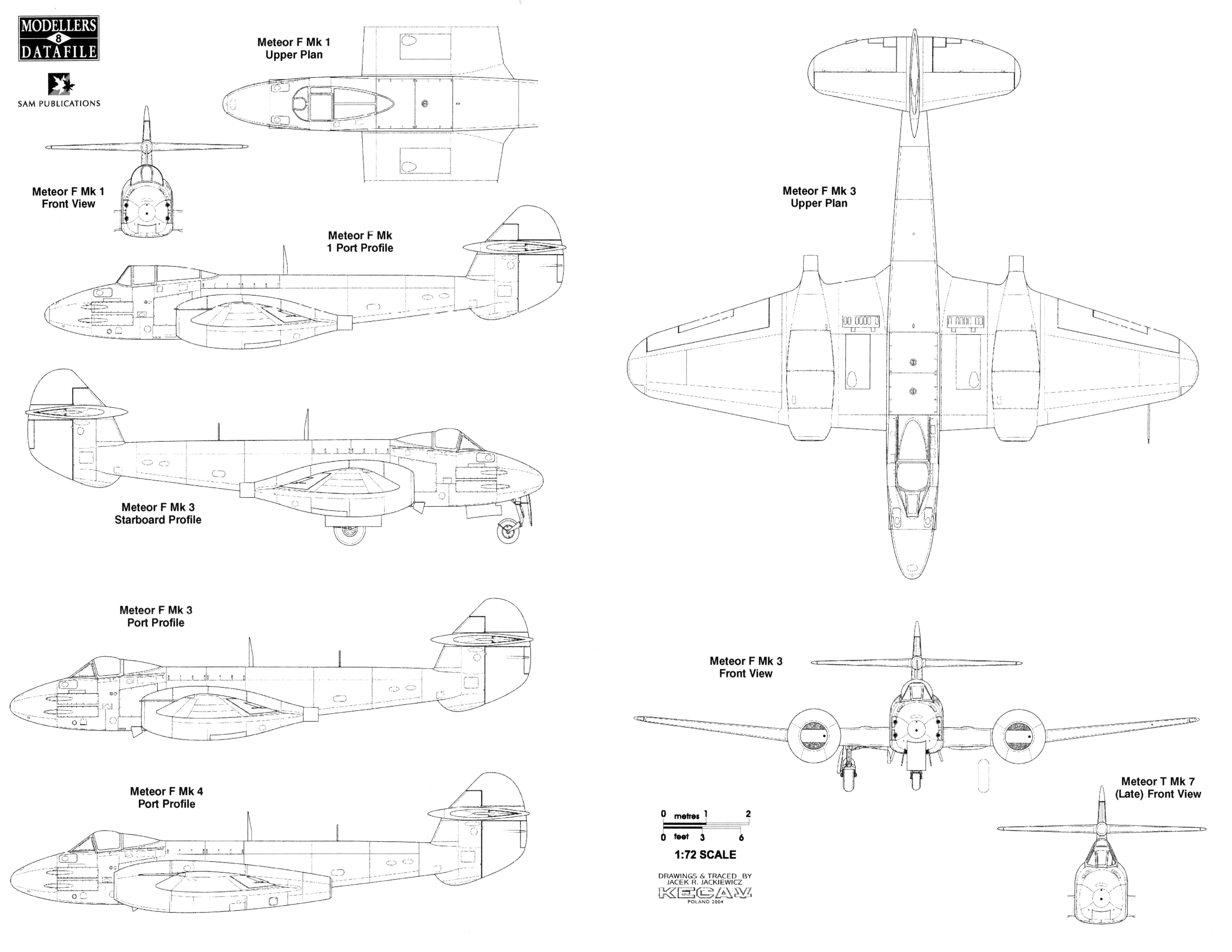
MODELLERS
8
DATAFILE
SAM PUBLICATIONS
Meteor F Mk 1
Upper Plan
Meteor F Mk 1
Front View
Meteor F Mk
1 Port Profile
Meteor F Mk 3
Starboard Profile
Meteor F Mk 3
Port Profile
Meteor F Mk 4
Port Profile
Meteor F Mk 3
Upper Plan
Meteor F Mk 3
Front View
Meteor T Mk 7
(Late) Front View
0 metres 1 2
0 feet 3 6
1:72 SCALE
DRAWINGS & TRACED BY
JACEK R. JACKIEWICZ
KECAY
POLAND 2004

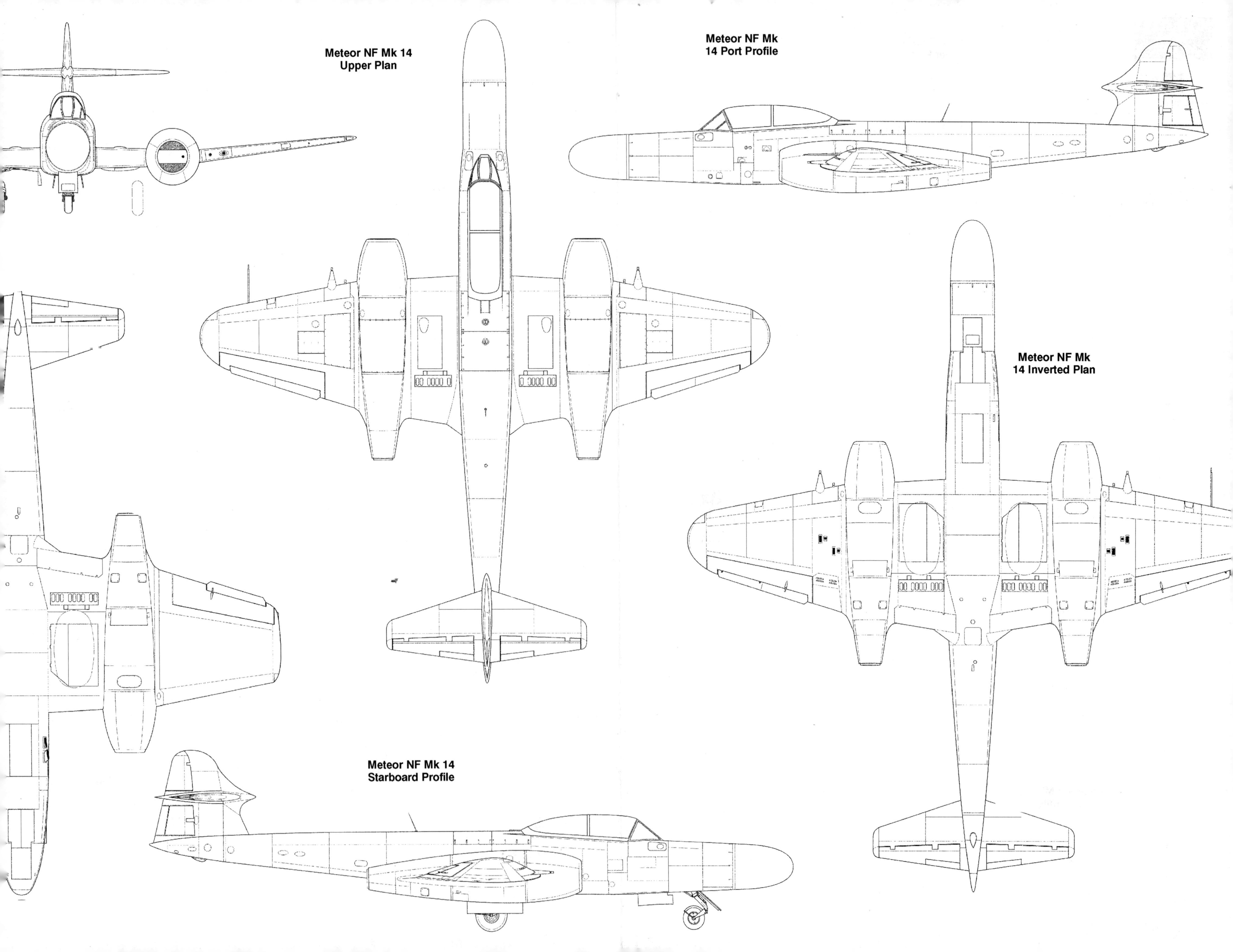
Meteor NF Mk 14
Upper Plan
Meteor NF Mk
14 Port Profile
Meteor NF Mk
14 Inverted Plan
Meteor NF Mk 14
Starboard Profile